KU-216-523

Albania

the Bradt Travel Guide

Gillian Gloyer

edition
5

www.bradtguides.com

Bradt Travel Guides Ltd, UK
The Globe Pequot Press Inc, USA

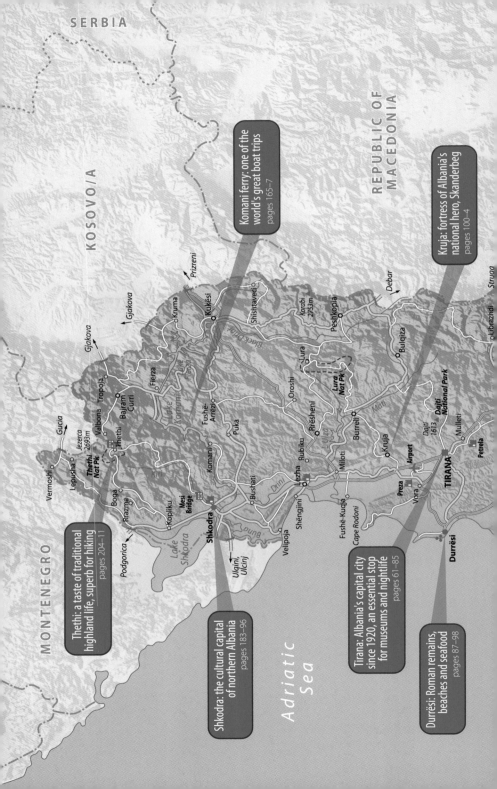

SERBIA

MONTENEGRO

KOSOVO/A

REPUBLIC OF MACEDONIA

Adriatic Sea

Komani ferry: one of the world's great boat trips
pages 165–7

Kruja: fortress of Albania's national hero, Skanderbeg
pages 100–4

Thethi: a taste of traditional highland life, superb for hiking
pages 204–11

Shkodra: the cultural capital of northern Albania
pages 183–96

Tirana: Albania's capital city since 1920, an essential stop for museums and nightlife
pages 61–85

Durrësi: Roman remains, beaches and seafood
pages 87–98

Prizreni

Gjakova

Kruma

Kukësi

Shishtavedjo

Korabi 2753m

Peshkopia

Debar

Gjakova

Gucia

Jezerca 2693m

Vermoshi

Lepusha

Thethi Nat Pk

Fierza

Liqeni i Fierzës

Lura

Lura Nat Pk

Bulqiza

Struga

Librazhdi

Valbona

Tropoja

Bajram Curri

Thethi

Black Drini

Oroshi

Rrësheni

Dajti National Park

Boga

Razma

Liqeni i Komanit

Fushë-Arrëzi

Puka

Komani

Rubiku

Burreli

Kruja

Dajti 1613

Mulleti

Kopliku

Mesi Bridge

Drini

Bushtati

Lezha

Miloti

Airport

Mati

Preza

TIRANA

Petrela

Podgorica

Shkodra

Lake Shkodra

Buna

Shëngjini

Fushë-Kuqja

Vora

Ulqini, Ulcinj

Velipoja

Cape Rodoni

Durrësi

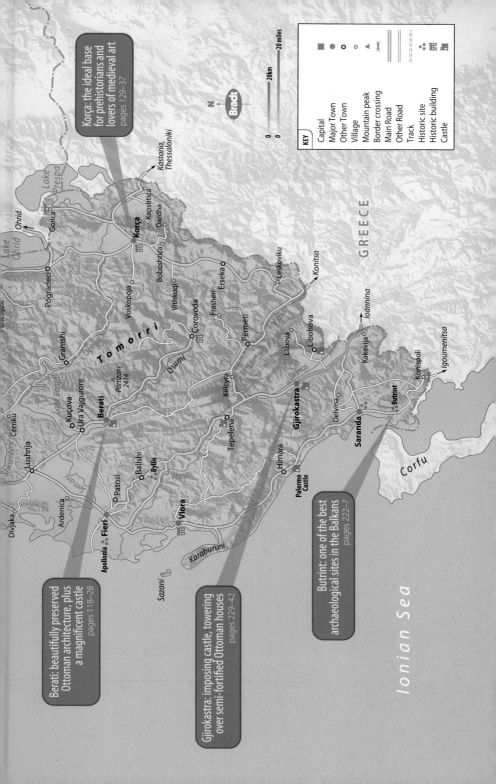

Korça: the ideal base for prehistorians and lovers of medieval art pages 129–37

Berati: beautifully preserved Ottoman architecture, plus a magnificent castle pages 118–28

Gjirokastra: imposing castle, towering over semi-fortified Ottoman houses pages 229–42

Butrint: one of the best archaeological sites in the Balkans pages 222–7

KEY
- Capital
- Major Town
- Other Town
- Village
- Mountain peak
- Border crossing
- Main Road
- Other Road
- Track
- Historic site
- Historic building
- Castle

Bradt

N

0   20km
0   20 miles

GREECE

Ionian Sea

Corfu

Lake Ohrid
Lake Prespa
Ohrid

Kastoria, Thessaloniki

Gorica
Pogradeci
Kapshtica
Dardha
Korça
Bobdshtica
Voskopoja
Vithkuqi
Çorovoda
Frashëri
Erseka
Leskoviku
Konitsa
Përmeti
Vjosa
Drinos
Libohova
Labova
Ioánnina
Kakavija
Konispoli
Igoumenitsa
Delvina
Saranda
Butrint
Gjirokastra
Palermo Castle
Himara
Tepelena
Këlcyra
Vjosa
Ballshi
Byllis
Viora
Karaburuni
Sazani
Apollonia Fieri
Ardenica
Patosi
Lushnja
Divjaka
Cërriku
Shkumbini
Semani
Lake Banja
Kuçova
Ura Vajgurore
Berati
Gramshi
Partizani 2414
Devolli
Osumi
Tomorri

Albania
Don't
miss...

Socialist Realist statues
The Monument to the Unknown Partisan is one of Tirana's best examples of this style
(PF/A) page 81

Gjirokastra
A UNESCO World Heritage Site since 2005, Gjirokastra is a town of whitewashed walls and steep, cobbled streets, such as Qafa e Pazarit, which is home to artisans' shops
(M/D) pages 229–42

Butrint
The Baptistery within this ancient archaeological site features a symbolic layout of concentric circles
(N/D) pages 222–7

Orthodox frescoes
The paintings in the 14th-century St Mary's Church, Mborja, show grisly scenes of the torments of sinners
(DD) pages 136–7

Shkodra
The Ebu Bekër Mosque, which lies at the heart of Shkodra city centre, was rebuilt in the 1990s as a replica of the historic mosque destroyed in 1967
(WB/AWL) page 194

Albania in colour

above   Skanderbeg Square is the *de facto* centre of Tirana and is overlooked by the Mosque of Et'hem Bey, the clock-tower, the Palace of Culture and the equestrian statue of Skanderbeg himself (P/D) page 75

left   The Mosque of Et'hem Bey dates from the 18th century and is one of the best-preserved old buildings in the capital, with frescoes inside and out (DD) page 75

below   The Lana River flows through the centre of Tirana (SS) page 64

right   The mosaic above the National Historical Museum portrays the sweep of Albania's history, from Illyrians to partisans (GG) pages 75–7

middle   Buildings in Tirana city centre have been painted in an array of bold colours (SS) page 61

below left   The imposing statue called 'Mother Albania' looks down over Tirana from the Martyrs' Cemetery (GG) page 82

below right   The Tanners' Bridge is one of the few remnants of Tirana's Ottoman past (SS) pages 78–9

We're **40**...
how did that happen?

How did it all happen? George (my then husband) and I wrote the first Bradt guide – about hiking in Peru and Bolivia – on an Amazon river barge, and typed it up on a borrowed typewriter. We had no money for the next two books so George went to work for a printer and was paid in books rather than money.

Forty years on, Bradt publishes over 200 titles that sell all over the world. I still suffer from Imposter Syndrome – how did it all happen? I hadn't even worked in an office before! Well, I've been extraordinarily lucky with the people around me. George provided the belief to get us started (and the mother to run our US office). Then, in 1977, I recruited a helper, Janet Mears, who is still working for us. She and the many dedicated staff who followed have been the foundations on which the company is built. But the bricks and mortar have been our authors and readers. Without them there would be no Bradt Travel Guides. Thank you all for making it happen.

Hilary Bradt

LIST OF MAPS

HOW TO USE THE MAPS IN THIS GUIDE

KEYS AND SYMBOLS Maps include alphabetical keys covering the locations of those places to stay, eat or drink that are featured in the book. Note that regional maps may not show all hotels and restaurants in the area: other establishments may be located in towns shown on the map.

GRIDS AND GRID REFERENCES The maps of Tirana use grid lines to allow easy location of sites. Map grid references are listed in square brackets after the name of the place or sight of interest in the text, with page number followed by grid number, eg: [68 C2]

FEEDBACK REQUEST AND UPDATES WEBSITE

At Bradt Travel Guides we're aware that guidebooks start to go out of date on the day they're published – and that you, our readers, are out there in the field doing research of your own. You'll find out before us when a fine new family-run hotel opens or a favourite restaurant changes hands and goes downhill. So why not write and tell us about your experiences? Contact us on ☏ 01753 893444 or ✉ info@bradtguides.com. We will forward emails to the author who may post updates on the Bradt website at www.bradtupdates.com/albania. Alternatively you can add a review of the book to www.bradtguides.com or Amazon.

FOLLOW BRADT

For the latest news, special offers and competitions, subscribe to the Bradt newsletter via the website www.bradtguides.com and follow Bradt on:

- 🅵 www.facebook.com/BradtTravelGuides
- 🐦 @BradtGuides
- 📷 @bradtguides
- ⓟ pinterest.com/bradtguides

SEND US YOUR SNAPS!

We'd love to follow your adventures using our *Albania* guide – why not send us your photos and stories via Twitter (@BradtGuides) and Instagram (@bradtguides) using the hashtag #Albania. Alternatively, you can upload your photos directly to the gallery on the Albania destination page via our website (*www.bradtguides.com*).

Part One

GENERAL INFORMATION

ALBANIA AT A GLANCE

Location Balkan peninsula
Neighbouring countries Montenegro, Kosova, Macedonia, Greece
Area 28,748km²
Climate Mediterranean
System of government Parliamentary democracy
Head of state President, elected by parliament every five years
Population 2,800,138 (2011 census)
Birth rate 1.5 children per woman of reproductive age; 12.73 births per 1,000 population (2014 estimate)
Life expectancy Males 75.33 years; females 80.86 years (2014 estimate)
Population growth rate 0.3% (2014 estimate)
Capital city Tirana (Tiranë)
GDP per capita €3,312 (2012)
GDP purchasing power parity (ppp) US$23.34 billion (2013 estimate; the grey economy may account for as much as 50% of official GDP)
GDP real growth rate +1.62% (2012)
Official language Albanian
Alphabet Roman
Currency Lek
Exchange rate £1 = 177 lek, €1 = 140 lek, US$1 = 110 lek (October 2014)
International telephone code +355
Electrical voltage 220V (in theory)
Weights and measures Metric
National anthem *Himni i Flamurit* (*The Flag Hymn*), composed in 1880
National flag Black double-headed eagle on red background
National holidays 1 January, 1 May, 28 November (see page 51 for other public holidays)

1

Background Information

GEOGRAPHY AND CLIMATE

Albania's surface area of 28,748km² (11,100 square miles) makes it slightly smaller than Belgium and slightly larger than the US state of Maryland. Much of its surface is mountainous – the average height above sea level is 708m, and its highest peak, Mount Korabi on the Macedonian border northeast of Peshkopia, is 2,751m high. Most of the population lives in the southern central lowlands and on the coastal plain.

Albania is in the southwest of the Balkan peninsula, bordered by Greece, the former Yugoslav republics of Macedonia and Montenegro, and the province of Kosova. It is separated from Italy by the Adriatic and Ionian seas, which divide at the Bay of Vlora, about 170km up the Albanian coast; at the narrowest point, the Straits of Otranto, the two countries are only 72km apart.

The climate is Mediterranean, with hot dry summers and mild rainy winters in the lowlands. The higher altitudes further inland make temperatures lower, and winter precipitation there often falls as snow. In the highest mountains, snow lies in the northeastern corries all year round. The lowlands have between 270 and 300 days of sunshine a year, and the sea is warm enough to swim in (comfortably) from May to October. The coldest month is January, when the mean lowland temperature is 5–10°C and inland it can fall to –10°C. The hottest month, July, can be very hot indeed, sometimes topping 40°C inland. Sea breezes keep the coastal towns cooler.

The southern Balkans are located on the boundary between the Eurasian and African tectonic plates, which makes them susceptible to seismic activity. Albania's complex geological development means the country has rich mineral resources – its silver mines were probably one of the attractions for the Greek colonists of the 7th century BC. It has fairly large oil reserves, which in recent years have attracted some Western investment. Under communism, Albania was the world's second-biggest producer of chrome, although production is now a fraction of what it was then.

Albania has 362km of sea coast, with the Adriatic running from the Montenegrin border south to the Bay of Vlora, where the Ionian Sea begins. In all but a few stretches the Adriatic coast is low-lying, with large protected bays (such as those of Vlora and Durrësi) which have been used as harbours since ancient times. The Ionian coast is very rugged, with rocky coves along the narrow coastal strip and steep mountains rising almost straight up along much of its length. The highest point is at the Llogoraja Pass, over 1,000m high. Abrasion and karstic activity have created many caves at the base of the cliffs, some of which were inhabited in prehistoric times.

The country is criss-crossed with rivers, which rise in the high mountains and pass through steep gorges, before reaching the plain and making their way to the sea. Most of the main rivers have been extensively managed, usually to generate hydro-electricity; the country's largest hydro-electric system is powered by its largest and most constant stream, the River Drini, which is 285km long and drains nearly 6,000km² within Albania. The longest rivers in southern Albania are the Semani, formed by the confluence of the Devolli and Osumi, and the Vjosa, which rises as the Aoos in northern Greece and runs northwestwards through the beautiful gorges between Përmeti and Tepelena.

NATURAL HISTORY AND CONSERVATION

Over a third of the territory of Albania – more than a million hectares – is forested, and the country is very rich in flora. More than 3,000 different species of plant grow in Albania and about 5% of those are either endemic or sub-endemic (meaning they also grow in neighbouring countries, but the centre of their distribution is in Albania). The box on pages 208–9 has more information about the flora of northern Albania. Many plants are used for medicinal purposes, in cities as well as villages; more information about these can be found in the box on pages 6–7.

The natural vegetation in the coastal strip is *maquis*, the scrubby bushes found all around the Mediterranean; in the north, where the coastal plain is wider, it is almost entirely under cultivation, while in the south many of the hillsides have been terraced and planted with olive and citrus trees. As the land rises, the *maquis* gives way to deciduous forest of beech and oak, with scattered patches of the rare Macedonian pine (*Pinus peuce*). Birch, fir and pine begin to predominate until the treeline is reached at around 2,000m; thereafter only mountain pastures break the harsh landscape. This subalpine and alpine zone occupies about one-eighth of Albania's territory. The forests are home to a great variety of wild animals, including wolves, bears, wild boar and chamois.

The rivers which flow into the low-lying Adriatic coast have created fertile alluvial plains and, at their mouths, exceptionally rich wetlands, which are home to many waterfowl and migratory birds. The coastal marshes were extensively drained in the 20th century to create agricultural land and eradicate malaria. Flora and fauna have also been affected by pollution, and unregulated hunting and fishing. Nonetheless, several outstanding wetland sites remain, at the mouths of the Buna, Drini and Mati rivers in the north of the country, and at the Karavastaja Lagoon south of Durrësi, all of which are wintering and breeding grounds for rare and unusual waterbirds. Even non-ornithologists will find many attractive birds to observe in these wetlands, including pelicans, cormorants, spoonbills, corncrakes and avocets. Among the rare ducks which winter in the Albanian wetlands are the ferruginous duck, or white-eyed pochard (*Aythya nyroca*), and the white-headed duck (*Oxyura leucocephala*), whose fully plumaged male is instantly recognisable from its extraordinary bright blue beak. See pages 199–202 for detailed information about birdwatching in the Albanian coastal wetlands.

Like the lagoons, Albania's large freshwater lakes also offer good opportunities for birdwatchers. The biggest of these is Lake Shkodra – indeed, at 370km² it is the largest lake in the Balkans – which straddles the border between Albania and Montenegro. Thousands of cormorants (*Phalacrocorax carbo* and *P. pygmeus*) winter on this lake. It is relatively shallow (44m at its deepest point) and is fed by many different rivers, as well as by springs, making it very varied in its fish life.

By contrast, the Ohrid and Prespa lakes, in the southeast of the country, are tectonic lakes. Lake Ohrid, which is shared between Albania and Macedonia, is exceptionally deep and fed mainly by karstic springs around the edges of the lake and on its bed. These springs, in turn, are fed from the Prespa Lakes, high up in the mountains, where Greece, Macedonia and Albania meet. Unique species of fish have evolved in Lake Ohrid, among them the delicious *koran* (*Salmo letnica*) and *belushka* (*Salmothymus ohridanus*).

The Prespa Lakes have very important breeding populations of Dalmatian and white pelicans (*Pelecanus crispus* and *P. onocrotalus*) and pygmy cormorants (*Phalacrocorax pygmeus*); their breeding sites are on the Greek and Macedonian sides of the lake, but they can be seen foraging all around the shores. Black-necked grebes (*Podiceps nigrocollis*) and coots (*Fulica atra*) winter on the Greater Prespa Lake. Additionally, whiskered terns (*Chlidonias hybridus*) and little bitterns (*Ixobrychus minutus*) are known to breed on the Lesser Prespa Lake. Lake Ohrid is also an important site for wintering waterfowl, with tens of thousands of coots recorded in different bird censuses of the 1990s. Black-necked grebes, pygmy cormorants, goldeneyes (*Bucephala clangula*) and red-crested pochard (*Netta rufina*) also winter at Lake Ohrid.

Some of the forests and wetlands which present particularly valuable ecosystems are designated as national parks or nature reserves, which is supposed to give them special protection. IUCN, an international partnership of governments and NGOs which sets the categories for nature reserves, defines a Protected Area as 'An area of land and/or sea especially dedicated to the protection and maintenance of biological diversity, and of natural and associated cultural resources, managed

BATS IN ALBANIA   *with thanks to Eva de Hullu*

Albania has no fewer than 32 species of bat, including some whose population is declining. Without specialist bat-detecting equipment it is next to impossible to determine the species of the bats flying around you in the evening. It is easier to go looking for bats in caves or empty sheds – some of the large bunkers might be good places, too.

In caves you are likely to spot different species of horseshoe bat, as well as the bentwing, or Schreiber's long-fingered bat (*Miniopterus schreibersii*), which is recognisable by its long, elegant wings. Colonies of Schreiber's bats can be very large – sometimes comprising as many as 10,000. Horseshoe bats usually fold their wings around their bodies when they sleep, which makes them easy to recognise. The Albanian NGO Protection and Preservation of Natural Environment in Albania (PPNEA; see page 57) has conducted some bat-monitoring in caves and bunkers in the Vjosa River area, during which they identified six species including the greater horseshoe bat (*Rhinolophus ferrumequinum*), the lesser horseshoe bat (*Rh. hipposideros*) and – observed for only the second time in Albania and with International Union for Conservation of Nature (IUCN) 'near-threatened' status – Bechstein's bat (*Myotis bechsteinii*). Other species which you might find in Albanian caves are Blasius's horseshoe bat (*Rh. Blasii*) and the long-fingered bat (*Myotis capaccinii*). Colonies of Savi's pipistrelle (*Pipistrellis savii*), a southern European species which is widespread in Albania, can be found in cracks in rocks or in buildings.

Sleeping bats are easily disturbed, which can endanger them while they are hibernating (from autumn to spring). You should take care not to pollute their environment, for example by smoking, and leave the bats in peace as soon as you have had a chance to look at them. Under no circumstances should you ever try to catch a bat. They can give painful bites and some harbour serious diseases such as rabies.

1

With thanks to Anika Dede

Herbal medicine is widely practised in Albania, in cities as well as the countryside. Many different plants are used for medicinal purposes; stalls selling them can be found in every town's market and villagers sometimes also sell them from the roadside. In recent years a few shops have opened, in Tirana and elsewhere, selling medicinal herbs in a more controlled and hygienic environment.

The most popular herbal tea in Albania is *çaj mali*, **'mountain tea'**, which is a type of ironwort (*Sideritis raeseri*). Its medicinal effectiveness is a matter of some dispute, but Albanians of all ages drink *çaj mali* to treat virtually any kind of minor ailment, from the common cold to indigestion.

Some of the most widely used herbal remedies are described below, with their Albanian and Latin names. It should be borne in mind, however, that some of them are toxic in the wrong doses or if the wrong part of the plant is used; this list should not be used for self-medication.

Wild **chamomile** (*lule kamomili, Chamomilla recutita*) is one of the most widely used medicinal herbs, and is native to southern and southeastern Europe. The flower heads with their stalks are gathered in the summer and dried – bundles of the herb can be bought throughout Albania. Chamomile is used for digestive and nervous disorders, and as an anti-inflammatory; it is usually drunk as an infusion, but it can also be added to bathwater to soothe dermatitis.

St John's wort (*lule basani, Hypericum perforatum*) is also very widely used to treat a variety of ailments. Bundles of its long stems can often be seen on market and street stalls all over Albania. It is used to treat diseases of the digestive and respiratory tracts, as well as kidney problems. It improves the circulation of the blood and helps against sleeplessness. St John's wort also has antiseptic properties, and an extract made from its flowers is used externally to prevent infection of wounds or burns.

The **lime** tree (*bliri i bardhë, Tilia*) has about 20 documented species, two of which are used medicinally. The flowers have anti-inflammatory, diuretic and mild anti-spasmodic properties, and also induce perspiration. The infusion made from them is used to treat colds and flu, and diseases of the kidneys and urinary tract. It helps to lower high temperatures and soothes nervous complaints.

The blue flowers of **borage** (*shaja, Borago officinalis*) have diuretic, antiseptic and anti-inflammatory properties, as well as being a culinary herb. Infusions of borage are used to treat urinary infections and problems of the nervous system; borage solution can also be applied externally to skin injuries and inflammations.

through legal or other effective means'. However, in Albania's case, legal designation has failed to prevent illegal felling of trees, pasturing of goats and other animals, or hunting. Very few national parks in Albania have any practical protection at all; their main safeguard is their remoteness and lack of infrastructure. National parks and reserves are administered by the Directorate of Forests and Pastures, part of the Ministry of Agriculture. Enquiries about access to the Category Ia reserves should be directed in the first instance to the prefecture of the respective area.

HISTORY

PREHISTORY The country now known as Albania has been inhabited for over ten millennia. The first Palaeolithic settlements to be excavated were in caves

Marshmallow (*mullanjadhja, Althaea officinalis*) has been cultivated in Europe for its medicinal properties since the Middle Ages, when it was grown in monasteries. Albanians use marshmallow, as an infusion of the roots and leaves, to treat coughs and stomach disorders; the leaves are made into poultices to heal external wounds and soften bruises.

Extracts of **hawthorn** (*murrizi, Crataegus laevigata* and other C. species) are used commercially in drops and pills for the treatment of heart and vascular problems. In Albania, the flowers and leaves of hawthorn are made into an infusion which improves heart rhythm and lowers blood pressure.

Fennel (*maraja, Foeniculum vulgare*) is a component of many commercially available herbal tea mixtures. As an infusion, the fruit is used to treat diseases of the digestive system and respiratory tract; a similar infusion can also be used as an eye wash for minor inflammations of the eyelid or conjunctivitis.

White horehound (*kapinoku, Marrubium vulgare*) has anti-inflammatory and antiseptic properties, and its flowering stems are used to treat mild digestive disorders and inflammation of the upper respiratory tract.

Cowslip and **oxlip**, both members of the primrose family (*aguliçore, primulaceae*) contain complex organic substances called saponins, which have an expectorant effect. Their roots or flowers are made into decoctions or infusions which are drunk to ease bronchitis and other diseases of the respiratory tract.

Blackthorn, or **sloe** (*kullumbria, Prunus spinosa*), is a spiny shrub whose white flowers have mildly diuretic and laxative properties. In Albania it is administered as an infusion to those suffering from problems of the digestive system, kidneys and urinary tract; it is also good for preventing chills and treating the symptoms of rheumatism.

Lungwort (*pulmonaria, Pulmonaria officinalis*) is one of the oldest medicinal herbs, used since the Middle Ages to treat respiratory problems. In Albania, its flowering stems are administered in the form of an infusion to treat those suffering from bronchitis.

Heartsease (*manushaqja tringjyrëshe, Viola tricolor*) is used internally and externally for its antiseptic and anti-inflammatory properties. The flowering stems are steeped in water and either administered as an infusion, to treat inflammation of the upper respiratory passages and infections of the urinary tract or kidneys; or used to soak gauze pads, which are applied as compresses to treat external wounds and dermatitis.

at Gajtan, near Shkodra, and Konispoli in the far southwest. More recent work has identified some open-air sites: Shkreli in the northwest and the area around Apollonia in central Albania, for example. The Neolithic period in this region is c6000–c2100BC and the Bronze Age is c2100–c1200BC; the Korça region is full of sites from these periods, including the tumulus site at Kamenica (see pages 138–9). It is in the Iron Age, starting around 1200BC, that it begins to be possible to recognise the culture known as Illyrian. Some archaeologists take the view that, during the Bronze Age, the inhabitants of the Balkan peninsula began to develop tribal differences and that one of the tribes which emerged as a result was the Illyrian people, who are the ancestors of modern Albanians. Others think that the Illyrians came from elsewhere and invaded Albania at some point between the 13th and the 10th centuries BC.

There is also considerable controversy over the question of where the boundary was between Hellenes (Greeks), Epirotes (whom the Hellenes considered to be sort of Greek, in the same way as Macedonians were) and Illyrians (who were definitely barbarians, ie: not Greek). It may be that Illyrian and Epirote settlements were interspersed in what is now southern Albania and northern Greece.

ILLYRIANS What is not in question is that Illyrian culture had many distinctive features and that the ancient Greeks considered the various Illyrian tribes as similar enough to each other to form a distinct group. They built large, well-fortified cities (almost all of which were in stunning locations with magnificent views), they traded with the Greek colonies on the Adriatic coast and beyond and they minted coins. The silver and copper which they mined was also used for personal adornments: *fibulae* (brooches) such as spiralling spectacle brooches; metal coils which women twisted into their hair; and the unique *byzylyk*, bracelets which were placed on the arms and legs of a dead person as part of the burial process. In one tumulus a skeleton was found with no fewer than six *byzylykë* on each limb.

In the 3rd century BC, a northern Illyrian tribe called the **Ardiaeans** established its capital in Shkodra. The Ardiaeans were seafarers – their coins (and the modern 20-lek coin) show a small, fast galley called a *liburnis*, which was a particular favourite of pirates – and in 229BC their attacks on Italian ships brought them to war with Rome, then emerging as the most powerful state in Italy. Queen Teuta of the Ardiaeans was forced to make terms, and the Romans gained their first foothold on the other side of the Adriatic. Sixty years later, in 168BC, they defeated the Ardiaeans in battle and besieged their king, Genti (known to the Romans as Gentius), in Rozafa Castle until he surrendered. Genti was the last Illyrian king.

ROMANS From the middle of the 2nd century BC, Roman control brought peace and prosperity to Albania. To connect the Adriatic coast with Thessalonica and Byzantium, the Romans built one of their great arterial roads, the Via Egnatia. The road was named after a Roman proconsul of Macedonia, Gnaeius Egnatius, who laid it and built bridges along it in the 2nd century BC, using an ancient route which linked southern Illyria with Macedonia. The starting points were Dyrrachium (now Durrësi) and Apollonia, and at the place where these two branches joined a town grew up which later acquired the name of Elbasani. The Romans built other roads too – one down the coast from Shkodra through Durrësi to Butrint and beyond, another from Shkodra east through Prizreni to Niš.

Julius Caesar visited the province of Illyricum in 56BC, while it was under his command, but the first time he is known to have come specifically to what is now Albania was in 48BC, pursuing his opponent in the Civil War, Pompey. Octavian studied in Apollonia before he became the Emperor Augustus, and rewarded the city afterwards with tax-free status. Many Roman citizens bought estates or settled in Albania. Lissus (Lezha) had a community of Roman citizens when Mark Antony landed there with Caesar's reinforcements in 48BC; a friend of Cicero's owned land near Buthrotum (Butrint). Dyrrachium, a free city in the Republic, became a Roman colony under Augustus, who also founded colonies at Byllis and Buthrotum.

On the final division of the Roman Empire in AD395, Albania came under Constantinople's authority, rather than Rome's. This meant that when the Western Empire collapsed in the 5th century, Albania became part of the Byzantine Empire.

BYZANTINES The 4th, 5th and 6th centuries saw destabilising invasions of Albania by Visigoths and then Ostrogoths, who occupied Dyrrachium in AD480 and used it as a base from which to invade Italy and set up a kingdom there. Shkodra was sacked in AD380 and Onchesmus (now Saranda) was completely destroyed in AD551. However, in between invasions, life went on. Bishops were installed and churches were built. The great builder-emperor, Justinian (AD527–65), ordered the fortification or refortification of several cities, including Dyrrachium and Byllis.

In the 10th century, Bulgaria captured large swathes of the Balkans, including all of Albania. The Byzantines were only able to recover this territory after 1018. However, the respite was short. In 1081 a large Norman army, under Robert Guiscard, landed at Avlona (Vlora) and proceeded up the coast to Dyrrachium. The ensuing battle is described in great detail by Anna Comnena, the daughter of the Byzantine emperor Alexius I Comnenus. (Among his allies were a people called the Albanoi.) Despite initial success, the Battle of Dyrrachium was a crushing defeat for Byzantium. Many of the empire's officers were killed; the European troops who had formed the backbone of its army proved to be undisciplined and useless and were replaced with foreign mercenaries. The decisive moment in the battle was a shock charge by the Norman cavalry, holding their lances ahead of them instead of throwing them. This innovation had been tested at the Battle of Hastings, and would be used to even more devastating effect in the First Crusade 15 years later.

After a siege lasting several months, the Normans went on to take Dyrrachium and other coastal towns, as a prelude to an advance to the east two years later; by the middle of the following year, the whole of Illyria was in their hands. Alexius I fought back, however. Allied with the Venetians, who wanted (and seized) control of Dyrrachium and Corfu, Byzantium had retaken most of its Balkan territories by the end of 1083.

Constantinople fell to the Fourth Crusade in 1204, and for the rest of that century competing successor states vied for pre-eminence. One of these became known as the **Despotate of Epirus**, whose capital was at Arta (now in northwestern Greece) and whose boundaries extended north to Dyrrachium and, at times, east to Macedonia and Thessalonica. It was founded soon after the fall of Constantinople by Michael I Comnenus Ducas, an illegitimate grandson of Alexius I Comnenus. His own illegitimate son, Michael II Comnenus Ducas, who ruled from about 1237 to 1271, seems to have been the first to use the title of Despot of Epirus. A despot was a kind of imperial regent and provincial administrator, and the title was usually awarded by the emperor.

In 1256, Michael II embarked on a campaign to capture Thessalonica, a city which was by then held by one of the other mini empires, that of Nicaea, and by early summer he was at the city's gates. Early in 1258, however, Durrësi, Vlora and Butrint fell to Prince Manfred of Sicily; Michael II reacted by offering him his daughter in marriage, with the conquered territory as her dowry, and forming an alliance with the kingdoms of Sicily and Achaia against Nicaea. The newly crowned co-Emperor of Nicaea, Michael Palaeologus, dispatched a large army to the Balkans which took the Epirote army by surprise at Kastoria. Michael II Comnenus Ducas regrouped with his allies at Vlora, but they were conclusively defeated at Pelagonia (now Monastir, in Macedonia) in the summer of 1259. The Nicaeans captured Arta and Michael II took refuge on the island of Cephalonia. He made his way back to Arta the following year, but it was too late for the Despotate of Epirus to reassert itself. On 15 August 1261, Michael VIII Palaeologus entered Constantinople in triumph after the fall of the Latin Empire.

Meanwhile, Albania continued to be tussled over. Manfred Hohenstaufen, by then King of Sicily, died in battle in 1266 against the crusade of Charles of Anjou, the younger brother of King Louis of France. In 1275, the Byzantines retook

Butrint and Berati, driving the Angevins back to the Adriatic coast. Five years later, Charles dispatched an army of about 8,000 eastwards across Albania to Berati; the garrison and people in the fortified citadel there held out until a relief army from Constantinople reached them in March 1281 and inflicted a crushing defeat on the Angevin troops. Albania was now back in Byzantine hands.

However, the Byzantine Empire had been fatally weakened during its years of exile from Constantinople and, in the 14th century, it was able to devote less and less energy to its western periphery. The Angevins recaptured Durrësi in 1307; the Serbian king Stefan Dušan invaded Albania in 1343, and got as far south as Vlora and Berati. The Serbs never exercised full control over the country, however. Instead it became a patchwork of semi-independent states run by powerful Albanian families; on Stefan Dušan's untimely death in 1355, they were left as the only functioning authorities. They included the Balshajs in northern Albania, the Muzakajs in the south, and the Topias in central Albania – in the 1380s, Karl Topia rebuilt the church of St Gjon Vladimir near Elbasani (see pages 116–17).

THE OTTOMAN CONQUEST The Ottomans had first settled on European soil in 1354, much to the alarm of John VI Cantacuzenus, the Byzantine historian and – at the time – co-emperor. In 1371, Sultan Murad I's troops routed the Serbian army at the river Maritsa; and in June 1389, a coalition of Serbs, Hungarians, Bosnians, Bulgarians and Albanians, under the leadership of the Serbian prince Lazar, met the Ottoman troops on the Field of Blackbirds (Kosovo Polje, in Serbian). The sultan was killed, but the coalition was routed and Prince Lazar executed. The few Serbian nobles who survived were obliged to swear a personal oath of allegiance to the new sultan, Murad's son Bayezid.

Bayezid marched against Constantinople in 1394, and the city remained under siege for eight years, until the Mongol army under **Tamurlane** swept into Asia Minor and defeated the Ottomans in 1402. Bayezid was taken prisoner and died in captivity. His successor as sultan, Mehmed I, returned to Albania; in 1417, Ottoman forces captured Vlora and then Gjirokastra. But their grip on the country was weak and Albania had not yet given up. The early 1430s saw rebellions, put down in 1433. In 1443, the Ottoman army was defeated at the Serbian town of Niš, by a crusade under a multi-national leadership which included the Hungarian hero János Hunyadi. At this point Skanderbeg, an Albanian nobleman who had been trained as a soldier in the Ottoman army, raised a rebellion from his family seat at Kruja (see box, pages 200–1). Thanks to Skanderbeg's ability to unify the Albanian clans against the enemy, they resisted the occupiers until 1479 – 26 years after the Ottomans had taken the Byzantine capital.

Under Islamic law, non-Muslims living under Muslim sovereignty are treated as 'protected infidels', a status quite different from that of non-Muslims under non-Muslim sovereignty, who can legitimately be killed or enslaved. The Christians in Albania (and elsewhere) were not obliged to convert to Islam, but they did have to pay a capitation tax. It was by virtue of this tax that their lives and property enjoyed legal protection.

Perhaps even more significant for Christian peasants was the 'Collection', or **devshirme**, whereby non-Turkish families throughout the empire were required to give up one of their sons to the sultan. Between the 14th and late 16th centuries, the Collection was the main source of recruitment into imperial service, and it must have meant a huge sacrifice for peasant families who needed their sons to work their land (although only sons, at least, were not taken). The best-looking youths in each intake were educated in the Palace Schools and sometimes worked their way up to become governors or other senior officials. Most of the 'collected' boys, though, became **Janissaries**, members of the sultan's personal infantry corps. Originally, the Janissaries consisted of a few hundred men who served as the sultan's bodyguards. Although their numbers grew over the years, they remained a small, elite corps – during the 16th century, they numbered around 10,000 at any one time. They were fiercely loyal to the Ottoman dynasty, although not necessarily to individual sultans; Janissary rebellions forced at least two sultans to abdicate.

As for those selected for the Palace Schools, after their education was complete they could become pages to the sultan, serve in the military palace guard or join one of the cavalry divisions attached to the palace; if they had a particular interest in Islamic law, they could become imams; if their aptitude lay in languages, they might become clerks. It was the sultan's personal pages, however, who stood the best chance of achieving the great offices of the empire – viziers, imperial treasurers and chancellors. Many Albanians became Grand Viziers, such as Daud Pasha, who was Grand Vizier from 1485 to 1497, and Koja Sinan Pasha a century later.

INDEPENDENCE In many cases, in fact, it was Ottoman civil servants who provided the intellectual framework and the creative impulse for the **Albanian nationalist movement** which began to emerge in the late 19th century. Abdyl Frashëri (see box, pages 150–1), for example, was Director of Finance for the *vilayet* (province) of Ioannina. He was a senior figure in the Prizren League, whose original goal was merely the unification of the four Albanian-speaking *vilayets*, but which by 1881 was campaigning for autonomy within the Ottoman Empire. The League succeeded in expelling the imperial administrators from Kosova, but it was crushed shortly afterwards and its leaders were imprisoned.

The nationalist movement now realised that the Albanian language could be a tool with which to build a sense of national unity, and the focus of its campaigning shifted to cultural and linguistic demands. Albanian books and magazines were published and Albanian-medium schools (that is, schools which teach subjects in the Albanian language) were opened (see page 135). A generation of great Albanian poets emerged, who embodied the national cultural renaissance (*Rilindja Kombëtare*) under way.

One obstacle to national unity was the fact that Albanians of different religious faiths wrote their language in different alphabets – Muslims used the Arabic script, Orthodox southerners the Greek alphabet, and northern Catholics the Roman. Agreement on a common alphabet therefore became a pressing aim of the *Rilindja* movement, and in 1909 a congress in Elbasani formally adopted the Roman alphabet which is used today.

The **First Balkan War** started on 8 October 1912 when Montenegro attacked northern Albania, which was still part of the Ottoman Empire. The other Balkan countries immediately joined in, the Ottoman army crumbled and Albania found itself invaded from all sides. Practically abandoned by their Ottoman rulers, the Albanians realised that if they did not obtain independence their territory would be swallowed up by their Balkan neighbours. Meanwhile, Austria-Hungary had become concerned that Greek, Serb and Italian designs on Albania would reduce its own influence in the Balkans – its southern backyard. Ismail Qemali, who had been one of the 26 Albanians elected to the Istanbul parliament, after the Young Turk revolution of 1908, travelled to Vienna and Budapest to obtain diplomatic support for Albanian independence.

By the time the war began, much of Albania was already up in arms and Albanian soldiers were deserting the Ottoman army, although others fought bravely with the

Ottoman forces against the Montenegrins. Rebels led by the Kosovar Isa Boletini occupied Skopje, took control of Kosova, and captured large tracts of what is now Albanian territory. When Ismail Qemali returned from his diplomatic tour, he learned that Serbian troops were approaching the Adriatic. Northern Albania was being invaded by the Balkan League and the Greek navy was attacking in the south – it was in difficult circumstances indeed that on 28 November 1912, 83 delegates from all parts of Albania gathered in Vlora and proclaimed Albania's independence.

The Great Powers – Austria-Hungary, Britain, France, Germany, Italy and Russia – formally recognised independent Albania in May 1913. In June, after 500 years, the last Ottoman troops left Albanian soil. The Great Powers appointed an International Commission of Control to draft a constitution, and Frontier Commissions to demarcate its borders. They refused to recognise the provisional government set up in Vlora and appointed a German prince as a puppet monarch. Prince Wilhelm of Wied never governed beyond Durrësi and gave up altogether after only six months (for more about this interlude, see box, page 97). Albania sank into anarchy as its leaders fought among themselves for power and, during World War I, it fragmented into a mess of 'autonomous' statelets under the influence of the various countries which had designs on its territory. It would not begin to recover until the 1920s.

KING ZOG One of the leaders who emerged during this chaotic period was Ahmet Zogu, a clan chief from the Mati district in northern central Albania. He participated in the Congress of Lushnja in January 1920, which appointed a senate and a cabinet to restore political order, and a High Council of State to oversee them. Zogu was made Interior Minister in the new government. Over the next few years he went on to consolidate his power base, and in December 1924 – after a brief period out of power – he marched on Tirana and overthrew the Democratic Party government of Fan Noli. He quickly abolished the High Council of State, became president, and set about rewriting the constitution and eliminating his opponents.

By the mid-1920s, Italian influence over Albania was increasing. Italian companies were building roads and improving harbours, Italian colonists were settling in parts of the south and, in November 1927, a large Italian military mission was installed in the country, with Italian officers attached to Albanian military units. In 1928, Zogu crowned himself Zog I, King of the Albanians, and promulgated a new constitution which gave him practically unrestricted powers.

Meanwhile, Italian 'advisers' were installing themselves in the ministries, Italian architects were redesigning Tirana and Italian businessmen were taking over the country's economy. By 1938, Italy accounted for 68.4% of Albania's exports and 36.3% of its imports. Eventually, on 7 April 1939, Mussolini annexed Albania and Italian troops invaded and occupied it. The king sent his wife, Queen Geraldine, and two-day-old son, Leka, to safety across the Greek border, following them himself later in the day. Zog would never return to Albania; he died in Paris in 1961, from where his remains were repatriated in 2012, as part of the commemoration of Albanian independence. His widow and son both died in Tirana: Geraldine, who by then styled herself the Queen Mother (Nëna Mbretëresha), in October 2002; Leka, in 2011.

WORLD WAR II Events in Albania during World War II are a matter of extreme controversy and political polarisation. The various liberation groups can be broadly categorised as 'nationalist', meaning those who wanted the post-war borders of Albania to include Kosova and other Albanian-speaking lands, and 'partisan', meaning those

SPECIAL OPERATIONS EXECUTIVE (SOE) – THE EARLY YEARS

M C Barrès-Baker

SOE was created in July 1940. Placed under the Minister of Economic Warfare and intended 'to co-ordinate … subversion and sabotage, against the enemy overseas', it combined Section D of MI6, the propaganda branch of the Foreign Office and a research branch of the War Office.

In November 1940, the exiled King Zog planned a revolt in northern Albania. SOE feared, possibly wrongly, that Zog was so unpopular that supporting him would actually weaken Albanian resistance. In any case the plan was opposed by the Greeks and just about everybody else; nothing came of it.

In April 1941, SOE sent Lieutenant-Colonel Dayrell Oakley-Hill, who had helped organise Zog's gendarmes before the war, into northern Albania, along with 300 resisters. He was to foment a rebellion but, when Germany invaded Yugoslavia, the operation turned into a diversion to support the Yugoslavs. The tiny invasion received little support and the situation rapidly became hopeless. Oakley-Hill eventually surrendered to the Germans in Belgrade.

In early 1942, SOE headquarters in Cairo began to plan subversion in Albania again. Until 1944, the ethnographer Margaret Hasluck (see box, pages 116–17) ran the SOE Albania desk. Since the British didn't recognise an Albanian government-in-exile, they were prepared to work with all Albanian resisters. In April 1943, Major Neil 'Billy' McLean and Captain David Smiley entered from northern Greece and contacted the National Liberation Movement (LNÇ, predominantly partisan) and the anti-communist, anti-Zog Balli Kombëtar. Weapons drops began in June. Initially the aircraft flew from Cyrenaica, moving in December to Italy from where sea sorties were also made. Most supplies went to the partisans, despite McLean and partisan leader Enver Hoxha having developed a growing mutual antipathy. A series of meetings between the LNÇ and Balli Kombëtar, possibly brokered by SOE and the Zogist Abas Kupi, led to the short-lived Mukje Agreements in August.

The Italian surrender exacerbated the divisions between the LNÇ and the nationalists, and civil war threatened. In October, SOE sent in an enlarged mission under Brigadier E F 'Trotsky' Davies, withdrawing McLean. Davies and his men continued to work with the resistance and carry out sabotage, despite growing civil conflict and large-scale German anti-partisan offensives over the winter. He was also charged with uniting the Albanians, or with recommending which group Britain should recognise. 'It sounded so simple,' Davies wrote later. 'In Albania I was to find the whole matter very complex and difficult.' Initially Davies recommended supporting all groups that fought the Germans, but in December he recommended limiting support to the partisans – by far the most active resisters. Davies was captured in January 1944. SOE, now based in Bari, followed his first recommendation.

Norman Wheeler, and later Alan Palmer, took over in the south. In April 1944, McLean and Smiley, along with Julian Amery, returned to northern Albania as part of a mission to Kupi. McLean became very close to Kupi, and hoped he could be built up as an alternative to the partisans. The aims of the two SOE missions rapidly diverged.

M C Barrès-Baker

By April 1944, the partisans were organised like a regular army. They had 13,000 soldiers, formed into 12 brigades. Despite their communist leadership, they were a broad-based popular resistance movement. Abas Kupi had only 5,000 men, and they were far less active than the partisans. Hoxha clearly mistrusted his SOE liaison officers, but his troops killed Germans. 'Billy' McLean's attempt to convince SOE in Bari to consider Kupi as a serious alternative to the partisans was therefore doomed. Although Bari officially supported both groups, the partisans continued to receive the bulk of air-dropped supplies.

Between spring 1943 and late 1944, about 50 British officers were sent to Albania. They were a varied group: Smiley was happiest when 'blowing things up'; Peter Kemp had fought as a nationalist volunteer in the Spanish Civil War; Davies ended the war in Colditz; Reginald Hibbert would become British Ambassador in Paris; and Julian Amery, who would later become a Conservative MP, got into trouble for wearing a beard while in uniform at Bari and, while moving in disguise around a Tirana full of occupying German soldiers in light summer uniforms, had a sudden insight into what it must be like to be a colonial subject of the British Empire. A sort of *Boy's Own* adventure atmosphere comes across in some SOE men's memoirs, but this was frustrating, gruelling and dangerous work. Several SOE men (not just officers) have graves in the Tirana Park Memorial Cemetery. The highest-ranking man buried there, Brigadier Arthur Nicholls, developed severe frostbite during the German offensive over the winter of 1943/44. Despite medical assistance from his Albanian colleagues, he died three days after his 33rd birthday. He was awarded a posthumous George Cross.

In July 1944, the partisans launched a major offensive, entering Kupi's heartland. Fearing all-out civil war, SOE stopped supplying them, but further partisan successes against the Germans led to this decision being reversed. Bari now signed military agreements with the LNÇ. Faced with this clear British move towards the partisans, Kupi and the Ballists both engaged the Germans more forcefully, but SOE was not impressed. In September 1944, it gave up on them completely. McLean and Smiley were ordered to return to Bari. Dismayed by the lack of support for Kupi, Smiley and Amery later claimed that SOE was bedazzled

who ultimately came out on top and took power after liberation. The former group included supporters of King Zog, such as Abas Kupi, who came to call themselves the Legality (Legaliteti) Movement, and supporters of the Noli government, such as Mit'hat Frashëri, who founded the National Front (Balli Kombëtar) Party in April 1939, immediately after the Italian invasion. The latter group included Enver Hoxha and Mehmet Shehu, and its core was the Albanian Communist Party.

Albania remained part of Italy for more than four years, although the Greek army occupied parts of the south when the Italian invasion of Greece went awry in late 1940. When Italy surrendered in September 1943, the occupying army in Albania disintegrated – some Italian soldiers became servants on Albanian farms in order to get enough food to survive. As in Italy itself, the Wehrmacht stepped into the gap; a Council of Regency was set up, consisting of four Albanian politicians who were prepared to collaborate with the Germans, and the country was formally independent once more.

by the partisans and infiltrated by communist agents. Their books were widely read, unlike Hibbert's memoir of his work with the partisans.

Fearing a partisan victory, many nationalists were by now fighting alongside the Germans. Kupi refused to do this, disbanding his forces instead. The British authorities in Italy refused to evacuate him, but he still managed to get out of Albania and across the Adriatic.

In October, British commandos helped liberate Saranda, making Hoxha very suspicious. Long Range Desert Group forward observers directed RAF air support during the battle for Tirana and SOE men accompanied the partisan brigades into the city.

The end of the war was not the end of British involvement in Albania. From 1949 to 1953, the American CIA and British military intelligence attempted to overthrow Hoxha by covert means. It has been claimed that Cambridge spy Kim Philby gave Moscow details of the operation, but the plans overestimated the ability of ordinary Albanians to rise up against the regime. Many infiltrators, code-named 'pixies' by their Anglo-American handlers, lost their lives.

After the war, Hoxha denied, or greatly played down, British aid to the partisans. Indeed, he destroyed all trace of the British War Cemetery, moving the bodies to an unmarked collective grave, with the result that, until 1995, men who had died in Albania had to be commemorated at Phaleron War Cemetery in Greece. Even now, the grave markers at Tirana Park Memorial Cemetery do not correspond precisely to where the men lie. On the other hand, some in the West accused SOE of having enabled the communists to seize power. Most historians now accept that the aid was very useful to the partisans, but that they would have defeated the other groups anyway.

Initially the post-communist government only recognised the achievements of SOE personnel who had not worked with the partisans, but for the Liberation Day celebrations in November 1994 they invited all the wartime British Liaison Officers they could. Only two managed to attend – Hibbert, who had worked with the partisans, and Smiley, who had not. Both men were awarded the Order of Liberty, First Class.

As mentioned above, several SOE agents who served in Albania subsequently wrote memoirs. For details of these, see *Appendix 2, Further Information*, page 272.

Many Albanians, however, refused to accept the German occupation. In the vicious war that followed, Albanians fought both against and alongside the Germans, and against each other. Beyond the intellectual elite of Tirana, Albanian politics is still essentially based on who did what to whom during the war.

Both nationalists and partisans were assisted by British officers, infiltrated into Albania from 1943 by the Special Operations Executive, or SOE (see boxes on page 13 and above). Gradually, however, Britain gave greater support to the partisans, supplying them with weapons, ammunition and clothing. In May 1944, at a congress in the southern town of Përmeti, a provisional government was elected. The Congress of Përmeti consolidated the exclusion which had begun the previous year of the non-communist forces, annulled various decisions and agreements made by the pre-war monarchist government, and specifically banned King Zog from returning to Albania.

In September, partisan brigades began to advance on Tirana. The Battle for the Liberation of Tirana lasted 19 days, from 29 October to 17 November; intense street fighting raged up and down the city, with the partisans receiving some air support from RAF Beaufighters. By the end of November, the Germans had been driven out of Shkodra, their last foothold in Albania, and the communist government controlled the whole country.

COMMUNISM Albania was impoverished and devastated at the end of the war. An estimated 28,000 people had been killed and thousands more were homeless. The United Nations implemented a relief programme and the new government – under its prime minister Enver Hoxha – organised brigades of peasants to repair roads and rebuild houses. Meanwhile, industry, banking and transport were nationalised, the property of those who had fled the country for political reasons was confiscated and, in 1945, an agrarian reform law broke up and redistributed privately owned estates. The following year all surplus agricultural land was taken over by state farms or co-operatives.

At this time, the relationship between Albania and Yugoslavia was still good – Belgrade gave generous economic assistance to its neighbour, despite its own need for reconstruction. As far as Britain and the USA were concerned, however, Albania suspected their embassies of encouraging opponents of the regime (probably with some justification) and started to restrict their diplomats' movements. Britain withdrew its diplomatic mission in April 1946, followed later that year by the USA.

Relations between Britain and Albania became even worse after the **Corfu Channel incident** of October 1946, when two British destroyers hit mines in the narrow strait between Ksamili and Corfu, and more than 40 crew members were killed. The mines had been recently laid, rather than forming part of a wartime minefield, and Britain accused Albania of deliberately laying them. The matter was the first-ever case referred to the International Court of Justice, which ruled against Albania and ordered it to pay compensation. Many historians now think that Yugoslav ships were responsible, although Albania's (and Britain's) role in the episode is still far from clear.

When Yugoslavia was expelled from Cominform (the post-war body which replaced Comintern) in 1948, Albania immediately sided with the Soviet Union and annulled all its economic agreements with its neighbour. This was also the year that the Albanian Communist Party changed its name to the Party of Labour (Partia e Punës së Shqipërisë, or PPSH).

The 1950s was a decade of **industrialisation**, with hydro-electric plants built to provide power for the new factories and mines. In 1954, the year after Stalin's death, Mehmet Shehu took over the position of prime minister, although Enver Hoxha stayed on as First Secretary of the party and continued to wield considerable power. Shehu had been one of the partisans' most illustrious generals; before the war he had attended Italian military school, been expelled for left-wing activities and fought in the Spanish Civil War. He was interned in France and returned to Albania on his release in 1942.

By the late 1950s, relations between China and the Soviet Union were deteriorating and Albania took China's side. In 1961, this culminated in a complete severance of diplomatic links between Albania and the USSR and, in 1968, Albania withdrew from the Warsaw Pact. In 1967, in the wake of the Chinese Cultural Revolution, Albania banned the practice of religion and declared itself the **world's first atheist state**. Priests and *hoxhas* (Muslim clerics) were shot or imprisoned, and churches and mosques were demolished or converted into warehouses or sports halls. Only a few very old or exceptionally beautiful religious buildings were spared.

After Mao's death in 1976, China lost interest in Albania and in 1978 it ended its aid programmes there. Albania now had no powerful ally to protect and subsidise it, and had little option but to begin to improve relations with its neighbours – first with Yugoslavia and later, after the restoration of democracy there, with Greece. However, most Albanians – those who did not take part in sporting or cultural delegations or get to attend trade fairs – were almost completely cut off from the rest of the world.

Rapprochement with Yugoslavia caused divisions within the party and the government, which Hoxha usually resolved by eliminating those who disagreed with him. Mehmet Shehu fell out of favour and was found dead in December 1981. It was rumoured that Hoxha had shot him, but Shehu's own sons believe their father committed suicide. They and their mother were imprisoned; Shehu's widow died in prison, while his sons were released in 1991. Hoxha himself died in 1985 and was succeeded as First Secretary by Ramiz Alia, one of the few northerners to have gained prominence in the PPSH.

Alia attempted to improve relations with Albania's neighbours, but internally there was little liberalisation of any sort until after the Berlin Wall had fallen. Then a few minor political reforms were announced and religious worship was again tolerated. In 1990, thousands of Albanians climbed over the walls of the Western embassy buildings in Tirana, in an attempt to flee the country. Students began demonstrations and hunger strikes, demanding, first of all, better living conditions in their halls of residence, then the removal of Enver Hoxha's name from that of Tirana's university, and finally 'freedom [and] democracy'. On 11 December 1990, the government at last agreed to allow independent political parties. When the Democratic Party (DP) was formed the following day, it was the first opposition party in Albania for half a century.

THE 1990S In February 1991, a march in support of the striking students turned into a symbolic and historic event, when the demonstrators poured into Skanderbeg Square and pulled down the 10m-high statue of Enver Hoxha which dominated it. A few weeks later tens of thousands of young men climbed aboard ships docked in the ports of Durrësi and Vlora, and forced their crews to take them across the Adriatic to Brindisi. It was in this tense environment that, on 31 March 1991, Albania's first multi-party elections were held. The DP and other newly formed parties contested the elections but were unable to make much headway against the PPSH electoral machine. Despite the parliamentary arithmetic, however, the PPSH government was brought down only weeks later by a general strike. A cross-party government took over and new elections were held on 22 March 1992, which the DP won by a landslide.

The PPSH subsequently rebranded itself as the Socialist Party and carried out internal reforms, in particular allowing considerable autonomy to its youth wing, whose members were not tainted by association with the party's communist past.

The DP governed until 1997, when it, too, was brought down. This time the cause of the unrest was the failure of pyramid investment schemes which had sprung up in 1995 and 1996. The 'pyramids' offered a rate of return which people with any experience of Western capitalism would have known was unsustainable. The Albanians, however, isolated as they had been, were easily convinced to deposit their savings there; some sold their houses or farms to raise cash to invest in the pyramids. Even educated people who knew deep down that it was too good to be true allowed themselves to be carried along. Towards the end of 1996, some of the smaller pyramid 'banks' began to fail, as was inevitable, and savers began to panic, which was also inevitable.

1

Street demonstrations spread and soon became riots. In the generally anti-DP cities of the south, the riots grew from simple protests against the disappearance of people's savings to a full-scale rebellion against the government, which quickly spread to other parts of the country. Police and army officers fled and looters broke into their weapons stores. Anything connected to the state was ransacked and destroyed, from DP offices and police stations to state-owned hotels and children's swing-parks.

The anarchy lasted for weeks and was only brought under any sort of control by the arrival of an international peacekeeping force, the promise of new elections, and the establishment of a caretaker, cross-party government. The elections of June 1997 were conducted in circumstances in which normal campaigning was impossible and voter intimidation was widespread. Nonetheless, the results were accepted by the DP president, who resigned just before the new, socialist-dominated parliament convened.

The incoming government restored its authority gradually over central Albania, but there was still considerable instability in much of the rest of the country. Over half a million weapons had been looted in the spring of 1997, and attempts to persuade people to hand them back were largely unsuccessful. In September 1998, the political situation took a turn for the worse with the assassination of a DP Member of Parliament, Azem Hajdari. For a few days, violence returned to the streets of Tirana, fortunately without spiralling out of control.

Gradually Albania pieced itself back together. Its central and local authorities won widespread praise for their response to the crisis in Kosova, which brought half a million refugees across its borders. Its Interior Ministry and police chiefs cleared the car-jackers off the highways and locked up the armed gangs who controlled some towns and cities. Ordinary Albanians were horrified by what happened to their country in 1997. This, perhaps more than anything else, has ensured that Albania has subsequently avoided sliding into similar turmoil, even when political tensions have run high.

GOVERNMENT AND POLITICS

Albania is a parliamentary democracy, governed by a constitution passed in 1998. One hundred and forty members, elected through regional party lists, sit in its parliament. Their mandate runs for four years and the last elections were held in 2009. Every five years, the parliament elects the country's president, who is the head of state.

In the most recent parliamentary elections, held in 2013, the Socialist Party, which had been in opposition for eight years, emerged as the largest single party and formed a government coalition with the Movement for Socialist Integration (LSI) and two smaller parties.

Local government is conducted by directly elected mayors and proportionally elected councils. In addition, there are 12 prefectures, each headed by an appointee of central government. The prefects co-ordinate the regional departments of the various ministries and have some oversight over the local councils' work. For macro-planning purposes, each local council elects delegates from its number to a regional authority (qark) whose boundaries correspond with those of the prefecture.

ECONOMY

The Democratic Party government elected in 1992 inherited an economy in ruins, where GDP had fallen by more than 50% since 1989. It launched an economic reform programme which included price and exchange system liberalisation, fiscal consolidation, monetary restraint and an incomes policy. These were complemented by a comprehensive package of structural reforms, including privatisation, enterprise and financial sector reform, and creation of the legal framework for a market economy and private sector activity.

These reforms were similar to those applied in other newly democratic countries of central and eastern Europe, and were popularly known as 'shock therapy'. The growth and currency stabilisation which they brought were accompanied by unemployment and a sharp reduction in state benefits. In 1995, GDP growth began to stall and inflation to increase – in 1996, it approached 20% and in 1997, the year of the civil uprising, it reached 50%.

Since 1998, however, the economy has stabilised and GDP has increased every year since, thanks mainly to the expansion of the services sector, which accounts for nearly half of GDP. Agriculture, mostly on small family farms, accounts for about half of employment but less than 20% of GDP. The construction industry has fallen back from its peak in 2008 to just over 10% of GDP. The economy is further bolstered by remittances from Albanians abroad, mainly in Greece and Italy, which, although they have declined in recent years, still account for 7% of GDP.

The grey economy may be as large as 50% of official GDP. Much of this comes from the cultivation and export of cannabis, which is widely grown throughout the country. Spectacular police raids on the cannabis growers of Lazarati and elsewhere made international headlines in 2014.

ETHNIC GROUPS

Most people who live in Albania are ethnically Albanian. There are several minority groups in the country, but accurate figures for their numbers are not available. The most recent census, conducted in 2011, was the first to include a question about ethnic and cultural affiliation, but this was one of several optional questions and nearly 16% of respondents chose not to answer it. The nationwide figures also give a misleading impression because most ethnic minorities are clustered in specific districts, rather than being evenly spread throughout the country.

The largest minority is the Greek-speaking community, which is concentrated in southwestern Albania. There are state-funded Greek-medium schools in that part of the country, and ethnic Greeks are active in the political and commercial life of Albania. The nationwide figure for the Greek community in the 2011 census is 0.87%, although it is likely that there is some underreporting. The Roma and the Vlachs make up the second-largest ethnic groups, with 0.3% each at national level. As in most other countries, Roma are almost completely excluded from the political process and many live in extremely precarious conditions of great poverty.

Vlachs (also known as Aroumanians) were originally transhumant shepherds and they are found all over the Balkans. The main centres of Vlach population in Albania are in villages in the Korça district (Voskopoja is one; Mborja is another) and across the central lowlands in towns such as Lushnja and Berati. Their language is very similar to Romanian and many Albanian Vlachs have emigrated to study or work in Romania. It is not known when the two groups divided, but the languages are close enough that a modern Romanian and an Albanian Vlach can converse with each other.

Egyptians and Slavs are the other main minorities in Albania. The Egyptian, or Jevg, community claims to be descended from Egyptian mercenaries who came to Albania with Alexander the Great's army. This community, too, exists in other Balkan countries; in Albanian-speaking lands their mother tongue is Albanian.

Egyptians are often lumped in with Roma, but they look different and are more integrated into Albanian society. The main thing the two communities have in common is the extreme discrimination they face.

There are Slav-speaking settlements around Lake Prespa, where they are ethnically Macedonian; in the border area between Peshkopia and Kukësi, where they are Gorani, like their cousins (often literally) across the border in Kosova; and around Lake Shkodra and in Malësia e Madhe, where they are ethnically Montenegrin.

LANGUAGE

Albanian is an Indo-European language, in the same large family as Greek, Italian and Serbo-Croat (and English), but in a separate linguistic branch from all of them. It shares certain grammatical features with Romanian, and the point at which the two languages diverged is a matter of great controversy among philologists of both countries.

Albania was part of the Ottoman Empire for more than 400 years, and Turkish words have naturally become assimilated into the Albanian language, including *reçel* (jam), *koltuk* (armchair), *sahat* (clock), *çantë* (handbag) and *kusur* (small) change). Greek words have also made their way into Albanian, and are used particularly in the south (for example: 'Are you hungry?', 'A ke oreks?').

The grammatical structure of Albanian is instantly recognisable to anyone who has studied other Indo-European languages. People who speak French or another Romance language will notice cognates such as *furrë* (*four*, oven), *qen* (*chien*, dog) and the numbers *dy* and *katër* (two and four). That said, however, it must be admitted that Albanian grammar is difficult and much of its vocabulary does not look familiar on first acquaintance.

Albanians themselves are secretly rather pleased that their language is reputed to be so difficult. They will waste no time in telling you with glee that the Albanian alphabet has 36 letters; they will regale you with stories of elderly peasants from opposite ends of the country who are unable to understand each other's dialect. They will be delighted if you learn some of their language, but somewhat taken aback if you speak it well.

THE ALPHABET The 36 letters of the alphabet include two letters with diacritic marks (ë and ç) and nine digraphs, meaning letters which are written using two consonants but which are considered to be a single letter (dh, gj, ll, nj, rr, sh, th, xh and zh). This makes the printed language look scarier than it really is – most of the 36 letters will cause no difficulty at all. Each of the consonants is always pronounced in the same way, wherever it appears in the word; vowels can be short or long, but the language is fairly phonetic, which makes it very easy to learn phrases. A guide to pronunciation and a list of everyday words and phrases can be found in *Appendix 1, Language*, pages 263–70.

DIALECTS A dialect is a language variant which is sufficiently different from another variant of the same language, and sufficiently consistent within itself, to be more than just an accent. Three dialects of Albanian are normally recognised: Arbëresh is spoken in parts of southern Italy, where Albanians settled after the Ottoman conquest of their country; Gheg is spoken in northern Albania, Kosova, Montenegro and northwestern Macedonia; and Tosk is spoken in southern Albania, southern Macedonia and Skopje, and in some mountain villages of northern

Greece. Some would argue that the language used in central Albania (Durrësi and Tirana) might also qualify as a dialect.

Within Albania a standard form of the language is used, known as 'the literary language' (*gjuha letrare*). The literary language was an official attempt to combine elements of Gheg and Tosk, although northern Albanians would contend that Tosk elements preponderate in it. It has been taught in Albanian schools for more than 40 years and is universally understood. People may use their own dialect when talking among themselves, but with anyone who is not local (ie: not only foreigners) they will switch to this standardised Albanian. Of course, it is true that an elderly shepherd is likely to be less fluent in 'literary language' than a 30-year-old bank clerk, but the chances are the shepherd will also make more of an effort to ensure that, as a guest in his or her land, you are happy and understand what is going on.

RELIGION

E mos shikoni kisha e xhamia/feja e shqyptarit asht shqyptaria!
(Pay no attention to churches and mosques/the Albanian's faith is Albanian-ness!)
O Moj Shqypni!, Pashko Vasa (1825–92)

During the five centuries that they formed part of the Ottoman Empire, Albanians converted to Islam in larger numbers than anywhere else in Ottoman Europe. Catholicism survived in the high mountains of the north and in coastal cities such as Shkodra; Orthodox Christians clung to their faith in the south. However, it is fairly clear that many (if not most) of those who converted did so for entirely pragmatic reasons, such as reducing their tax demands, gaining the right to bear arms or keeping their sons from the *devshirme* (see pages 10–11). Often the man of the household would convert, while his wife retained her Christian faith. There were also cases of 'crypto-Christianity', where people would adopt Islamic names and attend prayers in the mosque, but in private would follow their old Christian rituals.

Perhaps this attitude helps to explain how it was possible for religion to be completely banned in 1967. In that year, Albania's communist government prohibited religious worship and the country became the world's only officially atheist state. Churches and mosques were demolished or turned into warehouses or sports halls, and the practice of religion would remain an offence until 1990. Albania remains an extremely secular society today.

The 2011 census was the first to include a question about the respondent's religious affiliation, but it was one of several optional questions and over 16% of people chose not to answer it. Unreliable though the data may be, they reveal an interesting shift from the traditional breakdown of 70% Muslim, 20% Orthodox and 10% Catholic. The 2011 figures show just under 57% Muslim, with a further 2% answering 'Bektashi' (see pages 22–3), 10% Catholic and only 7% Orthodox. A fraction of one percent identified themselves as belonging to another Christian religion – the evangelical Protestant churches which have become popular in the cities in the past decade or so – and 2.5% continue to describe themselves as atheists.

THE AUTOCEPHALOUS CHURCH The Albanian Orthodox Church is autocephalous, meaning that it ordains its own bishops and is its own authority. Autonomy from the Greek Church was a campaign issue for Orthodox Albanians in the *Rilindja* years of the early 20th century, particularly in Korça and among diaspora Albanians in the USA (many of whom were originally from Korça). The first liturgy in Albanian was celebrated in Boston in 1908, by a priest who had been ordained two weeks before by the Russian Archbishop of New York. The Albanian priest's name was Fan Noli, and in 1924 he also served for six months as Prime Minister of Albania.

After the end of communism and the restoration of religious freedom, a new archbishop was enthroned in 1992, and the Albanian Church has regained its autocephalous status. The website of the Orthodox Autocephalous Church (*http://orthodoxalbania.org/old*) has information about the Church's history and activities, although it is mostly in Albanian. There is also a breakaway Orthodox Autocephalous Church, based in Elbasani (see pages 114–15).

THE CATHOLIC CHURCH Albania's Catholics are mostly concentrated in the northwest of the country: Shkodra, Mirdita and villages hidden in the mountains, too remote for the Ottomans to have bothered trying to convert them to Islam. Their perceived allegiance to Rome brought them under particular suspicion from the Partisans who came to power in 1944. Priests were arrested and shot; others were imprisoned and died in labour camps. Lay Catholics were arrested too, including a young woman from Mirdita called Maria Tuci, who had been a postulant with the Stigmatine Sisters in Shkodra until the government closed the convent. Imprisoned in 1949, she died the following year, aged only 21. Some of the Catholics who died for their faith under communism are commemorated in Shkodra Cathedral and (in English) on the website of the Catholic church in Shkodra (*www.kishakatolikeshkoder.com*).

JUDAISM Despite the German occupation of Albania, the country's small Jewish community survived World War II; indeed, during the war, Albania provided a haven for Jewish refugees from other countries and some of the Albanians who sheltered Jews are honoured at the Holocaust memorial Yad Vashem as 'Righteous among the Nations'. Nor were Jews treated any worse than members of other religions during the atheism campaign. The Jewish community emigrated en masse to Israel as soon as the borders opened, not because they had been badly treated in Albania but simply because, unlike most Albanians, they were lucky enough to have a country which would welcome them.

BEKTASHISM Albania's 'fourth religion' is Bektashism, a Sufi order of Islam founded in the 13th century. The Ottoman Empire's 'official' Islam was Sunni, and was followed mainly by the intelligentsia, the civil servants and functionaries. Ordinary people in the Balkan provinces were much more attracted by the Sufi sects, whose rituals and rite system were closer to folk beliefs. The followers of Sufism believe that individuals can achieve communion with God through their own personal qualities and experience, with the help of contemplation.

Bektashism came to Albania gradually, brought by clerics known as dervishes or *babas* (fathers) travelling alone or in very small groups. They actively sought to assimilate local traditions into the religious ideas they taught, including relics of paganism such as mountain worship. Their religious centres – places of preaching, study and initiation which are called *teqe* (spelt '*tekke*' in Turkish, and sometimes in English too) – were often established near the tomb of some righteous person, who with time became venerated in the same way as Christian saints.

Bektashism took hold in Albania and began to expand dramatically in the early 19th century; Ali Pasha Tepelena (see box, pages 246–7) was a convert. Alarmed by the sect's popularity, the Ottoman authorities attempted to suppress it; in response, the *babas* moved up into the mountains and built *teqes* in high, remote places such as Mount Tomorri in Skrapari and Melani, above Libohova. Many of these *teqes* are still used today, especially for pilgrimages on holy days.

The Bektashi order was expelled from Turkey in 1925 and its world headquarters have been in Albania ever since. Further information about the history of and modern developments in Bektashism can be found at http://bektashiorder.com.

EDUCATION

School education in Albania follows a pattern which is unfamiliar to British visitors. Most children attend the same school for nine years, then go on to either a General High School (*Shkolla e Mesme e Përgjithshme*) or a Professional High School (*Shkolla e Mesme Profesional*). The latter trains students for specific professions – for example, economics and accounting, mechanics, construction, hotel management or sports. In very rural areas, the elementary schools tend to take only five classes; after their fifth year, the children have to commute to school in a larger village or town, or even board with relatives or in a school dormitory (*konvikt*).

More than half of those who finish high school go on to higher education. Albania's state university was founded in the 1950s. It has branches in each city, offering a range of faculties such as engineering, medicine, science, law and economics; the Agricultural Institute in Kamza (near Tirana) and the Conservatoire (in Tirana) are also part of the state university system. The first private university in the country opened its doors in 2002 and since then there has been a huge increase in the number of such institutions. They are of varying quality; some are very good and have close academic relations with universities in Italy, France or other western European countries. Many Albanian families continue to make huge sacrifices so that their children can go to universities abroad.

CULTURE

LITERATURE The earliest documents written in Albanian were religious works produced by Catholic priests – a 16th-century missal and some doctrinal poetry survive. However, Albanian literature did not emerge until the 19th century, in a cultural phenomenon known as the National Renaissance (*Rilindja Kombëtare*) which was closely linked to the rise of Albanian nationalism.

The 19th-century writers included essayists and dramatists, but the predominant literary form was lyric poetry, and its exponents came from all parts of the Albanian-speaking world. Pashko Vasa (1825–92) and Gjergj Fishta (1871–1940) were Shkodran; Çajupi (1866–1930) and Naim Frashëri (1843–1900) came from the south; Jeronim de Rada (1814–1903) was Arbëresh; and Fan Noli (1880–1965) was born in an Albanian settlement near Adrianople, now the Turkish city of Edirne. Other notable literary figures of the period were Asdreni (1872–1947), the author of the poem which later became the national anthem, and the essayist Faik Konica (1875–1942), who was Albania's ambassador to the USA from 1926 until his sudden death in 1942.

The lyric tradition continued into the 20th century, represented by the Shkodran poets Migjeni (1911–38) and Martin Çamaj (1925–93), and was complemented with novels, plays and short stories. The extracts from Albanian folk tales throughout this book are translated from the versions by Mitrush Kuteli (the pseudonym of Dhimitër Pasko, 1907–67). Dritëro Agolli (b1931) made a delightful translation of some of Robert Burns's poems into Albanian. These writers, like others such as

Fatos Arapi (b1930), the Kosovar Rexhep Qosja (b1936) and Vath Koreshi (1936–2006), are almost unknown in the English-speaking world.

The only novelist of that generation who is at all widely read there is Ismail Kadare, born in Gjirokastra in 1936. Kadare's works, in addition to being fine literature, make very good background reading if you are planning to visit Albania. *Chronicle in Stone, Broken April* and *The General of the Dead Army* are perhaps the most accessible. These novels are available in English, but the translations are made from the French version rather than coming directly from Albanian. Those who read the language may well prefer the French translations, which were made by the great Albanian–French translator Jusuf Vrioni (1916–2001), and give a more accurate flavour of the original. Affordable paperback editions are published in Fayard's *Le Livre de Poche* series. Ismail Kadare was awarded the inaugural Man Booker International prize in 2005; see page 232 and box, page 238 for further information about Kadare and his work.

Younger Albanian writers include Bardhyl Londo (b1948), Besnik Mustafaj (b1958), Preç Zogaj (b1957) and Visar Zhiti (b1952), whose first volume of poetry was deemed so subversive that it earned him ten years in communist labour camps.

FILM In the 1960s and 1970s, Albania developed a thriving film industry. A film studio, Kinostudio, was opened in 1952 and *Skanderbeg*, a Soviet–Albanian co-production, was released the following year. Initially, post-production was done in the Soviet Union or Yugoslavia; the first feature film entirely produced in Albania was *Tana*, in 1958. By the 1970s, Kinostudio was making 14 films a year. There were 26 cinemas, in towns all over the country, and portable cinemas took films to the villages. The Albanian Film Archive (*www.aqshf.gov.al*) holds a huge stock of communist-era films, much of it in very precarious condition. Work is under way to conserve, restore and digitise some of the films and, in due course, they may become commercially available on DVD.

In the late 1990s, Albanian scriptwriters and directors began to produce films again and several have had international success. Directors to look out for include Kujtim Çashku (*Colonel Bunker*, 1996), Gjergj Xhuvani (*Slogans*, 2001; *Dear Enemy*, 2004; *East West East*, 2009) and Fatmir Koçi (*Time of the Comet*, 2008). Art-house cinemas in Britain and other western European countries screen Albanian films from time to time, and they can sometimes be sourced from the internet.

MUSIC There are three distinct strands to Albanian folk music – the diatonic music of the north, the pentatonic tradition of the south and urban music (*ahengu qytetar*) in which chromatic melodies often prevail.

The music of northern Albania (and of Albanians in Montenegro and Kosova) is characterised by solo male singers, accompanied on long-necked stringed instruments called *çiftelia* and *lahuta*. The *lahutë* is a bowed instrument, making it suitable for accompanying diatonic melodies, while the *çifteli* has frets and is used to create a kind of drone effect, which is very atmospheric. A single-drone bagpipe called the *gajde* is also played in the north and sounds remarkably Celtic.

Albanian polyphonic music has a very wide geographic spread. It is found not only in southern Albania, but also across the modern borders in Greek Epirus and southwestern Macedonia, as far north as parts of Kosova, and in the Arbëresh settlements in southern Italy. In its core area of southwestern Albania, its basis is pentatonic and it is usually sung unaccompanied, by two or three or – in rare cases – four voices (in the musical sense of 'voices'; there might well be more than three or four people singing). The most characteristic instrument of the south is the clarinet.

The chromatic intervals of Albanian urban folk music were inherited from Turkish musical traditions during the Ottoman period. This type of music is found mainly in the towns of central Albania, especially Elbasani, and also in Shkodra and Berati. It can be sung with an instrumental accompaniment, or played by a small orchestra. Musical instruments which are typical of this tradition are the accordion, the mandolin, the tambourine and a fretted instrument called the *sharki*. Urban folk music has heavily influenced the development of 'popular music', *musika popullore*, which is the only type of traditional music it is at all easy to hear live in Albania.

The folklore festivals at Gjirokastra (every four years, more or less) and Peshkopia (annually, in September) are the best places to hear all the different Albanian musical traditions, including performers from other Albanian-speaking lands. Smaller festivals of traditional music take place from time to time in other parts of the country; the Përmeti Folk Festival, held annually in June, brings together traditional musicians from all over the Balkans, with a special focus on a different country each year.

Background Information CULTURE

1

2

Practical Information

WHEN TO VISIT

For most purposes, the best times of year to visit Albania are spring and autumn. The countryside is particularly beautiful in those seasons; in autumn the orchards blaze with the bright orange of the persimmons and the cooler colours of the citrus fruits, while in spring the apple and cherry blossoms form little pastel-toned drifts by the roadside. The long spring evenings are a good time to enjoy the terrace cafés in Tirana and the coastal towns. In September and October it is still warm enough to swim at the Ionian beaches. Spring and autumn are ideal for relatively low-level hiking or cycle-touring.

Albania has a Mediterranean climate and in the lowlands it never gets really cold. The southwest coast in particular is very clement, with average winter temperatures of 8–10°C. The problem in winter tends to be rain, which makes the city streets and minor roads muddy and slippery. Most of Albania's annual rainfall occurs between late autumn and early spring; outside the high mountain areas, it is unusual for it to rain in summer.

In the highlands, winter is a much more serious proposition; snow can fall from November until March. Major roads, such as those linking Shkodra with Kukësi or Përmeti with Korça, are cleared quickly (usually within a day), but the high passes on minor roads are normally closed for two or three months – or even longer in a harsh winter. Mountain towns such as Korça and Peshkopia are very cold at this time of year. In Tirana, however, it is unusual for temperatures to stay below zero for more than a few days at a time, whereas on the coast snow is practically unheard of.

In summer, on the other hand, inland towns can become oppressively hot; July is usually the warmest month. Sightseeing in high summer is an exhausting business. In Tirana, for example, temperatures in the high 30°Cs are common, and there are a few days in most summers when the thermometer tops 40°C. Hotels and restaurants of a reasonable standard have air conditioning, but museums do not. On the coast, sea breezes keep the average temperatures down to a more tolerable 25–30°C; but during July and August the coastal resorts are crowded and the beaches covered in litter. The best place to be at the height of summer is in the high mountains. Hikers and cyclists should be sure to have enough water with them; everyone else will never be far from a café.

HIGHLIGHTS

Albania has something for almost everyone. Lovers of the outdoors will be happy just about anywhere in the country. The Albanian Alps in the far north and the mountains between Berati and Përmeti in the south are probably the best organised in terms of accommodation, guides and so forth. The Lura Lakes, between Rrësheni and Peshkopia, and the Lunxhëria and Nemerçka ranges in the southwest, are more remote but offer fantastic hiking or cycling opportunities for those with more time at their disposal.

Those who are interested in archaeology and history will find Albania full of delights. In the southwest of the country, the ancient city of Butrint already draws thousands of visitors every year across the Corfu Channel. It richly deserves its status as the country's best-known archaeological site, but there are many other interesting Illyrian, Greek and Roman remains. No visit to southern Albania would be complete without the ancient cities of Gjirokastra and Berati, with their hilltop castles and unique architecture. In the north, the castles of Shkodra and Kruja embody centuries of history, one layer upon another.

Lovers of medieval art should visit the icon collections in Berati, Korça and Tirana; the whole of central and southern Albania is full of half-forgotten churches with magnificent frescoes. Ornithologists will want to head for the coastal wetlands at Karavastaja, Kune-Vaini and Velipoja. Finally, connoisseurs of beaches could easily spend a couple of weeks happily working their way up or down the Albanian Riviera.

SUGGESTED ITINERARIES

Where you go in Albania depends not only on what you like doing, but also where you enter the country. The main points of entry are Tirana International Airport, and Saranda, on the ferry from Corfu. Those who approach Albania from other directions – from Montenegro, Kosova, Macedonia, Greece or Italy – will need to tweak these suggested routes to suit their starting points. All the itineraries which follow can be done by public transport, although the occasional taxi will speed things up considerably.

LONG WEEKEND
Coming from Corfu
Friday: Arriving in Saranda on the morning hydrofoil will allow you to head straight for Butrint, possibly spending the night at the Livia Hotel there.
Saturday: Gjirokastra: visiting the castle and one or two of the traditional houses; staying overnight there or returning to Saranda in the evening.
Sunday: The Riviera: Ali Pasha's fortress at Porto Palermo; possibly Borshi Castle; a swim at Borshi or Himara; back to Saranda for the Monday morning hydrofoil back to Corfu.

It is possible to rent a car in Saranda and for such a short visit this would be a good option. See *Car hire* on page 42 for more details.

Flying into Tirana
Friday: Day in Tirana: National Historical Museum; National Art Gallery; a short or long walk around town.
Saturday: Hike to Pëllumbasi Cave; return to Tirana that evening; or take the bus to Durrësi (beach or historical sites in city centre, depending on weather and preferences), either returning to Tirana or staying overnight in Durrësi.
Sunday: Travel to Kruja; visit the castle and museums; straight to the airport for the evening flight, or stay overnight and travel to the airport from Kruja the next morning.

ONE WEEK
Coming from Corfu
Day 1: As Friday, above.
Day 2: As Saturday, above, staying overnight in Gjirokastra.
Day 3: Visit Antigonea and/or Libohova; overnight in Gjirokastra.
Day 4: Day trip to Byllis; return to Gjirokastra or Saranda in the afternoon.
Days 5–6: The Riviera: as Sunday, above, but staying at Borshi, Himara or Dhërmiu; swim and eat fish, or continue to the Llogoraja Pass and go hiking in the forest (a hire car would be especially useful on these two days).
Day 7: Return to Saranda; afternoon ferry back to Corfu.

Flying into Tirana
Day 1: As Friday, above.
Day 2: Berati: visit the castle and Ethnographic Museum; walk around town; stay overnight.
Day 3: Day trip to Byllis; overnight in Berati.
Day 4: Return to Tirana via Elbasani.
Day 5: As Saturday, above.
Day 6: Day in Tirana: combination of cable-car trip to Mount Dajti; Petrela Castle; Archaeological Museum; Tirana Mosaic; a short or long walk around the city.
Day 7: As Sunday, above.

TWO WEEKS
Coming from Corfu
Day 1: As above
Day 2: Further exploration of Butrint site; boat trips and/or hiking. Overnight in Saranda or Gjirokastra.
Days 3–5: As days 2–4, above, with final night in Gjirokastra or Përmeti.
Day 6: To Korça via Përmeti and Erseka.
Day 7: Korça and environs (archaeological sites or Prespa Lakes, depending on preferences).
Days 8–10: To Tirana; follow Tirana weekend itinerary (staying a third night in Kruja or Tirana).
Day 11: Vlora.
Days 12–13: As days 5–6, above, returning slowly to Saranda down the Riviera.
Day 14: Morning or afternoon ferry back to Corfu.

Flying into Tirana
Days 1–4: As above, with night 4 in Elbasani.
Day 5: To Korça (archaeological sites or Prespa Lakes, depending on preferences); overnight in Korça.
Day 6: To Gjirokastra via Erseka and Përmeti.
Day 7: Gjirokastra: visiting the castle and one or two of the traditional houses; staying overnight there or continuing to Saranda in the evening.
Day 8: Saranda and Butrint.
Day 9: Return to Tirana via Riviera (Himara and Vlora).
Day 10: As day 6 above.
Day 11: As day 5 above.
Days 12–13: Lezha, Shkodra and Drishti or Rubiku. Overnight in Shkodra.
Day 14: As day 7, above.

THREE WEEKS A three-week itinerary might combine the two one-week itineraries (regardless of the point of entry into Albania; the order of the itineraries can be tweaked so that you finish where you want to leave from, rather than at the other end of the country), and then focus on either (a) the cultural and historical heritage or (b) outdoor activities in the mountains (see following sections).

Option (a)

Add three nights to 'Corfu' days 1–3, staying in Gjirokastra and Saranda, to visit the Islamic sites at Delvina, Phoinike, Hadrianopolis.

Add two nights to 'Tirana' day 5, to allow a day trip to Voskopoja, a detour to Selca e Poshtme and more time to explore Korça.

Days 19–20: Add two nights to 'Tirana' days 12–13, for an overnight trip to Thethi, Puka or Mirdita.

Day 21: As Day 7, above.

Option (b)

Add two nights to 'Tirana' days 2–3, continuing from Berati to Çorovoda for rafting or hiking, depending on the time of year.

Day 16: To Shkodra.

Days 17–20: Bus to Thethi; overnight there; hike to Valbona; overnight in Tropoja; return to Shkodra on Komani ferry.

Day 21: Return to airport either directly from Shkodra or with detour to Kruja (as day 7, above), depending on flight departure time.

ONE MONTH If you are lucky enough to have a whole month to spend in Albania, you will probably have torn up any itinerary by the end of your first week. If you like mountains, you will want to spend more time in the Albanian Alps or perhaps explore Puka or Mirdita. If you like cultural heritage, you may want to spend an extra day or two in Shkodra and then visit Mati and Mirdita on the way back to Kruja (or Saranda). Or perhaps you will have had enough of travelling and just want to relax on the Riviera or at one of the lakes. It is worth repeating that Albania has something for almost everyone.

TOUR OPERATORS

UK-BASED OPERATORS

The number and range of organised tours to Albania from western Europe increases every year. The tours range from general introductions, often including one or more of Albania's neighbouring countries, to specialist archaeological or cultural visits. The doyen of the UK-based tour operators is Regent Holidays, which has been leading trips to Albania since 1971. Regent also offers a four-night city break to Tirana and – like other agencies – can tailor-make individual itineraries.

Andante Travels The Old Barn, Old Rd, Alderbury, Salisbury SP5 3AR; ☎ 01722 713800; e tours@andantetravels.co.uk; www.andantetravels.co.uk

Brightwater Holidays Eden Park Hse, Cupar, Fife KY15 4HS; ☎ 01334 657155; e info@brightwaterholidays.com; www. brightwaterholidays.com

Regent Holidays (see ad, page 26) ☎ 020 7666 1244; www.regent-holidays.co.uk

ALBANIA-BASED OPERATORS

Although there are many travel agencies within Albania, almost all of them cater for the outbound market. As a rule, those which act as agents for foreign tour operators also offer tours and bespoke itineraries for independent travellers.

Albania Holidays (see ad, 1st colour section) Tirana; ☎04 223 5688, 223 5498; e contact@albania-holidays.com; www.albania-holidays.com
Elite Travel Elbasani; ☎05 424 4094, 425 9934; e info@elitetravel-albania.com; www.elitetravel-albania.com
Gjolek Mera m 069 21 22 555; e gjolekmera@yahoo.com
Tours Albania (see ad, page 57) Tirana; m 068 40 29 914; e toursalbania@yahoo.com; www.tours-albania.com

TREKKING HOLIDAYS
Caravan Travel m 069 53 75 743, 069 22 34 137; e travelcaravan@ymail.com; http://caravanhorseriding.com; Facebook: Caravan Riding Centre Albania. Based in Gjirokastra, Caravan Travel runs horseback tours of varying lengths in the surrounding mountains.
Outdoor Albania Rr Sami Frashëri, Pallati 'Metropol', Tirana; ☎04 222 7121; Skype: Outdoor Albania; e info@outdooralbania.com; www.

outdooralbania.com. Specialist operator Outdoor Albania organises guided hiking holidays of varying durations throughout the spring & summer. In winter, it offers guided ski tours & snowshoeing trips, led by an experienced climber & skier. Outdoor Albania also has a range of 1-day & w/end activities, including day hikes in the countryside around Tirana, & can design bespoke tours for individuals or small groups, to suit the participants' abilities & interests.
Walks Worldwide Long Barn South, Sutton Manor Farm, Bishop's Sutton, Alresford SO24 0AA, UK; ☎0845 301 4737, 01962 737565; e sales@walksworldwide.com; www.walksworldwide.com. Offers several hiking tours in northern & southern Albania & can arrange tailor-made walking holidays there.
Zbulo (Discover Albania) m 069 67 31 932; e welcome@zbulo.org; www.zbulo.org. Zbulo, based in Thethi, is a more recent arrival on the outdoor-activity scene, but offers some interesting hiking itineraries.

RED TAPE

Citizens of most Western countries are not required to obtain Albanian visas in advance. Countries to which this visa-free system applies include all those in the European Union and EFTA, all of Albania's neighbours (including Serbia), Australia, Canada, Japan, New Zealand, the USA and Turkey. Visitors to Albania are no longer required to pay an entry tax.

The Albanian Foreign Ministry's website (*www.punetejashtme.gov.al/en/services/services-for-foreign-citizens*) carries information in English and Albanian about visa requirements, and information on Albanian embassies throughout the world.

EMBASSIES

ALBANIAN EMBASSIES OVERSEAS
Albanian embassies do not provide guidance to tourists beyond visa requirements and similar queries. Nor does the country have any tourist information offices overseas.

🇨 **Canada** 130 Albert St, Suite 302, Ottawa, Ontario, K1P 5G4; ☎+1 613 236 3053; e embassy.ottawa@mfa.gov.al; www.ambasadat.gov.al/canada/en/
🇨 **UK** (also covers the Republic of Ireland) 33 St George's Drive, London SW1V 4DG; ☎020 7828 8897; e embassy.london@mfa.gov.al; www.ambasadat.gov.al/united-kingdom/en
🇨 **US** 2100 S Street NW, Washington DC 20008;

☎+1 202 223 4942; e embassy.washington@mfa.gov.al; www.ambasadat.gov.al/usa/en

WESTERN EMBASSIES IN ALBANIA
The Albanian Foreign Ministry's website (*www.punetejashtme.gov.al*) has a full list of diplomatic representation in Albania, with contact details and consular opening hours, including for countries (such as Canada and Sweden) which cover Albania from their embassies in other countries.

🇨 **Austria** Rr Frederik Shiroka 3; ☎04 227 4855/6; e tirana-ob@bmeia.gv.at; www.bmeia.gv.at/botschaft/tirana.html (also consulate in Shkodra)

e **Denmark** Rr Nikolla Tupe 1, 4th Floor; ☏ 04 228 0600; e tiaamb@um.dk; http://albanien.um.dk
e **France** Rr Skënderbeu 14; ☏ 04 238 9700; e ambafrance.tr@adanet.com.al, consulat.tirana-amba@diplomatie.gouv.fr; www.ambafrance-al.org
e **Germany** Rr Skënderbeu 8; ☏ 04 227 4505; e info@tirana.diplo.de; www.tirana.diplo.de
e **Greece** Rr Frederik Shiroka 3; ☏ 04 227 4670, 227 4669, 223 4668; e gremb.tir@mfa.gr; www.mfa.gr/missionsabroad/en/albania-en (also consulates in Korça & Gjirokastra)
e **Italy** Rr Gjon Pali II 2; ☏ 04 227 5900; e segramb.tirana@esteri.it; www.ambtirana.esteri.it (also consulates in Gjirokastra, Shkodra & Vlora)
e **Netherlands** Rr Asim Zeneli 10; ☏ 04 224 0828; e tir@minbuza.nl; http://albanie.nlambassade.org

e **Poland** Rr e Durrësit 123; ☏ 04 451 0020; e tirana.amb.sekretariat@msz.gov.pl; www.tirana.msz.gov.pl
e **Spain** Rr Skënderbeu 43; ☏ 04 227 4960/1; e Emb.Tirana@maec.es; www.exteriores.gob.es/Embajadas/TIRANA
e **Switzerland** Rr Ibrahim Rugova 3/1; ☏ 04 223 4888, 225 6535; e helpline@eda.admin.ch; www.eda.admin.ch/tirana
e **UK** Rr Skënderbeu 12; ☏ 04 223 4973/4/5; www.gov.uk/government/world/organisations/british-embassy-tirana
e **USA** Rr e Elbasanit 103; ☏ 04 224 7285; e TiranaUSConsulate@state.gov; http://tirana.usembassy.gov

GETTING THERE AND AWAY

BY AIR British Airways (*www.ba.com*) has direct flights from London Gatwick to Tirana (TIA). At the time of writing, 14 airlines operate scheduled flights into Tirana. A full list, with the addresses of their websites and the telephone numbers of their offices in Tirana, is available on Tirana International Airport's website (*www.tirana-airport.com*). This also has real-time listings for arrivals and departures, details about flight schedules and other useful information. There are also flights from the UK to Podgorica and Prishtina. For information about getting to Albania from Montenegro, see pages 183–4 and 213, and from Kosova, see pages 165 and 172.

Tirana is Albania's only international airport. Officially called 'Mother Teresa International Airport' and usually referred to as Rinas (the name of the nearest village), it has been completely modernised and has a bright and airy passenger terminal with all the usual facilities, including free Wi-Fi throughout. Smoking is prohibited, except in the smoking lounge airside.

An ATM in the arrivals hall accepts Visa, MasterCard and Maestro cards, and issues Albanian lek. There is also an information kiosk and a bureau de change (currency exchange desk). Beyond immigration and customs control are car-hire agencies (see page 42), mobile phone shops, cafés and a bookshop. There are several hotels in the vicinity of the airport; for further information, see the hotel listings in *Chapter 3*, pages 66–70.

It takes about half an hour from the airport to Tirana, 17km away. A slip road in the opposite direction leads to the Fushë–Kruja junction of the main north–south highway, 2.8km from the airport; this is the most convenient route to northern Albania. The minibuses from Shkodra and other towns in the north can drop passengers at the airport, on request and for a small surcharge.

Approved airport taxis can be booked at a kiosk in the baggage reclaim area, or hired from one of the taxi drivers who wait where passengers exit into the arrivals hall. You should agree a fare with the driver before accepting his services – the going rate into Tirana is €20. Alternatively, unofficial taxis park across the road from the airport perimeter fence and charge slightly less. A taxi to Shkodra from the airport should cost no more than €50.

From 07.00 to 19.00, an hourly bus service runs from outside the airport perimeter fence into the centre of Tirana: the one-way fare for this journey is 250 lek. In the city centre, the bus leaves from the junction of Rruga e Durrësit with Rruga Mine Peza, where there is a clearly marked bus stop with a timetable.

On the way out of Albania, airport check-in and security procedures are reasonably efficient. Leks can be changed back into euros, US dollars or sterling at the landside bureau de change, but the rates are as poor as one might expect. It is likely to be a better deal to spend any surplus leks in the duty-free shops airside. These sell Albanian souvenirs and foodstuffs such as olive oil and mountain tea (see box, page 6), as well as the usual things one finds in airports, including competitively priced spirits.

BY SEA AND LAKE For many northern Europeans, the cheapest and most convenient way to get to southern Albania is to take a charter flight to Corfu and from there the ferry or hydrofoil to Saranda. There is a **hydrofoil** crossing every morning and a **ferry** crossing every afternoon, all year round; additional ferries operate in summer. See pages 215–18 for further details of this route.

Albania has good sea connections with Italy. The busiest route is Bari–Durrësi, with several ferry companies operating throughout the year. The crossing takes about nine hours. There are also ferries to Durrësi from Ancona and Trieste (18 and 24 hours, respectively), and to Vlora from Brindisi (eight hours overnight). The Italian ferry websites (eg: *www.traghettiweb.it, www.traghettiamo.it*) have details of all the routes between Italy and Albania. See pages 90–1 and 253 for further information about getting to Durrësi or Vlora by sea.

A **passenger-only ferry** across Lake Ohrid was piloted in the summer of 2014, linking the Macedonian towns of Ohrid and Struga with the Albanian resort of Pogradeci (see page 140). The return fare on the once-weekly service was 3,000 lek or €30. Assuming it continues in the future, it will be an attractive, although pricier, alternative to the bus journey around the northern or southern end of the lake.

Those fortunate enough to have the use of a **private yacht** will find their mooring options rather limited in Albania. The country's only marina (at least at the time of writing) is on the Bay of Vlora, at Orikumi (see pages 261–2). It is also possible to anchor or berth in Durrësi, Shëngjini, Vlora and Himara. Sail Albania, based in Vlora, can advise; they are the port agents for the Orikum marina and for Vlora. Yachts can also be chartered from them.

Orikum Yachting Club (*Marina e Orikumit*) 40 20′ 32″ N 19 28′ 18″ E; ☎ 0391 22248, Italian number ☎ +39 0565 252040; m 069 53 50 233; e marinaorikum@hotmail.it; www.orikum.it

Sail Albania Rr Murat Terbaçi, Uji i Ftohtë, Vlora; m 069 73 24 138, 069 77 10 739; e sailalbania@gmail.com; www.sail-albania.com

BY LAND Visitors who bring their own **cars** into Albania should ensure that their vehicle insurance is valid there. There is no longer a 'circulation tax'. Petrol and diesel are widely available everywhere except the most remote mountain areas. Liquid Petroleum Gas (LPG) is available at selected garages in cities and large towns.

Crossing into Albania by **bus** is usually a straightforward process. Finding out about these cross-border buses, however, can be more of a challenge. At Greek bus stations and tourist information offices, staff will usually deny the existence of any public transport to Albania. It is unclear whether this is because they are genuinely unaware of the many buses that travel between Greek and Albanian towns and cities, or are trying to prevent tourists from leaving their country.

There is always the alternative of taking a local bus to the border, going through both passport controls on foot, and continuing onward in one of the taxis or minibuses waiting on the Albanian side. At the major land crossings – Kakavija and Kapshtica from Greece, Qafa e Thanës from Macedonia and Hani i Hotit from Montenegro – there will always be onward transport during the daytime. At the smaller crossings the drivers tend to have given up waiting for custom by about midday.

If crossing into Albania from Kosova, there are practically no formalities apart from showing your passport. Women aged under 18 travelling without either of their parents should carry a notarised authorisation; this is intended to make life difficult for criminals trafficking women, rather than for the legitimate female traveller. In the other direction, the Kosovar authorities require a minimum of 15 days' (additional) insurance to be purchased for foreign-registered vehicles (€30 for a car, at the time of writing). Vehicles with Kosova or Albania plates are exempt. This means that, unlike at other international crossings, local buses and minibuses travel freely across the border at Qafë e Morinës. See page 172 for further information about public transport on this route.

There are no international passenger **trains** at the time of writing, although the line from Podgorica to Shkodra is open and used for freight.

HEALTH   *With thanks to Dr Felicity Nicholson*

BEFORE YOU GO   Albania is no more dangerous from a health point of view than any other country in southeastern Europe. It is a good idea in general to keep up to date with vaccinations against tetanus, polio and diphtheria. In the UK these are normally given together and should be boosted every ten years.

Other vaccinations which are worth considering are those against typhoid, hepatitis A and hepatitis B. The first two infections are transmitted by contaminated food or water. Washing your hands before and after eating, and taking care over what you consume will greatly reduce the risk of contracting either typhoid or hepatitis A. If you plan to camp wild or stay in mountain-village homes where it may be more difficult to take these precautions, you might wish to consider being vaccinated before you travel.

Hepatitis B is transmitted by sexual contact with an infected person, or by puncture wounds from contaminated instruments, such as needles. In the UK, the course of vaccinations is usually given only to health workers and other people who are likely to be at high risk. Albania is considered to have an intermediate carriage rate for hepatitis B of 2–8%. For travellers, the risk of hepatitis B can be avoided by not indulging in risky behaviour such as unsafe sex, body piercing, tattooing or acupuncture. There is also an increased risk when working with small children or playing contact sports. There are two types of vaccination, but even the shorter course (Engerix) must be started at least 21 days before travel for those aged 16 or over. Tuberculosis (TB) is transmitted by close contact with infected people and through improperly pasteurised dairy products (see page 36). Although it is on the increase throughout the world, it is relatively rare in Albania; travellers should stick to UHT milk, to reduce the risk not only of TB but also of brucellosis.

INSECT-BORNE DISEASES   These include tick-borne encephalitis and leishmaniasis; malaria was eradicated from Albania in the 1930s. **Leishmaniasis** is transmitted by sandflies, very small insects (a third of the size of mosquitoes), which bite mainly between dusk and dawn. They breed quickly in unsanitary conditions, so if you are in this kind of environment you should minimise outdoor activities after dusk, use protective clothing and insect repellent, and consider using a fine-meshed bed net (the mesh in mosquito nets is too big to keep sandflies out). The bite is painful, so you will know if you have been bitten. Leishmaniasis has two forms: cutaneous, which causes skin ulcers and lesions, and visceral, which weakens the immune system and can be fatal. There is no vaccine to prevent leishmaniasis, but both forms can be treated.

Tick-borne encephalitis This is spread through the bites of infected ticks. You can protect yourself to a large extent by preventing ticks from attaching themselves to you, and removing any which succeed. If you are hiking in the forests, you should cover your arms and legs; wear long trousers tucked into your boots, and a hat. There is some evidence that insect repellents containing DEET or permethrin can discourage ticks. Tick repellent and tick-removal gadgets can be bought before you travel, but they are not available in Albania.

Always check for ticks at the end of your day out. Ticks should be removed as soon as possible; the longer they are on your body, the greater the chance of infection. Grasp the tick as close as you can to your skin, with tick tweezers or your fingernails, and then pull it steadily and firmly away, at right angles to your skin. The tick will come away complete, as long as you do not jerk or twist. Clean the skin, and your hands, afterwards with soap and water or skin disinfectant, if possible. Don't try to burn the tick off or remove it with Vaseline, alcohol or other irritants, since they can cause the ticks to regurgitate and therefore increase the risk of disease. If you are travelling with a companion, you can check each other for ticks; if you are hiking with small children remember to check their heads, and particularly behind the ears. Seek medical attention if you feel flu-like symptoms within one to four weeks after being bitten by a tick. In 20–30% of cases, the disease can then progress, with symptoms including a high fever and headache. There is a safe and effective vaccine (TicoVac and TicoVac Junior) available in the UK, although not on the NHS – the full schedule is three doses over 12 months. Two doses given a minimum of two weeks apart will offer some protection, although you should continue to take the precautions outlined above.

TRAVEL CLINICS AND HEALTH INFORMATION Healthcare professionals worldwide who are members of **ISTM** (International Society of Travel Medicine) are listed with their contact information on www.istm.org; for the UK, **MASTA** clinics are listed, with contact information, on www.masta.org. For other journey preparation information, consult www.fitfortravel.scot.nhs.uk. The MASTA website can generate a specific health brief for you.

HEALTHCARE IN ALBANIA If you are involved in an accident or a medical emergency, you should get yourself or the injured person into a taxi and say to the driver 'tek urgjenca', meaning 'to accident and emergency'. You will be given the best treatment possible. There is also an ambulance service, reached by dialling 127, but a taxi is probably quicker, at least outside the big cities.

In Tirana and other cities, there are now good non-state hospitals, with the latest technological equipment, which offer a full range of medical services up to and including heart bypasses and neurosurgery. In small towns and rural areas, healthcare can be a problem. State hospitals are often short-staffed and their equipment is old and sometimes does not work at all; many rural clinics have closed altogether. If you intend to travel outside the cities and are reliant on a specific medication, you should ensure you take an adequate supply with you.

⊞ **American Hospital** Behind Military Hospital, Lapraka; ✆04 235 7535, 235 7011; www. spitaliamerikan.com. Also clinics in Durrësi (✆05 222 2333) & Fieri (✆034 232 121, 232 123).

⊞ **Hygeia Hospital** Opposite Casa Italia, Kthesa e Kamzës; ✆04 239 0000; www.hygeia.al

For minor ailments, pharmacies can sell you almost anything over the counter, including antibiotics and contraceptive pills. Opticians can make repairs to spectacle frames or replace lenses fairly quickly. Disinfecting solution for contact lenses is stocked by a few opticians in Tirana, but probably not elsewhere. The standard of dental practices is very variable – there are some good ones in Tirana – and you should seek local advice, perhaps at your hotel. The international-style supermarkets in Tirana, and possibly in other large cities, stock tampons.

Albanian **tap water** is treated and is fine for brushing teeth, but it would not meet European Union standards. Most urban Albanians prefer mineral water. In the mountains, everybody drinks spring water, often from their own spring.

You should avoid drinking **unpasteurised milk** while you are in Albania; in cafés and restaurants the milk is always UHT, and therefore safe. There is TB and brucellosis in the Albanian dairy herd, and not all milk and yoghurt is properly pasteurised. Cheese is safe and imported UHT milk is always available in shops. The problem only really arises if you are staying with a family in a rural area, when you will almost certainly be offered fresh milk for breakfast. You might want to think in advance about how to refuse it tactfully; the Albanian for 'I don't eat dairy products' is '*nuk ha bulmet*', although this excuse will mean that you also miss the chance to try the family's delicious homemade cheese the evening before.

SAFETY

Albania is a safe country for visitors. Its traditions of hospitality mean foreigners are treated with great respect; almost all Albanians will go out of their way to help you if you are lost or in trouble. In general, violent crime in Albania happens either within the underworld of organised crime or in the context of a blood feud. A foreign visitor is highly unlikely to come into contact with either of these categories.

Nevertheless, there are poor and desperate people in Albania, as there are in any other country, and thefts and muggings do occur. It is foolish to flash expensive watches or cameras around, especially in the peripheral areas of towns where the poorest people tend to live. Many travellers carry a dummy wallet with a small amount of cash in it, so that in the event of a mugging they can hand this over instead of their 'real' wallet full of dollars or euros.

The greatest risk most people in Albania face is on the roads, where traffic accidents are very frequent and the fatality rate is one of the highest in Europe. Until a few years ago, Albanian roads were so bad that it was difficult to drive fast enough to kill anyone. Now, though, cars zip along newly upgraded highways which are also used by villagers and their livestock. There is no stigma attached to drink-driving and practically no attempt is made to check it.

WOMEN TRAVELLERS

Foreign women are treated with respect in Albania, although the same respect is not always shown to Albanian women. Domestic violence, in particular, is very prevalent and almost always unreported. Outside the home, however, women are at less risk of sexual assault or rape than in any northern European country. Of course these crimes are not completely unknown, but they are rare enough to make headline news when they happen.

BLACK AND MINORITY ETHNIC TRAVELLERS

Black and minority ethnic (BME) visitors to Albania sometimes find themselves on the receiving end of treatment which, although not racist in its intent, can make the visitor feel uncomfortable – for example, children or even adults stroking or pinching your skin out of curiosity. Occasionally, however, BME visitors have been verbally and even physically abused by groups of racists. There have also been sporadic reports of racist treatment by some hotel owners. Saranda seems to be especially problematic.

LGBT TRAVELLERS

Although homosexuality is legal in Albania – indeed, a 2010 law specifically protects its citizens against discrimination on grounds of sexual orientation – it is still fairly taboo and the LGBT (lesbian, gay, bisexual and transgender) community remains very underground. Almost no public figures are openly gay. A contestant on Albania's version of *Big Brother* came out in 2010, after the anti-discrimination law had been passed, but this led to his parents being driven out of their home town. That said, however, LGBT travellers are unlikely to encounter hostility or discrimination in Albania, assuming they behave with reasonable discretion (as they probably would in an unfamiliar town in their own country). A couple of bars in Tirana advertise 'gay-friendly' evenings.

Although the LGBT movement is still in its early stages, some advocacy and support organisations do exist: for example, the Alliance Against Discrimination (*www.aleancalgbt.org*) and the Pink Embassy (*www.pinkembassy.al*). They provide information, advice and counselling on LGBT matters and organise empowering events for members of the LGBT community.

TRAVELLERS WITH DISABILITIES

In 2010, Albania signed the UN Convention on the Rights of People with Disabilities. The next step in the journey towards achieving a society based on equality for all will be the ratification of this Convention, which will set targets for improving legislation, access and employment for people with disabilities. While this is all positive, Albania remains a deeply problematic destination for people with physical disabilities, particularly users of wheelchairs. Most pavements in Albania are not accessible, which makes independent movement nearly impossible, and most communist-era public and cultural buildings are entirely inaccessible, often with steep stairs. Traffic lights do not have acoustic signals; public transport is completely inaccessible for wheelchair users; and the use of Braille is pretty much non-existent. All that said, however, people with reduced mobility will find Albanians eager (possibly overeager) to assist when necessary.

Some more recent buildings have been designed to take people with disabilities into account. The Sheraton and Rogner Europapark hotels are accessible and have specifically designed guest rooms. Tirana International Airport is accessible throughout, including the toilets, and has dedicated parking spaces at the entrance to the terminal. However, disability assistance at the airport is inexperienced and no lifts are available to get off the aircraft. Some of the new shopping malls in Tirana and other big cities are also accessible. See *Travelling positively*, page 56, for contact information for the Albanian Disability Rights Foundation. (Thanks to Clare Sears for her help with this section.)

TRAVELLING WITH CHILDREN

Older children are likely to have a wonderful time in Albania, as long as they are reasonably flexible when things do not go exactly as planned. Travelling with young children, however, does present some practical problems. Pavements tend to be rather high, which can make pushchairs awkward to manoeuvre, and restaurants rarely have high chairs available. Outside Tirana, healthcare is not up to Western standards and it may be hard to find exactly the medication you need, should this be required. Entertainment specifically for children is not usually available, apart from the swing-parks in which every town abounds. On the outskirts of Tirana, strung out along the Elbasani road, there are several day resorts which have pools and other activities for children.

Two particularly appealing places for children of almost any age are the Llogora Tourist Village, between Vlora and Saranda, and Farma Sotira, in the mountains between Përmeti and Korça. The Llogora resort has sports facilities including tennis courts and a large indoor swimming pool. Activities are organised for youngsters and a babysitting service is offered. The whole resort, over 1ha in extent, is designed to blend in harmoniously with the natural beauty of the park. Several roe deer live in a large enclosure at the edge of the forest and are let out during the day to wander freely around the complex. Farma Sotira is a working farm, with sheep, cattle, chickens and horses. There is an outdoor pool with a separate shallow section for children. It is surrounded by meadows and forests; more strenuous hikes are also possible.

WHAT TO TAKE

It is not strictly necessary to take anything at all to Albania. Imported toiletries, first-aid items and AA batteries can all be bought in any reasonably sized town. Tampons are available in the Western-style supermarkets in Tirana and probably other cities. The street markets have the same cheap Chinese clothes as those sold in Western supermarkets, at about the same prices. Even cash is now relatively easy to obtain – all towns have ATMs (cash machines) linked to the Visa or Maestro (or both) international networks. However, it should be noted that credit cards can be used only in top-of-the-range hotels and restaurants. Travellers' cheques are not accepted as payment anywhere.

The most useful item to bring is undoubtedly a pocket- or head-torch (flashlight). The electricity supply in towns is much more reliable than it used to be, but there are still power cuts from time to time. In rural areas, these are much more frequent and the lights can be out for several hours, or even weeks. Even if you are not planning to venture out of the cities, you will find a torch useful. The streets of Albanian towns are badly lit, as are some museums; a torch can come in very handy for seeing what is in the display cases. British travellers should remember to pack an adaptor for electronic equipment (phone, camera, etc) which does not have European two-pin plugs.

Mosquitoes can be a problem in the summer, especially on the coast. Insect repellent can be purchased in Albania, but you may prefer to come prepared with an extra-powerful brand. Plug-in devices which emit repellent are useful at night but, if you are likely to be staying anywhere with an uncertain power supply, a mosquito coil is more practical.

If you plan to travel around the country, particularly by public transport, a supply of baby wipes or a tube of antibacterial hand gel will come in useful. The roadside restaurants where the buses and minibuses stop for breaks usually have running water nowadays, but not always anything with which to dry your hands. Smart girls keep some toilet paper or tissues in their handbags.

In the cities, especially Tirana, the summer dust can irritate eyes and throats; eye drops and cough sweets help, and some contact lens wearers give up and revert to wearing glasses.

ELECTRICITY The electricity supply in Albania is theoretically 220 volts AC. In practice it is often very much lower. Laptop batteries are usually resilient enough to cope with power spikes, but if you are travelling with sensitive equipment which could be damaged by voltage surges or brownout, you should obtain a line conditioner – the computer shops in Tirana sell them for about €50. Electrical sockets are almost always the two-pronged ones usual in continental Europe. There is an older type, rarely encountered in tourist accommodation, where the round prongs are slightly closer together than normal, too close for all but the most flexible of European plugs; hotels with these old sockets usually have at least a couple of adaptors for their own use, which they will probably agree to lend you for long enough to charge your phone or your camera battery. For trips into the mountains of more than a day or two, a portable solar charger is a good way to keep phones and cameras powered up.

MONEY

CURRENCY The Albanian monetary unit is called the lek, which is also one of the words for 'money'. The currency floats freely but is fairly stable; at the time of going to press, there are about 177 lek to the pound sterling, about 140 to the euro, and about 110 to the US dollar. On the rate boards in banks and bureaux de change, the initials 'ALL' are sometimes used instead of the word 'lek'.

In the 1970s, the lek was revalued and a zero was dropped. Albanians of all ages still insist on using the old number of zeros, although people who have regular dealings with foreigners sometimes try to remember not to. The systems are differentiated by the adjectives 'old' (*të vjetra*) and 'new' (*të reja*). In modern supermarkets the prices are displayed in 'new' lek; in markets and small shops, particularly outside the cities, if prices are displayed at all they might be in either system. While it is fairly easy to guess that the price of a bottle of mineral water is about 30p rather than £3.00 (50 'new' lek rather than 500), it can in other cases be quite unclear which is meant. Fortunately, most Albanians are very honest about this and will put you right if you try to give them ten times more money than they expect.

Matters are made even more confusing by a tendency to quote large numbers without mentioning the word 'thousand' – so a hotel receptionist might well quote a room rate simply as 'fifty'. The only way to find out if this means 50 dollars, 50 euros or 5,000 (new) lek is by asking. The rates of exchange to major currencies, at the time of going to press, can be found on the inside front cover of this book. Up-to-date rates can be consulted on many websites, such as www.exchangerates.org.uk.

CHANGING MONEY Cash machines (ATMs) issuing Albanian lek can be found in every town of any size. Some ATMs are linked only to the MasterCard/Visa/

Cirrus network; others (eg: those of the ProCredit and Raiffeisen banks) are also connected to the Maestro network. ProCredit ATMs issue euro notes as well as lek. Some banks have ATMs which only work with cards issued by that bank; the security guards will usually try to put obvious foreigners right if they see you approaching such an ATM.

Although credit cards can be used to withdraw cash, they cannot be used to pay for goods or services except in a few of the most upmarket hotels and restaurants. Similarly, travellers' cheques are not accepted as payment by hotels or anywhere else. This is especially important to bear in mind if you are setting off to travel in the Albanian mountains, where you will need sufficient cash to pay for all your accommodation and, if you are driving, fuel. The Albanian Riviera is also a cash-only economy along almost the whole of its length.

Foreign currency can be changed in banks, at bureaux de change, and on the street; the euro is by far the most widely accepted. Banks and bureaux de change will have rates for major currencies other than the US dollar and the euro. In cities where there are bureaux de change, these offer a speedier, less bureaucratic procedure than banks, and offer practically the same rate for the amounts which most visitors will be changing.

Money changers operate in every town, because the Albanian economy functions through remittances – cash sent home by family members working abroad. The money changers usually hang around where the remittances are collected, outside the post office or the Western Union branch. You can ask in either of these places if there are no changers to be seen – they are probably having a coffee somewhere nearby. Where a bureau de change exists, the money changers do not offer a significantly better rate. In Tirana and other big cities a minority of unscrupulous on-street changers circulate counterfeit notes.

You may also be able to change cash at your hotel, although you should not rely on this option. You will almost certainly be able to pay for your room in euros, although if you have been quoted a price in lek, the hotel will use a rule-of-thumb exchange rate which may not be in your favour. Restaurants also sometimes accept euros.

BUDGETING

How much you spend in Albania depends on what you want to do and where you want to sleep. If you base yourself in Tirana, stay in one of the top-of-the-range hotels, hire a car with a driver to move around in, and eat in the best fish restaurants, you could just about get through €300 a day (hotel: €130–160; car: €100 per day, if long tours are involved; dinner with wine in an expensive restaurant: €40–50 per head). If, at the other budgetary extreme, you stay in backpackers' hostels (€12–15 per person), travel everywhere by bus (an hour-long journey costs about €1), buy lunch from the market (bread, cheese, tomatoes and fruit for under €5), and dine on pasta or pizza (€10 maximum), you could equally easily keep within a budget of a tenth of that amount.

Most people will probably fall somewhere between these two extremes. A 1.5-litre bottle of water in a shop (as opposed to a café) costs between 50 and 70 lek; a half-litre bottle of Albanian beer in a bar usually ranges from 150 to 200 lek; a small loaf of bread from a bakery costs between 40 and 50 lek; small, triangular byrek (see Eating and drinking, pages 48–51) are usually 30 lek; a medium-sized Mars bar, or similar imported chocolate, costs 60 lek in a supermarket, a bit more in a kiosk; and a litre of petrol, at the time of writing, is around 200 lek – diesel is

10 lek or so cheaper. Bars and cafés on the coast tend to charge more, especially in summer, than their inland equivalents.

Most museums, castles and archaeological sites have a small admission charge, usually 200 lek. Some sites are unstaffed and do not have any explanatory information for visitors; when access is possible, it is free. Mosques and churches invariably have a donation box where visitors are expected to leave a contribution; 100 or 200 lek per person is reasonable.

GETTING AROUND

MAPS After many years when almost all road maps of Albania were based on an out-of-date and inaccurate source from the early 1990s, it is a huge relief that usable maps are at last available. While they are usable, however, none is absolutely reliable – distances and spot heights, in particular, vary wildly from one map to another – and the speed of Albania's road improvement programme means that road classification is likely to go out of date quite quickly (this warning even applies to the maps in this guide).

The only commercially available **hiking maps** are published by the German company Huber Kartographie. At the time of going to press, only the far north of Albania is covered: 1:50,000 maps of Tropoja (see *Chapter 6*, pages 164–71), Thethi and Kelmendi (see *Chapter 7*, pages 202–14), and a 1:60,000 map of the cross-border hiking trail known as Peaks of the Balkans (see page 45). Further maps in this series are planned. The maps have contours at 50m intervals and include descriptions, in English, of selected hiking trails and cycling routes. Better still, they show, in grey dotted lines, the routes of old paths; these were the best routes 40 years ago and in most cases are still used by local people.

Once you get to the Albanian Alps, 1:30,000 hiking maps of the mountains in the north can also be purchased, at very reasonable cost, from Journey to Valbona, a multifaceted organisation based in the Valbona Valley (*www.journeytovalbona. com*). The only reliably marked trails in Valbona are being maintained and expanded by a group of local volunteers, and these beautiful maps are being produced in tandem with that work. They differentiate between marked trails, unmarked but clear trails, and invisible but plausible routes for confident navigators. Contours are shown at 10m intervals, 4x4 tracks are also indicated and there are extensive trail notes. The maps are printed to a high quality on waterproof paper. Maps of five different areas are available; the whole map, with hiking routes from Thethi to Gashi, can be consulted at the Rilindja Hotel (see page 169), where the smaller maps can be bought. Some of the purchase price goes to finance the work of maintaining and expanding the trail system.

The Albanian Military Geographical Institute (IGUS) has mapped the whole country in 1:50,000, but at the time of writing the sheets are not on sale. The only option at that scale, outside the Albanian Alps, is to refer to the 1:50,000 Soviet topographic maps, available to download for a small charge at www.mapstor.com. These maps are based on very old data but are still useful for planning hikes or cycling tours in most of Albania. In some parts of the country the topography has changed quite substantially since they were produced – for example, the old village of Kukësi is now under Lake Fierza – and they should be used with caution everywhere, since new roads and dams have been built and old tracks have become blocked by landslides or washed away by floods. The names on the maps are in the Cyrillic alphabet. It should also be noted that the projection used is one from which amateur GPS equipment is unlikely to be able to set co-ordinates.

Freytag & Berndt *Albania*, 1:400,000, single-sided, index on reverse, some topographical detail, also covers all of Montenegro & Kosova, most of Macedonia & part of northern Greece.

Freytag & Berndt *Albania*, 1:200,000, double-sided, index booklet, some topographical detail, shows administrative boundaries.

Huber Kartographie GmBH *Peaks of the Balkans*, 1:60,000, contoured, GPS-compatible, relief shading, shows national park boundaries and recommended overnight stops. Detailed route description on reverse, with GPS waypoints.

Huber Kartographie GmBH *Tropoja−B. Curri−Valbona & Vermoshi−Tamare−Razma−Thethi*, 1:50,000, contoured at 50m intervals, spot heights, GPS-compatible, extensive topographic information. Recommended hiking and cycling routes are prominently marked & cross-referenced to descriptions on the reverse of each map. The old, traditional paths are also shown.

ITMB *Albania*, 1:210,000, double-sided, indexed, some topographical details, street plans of 7 cities & towns. Not a hiking map, but shows many of the old, traditional paths. Inexplicably, some well-established roads are missing altogether, including at least 2 border crossings.

Reise Know-How *Albanien*, 1:220,000, double-sided, indexed, waterproof, tear-resistant, good topographical detail with contour colouring & spot heights. Awkward to use on the road.

CAR HIRE Self-drive cars can be hired in Tirana, the airport and a handful of other locations. Only Tirana Car Rentals currently offers the option of dropping the vehicle off in a different town from where it was picked up. Car hire is relatively expensive (€50–100 per day for the cheapest compact car) and, for some of the routes described in this book, a small saloon will not be adequate. Some of the car-hire agencies have 4x4 vehicles available, although of course these are considerably more expensive.

The car-hire desks at the airport are not open 24 hours a day; in any case, if you want to be sure of being able to rent a car as soon as you arrive, you should book it in advance. Several small, local companies also offer car hire from offices located just beyond the airport perimeter fence, across the roundabout with Mother Teresa's statue on it.

It is reasonably economical to hire a taxi with its driver, either through Albania Holidays (see page 31) or any other local travel agency, or independently at the main taxi rank in each of the towns you visit.

Avis Sheraton Hotel; 04 226 6389; or Rogner Hotel; 04 223 5011; www.avis.com

Europcar Rr e Durrësit 61; 04 222 7888; www.europcar.com

Hertz Tirana International Hotel, Skanderbeg Sq; 04 226 2511; www.hertz.com

Sixt Rr e Kavajës 116, Volkswagen dealership; m 068 206 8500; www.sixt.com

Tirana Car Rentals Rr Abdyl Frashëri 11, sh 4 (offices also in Durrësi, Vlora & Saranda) 04 630 1255; m 068 403 0505; www.tirana-car-rentals.com

INTERURBAN TRANSPORT Albanians use three main methods of public transport between towns: buses, minibuses and shared taxis. Buses have about 40 seats and run to timetables. Minibuses have 12 or 15 seats and leave when they are full. Where both types of vehicle operate, the bus is cheaper and tends to take a bit longer, but is often more comfortable. A government initiative in 2014 attempted to rationalise the intercity transport network; this has meant that, at the time of writing, minibuses no longer operate on some routes. Rural and mountainous routes, though, are often not served by buses at all, only minibuses and taxis. Buses and minibuses operate daily, except on some very remote routes where there is no service on a Sunday. The cost of a shared taxi is based on four paying passengers, including children and luggage if necessary. The trains are cheap, but they are so slow and infrequent that nobody uses them for any but the shortest journeys. There are no internal civilian flights at the time of writing.

When travelling, the crucial thing to bear in mind is that Albanians are early risers. Bus services start very early indeed, often before 06.00. Where there are minibuses, the earliest ones fill up quickly with people who are travelling all the way to the final destination. Later in the morning, you could spend half an hour, or more, waiting around for more passengers to turn up. The earlier you set off, the quicker your journey will be. Getting to the terminus early also gives you a choice of vehicles; for example, some models of minibus have more room for luggage than others and newer buses tend to have better suspension.

The time of departure of the last bus depends to some extent on how far away the destination is – Tirana–Shkodra, for example, is only a couple of hours, and there are buses until 17.00. The latest departures from provincial towns tend to be earlier than those from Tirana; for example, the last bus from Shkodra to Tirana leaves at 16.00. As a rule, you should not rely on being able to find any public transport much later than midday, unless otherwise specified in this guide. After the last bus has left, there are likely to be taxis hanging around hopefully but, unless you are prepared to pay for all four seats in the taxi, you may still have a long wait.

Getting to and from Tirana is easy – every town in Albania has daily transport to the capital, although from very faraway places the bus might leave unfeasibly early. Intercity bus and minibus schedules can be consulted on the user-curated website www.matinic.us/albania/furgon.php. Links between minor towns and their regional capitals are usually good. The only real challenge for non-Albanians is working out which vehicle is going where. Some of them have signs above the dashboard with the name of their destination, while others do not. Fortunately there are lots of people around you can ask.

There is always some kind of public transport between the main villages and their district capitals (the 'main village' is referred to in Albanian as *komuna*, ie: the administrative centre of a group of villages). But the 'early start' logic has an extra twist to it in these cases: rural buses (or minibuses) are normally driven by somebody who lives in the village, not the town, which means that the bus spends the night in the village and is driven down to the town in the early morning, to arrive there at the start of the working day. The passengers then go off and do whatever administrative tasks or shopping they have come to town to do. Then, when everybody has finished, the driver takes them all back to the village. This is usually around lunchtime – 13.00 or thereabouts – but the only way to be certain is to ask the driver. This means if you want to go to a village by bus (and there are a lot in this guide, either as attractive destinations in their own right or as the nearest accessible point to an archaeological site), you will probably spend quite a lot of time hanging around, sitting alone on the bus or drinking coffee with the driver. You will probably also have to spend the night in the village, unless you plan to walk out. In very remote areas, it is sometimes possible to hitch a lift on the school buses which ferry the teachers, first thing in the morning, from the district capital to the elementary schools in the villages.

Bus (and minibus) terminuses are often in the outskirts of towns, but there are almost always taxis hanging around to provide onward transport.

INTRA-URBAN TRANSPORT In most Albanian towns and cities, the urban **bus** system is – frankly – opaque. It is designed for people who live in that town and who know that Ilir's boy drives the bus that goes up past the tractor factory. Visitors who do not know Ilir, or what his son looks like, or that those ruined buildings on the hill used to be the tractor factory, until it was burnt down in 1991, have little chance of identifying the bus which will take them where they want to go. In Tirana things are somewhat easier – at least there the buses display their destinations and there are bus stops showing the routes served – but the buses get so crowded at peak times of day that using them then is not a comfortable option.

Fortunately, there are plenty of **taxis** in every town of any size. They usually have a flat fare for short journeys within the town centre; for longer journeys you should agree a fare before getting into the car. Taxis can be hired for half a day, or a day, or even longer – the Albanian expression for this is '*në dispozicion*' – and again the rate should be negotiated in advance. If meal breaks are involved you will be expected to pay for the driver's food, unless this has been specifically excluded from the deal.

Taxis are usually old Mercedes-Benz models, like the 190 series, and with their robust suspension they can get to most places in this guide. Where a road is not suitable for a taxi, this is indicated in the text.

Taxi licences are issued by the relevant local council. Licensed taxis have yellow registration plates with the word TA-XI on them, and a shield-shaped sticker on the door with the licence number on it. In Tirana and some other cities, the cars themselves are often yellow too; in Korça, for some reason, they are electric blue. In very small towns the cars might have only the council's stickers, not the yellow number plates. Pirate taxis are not usually any cheaper for short journeys. Licences are quite expensive and the legitimate taxi drivers are understandably resentful of the pirates.

Taxis do not usually cross international borders (the Kosova–Albania border does not count as international). At the busier, longer-established crossings there are usually taxis or minibuses waiting on the Albanian side to collect people who have been dropped off on the other side and walked across. This is common practice and the drivers will have a going rate for the trip, although whether they let a foreigner in on this secret is another matter. The smaller, more recently opened crossings do not have reliable transport of this sort.

It can sometimes be a challenge to find museums, galleries and other places of interest. Street names are rarely used in Albania and, even when they are, matters are complicated by the fact that everybody still uses the old, communist-era names instead of the new ones which are on street maps. Albanians navigate by landmarks rather than addresses so, if you ask for directions to, say, the Vila Bekteshi restaurant in Shkodra, you will not be told it is on Rruga Hazan Riza Pasha, but that it is just along from the Orthodox cathedral, behind the mosque.

HIKING, BIKING AND WINTER SPORTS
Albania offers magnificent opportunities to explore wild, remote places, on foot, by mountain bike, or on skis or snowshoes. However, only a few of the national parks have any kind of infrastructure in place to support outdoor activities; accommodation, where it exists at all, is usually in family homes with conditions which are sometimes rather basic. Indeed, just reaching many of Albania's national parks and nature reserves involves a difficult journey by 4x4 or several hours' walk from the nearest village served by public transport.

The mountain areas of Albania are now very sparsely populated, because many villagers have given up subsistence farming in exchange for a slightly less tough life in a town or city. If you sprain your ankle or run into other problems, the nearest help could well be several hours' walk away. Remote mountain areas do not usually have mobile phone coverage. You should never set off on a hike alone. Great caution is also needed when approaching sheepdogs in the mountains; they are trained to attack anything which they think might be a threat to the livestock they are protecting. If you are confronted by a sheepdog, stop; if you have the presence of mind, back slowly away from it. Do not go any further into the dog's territory until the shepherd, who will be somewhere around, makes his or her way to you and calls the dog off.

Two long-distance, cross-border **hiking trails** have been developed in recent years: Peaks of the Balkans (*www.peaksofthebalkans.com*) and Via Dinarica (*www.viadinarica.com*). The main problem with both of these initiatives is that it is practically impossible for an independent hiker to obtain permission to cross the borders between Montenegro, Kosova and Albania. In theory, all three countries have systems in place to enable this; in practice, you need to be physically present at the relevant police station in order either to pay the permit fee (Montenegro) or to process the paperwork (Albania and Kosova). The Thethi-based agency Zbulo (see page 31; *www.zbulo.org*) can submit your paperwork, chase up your application and inform you when your permit is approved, for a small fee. If you are travelling as part of an organised hiking tour, the agency you have booked with will deal with permits for the whole group.

There are few formal campsites; **wild camping** is tolerated, but if you want to camp, you should follow the usual codes of conduct (the Mountaineering Council of Scotland's website – *www.mcofs.org.uk/assets/pdfs/wildcamping.pdf* – has useful guidelines, although obviously its legal advice does not apply in Albania). In particular, it is not always easy to tell if you are pitching your tent on private property. If there is an inhabited house within sight, you should make yourself known to the inhabitants. Apart from anything else, if they discover in the middle of the night that there are strangers roaming around their property, they are almost certain to reach for their guns before leaving the house to find out who is there. Albanian highlanders have ancient traditions of hospitality and may well invite you to sleep in their house. If you prefer to be in your tent, a polite compromise might be for you to pitch your camp in their garden. If the head of the family refuses payment, it is a nice gesture to press a few hundred lek, 'for the children' ('*për femijët*'), into the hand of the oldest child.

Hikers are unlikely to be robbed, but it is not impossible either; if you are attacked, your assailant is almost certain to be armed with a gun. Sleeping rough in the Albanian mountains might also bring you into closer proximity with the carnivorous fauna of the country than you would like. Wolves do not eat people, although hearing them howl around your tent is probably quite disconcerting; bears, on the other hand, have been known to attack humans and they don't howl first. Albania also has some venomous snakes, among them the dangerous horn-nosed viper (*Vipera ammodytes*).

Cyclists will be spoilt for choice with all the ancient tracks across Albania's mountain passes and along remote valleys. Suitable bikes cannot be hired in Albania, except as part of an organised excursion or for day trips from Tirana. Some ideas for routes are suggested in the relevant chapters.

Road surfaces are very variable and 'touring' or off-road tyres are essential. The cobbled surfaces of some of the old Italian-built roads become very slippery in wet weather and may not be rideable then. Gradients are often much steeper than cyclists used to the Alps, for example, might expect. The unreliability of maps of Albania (see page 41) can make these gradients even more of a surprise (or shock). Softies can always fall back on the option of putting the bikes on a bus and doing the toughest stretches the easy way. See pages 42–4, and throughout, for advice on public transport.

Albanian drivers are now becoming more used to sharing their roads with foreign cyclists and, in the main, they are reasonably courteous to them. However, it is safer as well as more enjoyable to travel as much as possible during the day and

2

on roads with light traffic. On busy highways, extreme caution and defensiveness are advisable. On some of the new highways, there are signs indicating that cyclists are not allowed. If there is an alternative route, it will probably make for more enjoyable riding; if there is not, it seems that the prohibition is not enforced, at least not on foreign cyclists.

As for security, if you are camping you should remove all loose items and lock the bike as securely as you possibly can, perhaps by chaining it to a tree. Hotel owners will be happy to find a space for your bike in the courtyard or somewhere else secure, although you should nonetheless lock it and keep loose items with you. (Thanks to Bruce Logan, Jaap de Boer and others for their comments on cycling in Albania.)

In the communist era, **skiing** was quite a popular pastime and several small resorts were developed. They do not have Western-style infrastructure, but for adventurous skiers they would be interesting to visit. The first snow usually falls in November and lasts until March or April, with average snowfall of 40–60cm and low maximum temperatures. At the time of writing, the best place to ski in Albania is **Puka**, in the north of the country, where skis (and ice skates) can be hired and which has a choice of good accommodation. For further information about Puka and its ski resort, see pages 161–4. For those who are prepared to bring their own skis, other resorts are:

Dardha 20km south of Korça; see pages 163–4. A traditional village, 1,344m above sea level, which is a tourist attraction in the summer, too. Hotel & guesthouse accommodation is available.

Shishtaveci 31km from Kukësi, right on the border with Kosova; see page 176. At the time of writing, the road is atrocious, although the village is served by a minibus. There are no hotels in Shishtaveci.

Voskopoja 26km west of Korça; see pages 137–8. The Akademia Hotel, 2,286m above sea level, was used in the communist period to accommodate groups of students on skiing trips. Alternative accommodation is available with local families in Voskopoja.

People who actually live in the Albanian mountains do not use skis to get around in winter, but snowshoes. These are an enjoyable way for non-skiers to explore the mountains in winter. Outdoor Albania (see page 31; *www.outdooralbania.com*), the Tirana-based specialist agency, runs snowshoeing excursions throughout the winter in the mountains around Tirana, as well as ski tours in different parts of the country. In spring and summer it offers treks of varying lengths and levels of difficulty.

Toilets The sit-down toilets which are standard in northern Europe and the USA are a fairly recent innovation in Albania. During the isolated years of communism, the porcelain surround known as a Turkish toilet was the norm in cities, while village families had an outhouse with a hole dug in the ground. In towns and in the restaurants and cafés along the highways, it is now unusual to come across a Turkish toilet.

In the main hiking destinations, such as Thethi and Valbona, the guesthouses and restaurants usually have modern flush toilets. However, time moves more slowly in the remote countryside. The 2011 census revealed that about 12% of rural homes still rely on a non-flush toilet. In these cases, you will usually find a large plastic container filled with water in or just outside the outhouse, and a small container with which to scoop out however much water you need. Hand-washing in these situations requires an element of juggling; a tube of antibacterial hand gel and/or a packet of pre-moistened wipes always come in useful.

ACCOMMODATION

Communist-era hotels in Albania were built to provide accommodation either for individuals travelling on official business or for families on holiday at the beach or in the mountains. Very few foreign tourists visited Albania and so – unlike other communist countries in central and eastern Europe – there were no hotels specifically built for them.

Every provincial capital had a centrally located hotel, with its own bar and restaurant, and usually with a large number of rooms. This was invariably referred to as 'Turizmi' ('The Tourism'), and it was where foreign tour groups stayed as well as Albanian sports teams or cultural ensembles. Because these hotels had been state-owned, they were often targeted by rioters during the civil uprising of spring 1997 and several were completely destroyed. Of those which survived, all have now been privatised. Typically this means that some rooms – one or two corridors – now have en-suite bathroom facilities, an electric heater in winter and sometimes a television set; these rooms usually cost about €30–40 euros for two people. The rest are aimed at the Albanian market and still share toilets and showers. These are not always offered to foreign visitors, but they are cheaper than the upgraded rooms, usually 1,000 lek per person per night. Hotels in this category do not always have running water all day and, although they may have generators, these are normally connected only to the public areas – reception, restaurant, bar, etc – and not the bedrooms.

In some cases, the new owners have invested heavily and their hotels meet reasonable international standards, with constant hot and cold running water, generators connected to the bedrooms as well as the public areas, and en-suite bathrooms as standard. Where this is so, it is indicated in the relevant listing here.

More recently built hotels are also very variable in their quality. Some target Albanians travelling for work reasons – bus drivers, sales representatives, etc – and are cheap but basic. Others have opted for the smaller but wealthier market of Albanian professionals and foreign visitors. The conditions in these hotels range from the comfortable to the very comfortable, although their room rates do not always reflect the facilities offered. These mid-range hotels have en-suite bathrooms, air conditioning and cable television as standard. In Tirana such hotels typically charge around €60; in the rest of the country it is more likely to be around €40–50. At the beach resorts in July and August, hotels charge whatever they think they can get away with; demand exceeds supply at the height of the Albanian holiday season and so haggling is unlikely to be very successful at that time of year. When the quoted price is for the room, not per person, single travellers can often negotiate a discount.

Room rates are usually given in euros, except at the budget end of the market where they tend to be quoted in lek. It is always possible to pay in either currency, although you will almost certainly be given change in lek. Sterling and US dollars

HOTEL PRICE CODES

Double room per night:

$$$$$	Luxury	over €100
$$$$	Upmarket	€60–100
$$$	Mid-range	€40–60
$$	Budget	€20–40
$	Cheap	under €20

are not usually accepted. Breakfast is sometimes included, sometimes not; it will almost always be available, even if you have to pay extra for it. Albanian hotel breakfasts usually consist of toast or bread with a hard-boiled or fried egg, cheese, jam, honey and/or ham. Often you will be invited to choose one or two of these options. Milk or tea is served with breakfast; coffee is almost never included and must be ordered separately.

Increasing numbers of hotels in Albania now have their own websites through which rooms can be booked. Otherwise, hotel accommodation throughout the country can be reserved through the Tirana-based agency **Albania Holidays** (` 04 223 5688, 223 5498; *www.albania-hotel.com*) and through international websites such as www.hostelworld.com and www.booking.com.

CAMPING Campsites are a new phenomenon in Albania and few stay open all year round. In summer, many of the beaches on the Riviera (see pages 245–52) have tented sites, of varying degrees of comfort, where travellers can either rent a tent or pitch their own. Information about these seasonal campsites will be available on the usual travellers' websites. Several of the year-round sites also provide facilities for camper vans and caravans; these are listed in the relevant chapters of this guidebook. See page 45 for advice on wild camping.

EATING AND DRINKING

Albanian cuisine is rich in Mediterranean ingredients such as olive oil, tomatoes and pimentos, although garlic is not widely used. Lamb, as you would expect in a mountainous country, is excellent, as is fish from Albania's rivers, seas and lakes. Those who like offal will welcome the chance to try dishes which BSE and changing consumer tastes have eliminated from northern European menus. In restaurants, tips are expected though not obligatory – rounding up to about 10% of the total bill is fine. Tipping practice in cafés is to leave a couple of coins on your table after you have paid your bill.

Fruit and vegetables in Albania are delicious. The tomatoes taste of tomato, the watermelons remind you of something other than water, and the citrus fruit is tangy and refreshing. Aubergines, courgettes, green beans and okra figure prominently in summer, with cabbages, carrots and potatoes taking over in winter. It is a frequent boast in restaurants that all the food is organic (*bio*), but there is no system in Albania for certifying organic produce.

In most places, it is almost impossible to find fresh fruit and vegetables out of their own season; the Western-style supermarkets and, sometimes, the central market in Tirana are the only places where you will find oranges in May or fresh tomatoes in December. Albanian housewives preserve vegetables in vinegar for the winter, when salads consist mainly of different sorts of pickle – not only the familiar gherkin, but also preserved peppers, aubergines and other treats.

The classic way to eat lamb is spit-roasted, and the classic place to eat it is at one of the out-of-town restaurants which specialise in this. At weekends and on public holidays these places are filled with extended families at huge tables, tucking into lamb, salad, chips and draught wine. A variation is *paidhaqe*, lamb ribs grilled over charcoal. Town restaurants are more likely to serve pork or veal (the calves are not kept in crates and are much older when they are slaughtered than the milk-fed veal calves which used to be eaten in Britain). Veal escalopes are ubiquitous; *biftek* is a cross-cut steak from the shoulder or loin, which can be fried or braised; and *rosto* is boned shoulder, oven-roasted and served with gravy.

RESTAURANT PRICE CODES

Average price of a main course:

$$$$$	Expensive	over 1,500 lek
$$$$	Above average	1,000–1,500 lek
$$$	Reasonable	500–1,000 lek
$$	Good deal	under 500 lek
$	Cheap	snacks, less than 200 lek per item

Sheep's heart, liver, kidneys, brains and other organs are very popular. In the big cities, it is not always easy to find restaurants which serve these things, but they always exist and can be tracked down by asking. Albanian specialities include *paçë koke*, a thick soup made with sheep's head which is a traditional breakfast dish, and *kukurec*, chopped innards in a gut casing.

The lake fish *koran* (a species of trout unique to Lake Ohrid) and carp are usually available only near the lakes where they are fished, although you can sometimes find them in Tirana, at a price. River trout, too, seldom travel far. Fresh sea fish is readily available all along the coast and in the inland cities. The varieties which appear most frequently on menus are *levrek* (sea bass) and *koçë* (sea bream), both usually farmed, and *barbun* (red mullet) and *merluc* (hake). Eels (*ngjalë*) are caught in the lakes and coastal lagoons and are much sought after there; they rarely make it to the cities. Prawns (*karkalec*) are landed by Albanian fishermen, and on the coast they are likely to be fresh; elsewhere you may wish to ask if they are frozen (ie: imported). Fresh lobster is sometimes available, although it is not cheap. Mussels (*midhje*) are harvested from the wild and also farmed in the Butrint Lagoon. Clams seem to be served only with pasta dishes in Italian restaurants. Finally, although it is not a fish, the edible variety of frog (*bretkosë*) is bred and its legs eaten – usually grilled – in central and southern Albania.

Traditional Albanian home cooking uses vegetables, yoghurt and cheese to make meat go further. Potatoes, aubergines, courgettes, peppers and cabbage are all stuffed with minced meat. Pieces of veal are simmered with aubergine, spinach or green beans, or braised in a terracotta pot with pickling onions (*mish çomlek*). For *turli*, different vegetables – carrots, aubergines, potatoes, okra or anything else the cook has to hand – are layered with slices of tomato around a veal joint and simmered. *Fergesë* is made with green peppers and onions, fried together and then mixed with egg and *gjizë*, a dry curd cheese, before being baked. Pieces of meat or liver are sometimes added to *fergesë*.

Shish qebap is cubes of meat – lamb, pork or beef – marinated and then grilled on skewers, alternated with onion slices; *qebap në letër* is the same ingredients plus chunks of feta cheese, wrapped in tinfoil and baked in the oven. In *tavë Elbasani*, or *tavë kosi*, yoghurt and eggs are beaten together and poured over pieces of lamb or mutton, before the whole thing is baked in the oven. *Qofta* are rissoles of minced lamb bound with egg: sometimes they are round and flat, like hamburgers, and sometimes they are cylindrical; sometimes they are served grilled with salad and chips, and sometimes with a tomato-based sauce, when they are usually called *Qoftë Korçe*.

Qofta also appear as fast food, sold at street kiosks straight from the grill. Doner kebab, called *sufllaqë* in central Albania and *pita* in the south, is served either in a circular piece of unleavened bread or in a hot-dog roll, topped with salad, chips and tomato ketchup or mustard. The other big player in the Albanian fast-food world is the *byrek*, which comes in many guises but is essentially filo pastry with something inside. The classic *byrek* is round and flat, and alternates layers of pastry with *gjizë*, or minced meat fried with chopped onions, or leeks. As a starter for the family lunch, it can be bought whole at the *byrektore* or made at home; as fast food, it is cut into quarters and eaten on the street. Another variant is the small triangular *byrek*, which can contain meat, or *gjizë*, or spinach, or tomato and onion, and is crispier and lighter than its circular relative. Finally there is the *pita*, for which the filo pastry is rolled up around the filling to make a long sausage shape, then coiled around itself and baked. All of these are tasty options when a full meal is not required.

Desserts are not usually eaten after meals in Albanian homes. On special occasions *xupa* might be served, a kind of blancmange sprinkled with walnuts. Sweetmeats are more often eaten with coffee during the *xhiro*, the early evening promenade. *Kadaif* and *halva* will be familiar to anyone who has visited Turkey or Greece, or indeed ever been in a Turkish café. *Tullumba* are cylinders of dough, deep-fried and tossed in syrup. *Sheqerpare* is made from little balls of sweet dough, baked in butter. *Shëndetlli* is a kind of fruit cake, steeped in honey.

There is almost never a vegetarian option among the meals on offer in restaurants, except in upmarket, Westernised establishments. Fish eaters will be fine in the cities and on the coast; vegetarians will generally be able to persuade the restaurant kitchen to rustle up an omelette or a simple tomato sauce for pasta. The Albanian highlands are resolutely carnivorous; non-carnivores will struggle to convince their puzzled hosts that all they want is cheese or eggs. Delicious though the cucumbers and tomatoes are, vegans are likely to have become quite tired of them after a couple of weeks in Albania.

DRINKING The draught **wine** in provincial restaurants is normally rather young, but can be very drinkable. Albanian wine in bottles is often excellent. The main wine-producing areas are around Korça and Berati and between Lezha and Shkodra. The Bardha vineyard near Tirana produces outstanding wine in small quantities, difficult to track down but on the wine lists of a few Tirana restaurants. Most Albanian vineyards use well-known grapes such as Sauvignon and Cabernet. Indigenous grapes include Shesh (red and white) and Kallmet (red). Çobo, in Ura Vajgurore near Berati, has moved towards producing all its wine solely from indigenous Albanian grapes, including almost-forgotten varieties such as Vllosh, Debinë and Puls. Çobo and Bardha wines are usually on sale in the duty-free shops at Tirana International Airport.

Beer is brewed commercially in Tirana (Birra Tirana and Kaon), Korça (Birra Korça) and Vlora (Norga); the Tirana and Korça breweries produce dark beer as well as the more widely available lager. Locally produced beer is available in a few other towns, such as Puka.

Of the other Albanian alcoholic drinks, **raki** is the most widely consumed. Despite its Turkish name, Albanian raki is not flavoured with aniseed as it is in Turkey. It is a clear spirit, usually distilled from grape juice, and drunk as a morning pick-me-up, an aperitif, a digestif, or at any other time of day. Albanians also make raki from mulberries (*mani*), brambles (*manaferre*) and practically any other soft fruit they can lay their hands on. In Slav-speaking villages raki is distilled from plums, as it is across the borders in former Yugoslavia. The Berati-based vineyard Çobo makes excellent walnut raki. Another unusual raki is that made from the fruit of the strawberry tree (*Arbutus unedo*) called *mare* in Albanian. The best raki is homemade; commercially bottled products are widely available in shops. Albanian brandy (*konjak*) can be quite good, or it can be appalling; the commercially available Skënderbeu brand is in the former category. *Fernet*, a drink made from herbs which tastes nothing like the Italian Fernet-Branca, is a popular aperitif, though something of an acquired taste.

Coffee is an even more integral part of Albanian life than raki. Over coffee, deals are done, jobs are offered and marriages arranged. Having a coffee with an Albanian takes an absolute minimum of half an hour. Traditionally it was made in the usual Balkan way, with very finely ground coffee, water and sugar all boiled together in an individual pot – in Albanian it is called *kafe turke*. This is usually what you will be offered in Albanians' houses. In cafés and restaurants in all but the very smallest towns, Italian espresso machines are the norm, when there is electricity to operate them. During power cuts, *kafe turke* comes back into its own. You will be asked how you take it, meaning how much sugar you want. Four possible answers are: '*e ëmbël*' (sweet); '*e mesme*' (standard, which is quite sweet); '*me pak sheqer*' (with a little sugar); and '*sade*' (unsweetened).

PRACTICAL INFORMATION Apart from the top-of-the-range restaurants in Tirana, most restaurants in Albania do not have fixed opening hours. They are family-run and they open when the owners think people might want to start eating – in the countryside this will be around 09.00 or 10.00, when Albanian farmers have breakfast (*paçë koke*, for example), while in towns it is usually a bit later. They close when there are no more customers – in the countryside this tends to be quite early in the evening, in small towns it will be around 21.00 and in cities an hour or so later. Some restaurants, particularly those which serve very traditional food, are open only in the mornings and at lunchtime; the listings in each section of the guide specify where this is the case.

It is rarely necessary to book a table in advance; indeed, most restaurants do not even have telephone numbers, other than the mobile phone of the owner. Where reservations are advisable, numbers are given in the listings in each section.

Restaurant bills are always in lek, although euros are usually accepted if necessary; however, the exchange rate is unlikely to be in the customer's favour.

PUBLIC HOLIDAYS

Albania shuts down on the following national holidays: 1 and 2 January (New Year); 1 May (International Workers' Day); and 28 November (Independence Day).

On other public holidays, including the major feast days of each of Albania's religions, banks and government offices are closed, while shops, bureaux de change and other private firms may or may not open. It varies to some extent from town to town – in Catholic Mirdita, for example, you will not find much commercial activity on 25 December. The holidays are: Orthodox Christmas (6 January); Summer Day (14 March); the Bektashi festival of Nevruz (22 March); Catholic and Orthodox Easters (moveable, usually on different Sundays in April); Beatification of Mother Teresa Day (19 October); Liberation Day (29 November; liberation, that is, at the end of World War II, which not everybody in Albania agrees is a reason for celebration); Bajram i Vogël (Eid al-Fitr, the end of Ramadan, moveable); Bajram i Madh (Eid ul-Adha, moveable); and Catholic Christmas (25 December).

'National' museums close on Mondays; others are more likely to be closed on Saturdays and Sundays.

SHOPPING

The best place in Albania to shop for souvenirs is Kruja, where all the shops are close together in the bazaar. There are traditional felt-makers, who produce slippers and the felt caps called *qeleshe*; shops selling hand-woven *qilime* (this is the same word as the Turkish *kilim*, a woven rug); and antique dealers. Many of the Kruja shops sell small souvenirs such as Albanian flags, copper plates and ashtrays in the shape of bunkers.

Elsewhere it can be quite difficult to find traditional crafts for sale; there are a few shops in Tirana, an artisans' co-operative in Gjirokastra and locally run souvenir stalls at Butrint. Please refer to the relevant chapters of this guide for further information. If all else fails, small souvenirs and bottles of wine, raki and cognac can be purchased at the airport.

ARTS AND ENTERTAINMENT

Albania, like many formerly communist countries, has a strong tradition of classical music. The country's main venue for this is the National Theatre of Opera and Ballet on Tirana's Skanderbeg Square; forthcoming concerts, operas and ballet performances are advertised outside the theatre. Classical recitals also take place in the Academy of Arts in Tirana and, occasionally, in other venues around the country (eg: the theatre at Butrint). It is far from easy to find out about these events; asking at the nearest tourist information office might yield results. Plays and similar performances are staged, generally in Albanian, in the main theatres in Tirana, Shkodra, Durrësi and Korça. Public institutions, such as theatres and museums, cannot normally deal with telephone enquiries from members of the public. The cinemas in several towns and cities usually screen Hollywood films, in the original version with Albanian subtitles. Screenings of Albanian films are much rarer.

It is almost as difficult to find performances of traditional Albanian music or dance. The best way to stumble across them is to be staying in a hotel where a wedding is being celebrated; Albanian weddings last three days, with the final big celebration always on a Sunday night. There are folk festivals at Gjirokastra (every four years, roughly), Peshkopia (annually, in September) and Përmeti (annually, in June). Please refer to the relevant chapters of this guide for further information.

PHOTOGRAPHY

Albanians are usually delighted to have their photographs taken but, like people in any other country, they prefer to be asked first. Once permission has been requested, you may well end up having to take photos of the entire family. The demise of the Polaroid camera means it is no longer possible to give the person you have just photographed an immediate copy of the shot, but the computer shops found in most towns may be able to print photographs from your memory card.

Again like everywhere else, the security and armed forces tend not to be very happy about people taking photos of military or government buildings. Bunkers are fine, as long as they are not surrounding a military base.

MEDIA AND COMMUNICATIONS

MEDIA Albanian television is very diverse. In addition to the state-owned public broadcaster, TVSH, several privately owned stations are licensed to broadcast in almost every district of the country. The main news broadcasts are generally between 07.00 and 08.00, between 15.00 and 16.00, and at around 19.00.

Where cable television is provided in hotels, it does not usually include any English-language channels. There are always dozens of Italian channels, plus a few in German and an apparently random selection of other languages. Monoglot news junkies may want to hunt out a hotel with BBC World or CNN via satellite. **Radio** plays a less significant role in Albania than in some other countries. There are many radio stations, but most of them are music channels. To the great dismay of many Albanians, the BBC World Service ended its Albanian service in 2011. The Voice of America broadcasts to Albania on medium and short wave; its website (*www.voa.gov*) has details of frequencies.

Newspapers are often very partisan – indeed, three widely available papers are actually owned by political parties. There are two English-language newspapers, the *Albanian Daily News* and the weekly *Tirana Times*, which carry summaries of the previous day's Albanian press as well as their own articles. Hard copies can be obtained at the upmarket hotels in Tirana and in the Adrion bookshop on Skanderbeg Square; see *Appendix 2, Further Information*, page 275, for details of the subscription-only websites at which they can be read online. In Tirana it is also possible to buy newspapers such as the *International Herald Tribune*, the *Financial Times* and *The Guardian*; they are transmitted digitally and printed locally, so that they are available in the mornings. If you have internet access, of course, you can access your preferred media source online, which will be substantially cheaper.

PEOPLE Communicating with Albanians is much easier than might be expected. They are among the most polyglot people in Europe, perhaps because the country was isolated for so long and so few foreigners speak their language. It is mainly younger people who speak English; it is not at all unusual for a young Albanian to speak three or four languages well. Most older people do not know English, but they may well speak good French, Greek or Italian.

Italian is widely spoken in coastal towns, such as Shkodra, Durrësi and Vlora, thanks to their historical links with, and geographical proximity to, Italy. Even during the later years of the communist regime, Albanians on the coast and in Tirana could watch Italian television, and so people now in their 30s and 40s more or less grew up with the language and often speak it extremely well. Younger people, however, are more likely to have English as their first foreign language.

Enver Hoxha (see box, page 83) studied in France, at the University of Montpellier, and during communism the French *lycées* in Korça and Gjirokastra continued to operate. Particularly in these towns, therefore, but also elsewhere, a sizeable number of Albanians speak French. In the south of the country, Greek is very widely spoken, even by people who are ethnically Albanian rather than Greek.

Those who were at school or university in the 1950s and 1960s learned Russian, although many of them have not used the language for 40 or more years and have forgotten most of it. In areas which border former Yugoslavia, there are Slavic-speaking ethnic minorities; see pages 19–20. Some people who are now in their 60s learned Chinese, usually because they studied in China; some academic exchanges have resumed since the advent of democracy in Albania, and one occasionally comes across younger people, too, who have studied in China and learned the language.

POST AND TELEPHONES The **fixed network** in Albania is run by a privatised monopoly, called Albtelecom but known locally as 'Telekomi'. Numbers in Tirana have seven digits; numbers elsewhere in the country have five or six. Every town in the country now has direct dialling, as do many villages, but calls are expensive and most people prefer to use their mobile phones. There are fewer than 240,000 fixed-line subscribers in Albania, whereas in 2014 there were 3.37 million active mobile phone numbers in use, although some of these are held by Albanians who live and work abroad.

There are three main **mobile phone** companies in Albania: Eagle, Vodafone and Plus. Between them, they have agreements with most other European companies, so if you have roaming enabled on your phone you should be able to use it in Albania. Alternatively, if your phone is network-unlocked, an Albanian prepay SIM card will cost a few hundred lek, most of it as call time. If you need a local phone with a call and data package, they can be rented in Tirana, for example at Easy Shop (*Rr Grigor Heba 5;* e *info@easyshop.al; Facebook: easyshopalbania*). Tariffs have come down in recent years and coverage is as good as it is ever likely to get in a mountainous country like Albania.

There are two ways to make a phone call in Albania if you do not have a mobile phone. One is to go to the Albtelecom office, which in most, but not all, towns is in a separate building from the post office, and ask to be connected to the number you want. In large towns there will be booths and your call will be transferred to one of these; in smaller places there will just be one phone. You pay for the call after you have made it. In cities, the other option is to use a public phone in the street. These take cards, not coins – of course you can buy a card (at Albtelecom) if you think you will use all the credit on it, but the normal system is for one of the men hanging around the phones to give you his card to use. You make your call, you give him the card back, he checks how much credit you have used and you give him the money. Either of these is a good option for calls within Albania; for international calls, Skype will certainly be cheaper and is available at practically any internet café.

The Albanian **postal service** (Albapost) is not 100% reliable, although it is not especially bad either. Important documents should be sent by courier. DHL and FedEx have offices in Tirana and a few other cities. An internal courier service called ACS operates within Albania.

INTERNET Every town in Albania, and almost every village with a school, has public internet access of some sort. In towns and cities, there are plenty of internet cafés, typically charging 60–100 lek per hour. They do tend to be full of young men playing online games or older people talking to their emigrant children on Skype, so you may have to wait for a computer. Many hotels now offer Wi-Fi, usually free of charge, and some also have computers on which their guests can access the internet.

If you need internet access while you are travelling in more remote areas, it is worth asking at the village school if you can use its connection. If it is working, the headteacher will probably be happy to help you.

ALBANIAN TIME AND BUSINESS

Albania is one hour ahead of GMT from October to March, and two hours ahead in summer; this is the same time as Italy and the countries of former Yugoslavia, but one hour behind Greece.

The traditional Albanian working day begins early – at 08.00, or in rural areas even earlier – and ends at 15.00, when everybody goes home for lunch, the main meal of the day. Many people then take a siesta, particularly in summer when the streets outside are melting, and re-emerge in the early evening for the *xhiro*. This is when families go out together and walk up and down the town's boulevard or – if it has a waterfront – its promenade. The *xhiro* may include an ice cream or a coffee, or a chat with casually met friends, but it does not have to involve anything other than walking. In some towns the main street is closed to traffic for the hour or two every evening when pedestrians are more important.

If you have business to do in Albania, it is best accomplished early in the day. Ministry and local government civil servants are supposed to work from 08.30 to 16.30, except on Fridays when they leave earlier. These hours do not fit at all well with the way Albanian families operate and so it is quite difficult to find civil servants in their offices after about 15.00, especially outside the big cities.

Shops are usually open from 09.00 or 09.30 to 15.00, and then again from about 18.00 to about 20.00. Other private businesses do not usually reopen in the evenings, but if you wish to meet the owner or manager, it is almost always possible to do this over a coffee at any reasonable hour.

Doing business or buying property in Albania is fraught with difficulty owing to the prevalence of corruption, the presence of organised crime, and the weakness of the judicial system. Anyone considering investing in the country should seek the advice of the commercial attaché at their embassy in Tirana.

CULTURAL ETIQUETTE

Albanians shake hands not only on being introduced to somebody but also on greeting or leaving people they already know. With friends, a kiss on both cheeks is exchanged by men as well as women. This is often combined with a hand on the other person's shoulder. After a long separation, or with really close friends, the number of kisses increases.

Normal Albanian etiquette is for people to shake hands the first time they see each other every day, and then again when they part. This is beginning to break down a little in office environments in Tirana, but is still very much expected everywhere else.

The usual way to indicate 'yes' is by moving the head horizontally from side to side. During a conversation, this movement is also used to indicate general agreement with what the other person is saying, or simply to show that you are listening. The usual sign for 'no' is a slight raising of the eyebrows, sometimes accompanied by a gentle click of the tongue. Raising the whole chin is a very emphatic 'no'. Unfortunately, exposure to foreign visitors has confused this simple state of affairs and people (especially in Tirana) sometimes try to be helpful by using non-Albanian head signals. The result is that it can be hard to tell whether the person shaking his or her head at you is saying 'yes' in Albanian, or 'no' in your language. Sometimes you just have to ask.

Albanians usually remove their shoes inside their homes or other people's houses. If you are visiting an Albanian home, you will be offered a pair of slippers or plastic sandals to wear while you are indoors.

Smoking is widespread. A ban on smoking in enclosed public places was introduced in 2007, but it is fully enforced in only a handful of restaurants and hotels. However, there is no smoking allowed on public transport, and people almost always respect this. On long journeys the bus or minibus will stop for a couple of cigarette breaks.

As might be expected in a country which for 50 years was starved of contact with foreigners, Albanians are always very keen to engage visitors in conversation, for

2

example, on bus journeys. Their questions often become very personal very quickly, although usually they do not mean to be intrusive. It is especially difficult to know how to answer questions about your salary from (for example) a pensioner whose income is probably less than €100 per month. Unmarried women can expect to be grilled about their entire sexual history, as their puzzled interlocutor attempts to work out the reason for this extraordinary state of affairs.

TRAVELLING POSITIVELY

The charitable sector in Albania is very weak compared with northern Europe or (especially) North America. Most Tirana-based not-for-profit organisations conduct research or lobbying rather than hands-on humanitarian assistance. The main organisations which actually feed hungry people and treat sick babies are the churches and mosques.

Albanian Disability Rights Foundation (ADRF) Rr Mujo Ulqinaku 26, Tirana; \04 226 6892, 226 9426; e adrf@icc.al.eu.org; www. adrf.org.al. Set up by Oxfam GB in 1994, ADRF (its Albanian acronym is FSHDPAK) promotes the rights of people with disabilities, mostly through lobbying & training.

Albanian Red Cross \04 225 7532/3; e kksh@ albaniaonline.com; www.kksh.org.al. This is the oldest humanitarian organisation in Albania, founded in 1921. It has been a member of the Federation of the International Red Cross & Red Crescent since 1923.

Home of Hope The Home of Hope children's home and day centre in Elbasani (Shtëpia e Shpresës; see page 117) is partly funded by a UK-registered Christian charity, Care & Relief for the Young (CRY) (\01489 788300; www.cry.org.uk). The Home of Hope welcomes gifts of books, CDs & games for the children's library. If you wish to donate cash, however, you should do this through CRY, which runs a child sponsorship scheme.

One area where there are some organisations actively trying to make a difference is that of the environment and sustainable tourism; they tend to call themselves 'Associations' (Shoqata) to differentiate them from the lobbying and research NGOs. The longest standing is the **Outdoor Albania Association (OAA)** (*Rr e Bogdanëve 3, Tirana;* m *068 31 33 451;* e *outdooralbaniaassociation@yahoo. com; www.outdooralbania-association.com*), founded in 2005 by people who were also involved in the specialist tour operator Outdoor Albania (see page 31). OAA works with local communities to improve access to remote attractions, bring visitors to these places, and train local people to create businesses that are sensitive to the environmental impact and the sustainability of their enterprises. For example, it is thanks to OAA that the Pëllumbasi Cave, near Tirana, is so easy to visit (see *Chapter 3*, pages 83–4). Every summer, it brings foreign and Albanian volunteers together in a village in southern Albania to work on projects such as rubbish collection, path clearing and signposting. OAA can always use donations of money as well as of time and labour; its website gives details of its bank account.

The **Balkans Peace Park Project (B3P)** (e *enquiries@balkanspeacepark.org; www.balkanspeacepark.org*) has activities throughout the area proposed for this cross-border park (see box, page 212, for further details); specifically in Albania, it has run a summer programme in the village of Thethi (see pages 204–11) every year since 2008 and, more recently, also in Kelmendi and Valbona (see pages 211–14 and 168–71). Albanian tutors train the local adults in environmental studies and in agricultural improvement techniques, while foreign volunteers teach English to both children and adults, as well as other skills – music, sports, photography, etc. B3P is registered as a charity in England but has a partner organisation, B3P-Albania, registered in Shkodra. Again, they welcome donations as well as volunteers.

Protection and Preservation of Natural Environment in Albania (PPNEA) (*Rr Vangjush Furxhi p16 sh1 a10, Tirana;* 04 225 6257; e *contact@ppnea.org; www. ppnea.org*) focuses on research and policy advocacy. Two of the major international projects PPNEA is involved in are the Balkan Lynx Recovery Programme (see page 209) and Save the Blue Heart of Europe, a campaign to protect the wild rivers of the Balkans from unbridled hydro-electric developments. PPNEA also has a number of smaller-scale but no less important projects, including monitoring pelicans and other waterbirds and campaigning against the keeping of bears in captivity. Donations can be made through its website.

Practical Information TRAVELLING POSITIVELY

2

Part Two

THE GUIDE

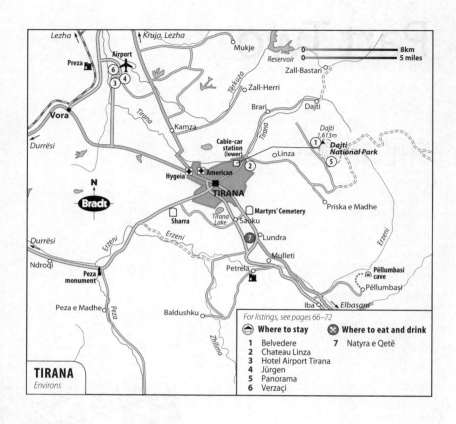

Lezha
Kruja, Lezha
Mukje
Reservoir
0   8km
0   5 miles
Zall-Bastari
Airport
Preza
6
3   4
Zall-Herri
Tërkuza
Brari
Dajti
Vora
Tirana
Kamza
Tirana
Dajti
1,613m
Durrësi
Cable-car
station
(lower)
Linza
1
Dajti
National Park
2
5
Hygeia   American
N
TIRANA
Bradt
Priska e Madhe
Martyrs' Cemetery
Durrësi
Erzeni
Sharra
Tirana
Lake
Sauku
Erzeni
Erzeni
7   Lundra
Peza
monument
Mulleti
Ndroqi
Petrela
Pëllumbasi
cave
Peza e Madhe
Peza
Baldushku
Iba   Elbasani
Pëllumbasi
Zhllima

For listings, see pages 66–72

🛏 **Where to stay**   ✖ **Where to eat and drink**

1	Belvedere	7	Natyra e Qetë
2	Chateau Linza		
3	Hotel Airport Tirana		
4	Jürgen		
5	Panorama		
6	Verzaçi		

TIRANA
Environs

3

Tirana

Telephone code: 04

Tirana was founded in the early 17th century by Sulejman Pasha of Mulleti, who built a settlement in the area around the modern intersection of Rruga e Barrikadave and Rruga Luigj Gurakuqi. His statue stands today in the little square near that crossroads. Until it was designated as the capital in 1920, Tirana was a small, unimportant town, whose main virtue for Albania's political leaders was its geographical position more or less in the centre of the recently independent country, on the fault line dividing the northern Ghegs from the southern Tosks. It remained a bit of a backwater town for several years afterwards, as Albania struggled to stabilise itself in the face of internal lawlessness and invasions by its hostile neighbours.

It was not until Italian influence became pervasive in the late 1920s that the centre of Tirana took on the appearance of a capital city. Italian planners created the huge new square – which was named after the national hero Skanderbeg – and the wide, typically Fascist boulevard; Italian architects designed the ministry buildings, the National Bank and the town hall at the square's southern end, as well as the Dajti Hotel, the royal palace on Rruga e Elbasanit, and some of the embassies. During the communist era, the few old buildings still standing on Skanderbeg Square were demolished and the opera house, the National Historical Museum and the Hotel Tirana were added, as were the public buildings further down the boulevard. All these 20th-century accretions, plus the destruction caused by various earthquakes and by the Battle for the Liberation of Tirana in 1944, means that there is not very much left of Ottoman Tirana. A good deal of what survived into the 1990s has subsequently disappeared under glittering high-rise apartment blocks and shopping centres.

Tirana has become well known for its brightly painted apartment blocks. This initiative began in the wake of the 2000 local elections, which saw an artist and former Minister of Culture becoming Mayor of Tirana. The new mayor, Edi Rama (at the time of writing, he is the country's prime minister), began by restoring to the ministries on and around Skanderbeg Square the ochre colour which they had when they were first built in the 1930s; he went on to give a lick of paint to the tatty apartment buildings in the streets nearby, choosing bold colours which – although they did not convince everybody – at least had the merit of brightening up the city. The colours and patterns became livelier and livelier, until even the more progressive of Tirana's citizens began to complain that their city was starting to look like a circus. Happily for them, the harsh summer sun bleaches out the most migraine-inducing colours after a year or two. As well as its intriguing mix of architectural styles, Tirana has several very good museums, lots of green spaces and a range of cultural activities. It has hundreds of cafés; dozens of modern bars, popular with younger people; numerous clubs, some with live music, particularly at the weekends; and an array of restaurants, many of them excellent. New bars and restaurants open all the time, and a complete list would certainly become out of date in the lifetime of a guide such as this. The more ephemeral

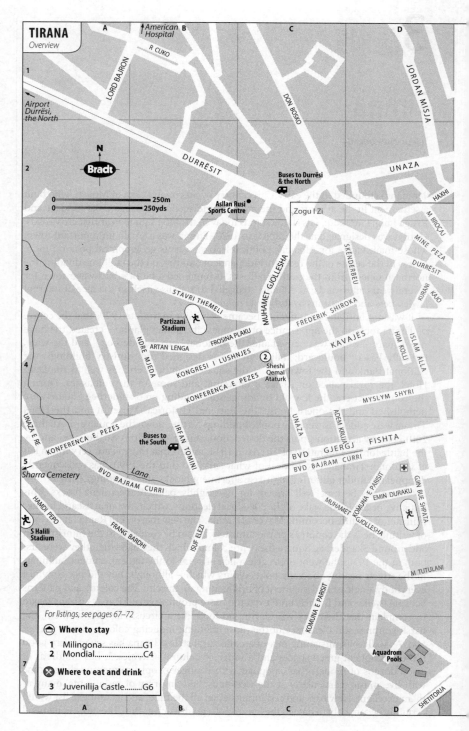

American Hospital

R CUKO

LORD BAJRON

1

Airport
Durrësi,
the North

DURRËSIT

DON BOSKO

JORDAN MISJA

UNAZA

HAXHI

Bradt

N

2

0 ———————— 250m
0 ———————— 250yds

**Buses to Durrësi
& the North**

Asllan Rusi
Sports Centre

Zogu I Zi

M BROÇAJ

MINE PEZA

DURRËSIT

KUJRANI KAVO

SKËNDERBEU

3

STAVRI THEMELI

FREDERIK SHIROKA

MUHAMET GJOLLESHA

Partizani
Stadium

FROSINA PLAKU

KAVAJËS

HIM KOLLI

ISLAM ALLA

NDRE MJEDA

ARTAN LENGA

KONGRESI I LUSHNJES

② Sheshi
Qemal
Ataturk

4

KONFERENCA E PEZES

MYSLYM SHYRI

ADEM KRUJAS

UNAZA E RE

KONFERENCA E PEZES

Buses to
the South

IRFAN TOMINI

UNAZA

BVD GJERGJ FISHTA

5

Sharra Cemetery

Lana

BVD BAJRAM CURRI

BVD BAJRAM CURRI

GJIN BUE SHPATA

HAMDI PEPO

S Halili
Stadium

FRANG BARDHI

ISUF ELEZI

MUHAMET GJOLLESHA

KOMUNA E PARISIT

EMIN DURAKU

M TUTULANI

6

KOMUNA E PARISIT

Aquadrom
Pools

7

For listings, see pages 67–72

🛏 **Where to stay**

1   Milingona....................G1
2   Mondial.......................C4

❌ **Where to eat and drink**

3   Juvenilija Castle.........G6

SHETITORJA

A   B   C   D

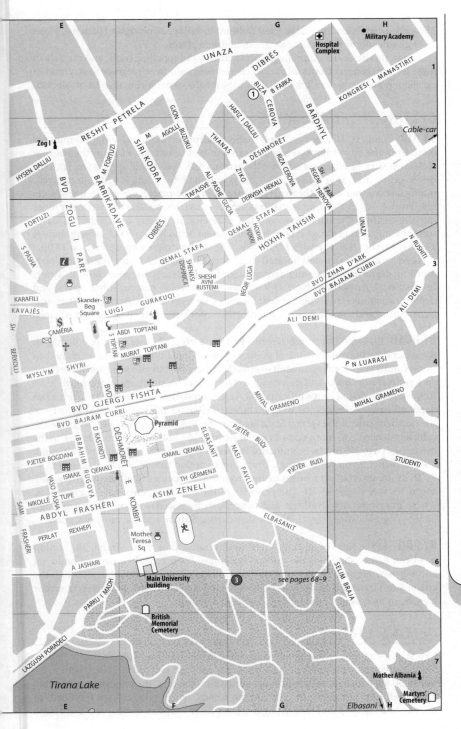

Military Academy

Hospital Complex

UNAZA

DIBRËS

RIZA CEROVA

B FARKA

KONGRESI I MANASTIRIT

RESHIT PETRELA

GJON BUZUKU

AGOLLI

THANAS

HAFIZ I DALLIU

4 DËSHMORËT

RIZA CEROVA

BARDHYL

Cable-car

Zog I

HYSEN DALLIU

M FORTUZI

SIRI KODRA

TAFAJSVE PASHE GUCIA

ALI PASHE GUCIA

ZIKO

DERVISH HEKALI

SRI FAIK

JEGENI TRENOVA

BVD BARRIKADAVE

FORTUZI

S PASHA

ZOGU I PARE

DIBRËS

QEMAL STAFA

QEMAL STAFA

HOXHE VIDRI

HOXHA TAHSIM

UNAZA

N RUSHIT

KARAFILI

KAVAJËS

SH

BERKOLLI

Skander-Beg Square

GURAKUQI

LUIGJ

CAMERIA

MYSLYM SHYRI

S TOPTANI

ABDI TOPTANI

MURAT TOPTANI

BEQIR LUGA

BVD ZHAN D'ARK

BVD BAJRAM CURRI

ALI DEMI

ALI DEMI

P N LUARASI

MIHAL GRAMENO

MIHAL GRAMENO

BVD GJERGJ FISHTA

BVD BAJRAM CURRI

Pyramid

D KASTRIOTI

DËSHMORËT

IBRAHIM RUGOVA

ISMAIL QEMALI

ELBASANIT

PJETËR BUDI

NASI PAVLLO

PJETËR BUDI

STUDENTI

PJETER BOGDANI

ISMAIL QEMALI

E KOMBIT

TH GERMENJI

ASIM ZENELI

VASO PASHA

TUPE

SAMI

NIKOLLË

ABDYL FRASHËRI

ELBASANIT

FRASHËRI

PERLAT

REXHEPI

A JASHARI

Mother Teresa Sq

SELIM BRAJA

Main University building

3

see pages 68–9

PARKU I MADH

British Memorial Cemetery

LAZGUSH PORADECI

Tirana Lake

Mother Albania

Elbasani

Martyrs' Cemetery

Tirana

3

63

Tirana in Your Pocket lists all the latest fashions in eating, drinking and dancing. Pages 71–3 give details of some of the longer-established places.

Tirana also has some infuriating aspects, mainly the appalling traffic and the Balkan noise level. In general, however, the city centre makes an attractive place to stay; and its excellent public transport links make it the best base for exploring the rest of Albania.

GETTING THERE AND AWAY

BY AIR Tirana is Albania's only international airport, 17km and about 30 minutes' drive from the city. Approved airport taxis can be booked at a kiosk in the baggage reclaim area, or hired as you exit into the arrivals hall. You should agree a fare with the driver before accepting his services – the going rate into Tirana is €20. Alternatively, unofficial taxis wait across the road from the airport perimeter fence and charge slightly less. From 07.00 to 19.00, an hourly bus service runs from outside the perimeter fence into the centre of Tirana; the one-way fare is 250 lek. In the city centre, the bus leaves from the junction of Rruga e Durrësit with Rruga Mine Peza [68 C2], where there is a clearly marked bus stop with a timetable. The last bus to the airport leaves at 18.00.

There are several hotels located near the airport, which are useful for early morning departures or late-night arrivals; for further details, see pages 66– 70. Tirana International Airport's website (*www.tirana-airport.com*) has real-time arrival and departure data, as well as flight schedules and other useful information. See *Chapter 2, Getting there and away*, pages 32–3, for further information about flying into Albania.

BY ROAD Buses and/or minibuses run to Tirana from all other parts of Albania. In the other direction, at the time of going to press, Tirana does not have a central bus station and it is sometimes difficult to establish where the bus you want will leave from. As a general rule, buses and minibuses to Durrësi and destinations in the north leave from near the Zogu i Zi roundabout [68 A1]; buses to the southwest leave from a bus depot off Rruga e Kavajës [62 B5]; and buses to Elbasani and the southeast leave from the northern side of the Qemal Stafa Stadium [69 F6]. The simplest way to locate the vehicle you need is to hire a taxi and say something like 'autobusët për në Durrës' to the driver (see page 269 for the grammatically correct form of other place names, although it won't matter if you get it wrong). Your hotel reception should also be able to help.

There are international buses to and from the main cities in all the neighbouring countries (see pages 33–4). The majority of the bus companies have their offices, where information is available and tickets can be purchased, on Bulevardi Zogu i Parë (Zogu I), which runs between Skanderbeg Square and the railway station.

BY RAIL At the time of writing, there are no trains to or from Tirana. The station has been demolished and the railway lines have been asphalted over to build yet another new highway. A new railway station may eventually be built, although the citizens of Tirana are unlikely to be holding their collective breath, given that they have been promised a bus station for at least a decade.

GETTING AROUND

Urban buses are run by private companies and licensed by the Municipality of Tirana. They can get very crowded in rush hour, but they are incredibly cheap, with a flat fare of 30 lek which is collected by a conductor on the bus. The two routes which are most useful for visitors to the city are the *Unaza*, which goes around the north of the city in a big loop and then along the Lana River – or vice versa – and the *Tirana e Re/Stacioni i Trenit*, which starts near the railway station and goes right down the Boulevard, before turning off along Rruga Abdyl Frashëri and making an even wider loop around the western part of the city. Other buses depart from the various bus-stops around Skanderbeg Square. The buses are different colours, depending on the line they serve, and can be boarded or alighted at any of the bus stops along their route. A tram route, which will cross the whole southeast to northwest axis of the city, is planned and may become operational within the lifetime of this book.

In the city centre, within the ring road ('Unaza'), taxis charge 400 or 500 lek. For longer journeys crossing the ring road, agree the fare before setting off. There are taxi ranks at several places in the city centre: along the sides of 'The Block' (see page 73); at various points along Boulevard Zogu I, convenient for the railway station and buses to and from the north; and beside the Academy of Arts on Mother Teresa Square. Tirana has a few radio-taxi companies; the easiest numbers to remember are 224 4444, 235 5555 and 237 7777, all of which are reliable firms with reasonably new cars.

Cars can be hired in the city centre and at the airport (see page 42 for contact information). Tirana's cycle hire scheme has bikes in racks at various points around the centre; the backpacker hostels also have bikes available to rent. It should be noted that driving and especially cycling in the centre of Tirana is not for the faint-hearted.

TOURIST INFORMATION

Tirana's tourist information office is located on Rruga Ded Gjo Luli, behind the National Historical Museum [68 D2]. Unfortunately, it is open only from 11.00 to 16.00 on weekdays and is closed altogether at weekends. It stocks a range of free leaflets and brochures about Tirana and other towns in Albania. English is spoken.

Tirana in Your Pocket is updated (a bit) about twice a year and is a good source of information about new restaurants, bars and clubs. The paper version is available in the Tirana bookshops, priced 500 lek, or it can be downloaded from www.inyourpocket. com. The Municipality of Tirana's website (*www.tirana.gov.al*) has information in Albanian about the city and contact information in English for some hotels.

The local travel agencies listed in Chapter 2 (see page 31) can arrange one-day (or longer) tours of Tirana on request. The backpacker hostels (see *Where to stay*, page 70) organise one-day hikes and cycling tours in the countryside around Tirana. Favourite destinations are Mount Dajti and the Pëllumbasi Cave (Shpella e Pëllumbasit); see pages 83–5. These day trips are an excellent option for lovers of the outdoors who are unable to spend enough time in Albania to embark on a more ambitious trek. Walking tours of Tirana (including a tour of the city's markets) can also be arranged.

 WHERE TO STAY   *Map, pages 68–9, unless otherwise indicated.*

Tirana has a wide range of hotels to suit every pocket. At the very top of the market, charging in excess of €100 a night, are the Sheraton, down by the university off Mother Teresa Square, the Rogner, on the Boulevard opposite the presidency building, and the Grand, on Rruga Ismail Qemali opposite Hoxha's villa. All are very well appointed, with comfortable rooms, good restaurants and swimming pools (indoor at the Grand, outdoor at the Rogner, both at the Sheraton).

There is a good range of comfortable hotels with rates around the €80–90 mark. Reception staff almost always speak some English and you can be reasonably confident that you will be able to use your credit card in such hotels. The **mid-range** hotels (**$$$**) have en-suite shower and toilet facilities, air conditioning and cable television as standard. Not all staff speak English, but there will be someone around who does. New hotels in this category open frequently and the list below is far from exhaustive.

Towards the **budget** end of the scale, hotels in the €20–40 price range (**$$**) are often perfectly adequate, although they do not always have air conditioning and language may be a problem. They do not usually have websites through which reservations can be made, but many of them are partnered with one or other of the usual international online booking agencies or with the Tirana-based www.albania-hotel.com. Anything much cheaper is likely to be a bit seedy; dorm accommodation in one of the backpackers' hostels will be a better option.

If you want to escape Tirana's noise and pollution at night but need to be in the city during the day, Mount Dajti might be the solution. The Belvedere is right next to the upper cable-car station; the Panorama operates shuttle buses from the cable-car station throughout the day. The upmarket Chateau Linza, part of the way up the mountain, also has a minibus to run its residents to and from the centre of Tirana.

LUXURY

⌂ **Chateau Linza** [map, page 60] (21 rooms, 45 apts) Rr Porcelanit, Qesarake, Linza; m 069 20 30 003/009; www.chateaulinzahotel.com. Beautiful setting on the way up Mt Dajti, overlooking Tirana. Shuttle bus for guests to city & airport. Open-air swimming pool with terrace bar, restaurants, wine bar, fitness centre, laundry service. All rooms are en suite, with Wi-Fi, TV, AC, direct-dial phone. Apts have 2 bedrooms, 2 bathrooms, kitchen, living room & balcony. **$$$$$**

⌂ **Diplomat Fashion** (26 rooms) Bd Bajram Curri 36; \ 223 5090; e reservation@diplomatfashion.com; www.diplomatfashion.com. Out on the ring road, rather far from the centre. Restaurant, garden cocktail bar & café, rooftop terrace bar, spa centre, library, Wi-Fi. 3 contemporary styles of room décor. All rooms en suite, with AC, satellite TV, direct-dial phone, internet connection. **$$$$$**

⌂ **Grand** (30 rooms, 1 suite) Rr Ismail Qemali 11; \ 225 3219/20; e info@grandhoteltirana.com; www.grandhoteltirana.com. Rooftop bar & restaurant, plus 1st-floor Italian restaurant; indoor pool & sauna. All rooms have AC, satellite TV & free Wi-Fi. **$$$$$**

⌂ **Green House** (6 rooms) Rr Jul Variboba 6; \ 222 2632, 225 1015; e info@greenhouse.al; www.greenhouse.al. Secure parking; excellent restaurant in garden below guest rooms. All rooms en suite, with dbl bed, AC, TV, Wi-Fi; quiet; some have bathtub, some have balcony. **$$$$$**

⌂ **Rogner Europapark** (137 rooms) Bd Dëshmorët e Kombit; \ 223 5035; e info.tirana@rogner.com; http://hotel-europapark.com. Good restaurant with Albanian & international cuisine; bar popular with politicians & expats; newsagent. Free Wi-Fi in public areas. Open-air pool & terrace bar in lovely gardens, tennis courts, fitness centre. Rooms have AC, satellite TV & free internet access. **$$$$$**

⌂ **Sheraton** (151 rooms) Sheshi Italia, off Mother Teresa Sq; \ 227 4707; e reservations.tirana@sheraton.com; www.starwood.com/sheraton. Piano bar, restaurant with Albanian & international menu, food court; Wi-Fi in public areas. Indoor & outdoor pools, health club. Big rooms with king-size beds, satellite TV, AC, high-speed internet (extra charge), minibar & views of the city or Tirana Park. **$$$$$**

⌂ **Sky Hotel** (33 rooms) Rr Ibrahim Rugova 5/1; \ 241 5995; e info@skyhotel-al.com; www.skyhotel-al.com. Right in 'The Block', in the iconic Sky Tower Bldg; lift, ground-floor bar, panoramic revolving restaurant, fitness centre & spa, secure parking. Enormous well-appointed guest rooms, all en suite with rain shower, AC, TV, Wi-Fi, safe. **$$$$$**

⌂ **Tirana International** (158 rooms, 12 suites) Skanderbeg Sq; \ 223 4185; m 068 223 4185; e reservation@hoteltirana.com.al; http://tiranainternational.com. Ground-floor bar, one of Tirana's main people-watching spots; restaurant with mainly Italian cuisine & terrace with view over the square; secure parking; free Wi-Fi in public areas; English-speaking reception staff. Indoor pool, spa centre, extensive conference room capacity. Rooms recently upgraded, all now have AC, HD TV, minibar, Wi-Fi, safe; those at the front have unbeatable views over the city & are slightly more expensive. **$$$$$**

⌂ **Xheko Imperial** (25 rooms) Rr Ibrahim Rugova; \ 225 9574/5/6/7; m 068 20 29 777; e contact@xheko-imperial.com; www.xheko-imperial.com. Lift to all floors; wine bar; restaurant & bar on roof terrace. Rooms have AC, satellite TV, phone, safe & Wi-Fi; well-equipped bathrooms with underfloor heating & hairdryers. **$$$$$**

UPMARKET

🏠 **Arbër** (24 rooms, 1 suite) Rr Bardhok Biba 59; 📞227 3811; e reservation@hotelarber.com; www. hotelarber.com. Lift, laundry service, free car park for guests, terrace bar, restaurant with Albanian & Italian menu. All rooms en suite, with CH, AC, satellite TV, minibar, direct-dial phone, internet access. Rooms are a good size – sgls have 1.2m beds, twins have an armchair & desk; 1 suite with 1 dbl bedroom, 2 bathrooms & a sitting room. **$$$$**

🏠 **Hotel Airport Tirana** [map, page 60] (50 rooms) Tirana International Airport (Rinas); 📞450 0190; m 068 20 04 243, 068 20 47 964, 068 20 55 133; e info@hotel-airporttirana.com; www.hotel-airporttirana.com. Just outside airport perimeter, no direct access, hotel shuttle bus picks up & drops off for free on request. Restaurant, garden bar, outdoor swimming pool with wooden loungers, lift, laundry service. Attentive, English-speaking staff, public areas non-smoking, some non-smoking rooms. Nicely furnished rooms, soundproofed, all en suite with AC, flat-screen TV, balcony, hairdryer, internet access; some have minibar, spa shower. **$$$$**

🏠 **Iliria** (20 rooms) Rr e Elbasanit; 📞237 1700; m 068 40 27 112; e info@hotelliriatirana.com; www.hotelliriatirana.com. Handy for US embassy. Restaurant & bar, secure parking, internet. All rooms en suite with CH, AC, satellite TV, minibar, Wi-Fi, safe, balcony; some overlooking Tirana Park. **$$$$**

🏠 **Mondial** [map, page 63] (28 rooms, 6 suites) Rr Muhamet Gjollesha 1023; 📞225 8121/2, 223 2372; m 068 20 04 642; e info@hotelmondial. com.al; www.hotelmondial.com.al. Rather far from the centre, out on the ring road, but convenient for

the airport & highways to the west & north. Good restaurant, rooftop & indoor bars, rooftop pool, sauna, laundry service, computer with internet access for guests' use. English spoken at reception. All rooms have satellite TV, AC, free Wi-Fi, safe, desk, minibar, direct-dial phone; suites have balcony. **$$$$**

🏠 **Theranda** (14 rooms) Rr Andon Z Çajupi 6&7; 📞227 3766; e reservations@therandahotel.com; www.therandahotel.com. Slightly hard to find but signposted off Rr Çajupi. The only mid-range hotel in Tirana which meets UK health & safety standards (eg: fire exits). 2 quiet villas linked by an attractive courtyard, bar, secure parking, computer for guests' use, good English spoken at reception. No restaurant on site, but b/fast inc. All rooms with alarmed door locks, good-sized en-suite bathroom, minibar, AC, TV, cable internet & free Wi-Fi. **$$$$**

🏠 **Vila Alba** (24 rooms & 3 in annexe) Rr Xhorxhi Martini 10; 📞225 5937; e office@vila-alba.com; www.vila-alba.com. On a quiet side street, English spoken, b/fast room on top floor with views over city; lift; key-cards for guest rooms. Nicely furnished, large rooms, all with en-suite bathroom & shower, LCD TV, Wi-Fi, minibar, AC, dressing table. **$$$$**

MID-RANGE

🏠 **Belvedere** [map, page 60] (24 rooms) Mt Dajti; m 067 40 11 035; e reservation@ dajtitower.com, marketing@dajtiekspres.com; www.dajtitower.com. Part of the complex around the upper station of the Dajti cable-car; magnificent views over Tirana on one side, forested mountainside on the other. Panoramic bar & restaurant, free transport on cable-car

Tirana **WHERE TO STAY**

3

67

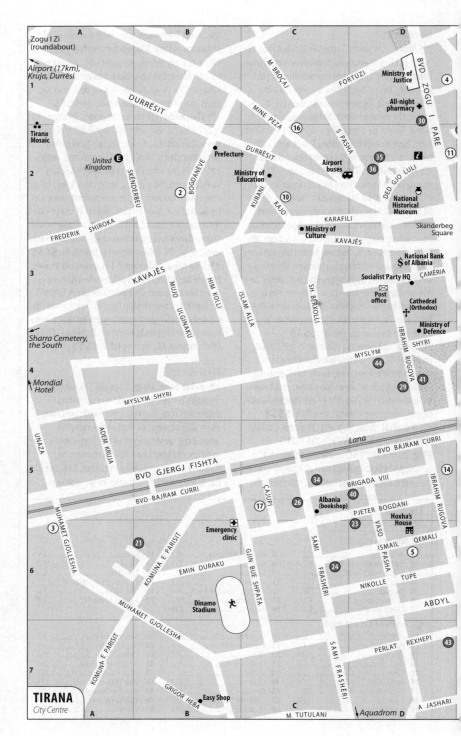

TIRANA
City Centre

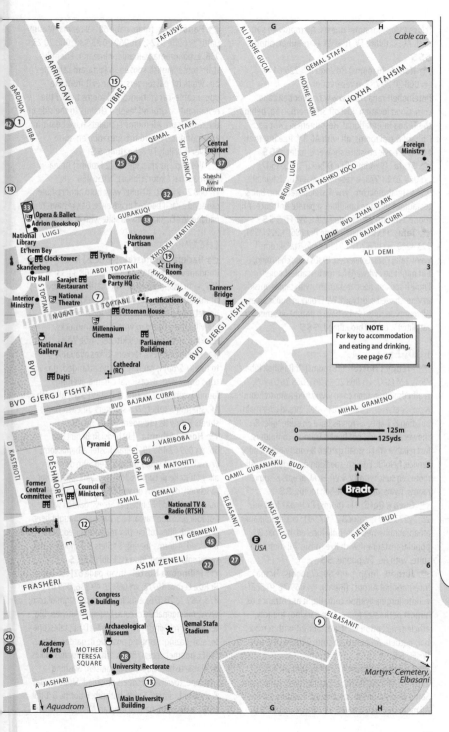

Cable car

E   F   TAFAJSVE   F   ALI PASHE GUCIA   G   H

BARDHOK BIBA

BARRIKADAVE

DIBRES

42 1

15

QEMAL STAFA

QEMAL STAFA

HOXHE VOKRI

HOXHA TAHSIM

QEMAL STAFA

SH DISHNICA

Central market

Foreign Ministry

18

25 47

37

8

BEQIR LUGA

TEFTA TASHKO KOÇO

Sheshi Avni Rustemi

32

GURAKUQI

38

BVD ZHAN D'ARK

Lana   BVD BAJRAM CURRI

32 33 Opera & Ballet
Adrion (bookshop)

National Library

LUIGJ

Unknown Partisan

XHORXH MARTINI

19

ALI DEMI

Et'hem Bey
Clock-tower   Tyrbe

Skanderbeg

City Hall

Sarajet Restaurant

ABDI TOPTANI

Democratic Party HQ

☆ Living Room

XHORXH W BUSH

Tanners' Bridge

Interior Ministry

S TOPTANI

National Theatre

7

TOPTANI

Fortifications

Ottoman House

31

BVD GJERGJ FISHTA

MURAT

National Art Gallery

Millennium Cinema

Parliament Building

NOTE
For key to accommodation and eating and drinking, see page 67

BVD

Dajti

BVD GJERGJ FISHTA

Cathedral (RC)

BVD BAJRAM CURRI

MIHAL GRAMENO

D KASTRIOTI

Pyramid

GJON PALI II

6

J VARIBOBA

46

M MATOHITI

0   125m
0   125yds

PJETER

QAMIL GURANJAKU BUDI

N

Bradt

DESHMORET

Former Central Committee

Council of Ministers

ISMAIL

QEMALI

National TV & Radio (RTSH)

ELBASANIT

NASI PAVLLO

PJETER   BUDI

Checkpoint

12

TH GËRMENJI

45

USA

ASIM ZENELI

22   27

FRASHËRI

KOMBIT

Congress building

ELBASANIT

9

Archaeological Museum

Qemal Stafa Stadium

20
39

Academy of Arts

MOTHER TERESA SQUARE

28

University Rectorate

Martyrs' Cemetery, Elbasani

A JASHARI

13

E   Aquadrom

Main University Building

E   F   G   H

69

(*closed Mon*) for hotel guests. All rooms en suite with AC, satellite TV, free Wi-Fi, minibar, phone. **$$$**

🏠 **Nobel** (6 rooms) Bd Zogu I; ☎ 225 6444; m 068 20 20 757; e reservations@ hotelnobeltirana.com; www.hotelnobeltirana. com. Good location, just off Skanderbeg Sq, behind the Tirana International. Restaurant & 24hr bar. Dbl, sgl & trpl rooms, all with AC, TV, free internet access & basic en-suite shower & toilet. **$$$**

🏠 **Stela** (9 rooms) Rr e Dibrës; ☎ 222 1547; m 068 20 13 978; e reservations@hotelstela.al, info@stelahotel.com; www.stelahotel.com. Bar & restaurant in same building, separate entrance. All rooms en suite with cable TV, AC, Wi-Fi. **$$$**

🏠 **Tafaj** (15 rooms) Rr Mine Peza 86; ☎ 222 7581, 223 4280; m 068 20 21 013; e info@tafaj.com; www.tafaj.com. Converted 1930s villa; charming, but might be awkward for the less able-bodied. English spoken; good restaurant, with tables outside in vine-shaded courtyard; Wi-Fi only in public areas. All rooms en suite (some have bathtub), AC, minibar, satellite TV, cabled broadband. **$$$**

BUDGET

🏠 **Freddy's Hostel** (18 rooms) Rr Bardhok Biba 75; ☎ 226 6077; m 068 20 35 261, 068 26 01 909; e alfredsalku@yahoo.com; www.freddyshostel.com. A cross between a hotel & a hostel, spread over main building & 2 apts; all rooms have en-suite toilet & shower, with beds, not bunks. Lounge, computers, fast reliable Wi-Fi; small garden & courtyard; laundry service; helpful, English-speaking management. All rooms en suite with TV & Wi-Fi, AC in apts & some rooms. Twins, dbls, tpl & 4-bed rooms. **$$**

🏠 **Guva e Qetë** (13 rooms) Rr Murat Toptani 25; ☎ 223 5491; m 068 27 07 901; e klidballkan@ albaniaonline.net. Centrally located, has bar & popular restaurant with live music. All rooms en suite, with AC, TV, phone. **$$**

🏠 **Jürgen** [map, page 60] (7 rooms) Tirana International Airport (Rinas); m 069 22 30 663; e hoteljurgen@yahoo.com. Right at entrance to airport perimeter fence; free parking; friendly, efficient reception staff. Restaurant with terrace; bar; garden. All rooms en suite with AC, TV, free Wi-Fi. **$$**

🏠 **Lugano** (8 rooms) Rr Mihal Duri 34; ☎/f 222 2023; m 068 20 98 788; e luganohotel@yahoo.com. Some English spoken at reception. Laundry service. All rooms en suite with AC, TV, Wi-Fi, minibar. **$$**

🏠 **Panorama** [map, page 60] (9 rooms) Mount Dajti; ☎/f 236 3124; m 069 20 23 936, 068 20 23 936; e panorama@albaniaonline.net. Friendly staff, some English spoken. A Panorama shuttle bus waits for passengers at the exit from the upper cable-car station. 5 dbl rooms below the restaurant, at ground level; 4 chalets to the side of the restaurant. All rooms & chalets have beautiful views (if it is clear, to the Adriatic), en-suite shower & toilet, TV & heating. **$$**

🏠 **Verzaçi** [map, page 60] (24 rooms) Tirana International Airport (Rinas); ☎ 056 460 118; m 068 20 25 542. 10 mins' walk from airport; hotel can send a car if booked in advance. Bar, restaurant, parking, Wi-Fi. All rooms en suite with AC & TV. **$$**

CHEAP

🏠 **Backpacker Hostel** (48 beds) Rr e Bogdanëve 3; m 068 46 82 353, 068 31 33 451; e tiranabackpacker@hotmail.com; www. tiranahostel.com. Albania's 1st backpackers' hostel, now in a(nother!) new location. Italian-era villa, large garden with bar, hammocks, relaxing area; equipped kitchen; free Wi-Fi, free internet access, lockers. Bikes available to hire (*€5/day*); car hire can be arranged; day trips organised; occasional cinema evenings; laundry service. 7 dorms & 2 dbls (**$$**), all with AC, sharing 3 toilets & 3 showers on each floor; sheets & towels provided; b/fast inc. **$**

🏠 **Hostel Albania** (30 beds) Rr Beqir Luga 56; m 069 67 48 779; e lira@hostel-albania.com; www.hostel-albania.com. Located 50m down an alley off Rr Beqir Luga, follow the signs for 'Nils Bor' (a school); directions on website. Kitchen, washing machine, free Wi-Fi, internet access; garden with outdoor relaxation area, bbq, bar with draught beer, b/fast with filter coffee. Day trips organised. Bedlinen provided. 4 dorms sharing 3 toilets & 2 showers, hot water solar-heated; lockers; 1 dbl (**$$**). **$**

🏠 **Milingona Hostel** [map, page 62] (50 beds) Rr Riza Cerova 197/2; m 069 20 49 836, 069 61 02 875, 069 20 70 076; e milingonahostel@gmail.com; www.milingonahostel.com. Equipped kitchen; big terrace for relaxing with view of Mt Dajti; telescope for star-gazing; camping possible in garden. Free Wi-Fi, internet access; BSL & other languages. Bikes available to hire; day trips organised; washing machine; towels and sheets provided. Shared toilet & shower facilities, 1 with bathtub. 6 dorms & 1 dbl (**$$**), each room named after an Albanian town. **$**

Tirana is probably the only capital city in Europe which does not have a McDonald's, although an ersatz McDonald's, called **Kolonat**, has branches across the city centre. Instead, it has a huge number of real restaurants, many of them excellent. In all but the most expensive establishments listed below, a main course with a salad or soup and a beer or a glass of wine should come in at around €15. Fish and seafood are always dearer than meat.

There are not many cheaper restaurants in central Tirana; the budget option is fast food (*sufllaqë* or *byrek* – see pages 49–50) at under a euro a portion. For spit-roasted lamb at weekends, Tirana residents go to one of the restaurants up on Mount Dajti (see page 85), or to Lundra or Sauku, villages off the Elbasani road.

EXPENSIVE

✗ **Otium** Rr Brigada VIII; ☎ 222 3570; m 069 20 50 778; ⊕ Tue–Sun. Small, intimate restaurant; excellent service; unusual but effective menu, blending high-quality Albanian ingredients with Western culinary inventiveness. $$$$$

✗ **Piazza** Rr Ded Gjo Luli, in the corner behind the fountain; ☎ 223 0706. Excellent menu, particularly the fish; outstanding wine list with the best Albanian wines; highly professional service; formal atmosphere. No longer has the monopoly on these virtues which it once had, but still very high quality. The **Piazza Café** ($$$) next door serves great sandwiches & burgers until late at night. $$$$$

✗ **Rozafa** Rr Luigj Gurakuqi 89; ☎ 222 2786, 223 9114; e restorant@rozafa.com.al; www.rozafa. com.al. The formal Rozafa is located down the alleyway around the corner from the Rozafa casino – bear left at the end of the alleyway to find the rather discreet entrance. The best fish in Tirana, inc excellent fish-based antipasto selection; good wine list; service not quite as stellar as in the past, but still very good. $$$$$

✗ **Vinum** Rr Qemal Stafa 60; ☎ 223 0822; m 068 26 84 900; ⊕ Tue–Sat. Signposted down an alleyway off Qemal Stafa. Excellent veal, lamb & poultry dishes, homemade pasta, interesting salads, all prepared in a very un-Albanian way. Professional, English-speaking service, good selection of Albanian & foreign wine. Quiet garden with tables outside in summer. $$$$$

ABOVE AVERAGE

✗ **Amor** Rr Muhamet Gjollesha; ☎ 224 1573; m 069 26 84 952, 068 40 10 403; ⊕ Mon–Sat. High-quality Italian dining in a weirdly out-of-the-way corner of Tirana. No printed menu; the waiter tells you what the chef proposes, based on what

they liked the look of in the market that morning. Difficult to find, in an alleyway among residential buildings behind the Dinamo Stadium. $$$$

✗ **Juvenilja Castle** [map, page 63] Rr Gjeneral Niko Pushkini; ☎ 226 6666; www.juvenilja.com. Lovely setting, in a curious castle-style building just on the edge of the Big Park (Parku i Madh). The usual range of salads & Italian dishes, with an unusually interesting selection of Albanian-style antipasti. Tables in garden right next to the park are for drinks only; the restaurant has a roofed gallery overlooking the garden & the park.$$$$

✗ **Oda** Rr Luigj Gurakuqi; ☎ 224 9541; m 069 20 94 911. The best traditional Albanian food in Tirana, with specialities from southern & central Albania, inc various offal dishes. In an old house near the central market; 2 small dining rooms, 1 with *sofra*, the other with Western tables & chairs; English spoken. Excellent selection of raki, inc *mani* & *mare* (see pages 50–1). $$$$

✗ **Sky Club** Rr Ibrahim Rugova; ☎ 222 1666, 222 1143. The Sky Tower, on the eastern edge of 'The Block', has Tirana's only revolving restaurant & bar. Drinks are also served at tables on the terrace around the outside of the restaurant. The views of the city are, as one might expect, magnificent. The revolution is quite slow – it takes almost an hour to turn the whole 360°. $$$$

✗ **Vila 100** Rr Myslym Shyri; m 068 20 74 576; www.vila100.com. Signposted between 2 apt buildings roughly opposite Albtelecom headquarters. Large garden, shaded with trees & vines; canvas covering for rain; good service, English spoken. High-quality meat & fish dishes, homemade pasta, interesting salads & antipasti, good wine list. $$$$

✗ **Vila Ambasador** Rr Asim Zeneli; ☎ 225 4855; m 069 20 66 257. The usual Italian-influenced menu, with some unusual mushroom dishes. Tables outside in pleasant garden in summer. $$$$

REASONABLE

✖ **Amsterdam** Rr Asim Zeneli, opposite the Netherlands Embassy (hence the name). Pleasant walled garden, pasta & pizzas, grilled meat, instant-heart-attack dishes such as fried cheese. $$$

✖ **Berlin** Rr Pjetër Bogdani, between Sami Frashëri & Vaso Pasha; ☎ 226 0737. Famous for its schnitzels; also has homemade pasta, good pizza, grilled meat & fish; good Albanian wine. $$$

✖ **Era** Rr Ismail Qemali between Vaso Pasha & Sami Frashëri; ☎ 225 7805, 226 0749. A good selection of traditional Albanian food, plus pizzas & pasta; the terrace is heated in winter; can get crowded, especially inside; one of the few restaurants in Tirana which stay open really late (until midnight at w/ends). $$$

✖ **Gloria** Rr Qemal Stafa; ☎ 224 7731. Friendly neighbourhood restaurant, interesting menu with some unusual main courses & excellent side dishes, as well as grilled meats & pasta. $$$

✖ **Green House** Rr Jul Variboba 6; ☎ 223 1015. Reliably good Italian-influenced menu, with a range of interesting meat & fish dishes, plus pizza from wood-fired oven. Sometimes has game dishes such as hare. Friendly, professional service. Tables outside in pleasant courtyard. $$$

✖ **Juvenilija** Rr Sami Frashëri at the T-junction with Rr Brigada VIII; m 068 20 22 802. Juvenilija has recovered from a spell of indifferent pizzas & is now back to its old form as a Tirana institution. Go with friends & share a couple of pizzas & cold beers. Also offers pasta, risotto, escalopes & some traditional Albanian dishes. $$$

✖ **Kaon Brewhouse** Rr Asim Zeneli. Outlet for the Kaon brewery (also a brewhouse, in the outskirts of Tirana), huge beer garden, tables also indoors. One of Albania's best beers on tap (lager & dark). Good salads & antipasti; meat grills; pizza & pasta. $$$

✖ **London** Bd Zogu I, on the left of the first block coming from Skanderbeg Sq; ☎ 223 8851. Good Italian food, courteous, professional service; both food & service have maintained a consistently high standard since the 1990s. More recent is the (enforced) smoking ban in the restaurant. The bar serves particularly good raki. $$$

✖ **Lulishte 1 Maji** Bd Xhorxh W Bush; ☎ 223 0151; m 069 20 97 621, 069 20 92 668. Huge

terrace with play area for children; live music on summer evenings. Brews its own beer, to a Czech recipe; menu of grilled meat, inc homemade sausages, Albanian dishes & the usual Italian-influenced meals. $$$

✖ **Qendër Stefan** (the Stephen Centre) Sheshi Avni Rustemi. On the corner of the square where the central market is, with a sign on the roof to identify it. Salads, Mexican food, other light meals. This is where the expatriates go for Sun brunch. $$$

✖ **Sarajet** Rr Abdi Toptani 7; ☎ 224 3038. Traditional Tirana dishes, such as *fergesë*, served at lunchtimes, but another reason for coming to this restaurant is that it is a beautiful example of Ottoman urban architecture, dating from 1780. For more information about this building, see page 79. English spoken. The restaurant garden is a particularly nice place to eat, set back from the road & shaded by old trees. $$$

✖ **Shakesbeer** Rr Brigada VIII. Good, keenly priced Korça beer (light & dark) to go with pub food such as meatballs & ribs. Tables outside in garden; Wi-Fi. $$$

✖ **Taiwan** Rr Ibrahim Rugova. The Taiwan (albanicised as 'Tajvani') complex in the park in the centre of Tirana (*Parku i Rinisë*) has 2 restaurants within it. Casa di Pasta, on the ground floor, has a range of interesting salads, fresh bread, good pizzas & a selection of pasta dishes. Slightly smarter steak restaurant on 1st floor ($$$$$). In summer it has tables outside, looking on to the park & the boulevard. $$$

✖ **Taverna e Kasapit** Rr Perlat Rexhepi. Good selection of traditional meat dishes (its name means 'The Butcher's Tavern'), *fergesë*, etc. $$$

✖ **Vila Logoreci** Rr Lek Dukagin 9; ☎ 224 7190. The usual pastas, pizzas & salad, good meat & fish grills. Outside tables set in lovely courtyard raised above street level. $$$

✖ **La Voglia** Rr Ibrahim Rugova, between Rr Myslym Shyri & the river. Pizzas, pasta, & excellent sandwiches of various sorts. Large terrace with tables outside. Free Wi-Fi for customers. $$$

GOOD DEAL

✖ **Natyra e Qetë** [map, page 60] Sauku; m 068 24 68 334. Tirana families come here at w/ends to eat spit-roasted lamb or *paidhaqe* (barbecued lamb ribs), with salad & chips, all washed down with red wine. Large outdoor seating area; lovely views of the surrounding countryside. $$

✗ **Serendipity** Rr Ibrahim Rugova; ☎ 225 9377. An essentially Tex-Mex menu – fajitas, enchiladas, burgers – with a leavening of Albanian & Italian options, inc pizza. Live music at w/ends. English-speaking waiters, mixed foreign & Albanian clientele. $$

✗ **Taverna Dajkua** In an alleyway between Bd Zogu I & Rr Bardhok Biba, behind the Arbër Hotel. Dajkua is one of the few restaurants in the city centre to specialise in *paidhaqe*, flame-grilled lamb ribs, which are traditionally eaten with Greek salad & chips. Grilled chicken is also available. Vegetarians will hate it. $$

ENTERTAINMENT AND NIGHTLIFE

In recent years, Tirana – and specifically the small area in the city centre known as 'The Block' (*Blloku*) – has become a major nightlife destination. 'The Block' is about 1km², reserved until 20 years ago for the townhouses of the country's leaders, and now absolutely crammed with bars, clubs and beautiful people. Tirana City Council clamped down in 2010 on noise in 'The Block' after midnight, much to the relief of the many people who live in the area; this has meant that the fashionable clubs have moved out of town, along the old road to Elbasani. Closer to the city centre, the **Living Room** [69 F3] (*Rruga Xhorxh W Bush, roughly opposite Parliament*) is perennially popular. Word of mouth is likely to be the best source of information about the constantly changing trends in the club scene.

Albania, like many formerly communist countries, has a strong tradition of **classical music**. The **National Theatre of Opera and Ballet (TKOBAP)** [69 E2], on Skanderbeg Square, displays the current season's schedule on the outside wall beside the ticket booth. The box office is open 09.00–13.00 and 17.00–20.00 Monday–Friday; tickets can be reserved by telephoning ☎ 222 7271 or 222 4753. Tickets are very reasonably priced (the first night is more expensive) and the performances are often excellent, although the level of noise from the audience can be rather irritating. In the past, the theatre has had a useful website and Facebook page and it is to be hoped that these will be revived in due course. Classical **concerts** usually take place in the Academy of Arts, on the western side of Mother Teresa Square, opposite the Archaeological Museum. The box office is just to the right of the main entrance, looking towards the building; prices vary according to the programme and performers.

Held annually in early December, Sofra e Tiranës is a festival of traditional and pop music and dance from the Tirana area. At other times of year, it is hard to find live folk music in Tirana; Guva e Qetë, on Rruga Murat Toptani (m *068 21 86 302*), sometimes has *musika popullore* – traditional light music. The national Song and Dance Ensemble (Ansambli e Këngëve dhe Valleve) occasionally performs at the TKOBAP. See page 25 for information about the regular folk festivals held in other parts of Albania.

Theatre performances in languages other than Albanian are rare and it is quite difficult to find out even about plays in Albanian. From time to time, the various western European cultural institutes hold festivals of their own countries' films, theatre or music. These festivals tend not to be well publicised and the best way to find out about them is by consulting the *Tirana Times* or *Albanian Daily News*.

Tickets for **football** matches can be bought at the Qemal Stafa Stadium [69 F7], off Mother Teresa Square. Two of the country's best teams – SK Tirana and KF Partizani – play there, and the matches are interesting cultural experiences, even for people who are not big football fans. Tirana's third team, Dinamo, plays at the small stadium on the other side of town, whose official name is Selman Stermasi but which is always called the Dinamo Stadium [68 B6].

3

SHOPPING

The centre of Tirana is full of shops, and the outskirts full of shopping malls, selling imported goods at higher prices than in the UK. There are a few places which stock things likely to be of interest to the visitor – the jewellery and ceramics shops on Bulevardi Gjergj Fishta between Ibrahim Rugova (formerly Dëshmorët e 4 Shkurtit) and Vaso Pasha, the souvenir shops on Rruga Luigj Gurakuqi on the way up to the central market, and a cluster of kiosks on Rruga e Barrikadave near the roundabout. Kruja, less than an hour's drive away (see pages 100–4) is a better place than Tirana to shop for souvenirs; the choice is wider and all the shops are together in one street.

The **Albania** bookshop [68 C5] on Rruga Sami Frashëri and **Adrion** International Bookstore [69 E3] on Skanderbeg Square stock books in English about Albania and the Balkans, and translations of Albanian literature.

The **central market** [69 F2] (*Pazari i Ri*), off Sheshi Avni Rustemi, is a cornucopia of organic fruit and vegetables, different sorts of olives and nuts, honey, eggs and homemade raki. The covered stalls on the square itself sell dried fruit and nuts, along with imported fruit and vegetables; the proper market is down the side street past the butcher's and the fish shops. Smaller, neighbourhood markets can be found elsewhere in the city; there is one along Rruga Mihal Grameno, for example, and another on Rruga Fortuzi.

OTHER PRACTICALITIES

There are ATMs (cashpoints, known in Albanian as *bankomat*) all over the city, most of them connected to the Visa and Maestro systems. ProCredit ATMs issue euros as well as Albanian leks. A few ATMs are not linked to the international networks, but only accept cards issued by that bank; the security guard will usually put you right if he spots you approaching the wrong sort of ATM.

Cash euros, sterling, Swiss francs and dollars of the Australian, Canadian and US varieties can all be readily changed in Tirana. There are many bureaux de change throughout the city, with clusters on Bulevardi Zogu I and around the junction of Rruga Myslym Shyri and Rruga Ibrahim Rugova. In general they stay open until at least 17.00; some close earlier on Saturdays and almost all are shut on Sundays. There are also money changers on the streets, particularly around the National Bank; the rate they offer for small sums is not significantly better than that of the bureaux, and counterfeit notes sometimes circulate on the street. Foreign currency can also be changed in any of the numerous banks in the city, although the process is a little swifter in the bureaux de change.

The central **post office** [68 D3] is on Rruga Çamëria, just behind the National Bank of Albania. It is open from 07.30 to 20.00 every day, including Saturdays and Sundays, although the full range of services is not available on Sundays. There are **internet cafés** all over the centre of town.

The city's all-night **pharmacy** [68 D1] is on Bulevardi Zogu I, on the left in the first block after the National Historical Museum, as you come from Skanderbeg Square. The accident and emergency clinic (*Urgjenca* in Albanian) is on Rruga Gjin Bue Shpata, near the Dinamo Stadium. Tirana has good private **hospitals**; see *Chapter 2*, pages 35–6 for details.

Tirana is a safe city, and the biggest danger is being struck by a bike or motorcycle jumping a red light, or whizzing the wrong way up a one-way street. The pavements are often rather uneven and, although young Albanian women seem to negotiate them flawlessly in precipitous heels, the less gazelle-like will find it easier to get around in flatter shoes. Along the main shopping streets in the city centre, an unexpected risk is that of falling down the (completely unprotected) steps of one of the many basement shops.

WHAT TO SEE AND DO

SKANDERBEG SQUARE [68 D3] Although it is no longer the hub of commercial or social life, Skanderbeg Square is still referred to as 'the centre' of Tirana, and it makes a convenient starting point for a cultural tour of the city.

On its northern side are the National Historical Museum and the Tirana International Hotel; to the west is the National Bank; and the eastern side is entirely taken up with what was once known as the Palace of Culture, which still houses the opera house and the National Library. The tables outside the Opera café are wonderfully cool in high summer, thanks to all the marble surrounding them. Bisecting the square is the wide **Boulevard**, designed by Mussolini's emissaries and perfect for Fascist parades. To the south, down to the main university building, it is called Bulevardi Dëshmorët e Kombit (the Martyrs of the Nation Boulevard). The northern section is Bulevardi Zogu i Parë (Zogu I Boulevard); a statue of King Zog now stands at its junction with the ring road.

An equestrian statue of **Skanderbeg** (see box, pages 200–1) stands at the head of Dëshmorët e Kombit. The sculptor was Odhisë Paskali (1903–85), a native of Përmeti in the far south of the country. Across the road from the statue are the **Mosque of Et'hem Bey** and, behind it, the **clocktower**. The 18th-century mosque is one of the few really old buildings left in Tirana, and is perhaps also the most beautiful. Its minaret was shattered in the Battle for the Liberation of Tirana, but it was subsequently repaired, and the mosque's status as a Cultural Monument kept it from being damaged or destroyed during the atheism campaigns of the late 1960s. There are frescoes on its exterior walls and more paintings inside the mosque – slim visitors can climb the tight spiral staircase to the gallery, from where there is a better view of these.

Excellent views of the city can be enjoyed from the top of the 35m-high clocktower (built in the 1820s). The opening hours are 09.00–13.00 on Mondays, 09.00–13.00 and 16.00–18.00 on Thursdays. Visits at other times may be requested by telephoning 224 3292. There is also a small exhibition of models of clocktowers in Albania, which can be seen on request.

MUSEUMS AND GALLERIES
National Historical Museum [68 D2] (*Muzeu Historik Kombëtar*; ⊕ *10.00–17.00 Tue–Sat, 09.00–14.00 Sun, last admission 30 mins before closing; 200 lek*) Dominating Skanderbeg Square is the National Historical Museum, with its huge mosaic mural above the entrance. The museum was opened in 1981 and the mural is an excellent example of the triumphalist art of the time. It depicts victorious Albanians from various points in history, from Illyrians to partisans via the fighters and intellectuals who won independence from the Ottoman Empire. You should allow at least two hours to go round the whole museum.

There are many interesting things on display and the labelling has greatly improved in recent years, with helpful maps and information on multilingual panels. Each display case usually has a summary in English and French. On the ground floor – the prehistory, antiquity and late antiquity sections – some of the individual exhibits are labelled in English and French as well as Albanian. The exhibition is arranged in rough chronological order, and starts with prehistoric finds from the Stone, Copper, Bronze and Iron ages. There are maps of Illyrian tribes and city-states at different points in time, and examples of Illyrian jewellery, coins and votive objects in terracotta and bronze from the 3rd to the 1st centuries BC. Two outstanding works of art date from the 4th century BC: a head of Apollo, discovered in the *orchestra* of the theatre at Butrint (see page 224), and known as 'The Goddess of Butrint'; and the first mosaic ever discovered in Albania, which portrays a woman's head and is called 'The Belle of Durrësi'. There is pottery from the Greek colonies in what is now Albania, 3rd-century armour and reconstructions of 2,000-year-old agricultural implements. Maps on the walls show the sites of uprisings and invasions during the turmoil of the 11th and 12th centuries.

The first floor covers the rise of the feudal states in the medieval period, the Ottoman conquest and Albania under Ottoman rule. The highlight of the medieval section is the 'Epitaph' of Gllavenica, a beautiful embroidered altar-cloth from 1373. The complete doorway of the church of St Gjon Vladimir, near Elbasani, has been re-erected – see pages 116–17 – and there are some interesting exhibits from other medieval churches, including a fragment of fresco from the 13th-century church at Vau i Dejës, near Shkodra, which was demolished (by *art students*) during the atheism campaign of 1967. A whole room is devoted to the role of Skanderbeg as leader of the Albanian resistance to the Ottomans. The section covering the 16th to 18th centuries gives a good overview of Ottoman administration and the development of Albania's cities.

The second floor of the museum covers the National Renaissance (*Rilindja Kombëtare*), the cultural and political movement of the late 19th and early 20th centuries, which culminated in Albania's declaration of independence on 28 November 1912. The explanatory panels are in English and French, although some prior knowledge of the *Rilindja* movement would be an advantage in understanding the exhibition. There are nice displays of 19th-century textiles, weapons and ethnographic items. The icon gallery on this floor is home to the magnificent iconostasis from the church of St Gjon Vladimir (see pages 116–17), by the 17th-century artist Kostandin Ieromonaku. There is a good selection of icons, including works by Onufri; however, the cream of Albania's Byzantine art is in Korça, home of the National Museum of Medieval Art, and in the Onufri Museum in Berati Castle (see pages 133–4 and 123–4).

Although the World War II exhibition still predominantly consists of displays about the communist-led LNÇ (see box, page 13) and the activities of the partisans, the curators have made an effort to include other sides of the story. There are panels explaining the parts played by Balli Kombëtar and the Legalitet movement, for example, and a display of photographs of the Councils of Regency which governed Albania in the period between Italy's capitulation and liberation. The role of SOE (see pages 13–15) and the contribution made during the war by the USA are also presented. The World War II section is quite extensive; those with a particular interest in this period might want to consider visiting it separately from the rest of the museum, since it could easily take over an hour to study the whole exhibition in detail.

The final hall of the museum is devoted to a fascinating exhibition about Albania during the communist period. Unfortunately, the information panels in the display cases are not translated, which makes it difficult for non-Albanian visitors to follow the historical development of the exhibition. A life-size mock-up of a solitary confinement cell brings home the terrible conditions in which so many Albanians were imprisoned. A rolling video, with some English subtitles, includes film of the student protests in 1991 which ultimately brought about the end of communist rule in Albania.

The museum shop stocks postcards, souvenirs and books. There are reasonable toilets on the ground floor.

Archaeological Museum [69 E7] (*Muzeu Arkeologjik; Sh Nënë Tereza;* ⊕ *10.30–14.30 Mon–Fri; 300 lek*) Although the National Historical Museum holds the best-known objects from Albania's archaeological heritage, the collection in the Archaeological Museum, located within the Centre for Albanology Studies in Mother Teresa Square, is much more extensive. Few of the artefacts are labelled in English, but in most cases the labels merely indicate provenance, so geographical rather than linguistic knowledge is what is required.

The first two rooms are devoted to the Stone, Bronze and Iron ages, with some particularly nice spear- and axe-heads, and a fine iron helmet. Then the artefacts from Illyrian cities begin, which will be of greater interest to visitors who are not prehistory specialists. Lovely little figurines in bronze and terracotta, including a delightful little bronze dog from Antigonea (see pages 240–1), are perhaps the most

THE MYSTERY OF THE MARTINI RIFLES

With thanks to M C Barrès-Baker

Fans of the 1964 film *Zulu* may wonder why the .45" Martini-Henry rifle, the weapon used to defend Rorke's Drift, appears in so many Albanian paintings and museum display cases. The answer is that they are not Martini-Henrys at all.

The British adopted the Martini-Henry in 1871, naming it after Friedrich von Martini, who designed its breech mechanism, and Scotsman Alexander Henry, who designed the barrel. In 1872, Khedive Ismail of Egypt gave the Ottoman sultan 50,000 Martini-Henrys. The sultan was so impressed that he ordered 600,000 copies from the Providence Tool Company of Rhode Island, USA. These were called Peabody-Martinis, after Henry O Peabody, an American who had patented the earliest version of the Martini breech.

Peabody-Martini rifles played a significant role during the 1877 siege of Plevna, inflicting heavy casualties on the attacking Russian (and Romanian) troops. Turkish payments for the rifles were constantly in arrears, however, and in 1885 this drove Providence Tool bankrupt. Its president was reduced to burning Peabody-Martini rifle butts to keep warm.

A few years later the Turkish army went over to using Mauser magazine rifles; Edith Durham, however, travelling in the early years of the 20th century, describes Albanian gendarmes 'armed with Peabody-Martini rifles of American pattern, which they call "Martinas" and cherish dearly'. By then the rifle had also become the weapon of choice among the Albanian civilian population, both because the cartridge cases were easy to refill and because it was a better man-stopper than more expensive bolt-action rifles.

Martinis could be used as part-payment in a *besa* (see box, pages 174–5) or to buy a wife; but keeping one's Martini in powder and lead could be nearly as expensive as keeping a wife. Men often decorated their Martinis, with silver filigree or with silver coins, one for each life taken. In *High Albania*, Durham describes a man singing a song to his Martini, 'in which he addressed it as his wife and his child, for he wanted no other.'

attractive items in these cases, but there is also jewellery and pottery to admire, and a well-preserved helmet complete with nose and cheek guards. The Roman period is represented with statuary, some fine glassware, inscribed tombstones, some of them with obviously Illyrian names, and inscriptions from Victorinus's Wall, built around the ancient city of Byllis.

On the walls there are enlarged photographs of archaeological sites and of some of the mosaics that have been discovered there. The museum has a selection of books for sale, some of them in English translation, about Albanian archaeology and archaeological sites.

National Art Gallery [69 E4] (*Bd Dëshmorët e Kombit;* ⊕ *10.00–17.00 Tue–Sat, 10.00–14.00 Sun; 200 lek*) The National Art Gallery has a fascinating collection of Albanian art, which puts into context the Socialist Realist work which can be seen in so many public spaces around the country. The chronological exhibition begins in the late 19th century with Albania's first non-religious painters, whose portraits and depictions of idealised rural life give an insight into the cultural atmosphere in Albania at that time. Albania's first art school was founded in 1931, and the paintings from the pre-war period show greater realism. The next rooms move Albanian art into the communist period, with the historical tableaux of artists such as Fatmir Haxhiu (1927–2001) and the Socialist Realist portrayals of idealised workers, including some splendid sculptures.

At the beginning of the 1970s, Albanian artists began to experiment with Formalism and produced some outstanding work in this genre. Although they tried to keep within the limits of Socialist Realism, their experimentation was not without risk: one of their number, Edison Gjergjo (1939–89) was arrested in 1974 for painting work 'displaying a pessimistic outlook and formalist traits'. The permanent exhibition ends with a display of post-1990 Albanian painting and sculpture, with work by artists such as Ksenofon Dilo (b1932) and Edi Rama (b1964), who at the time of writing is the prime minister of Albania.

The rear hall on the ground floor of the gallery is used for temporary exhibitions, which are often worth a look if you have time.

The National Art Gallery's website (*www.gka.al*) is an excellent introduction, in English, not only to the collection, but also to the history of Albanian art.

WALKS AROUND TIRANA A **half-hour walk** around some of Tirana's architectural highlights starts at the clocktower [69 E3] just off Skanderbeg Square. A park runs down the side of Rruga Luigj Gurakuqi, separating the moving traffic from the waiting buses and taxis. At the end of this park, half-concealed behind yet another high-rise building, is a curious circular construction, called the **Tyrbe of Kapllan Pasha** [69 E3]. A *tyrbe* is a Bektashi shrine (see pages 22–3) commemorating the burial place of a holy person, although it seems Kapllan Pasha is not, in fact, buried here and modern Bektashis do not treat this cenotaph with special reverence. It is thanks to its designation as a Cultural Monument that it has been conserved despite the building which now overshadows it.

Turning right here will bring you to the **Albanian Parliament** [69 F4], built in 1924 to an Italian design and set in attractive gardens. Information panels at the northern entrance to the gardens show the location of the various buildings. The city's main mosque stood in these gardens until it was destroyed in 1944, during the Battle for the Liberation of Tirana; a large new mosque is now being built to replace it. Across the road and down to the left, past the Lulishte 1 Maji restaurant, is a cute little 19th-century bridge called the **Tanners' Bridge** (Ura e Tabakëve) [69 G3]. It sits a little forlornly at the junction of Xhorxh W Bush and Bulevardi Gjergj Fishta, the main road on this side of the Lana River.

Now retrace your steps to the Parliament building and turn left around the corner of the gardens, passing the information panels. You are now on Rruga Murat Toptani, one of the streets bounding a block of buildings once owned by the powerful Toptani family. The archaeological remains which are conserved and exposed ahead of you are traces of the fortifications built in the 17th century, during the struggle for control of Tirana between the Toptanis and another feudal family. A short stretch of the Ottoman-era city wall still stands – again to your left – just beyond the excavations. Set back from the street to the left, the beautiful **Ottoman house** [69 F3] which can be glimpsed through an archway was, until 2005, the headquarters of the Centre for Geographical Studies. It was built at the beginning of the 19th century and, although it is known as 'the Toptani house', it is in fact the property of the Libohova family (see page 243).

Almost at the end of Rruga Murat Toptani is the **National Art Gallery** [69 E4]; just opposite the low gate into the gallery grounds, on the other side of the street and at right-angles to it, is Rruga Sermedin Toptani. Turning into this street, to your left are various ministries, including the Interior Ministry, which explains the large number of police often to be seen in the vicinity. On your right as you walk up this street is the **National Theatre** [69 E3], set in attractive gardens with a fountain.

Across the end of Rruga Sermedin Toptani runs Rruga Abdi Toptani. **Tirana City Hall** [69 E3] is side-on to you, with the **clocktower** and the **Et'hem Bey Mosque** visible beyond it. Turn right up Rruga Abdi Toptani to finish your walk with a drink or a meal in one of Tirana's finest examples of Ottoman urban architecture, now the **Sarajet Restaurant** [69 E3]. This house was built by the Toptani family in 1780; it stands behind trees on the right as you go up Rruga Abdi Toptani from Skanderbeg Square. The exterior of the building has been sympathetically restored and the function rooms on the first floor have intricately carved wooden ceilings. The house also has a tiny steam room (*hamam*), which was built for the family's private use; this cannot be viewed at the time of writing. The building was returned to its pre-communist owners in 2002, after many years as the headquarters of the Institute of Cultural Monuments, and they should be commended for the responsible way in which they have turned it to commercial use.

A detour on the other side of Skanderbeg Square, out along Rruga e Durrësit to the ring road (Unaza), will allow you to include Tirana's only visible Roman remains, the **Tirana Mosaic** [68 A2] (⊕ *08.00–17.00 daily; free admission*). The structure was discovered during construction work in 1972, and seems to have been the villa of a 1st-century AD winemaker, two of whose amphorae are on display here. The villa was converted into a basilica in the 4th or 5th century, when the mosaic floor was laid. It has been conserved and stabilised and is one of the few mosaics in Albania which can be viewed *in situ* by the general public. It is a little tricky to find, hidden among residential buildings, but it is signposted from the ring road.

A **longer walk**, but one which is particularly pleasant on a fine spring or autumn day, takes you down the Boulevard to the main park. To the right of the Boulevard, just beyond Skanderbeg Square, is the central park, still known to older people by its communist name of the Youth Park (Parku i Rinisë). In fine weather, the park is always full of people of all ages, relaxing with their friends or family. The curiously space-age building on the opposite side of the park – facing on to Rruga Ibrahim Rugova – is a recreation complex known as 'Taiwan' (albanicised as 'Tajvani'), in honour of the country which donated the splendid fountains beside it. Beyond the park, to the left of the Boulevard rises the **Pyramid** [69 E5],

3

an extraordinary structure built as a mausoleum for Enver Hoxha (see box, page 83), used for 20-odd years as a cultural and conference centre and – at the time of writing – closed pending development and becoming increasingly dilapidated. The large bell hanging above the walkway outside it is the Bell of Peace, an initiative of schoolchildren from northern Albania who collected spent bullet casings from the 1997 uprising (see pages 17–18), and used them to cast this testimonial to the country's near-collapse.

Turn right at the university and then up the hill to the left, where you will enter the park. If you keep bearing left uphill, you will get to an attractively painted wooden sign indicating the start of the 'Memorials'. The first you come to is the graveyard of German soldiers who died in Albania during World War II; a little further on are the graves and busts of four highly influential figures in the Albanian cultural renaissance (*Rilindja Kombëtare*) of the late 19th and early 20th centuries – the three Frashëri brothers, Abdyl, Naim and Sami (see box, pages 150–1); and, a little apart from them, Faik Konica (see page 23).

A little beyond the Frashëris, the **British Memorial Cemetery** [63 F6] commemorates 40 British and Commonwealth soldiers and airmen who died in Albania during World War II. See pages 13–15 for further information about their war work. They are not buried here, however; their remains were painstakingly collected and reburied by the British Army's Graves Registration Unit in 1946, but were later dug up and moved. Nobody knows now where the bodies lie. The British embassy organises a memorial service here on Remembrance Sunday (around the 11th of November) every year, which anyone can attend.

If you bear right instead of left at the park entrance, you will come to the **Artificial Lake**, with a promenade along the top of its dam. On the other side of the dam, the **Aquadrom swimming-pool complex** [62 D7] (⊕ *1 May–1st w/end in Oct; adult admission Jul/Aug: 09.00–14.00 500 lek, 14.00–19.00 300 lek; cheaper in spring/autumn*) has several separate pools, including a dedicated high-diving pool, and a flume. There is a café and a sandwich bar within the complex.

COMMUNIST NOSTALGIA Many communist monuments were destroyed in the unrest which accompanied Albania's transition to democracy. However, those interested in this period of the country's history will nonetheless find plenty to see in Tirana.

A tour of the city's communist relics can be done in a single day by the very committed. If you plan to spend some time in Tirana, you might prefer to spread it out into more manageable chunks. A combination of walking, taxis and buses is the most efficient way to do it in terms of cost and time; at peak traffic times it is quicker to walk some of the stretches, but it would be very tiring to do the whole circuit below on foot in one day.

As ever, Skanderbeg Square is a good starting point. In the square itself, the recently renovated mural above the entrance to the National Historical Museum [68 D2] is an excellent example of Socialist Realist art, even without the red star which formerly graced the partisans' flag. The **Tirana International Hotel** [69 E2] and the huge building which houses the opera – the **Palace of Culture** [69 E2] – were both designed by Soviet architects in the 1960s. The hotel has been completely overhauled, but the interior of the opera house still feels distinctly communist. You are not usually allowed in unless you are attending an event, but tickets are very reasonably priced.

Communist slogans can still occasionally be spotted on the walls of the older-style, four-storey apartment buildings. They were created by setting differently coloured bricks into the structure, which makes them rather difficult to remove, although the passage of time is wearing them out gradually. An easy-to-find example is the party's initials, PPSH, on a building about 90m on the left down Rruga Fortuzi, which goes off Zogu I alongside the Ministry of Justice [68 D1].

Apart from the Socialist Realist art in the National Art Gallery (see page 78) and the museum mural, the best example of this style in the centre of town is probably the **monument to the Unknown Partisan** [69 F3]. It stands in a little square beside the junction of Xhorxh W Bush and Luigj Gurakuqi. The partisan rises above the people and the traffic, waving his comrades on into battle with one hand and gripping his rifle in the other.

Back on the Boulevard, the **Dajti Hotel** [69 E4] played a pivotal role in its first half-century – during the communist period, at least until what is now the Tirana International opened, almost all foreign visitors stayed here. Ordinary Albanians were not allowed through the doors until the advent of democracy. Countless treaties were negotiated and plots hatched in the Dajti Hotel. The doors of this historic hotel closed in December 2005 and the building has become increasingly derelict. Peter and Andrea Dawson described the Dajti in 1989; it was still almost the same ten years later, although obviously the statues of Lenin and Stalin had gone by then. The bar used to be wonderful and its loss is lamented.

> We decide that the other large hotel in Tiranë, the Dajti, is worth investigation. We walk down the Avenue of the Martyrs of the Nation, past the bronze Lenin statue and the National Art Gallery and, behind the trees opposite the statue of Stalin, are the party cars: Mercedes and black Volvos. The red 'Dajti' lettering fronts a heavy stone and glass canopy, shielding the steps to the entrance.
>
> Inside, a vast reception area and hall contains a bookshop, a souvenir shop and, in a lounge, a television is showing Albanian programmes, watched by some of the foreign businessmen, who, along with trade and political delegations, form the bulk of the Dajti's clientele.
>
> A corridor to the right leads to the bar, and we have cappuccinos and bottled Albanian beer, sitting in comfortable armchairs at a low walnut table.
>
> Peter and Andrea Dawson, *Albania: A Guide and Illustrated Journal*

The Pyramid, just across the little Lana River from the Dajti, is a remarkable piece of architecture, with its sloping walls at the front leading round to vertical faces at the back. It was designed by Hoxha's daughter, Pranvera, and his son-in-law, who were also the architects of the Congress Building (Pallati i Kongresëve), just beyond the Rogner Hotel further down the Boulevard, and of the Skanderbeg Museum in Kruja. It was commissioned as a memorial museum to Enver Hoxha (see box, page 83); after the end of one-party rule and until the end of the first decade of the 21st century, it was used for conferences and trade fairs, with offices at the rear let to various companies, including a private national TV station. An ill-advised proposal to demolish the Pyramid appears to have been abandoned and it is to be hoped that the white marble tiles which used to clad its walls will now be restored.

On the Boulevard next to the Pyramid is the prime minister's office building, known as the **Council of Ministers** [69 E5], which used to house the government in communist days as well – a Socialist Realist bas-relief has been preserved on the wall facing the Boulevard. Across the road is the Checkpoint memorial, an installation commemorating Albania's isolation under communism. A piece of the Berlin Wall, a real bunker and – most chilling of all – part of the concrete mineshaft supports from the prison camp at Spaçi (see page 158) have been set in a little garden. The memorial has been installed opposite the building where the party's Central Committee met and where its senior members, including Hoxha, had their offices; this now houses various state institutions, such as the Parliament and the Constitutional Court. It is said that there is a tunnel from this building to **Enver Hoxha's house** [68 D6], 270m down Rruga Ismail Qemali. This street and those around it – almost a square mile – were closed to ordinary Albanians until the fall of the communist regime. The area was called 'The Block' (*Blloku*) and it was reserved for the families of the party elite, who were later referred to disparagingly as 'Bllok-men'. The bunker in the Checkpoint memorial came from one of the entrances to the Block. Hoxha's house is between Ismail Qemali and Vaso Pasha; the white section surrounded by lawns was his private office (it is still a government building, hence the guards), and he and his family lived in the half of the building closer to Rruga Vaso Pasha. Part of that section has now been taken over by an English-language school, while the other part is occupied by one of The Block's trendy bars – both of which must have the xenophobic Hoxha turning in his grave (read on to find where that is).

The best Socialist Realist statues in Tirana are those of the Unknown Partisan (see page 81) and of **Mother Albania**, who overlooks the city at the **Martyrs' Cemetery** (Varreza e Dëshmorëve) [63 H7]. The latter is a long walk uphill from The Block (about 30 minutes); alternatively, a taxi will take between 15 and 45 minutes, depending on the traffic on Rruga e Elbasanit. The *Qendër–Sauk* buses from Skanderbeg Square can be boarded at the beginning of Rruga e Elbasanit and pass the entrance gates to the cemetery, on the left-hand side of the road. The cemetery is open on weekdays until early afternoon. A flight of steps on the left of the path leads up to the *parvis* where Mother Albania stands, clutching a laurel wreath with a star and looking out over Tirana spread below her.

In April 1985 Enver Hoxha, former teacher of French, tobacconist and partisan leader, secretary of the Party of Labour, was buried here, and his polished red granite tombstone is on the stepped platform next to Mother Albania. A small red and black double-eagle flag flies at the head of the tombstone, and it is guarded by two soldiers at attention, with high black polished boots and automatic rifles: the smartest soldiers in Albania, according to Andrea.

Nearby are the graves of the party officials, and down the gentle slopes are the graves, many with star and laurel denoting a People's Hero, of 900 men and women killed during the War of National Liberation.

From here you can look down on Tiranë, with the minaret, clock-tower and Hotel Tirana clearly visible. On the left, almost hidden by poplars, is the former palace of King Zog, which was an important seizure for the partisan brigades liberating the capital.

Peter and Andrea Dawson, *Albania: A Guide and Illustrated Journal*

The inscription below Mother Albania reads 'Eternal Glory to the Martyrs of the Fatherland', a reminder that this cemetery is much more than a relic of communism – it commemorates many of those who died in World War II, struggling against Fascist Italy and then Nazi Germany. Resistance fighters who were opposed to the nascent Communist Party were not buried here. The rows of graves run down the hillside beyond the statue, beginning with the best-known partisan fighters, including women such as Margarita Tutulani, who was shot by the Italians in 1943 aged only 19. Hundreds of others follow in approximate alphabetical order of their first names, as was standard practice in Albania. Beside Mother Albania is the tomb

Enver Hoxha was born in Gjirokastra in 1908; his family home is now that city's Ethnographic Museum. Hoxha studied in Gjirokastra and Korça and was then given an Albanian state scholarship to attend the University of Montpellier. During his time in France, he met Ali Kelmendi, the most senior of the small number of Albanian communists at the time. When Hoxha returned to Albania in 1936, he got a job teaching at his old school, the French *lycée* in Korça, and became involved in the fledgling Communist Party there.

The party remained very small and fragmented until, in 1941, the Yugoslav communists sent two delegates to help reorganise it and recruit new members. The Albanian Communist Party was officially founded in November 1941, and the following year Enver Hoxha was appointed party secretary. He became prime minister of the Provisional Government of Albania in October 1944, and went on to consolidate his power within the party over the next few years. He continued as prime minister until 1954, when he handed over the position to his wartime comrade Mehmet Shehu (see pages 14 and 16–17); but Hoxha continued to exercise considerable authority over the government, the party and the country until his death in April 1985.

of the young partisan Qemal Stafa, a founding member of the Albanian Communist Youth; next to that is a rectangular patch where Enver Hoxha's body lay until April 1992, when it was exhumed and reburied in the main cemetery (Varreza e Sharrës), on the other side of the city.

To get to Sharra from the Martyrs' Cemetery, transport is required. The nearest taxi rank is just over 1km back down the hill, opposite the Faculty of Economics. Alternatively you could walk, or catch any passing bus, to Skanderbeg Square and then jump on a bus to Sharra. Once the trams are operational, they will go to Kombinati, a ten-minute walk from the Sharra Cemetery. The turn-off uphill to the cemetery can easily be recognised by the flower stalls just before it. The graves are grouped chronologically, but you need to bear in mind that Hoxha's coffin was exhumed and reburied in 1992, and so that is his chronological position, not 1985 when he died. Once you are in roughly the right section, the large brown marble headstone is easy to spot; there are often fresh flowers on the grave. Mehmet Shehu, Albania's prime minister until his fall from grace in 1981, has also been reinterred in the main cemetery. The whereabouts of his remains were unknown until 2001, when one of his sons tracked down his unmarked grave in a village near Tirana.

PËLLUMBASI CAVE The hike up to Pëllumbasi Cave (Shpella e Pëllumbasit) makes for a very pleasant day out if the weather is good. Also known as the Black Cave, it was home to humans at various points between the Stone Age and the early Middle Ages, and to cave-bears (*Ursus spelaeus*) a long time before that. (Cave-bears became extinct about 27,500 years ago.) The cave is 360m long and has chambers filled with wonderful stalagmites and stalactites. There are also, as one would expect, many bats – see box, page 5.

The path up to the cave starts at the village of Pëllumbasi, 27km from Tirana off the Elbasani road. The caretaker and guide lives near the start of the path and will accompany you if you wish; the loan of a headtorch is included in the price of admission (100 lek). The path climbs steeply through fields and then emerges at the side of the beautiful Skorana Gorge, with the Erzeni River flowing far below you. There are wooden signs, steps at the steepest parts and handrails at the most slippery parts. It takes about an hour to walk up to the cave entrance.

The turn-off for Pëllumbasi is just before the village of Iba; it is signposted at the junction for 'Ujvara Resort' and, less obviously, 'Pëllumbasi 2km'. A shop at the junction sells drinks and torches. There are two buses to Pëllumbasi from Tirana in the early morning, returning at 18.00; otherwise, you can take a minibus to Iba and walk from there. Full directions, a map of the hiking route and a diagram of the cave can be downloaded from the Pëllumbasi Cave website (*http://pellumbascave.weebly.com*). The cave also has a Facebook page: The Cave of Pellumbas. All these developments – the map, the website, the signs, the handrails and everything else besides – are thanks to the efforts of the Outdoor Albania Association, which first reopened the path and began to take hiking groups on this lovely excursion. For further details of how to contact the Outdoor Albania Association, see page 56, or the OAA website (*www.outdooralbania-association.com*).

CASTLES South of Tirana, beyond the lamb restaurants of Lundra and Sauku, the old road to Elbasani (see page 111) starts to climb gradually. As it crosses the Erzeni River, which rises in the mountains to the east of the city, **Petrela Castle** (and the completely incongruous restaurant built on one of its towers) can be seen perched high up on a rock on the other side of the river. Petrela was a strategic link in the defensive system used by Skanderbeg (see box, pages 200–1), and is said to have been where his sister Mamica lived. The restaurant within it opens at 11.00, after which time it is possible to enter the castle precincts and look around the surviving walls and towers. A good, asphalted road just after the bridge runs up to the village of Petrela, to the right, off the main road. Cars can be parked in the village square, from where it is a five-minute walk up to the castle.

In the other direction, towards the airport, **Preza Castle** occupies a splendid position overlooking the plains westward to the Adriatic and eastward to Mount Dajti. It was probably built in the mid-15th century, as an element in the Ottomans' efforts to capture Kruja (see pages 100–4), then reconstructed in the 16th century. It is so close to the airport and has such good views that it makes a nice farewell stop, if you have a little time to spare before checking in.

MOUNT DAJTI The Dajti National Park, 25km to the east of Tirana, is one of the most accessible mountain reserves in the country. It covers 3,000ha centred on Mount Dajti, which overlooks Tirana and can be seen, smog permitting, from Skanderbeg Square. At 1,613m, Mount Dajti is not very high by Albanian standards (although it is 269m higher than Ben Nevis, Britain's highest mountain); this means that there is forest almost all the way to the summit, which makes for very pleasant, shady walking, especially in the heat of summer.

The woodland is mostly beech, with some pines and firs. In the summer, alpine strawberries grow among the trees, and foxes, hares, red squirrels, weasels and beech martens live in the forest. Dajti is too close to civilisation though for large mammals like the wild boar and wolf, which are otherwise widespread throughout the Albanian mountains.

The Backpacker and Milingona hostels in Tirana (see *Where to stay*, page 70) offer an exciting excursion to Mount Dajti: participants go up in the cable-car while bikes are brought up in a van to meet them. The group spends the day cycling around the network of paths on the mountain and having a picnic lunch, before cycling (or freewheeling) back down to the city. It is perfectly possible to hike around the park independently; a map of the path network is posted at the exit from the upper cable-car station. You should wear sensible footwear and be sure to take sufficient water with you.

Getting there and away By far the best way to get up to Mount Dajti, unless you are afraid of heights, is on the cable-car (⏲ *summer 09.00–22.00 Tue–Sun; winter 09.00–19.00 Tue–Sun; closed Mon except if public holiday; 400 lek sgl, 700 lek return*). The lower station is on the outskirts of Tirana, at the end of Rruga Qemal Stafa; it is tricky to find if you are driving (or cycling) yourself. Follow the (sporadic) signs through the brand-new apartment buildings, even when you are sure you are lost. The 'Porcelani' buses go from the clocktower in the city centre and up Rruga Hoxha Tahsim to their terminus; there, shuttle buses wait to run passengers up to the cable-car station, every half hour or so. The upper station is within the national park, but well before the summit.

If you have your own vehicle or a hire car, it is also possible to drive up the mountain, although the road is in rather poor condition now that it is rarely used. It takes about 45 minutes from the city centre, through the suburbs and then into beautiful forests with occasional views out over Tirana. The Dajti road leaves Tirana on Rruga Qemal Stafa and passes the Chateau Linza Hotel. An entrance fee of 50 lek per car plus 50 lek per person is payable as you drive into the national park. There is a car park at the upper cable-car station.

✕ Where to eat and drink

✕ **Ballkon i Dajtit** m 068 40 11 021. Part of the complex around the upper station of the cable-car (see page 67 for the Belvedere hotel listing). Standard Albanian restaurant fare – pasta, salads, pizza, grilled meat – with amazing views over Tirana &, on a clear day, out to the Adriatic. **$$$**

✕ **Gurra e Përrisë** m 068 20 60 720. A trout farm, with the fish in pools in the restaurant's grounds. As well as fish, spit-roasted lamb is a speciality. In summer, tables outside around the trout pools; in winter, traditional-style dining room with log fire. Lovely views of the forested hillsides. **$$$**

✕ **Panorama** ☎ 236 3124; m 069 20 23 936, 068 20 23 936. The speciality is spit-roasted lamb, served with chips, salad & red wine; the restaurant is also well known for its game dishes, such as hare & pheasant. It is famous, too, for the spectacular views of Tirana from the dining room & terrace. The Panorama also has rooms & chalets; see page 70 for details. **$$$**

4

Excursions from Tirana

DURRËSI   *Telephone code: 052*

The headland at the north of Durrësi Bay forms a natural harbour in which ships have anchored since the 7th century BC. In antiquity it was known as Epidamnos, and the city which was built around it was called Dyrrhachion. In the 5th century BC, a popular uprising in Dyrrhachion became one of the causes of the Peloponnesian War which engulfed the whole of Greece from 431BC to 404BC.

Under Roman rule, Dyrrachium (as it was by then known) became a vital staging post, one of the two starting points of the Egnatian Way (Via Egnatia), the great road which linked the Adriatic coast with Byzantium. The city thrived during the Roman and Byzantine periods, and the amphitheatre which the Romans built there was the largest in the Balkan peninsula. In the Middle Ages Dyrrachium was coveted by Normans, Angevins and Venetians, and for a few years after independence Durrësi was the capital of Albania. This rich past is reflected in the town's Archaeological Museum, with its collection of Illyrian, Greek and Roman artefacts.

Most Albanians visit Durrësi not for its history, however, but for its beaches, with their golden sand and safe swimming. In the summer, these beaches become very crowded; but out of season, in late spring and early autumn, the sea is still warm enough to swim in and the evenings are pleasantly cool. In the city, a lively promenade runs along the seafront, parallel with Taulantia Boulevard, and ends in a small area of beach.

HISTORY Durrësi has probably been inhabited for about 3,000 years, but it enters history in 627BC, when it was colonised by settlers from the Greek island of Corfu (Corcyra), who may have been attracted by the silver mines further inland in Illyria. The new colony prospered for many years, until internal political unrest led to a war between Corcyra and Corinth. The Athenian historian Thucydides describes the aftermath of this war as one of the causes of the great war fought, between 431BC and 404BC, between Athens and its allies on the one hand, and the Peloponnesians, including Sparta, on the other.

Dyrrhachion flourished during the 4th to 2nd centuries BC. The city continued to benefit from Greek cultural influence, and temples were built to Greek deities such as Aphrodite and Artemis. The late 4th-century mosaic known as the 'Belle of Durrësi' is the best example of the Hellenistic art of this period. Politically and economically, too, Dyrrhachion was thriving. The Illyrian kings Glaukias (late 4th century BC) and Monun (around 280–270BC) ruled over a city whose population was growing and which had minted its own coins since the middle of the 4th century BC – some of these can be seen in Durrësi's Archaeological Museum.

EXCURSIONS FROM TIRANA

For listings, see pages 67–70, 91–3, 99 & 122

Where to stay
1 Adriatik
2 Ballkan Resort
3 Berat Caravan
    Camping
4 Familja
5 Hotel Airport Tirana
6 Jürgen
7 Kamping Pa Emër
8 Mali i Robit
9 Park Nosi Spa Resort
10 Verzaçi

Where to eat and drink
11 Ali Kali
12 Samiu

0   16km
0   10 miles

Adriatic Sea

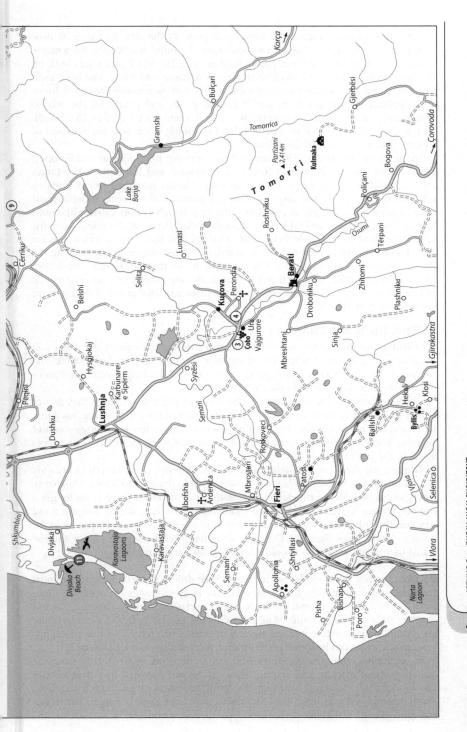

After the Roman conquest of 229BC (see page 8) the city, its name by now Latinised to Dyrrachium and with a population of around 40,000, became a major transit point between Italy and points further east. The Via Egnatia was built by Roman engineers along the route of an already ancient road which had been used by Illyrian and other traders for centuries; its two starting points were Dyrrachium and Apollonia (see pages 8–9), and it carried goods and people all the way to Byzantium, later called Constantinople. The Roman poet Catullus (84–54BC), mentions the city in one of his poems (C36.15), calling it – as one might expect of a port – 'the road-house of the Adriatic'.

In the second phase of the Roman civil war, between Julius Caesar and Pompey, Dyrrachium was the Pompeian forces' main arsenal and therefore a key target for Caesar after he landed in Albania in 48BC. Caesar managed to cut Pompey off from his arsenal, but in response Pompey entrenched his army in what must have seemed an impregnable position – the crag which is now called Shkëmbi i Kavajës, near Golemi, and which the Romans called Petra. With typical audacity, Caesar decided to blockade Petra and, although his forces were much smaller than Pompey's, not to mention less well fed, he almost succeeded in starving the Pompeian troops into surrender. Pompey then broke through Caesar's lines and, in the ensuing battle, inflicted heavy losses on the opposing side. Caesar managed to free his army and retreated east, where the third and final phase of the civil war would unfold in Thessaly.

GETTING THERE AND AWAY

By land Buses to Durrësi leave Tirana from the western side of the Zogu i Zi roundabout, at frequent intervals throughout the day, until at least 18.00. The journey time is almost entirely dependent on how bad the traffic is coming into or out of Tirana; a clear run will take about 40 minutes.

There are buses to Durrësi from all other cities in Albania, although they do not run as frequently as those to Tirana. From the south of the country, any bus going to Tirana will let you alight at the highway interchange a few kilometres south of Durrësi, known as Plepat; there are always taxis waiting there to ferry passengers along to the city centre.

Durrësi was the country's main **rail** terminus, although nowadays there are only four trains a day, to Librazhdi via Elbasani, to Shkodra and to Vlora. Departure times are shown on the timetable outside the station. Sadly, there is no longer a railway service to Tirana. Trains are agonisingly slow and, unless you are a rail devotee, the only journey which makes any kind of sense is the short run down the coast to Golemi (see page 98). Durrësi station has a certain scruffy charm and the trains themselves are worth a look, even when they are stationary.

By sea Durrësi is served by ferries from three different ports in Italy, the most frequent – and cheapest – being the daily car ferry crossings from Bari, a nine-hour journey. All year round, the ferries travel overnight, leaving Bari at 23.00 and arriving in Durrësi at around 08.00 the following morning. In the summer there are, additionally, daytime sailings. Several operators run ferries on this route; up-to-date schedules can be found on the Italian ferry website www.traghetti.it.

In addition to the crossings from Bari, car ferries operate to Durrësi from the Italian ports of Ancona and Trieste. These routes are operated by **Adria Ferries** (✆+39 (0)71 5021 1621; www.adriaferries.com), three days a week in each direction. From Ancona, the journey takes 20 hours; from Trieste, slightly longer. The ferries run all year round, with more frequent departures in summer.

The Port of Durrësi has been completely redeveloped, with a new passenger terminal which makes arriving on a ferry a much less intimidating and stressful experience than before.

By air Durrësi is less than an hour's drive from Albania's only international airport at Rinas. See *Chapter 2*, pages 32–3, for information about the airport and details of the airlines which fly to Albania.

GETTING AROUND The main sights in the city are all fairly central and walking between them is not at all arduous, except in very hot or very wet weather. There is a taxi rank at the bus station in Durrësi, where a driver can be hired for a single journey or for a day's or a half-day's sightseeing.

Red city buses run frequently between the beaches south of Durrësi and the post office on Rruga e Dëshmorëve, from early morning until about 21.00 in the summer. To get to Mali i Robit, you can either catch a minibus for Kavaja and ask the driver to let you off at the road-end, or agree a fare in advance with a taxi driver in Durrësi.

WHERE TO STAY *Map, page 92, unless otherwise indicated.*

There is no shortage of hotels in Durrësi, ranging from the expensive and luxurious to the cheap and cheerful. Several of them can be booked through the Tirana-based agency Albania Holidays (*www.albania-hotel.com*) and through international websites such as www.booking.com.

The coast to the south of the town has become heavily built up as far as Kavaja, with dozens of hotels lining the beaches. In high summer (July and August) the beaches are crowded and dirty, and there are often problems with the water supply in cheaper hotels during this time. The only hotels in this area of a high international standard are the Adriatik at Durrësi Beach and the Mali i Robit resort near Kavaja. Currilat Beach, to the north of the city centre, is quieter and has better hotels at the curve in the road known as Bërryli i Currilave ('the Currilat Elbow').

Mali i Robit Resort [map, page 88] (5 villas, 45 apts) Mali i Robit; m 069 20 24 734, 069 40 55 558; www.malirobitresort.com. 10km from Durrësi, set among pine trees. Outdoor swimming pool, fitness centre, tennis courts, restaurant, bar, disco, children's activities. All rooms have AC, satellite TV, direct-dial phone, internet connection; apts have 2 bedrooms, bathroom, living room, kitchen & balcony with sea view. **$$$$$**

Adriatik [map, page 88] (63 rooms, 6 suites) Lagja 13, Plazh; ℡ 260 850/1; e info@ adriatikhotel.com; www.adriatikhotel.com. 2 restaurants, bars, large & small swimming pools in palm-fringed garden, reserved section of sandy beach with sun-loungers & parasols, casino, tennis court, sauna, gym. Wi-Fi throughout; parking, business facilities, souvenir shop. Airport pick-ups & tours can be

arranged for guests. All rooms have en-suite bathroom with tub or jacuzzi & hairdryer; AC, satellite TV, direct-dial phone, minibar, safe; 'standard' rooms have view of gardens, others have sea view, 'executive' rooms have balcony. **$$$$–$$$$$**

Arvi (35 rooms, 7 suites) Bd Taulantia; ℡230 403; m 068 60 47 177; e arvishpk@msn.com, info@hotelarvi.com; www.hotelarvi.com. Modern & well appointed, excellent location on the seafront but close to city centre; English spoken. Restaurant, bars, business facilities, secure parking. Twin & dbl rooms all en suite with sea view, AC, satellite TV, Wi-Fi, direct-dial phone & minibar; suites also have WLAN internet access, balcony & jacuzzi. **$$$$**

Ani (14 rooms) Bd Taulantia; ℡224 228; m 069 86 58 612; e anihoteldurres@yahoo.it. Good location on the seafront; English spoken; bar, secure parking. Twin & dbl rooms, some with

4

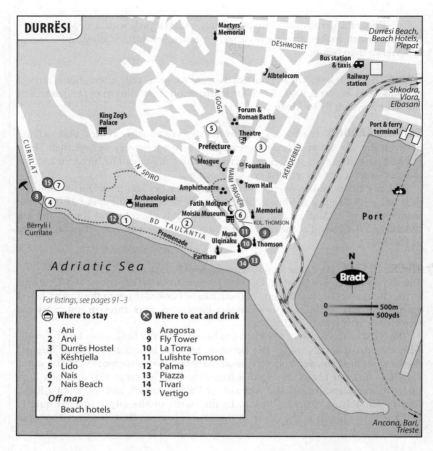

DURRËSI

Martyrs' Memorial

DÉSHMORÉT

Durrësi Beach, Beach Hotels, Plepat

Bus station & taxis

Albtelecom

Railway station

Shkodra, Vlora, Elbasani

King Zog's Palace

Forum & Roman Baths

Theatre

Port & ferry terminal

Prefecture

Mosque

Fountain

Town Hall

Amphitheatre

Archaeological Museum

Fatih Mosque

Moisiu Museum

Memorial

KOL. THOMSON

Musa Ulqinaku

Thomson

Partisan

Adriatic Sea

Port

N

Bradt

0   500m
0   500yds

Ancona, Bari, Trieste

For listings, see pages 91–3

Where to stay
1 Ani
2 Arvi
3 Durrës Hostel
4 Kështjella
5 Lido
6 Nais
7 Nais Beach

Off map
Beach hotels

Where to eat and drink
8 Aragosta
9 Fly Tower
10 La Torra
11 Lulishte Tomson
12 Palma
13 Piazza
14 Tivari
15 Vertigo

sea view, all en suite with AC, satellite TV, Wi-Fi & fridge. **$$$**

Kështjella (13 rooms) Bd Taulantia, Bërryli i Currilave; 221 817; m 068 90 38 684; e keshtjella01@hotmail.com; Facebook: Hotel Keshtjella Durres. Large beachside restaurant, terrace bar, friendly service. Room rate inc secure parking & use of sun-loungers & parasols on the hotel's section of the beach. Pedalos & boats for hire. All rooms with 1 dbl & 2 sgl beds, en-suite toilet & shower, Wi-Fi, TV, AC, phone, hairdryer, balcony with sea view. **$$$**

Lido (13 rooms, 1 suite) Rr A Goga; 227 941; m 068 20 43 719. Opposite Byzantine forum, set back from main road. Friendly, helpful staff; English spoken; bar & restaurant. Spacious rooms, twin & dbl, all en suite with Wi-Fi, AC, TV, direct-dial phone, fridge. **$$$**

Nais (16 rooms) Rr Naim Frashëri 46; 230 375, 224 940; e hotelnais@hotmail.com;

Facebook: hotelnaisdurres. Lift; friendly, helpful staff, English spoken; bar & conference room. All rooms en suite with Wi-Fi, small TV, fridge, phone, AC, some have balconies. **$$$**

Nais Beach (24 rooms) Bd Taulantia, Bërryli i Currilave; 223 130; e info@hotelnais.al; www.hotelsnais.al. Lift; English spoken; b/fast room; arrangement with Vertigo restaurant (see opposite). All rooms en suite with Wi-Fi, TV, fridge, phone, AC, balcony; upper floors have sea view. **$$$**

Durrës Hostel (8 rooms) Sheshi Liria; m 069 89 16 810 e info@durreshostel.com; www.durreshostel.com; Facebook: durreshostel. Superb location, just off Durrësi's main square, but quiet, in a modernised old townhouse with beautiful tree-shaded gardens. Bar open to public; garden areas reserved for hostel guests; balconies at front & rear of building; roof terrace; fully equipped kitchen; indoor sitting area; laundry; lockers. English spoken;

Wi-Fi throughout; bikes available to hire; day trips organised. All rooms high-ceilinged & airy; 36 dorm beds sharing ample shower & toilet facilities. Dorms **$**; 2 en-suite doubles **$$**

⋏ **Kamping Pa Emër** [map, page 88] Synej-Karpen, near Kavaja; ✆ 04 234 0387; m 069 36 03 122; e info@kampingpaemer.com; www.

kampingpaemer.com. About 10km from the highway, set in lovely grounds 30m from the beach; open year-round; poorly maintained and managed. Bar & restaurant overlooking the sea; some French spoken. Chalets (**$$$$**) & rooms (**$$$**) also available. Beachside pitches for 50 mobile homes & 50 tents. **$**

✖ WHERE TO EAT AND DRINK *Map, opposite.*

The promenade behind Taulantia Boulevard is lined with a string of restaurants, most of them offering the standard Italian dishes such as pasta, risotto and pizza, all of which Albanian chefs often do very well, plus fish which is usually fresh and good. All of the promenade restaurants have outside tables available during the summer months.

✖ **Aragosta** Bd Taulantia (Bërryli i Currilave); ✆ 226 477, 232 669; www.aragosta.al. Lovely setting overlooking the sea on the outskirts of town; hotel rooms also available. Good fresh fish & seafood, excellent antipasto buffet. Service can be rather slow, & the waiters have a tendency to suggest off-menu dishes which end up costing far more than you had planned to spend. **$$$$$**

✖ **Piazza** Bd Taulantia, opposite the Musa Ulqinaku statue. Good-quality seafood & fish; professional service. **$$$–$$$$$**

✖ **Vertigo** Bd Taulantia (Bërryli i Currilave) on top floor of Nais Beach Hotel (under different management). Spectacular sea views, Italian-influenced menu, good service, live music at w/ends. **$$$$**

✖ **Dy Kitarrat** Bd Taulantia; ✆ 235 802. The usual Italian menu, with the added attraction of

live music every evening in the summer months. The owner joins other performers in Albanian traditional music as well as Neapolitan & Greek songs. Very popular in the summer; advisable to book. **$$$**

✖ **Palma** Bd Taulantia. Reasonably priced fish & meat, pizzas, pasta, etc; tables outside in garden with sea view. **$$$**

✖ **Tivari** Bd Taulantia. Lovely location on the seafront where the promenade begins, tables outside on large terrace. The usual fish, grilled meat, pasta & pizza; also serves Italian-style sandwiches. **$$$**

✖ **Lulishte Tomson** Rr Naim Frashëri. Set in a shady garden (*lulishte*) behind Lodewijk Thomson's statue (see page 96). An unpretentious menu of grilled meat & chicken, salads, etc. **$$**

WHAT TO SEE AND DO

The amphitheatre (⊕ *09.00–19.00 daily; 300 lek, inc admission to Archaeological Museum; English-speaking guides sometimes available*) The huge Roman amphitheatre, which is one of Durrësi's main attractions, was built in the early 2nd century AD. The largest in the Balkans, it is elliptical in shape, about 130m at its longest point, with the arena itself measuring about 60m by 40m across. On the terraced seats there would have been room for about 15,000 spectators, about a third of the capacity of the Colosseum in Rome.

You can go down into the vaults below the rows of seats – the original steps, supplemented with less slippery modern ones, are just after the ticket booth – and see how the amphitheatre was constructed. The Romans alternated rows of brick with *opus incertum*, a mixture of stones and mortar, a technique designed to resist earthquakes. You can see this *opus incertum* in several places around the amphitheatre, including three full rows, well over 2m high, in one of the galleries. The technique was evidently quite successful, since most of the amphitheatre is still standing, despite Durrësi being hit by several strong earthquakes over the centuries. Behind the gallery, you can see the pens where the lions were kept; and leading out from it is the tunnel through which the gladiators entered the arena. When the site was first excavated, 40 skeletons were discovered with their necks broken – could they have been unsuccessful gladiators?

Down in these galleries there is also a Byzantine chapel, with mosaics of saints and archangels on the walls. They are the only wall mosaics ever found in Albania, and those on the back wall are rather badly damaged. The 6th-century mosaic on the side wall is thought to depict the sponsor of the whole chapel, a man identified only as Alexander, and his wife. The local Christian community took the amphitheatre over in the 5th century, after gladiatorial combat had been banned and the amphitheatre was abandoned. The arena became a cemetery and the little church was built for funeral services. There is a baptismal well at the entrance.

Back out in the sunlight, the entrance halfway round the terracing is where Dyrrachium's aristocracy arrived in their carriages. The horses were led off to the left while their owners took their seats above the entranceway. The tunnel through which they rode is said to extend right to where the town centre is now, nearly half a kilometre away. Further round to the left, through the beautifully built tunnel where the horses were taken, is another chapel, with faint traces of badly damaged fresco still just about visible.

The amphitheatre was discovered only in 1966 and has not been fully excavated, because people still live in the houses which were unwittingly built on top of it. The Albanian Institute of Archaeology and various Italian universities continue to research the site. Excavations between 2004 and 2007 revealed the southern exit from the amphitheatre, which was destroyed by an earthquake in the 13th century. A number of important medieval structures have also been discovered in this area, including shops which were still in use within living memory.

The Archaeological Museum *(Bd Taulantia; ⊕ 09.00–15.00 Tue–Sun; 200 lek (joint ticket with amphitheatre available), Albanian citizens 100 lek)* Durrësi's Archaeological Museum, closed for several years for structural maintenance and object conservation, reopened in 2014. On the ground floor, artefacts from the Greek, Hellenistic and Roman periods are displayed. It has still not proved possible to open the upper floor, which will, eventually, be used for the museum's Byzantine collection. The fact that the city has been more or less continuously inhabited throughout its history means that most of it has never been systematically excavated. Many of the items in the museum were discovered by chance, as local people ploughed their land or as foundations were dug for the new high-rise apartment blocks.

The exhibition is put together well and, although not all the artefacts are labelled, the general flow of the display is explained on panels in English as well as Albanian. A highlight of the Greek section is a whole case of terracotta faces and other body parts, votive offerings found at the sanctuary of Aphrodite, the Greek goddess of love; Catullus, in his Poem 36 referred to above, indicates that Dyrrachium was a centre of worship of Venus (the Roman name for Aphrodite), and this certainly appears to be borne out by the offerings found here.

Around the middle of the 4th century BC, Dyrrhachion began to mint and circulate its own coins. The silver *stater* bore the old Corcyran emblem of a cow suckling a calf, with the Greek initials DYRR. Lower-denomination bronze coins were also minted. Dyrrhachion's currency has been found as far away as the Danube territories of Dacia (modern Romania) and Thrace. A collection of amphorae (two-handled urns), some of them encrusted with shells from centuries of immersion in the sea, shows the city's importance as a maritime trading centre – their lids are marked with the initials of the exporter.

In the Roman section are *stelae* (tombstones) with engravings and inscriptions – one is to a certain Quintus Dyrracinus Phileros, the middle name showing that people were beginning to identify themselves as being from this city. A large kiln for firing pottery was found intact near Currilat Beach, and some fragments of fresco came from the rescue excavation of a private bathhouse discovered while the foundations were being dug for one of the new high-rise apartment blocks. There is a milestone from the Via Egnatia, a limestone doorframe with elegantly carved dolphins and a case of locally produced glassware, mostly the long-necked jars in which, it was popularly supposed, the tears of a deceased's loved ones were collected so that they could be interred with the body (in unromantic fact, they probably just contained ointments and perfumes).

Controversially, the large mosaic known as 'the Belle of Durrësi' has been kept by the National Historical Museum in Tirana. The staff of the museum had prepared a prime spot for the mosaic and were disappointed to learn that it was not coming home after all. In its place, at the entrance to the museum, is a statue of Gaia, the goddess of the earth, and other statuary.

There are attractive replicas for sale of some of the artefacts on display, as well as books in Albanian and English about the history of Durrësi and other archaeological sites.

The city walls Durrësi was first fortified in the Hellenistic period and then refortified shortly after the Roman conquest, in the 1st century BC. However, the oldest surviving walls are Byzantine, built during the reign of the emperor Anastasios (AD491–518) to replace earlier fortifications which a catastrophic earthquake in AD348 had destroyed. These walls protected the city for several centuries, until the Byzantine Empire began to collapse and Dyrrachium and its valuable port fell prey to one invader after another. The medieval city within the walls covered an area of around 120ha.

Dyrrachium – or Durazzo, as it was by then known – was part of the Venetian Republic for the whole of the 15th century. One of the towers which the Venetians built, at the southern corner of their walls, can even be seen from within – it has been converted into a bar, called **La Torra**, with tables in the alcoves where cannons would once have stood. Finally, in 1502, the Ottomans rebuilt the old fortifications and garrisoned their troops within them. An information panel at the city gate, which leads to the amphitheatre, shows an outline map of the fortifications as they changed over the centuries. There is a very good view of the line of the Venetian fortifications – and of the amphitheatre – from the rooftop bar in the high-rise building called the Fly Tower.

The forum and baths Turning in from La Torra, through the city walls and up Rruga Naim Frashëri, will bring you to Durrësi's main square, with the town hall and the theatre facing each other across it and a large, modern mosque to your left. Behind the theatre is the Byzantine forum, thought to date from the end of the 5th century AD. The forum was a circular area 40m in diameter, which was paved with marble and surrounded with an elegant colonnade. Several of the Corinthian columns are still standing, a little incongruous amid the communist-era apartment buildings which flank the forum. In the centre of the forum was a podium, and around the colonnade were shops, which were in use until the 7th century. The forum was then abandoned and – like the arena of the amphitheatre – used as a cemetery.

Right up against the back wall of the theatre, the remaining walls of part of a Roman bathhouse can also be seen. This predates the forum – it was built in the early 2nd century AD – and was discovered during the construction of the modern theatre in the main square. It is rather overgrown and the black-and-white marble tiles which lined the *piscina* (plunge-pool) are hidden from sight.

Ottoman buildings Durrësi was occupied by the Ottomans in August 1501, and a period of economic and cultural decline began. The harbour which had been such an important link across the Adriatic was of little interest to an empire centred far to the east. For the next 200 years, Durrësi became an insignificant little town of no more than 120 houses.

Almost immediately after the occupation, the Ottomans built a mosque on the site of a 10th- or 11th-century basilica, which is called the **Fatih Mosque**; Sultan Mehmed II, who was called the Conqueror (Fatih) after he took Constantinople in 1453, was dead by then, but his memory was not. The mosque is on a corner of a side street off Rruga Naim Frashëri, a restrained, whitewashed building with intricate wrought-iron windows. The minaret is a recent addition.

Just before the corner on which the mosque stands, a left turn will bring you to one of Durrësi's few remaining Ottoman houses, a delightful building with a traditional *çardak* or enclosed balcony. This was the home of Alexander Moisiu, an Albanian actor who was renowned across Europe in the early part of the 20th century. Moisiu was born in 1879, to an Italian mother and Albanian father in Trieste. He applied for Albanian citizenship five years after the country became independent, but was awarded it only in 1934. He died in Switzerland the following year, aged 55. Alexander Moisiu's house is now a **museum** (☉ *09.00–13.00 Tue–Sat; 100 lek*), which contains an exhibition of photographs and documents relating to the actor's family and professional career, and (perhaps of greater interest to most non-Albanian visitors) a display of folk costumes and other ethnographic material. Those with a particular interest in Alexander Moisiu might like to visit his father's family home in nearby Kavaja, which has also been preserved as a museum.

King Zog's Palace It was not until the Balkan Wars and Albania's independence that the city re-emerged from obscurity; it was the new nation's capital in 1914, under Prince Wilhelm of Wied (see box, opposite), and then again from 1918 until the final decision to site the capital in Tirana. King Zog I (see page 12) had a palace built here in 1927, a cream and pink villa up on the hill with marvellous views over the city and the bay. The building has now been returned to Zog's descendants and is not open to the public.

Monuments On 7 April 1939, Italian troops disembarked in Durrësi as part of their mission to occupy Albania. British-trained gendarmes, under the command of Abas Kupi (see page 14), resisted the invasion but were outnumbered and eventually defeated. Across from La Torra stands a Socialist Realist monument to this attempt, which the anti-communist Kupi would probably have hated. Perhaps it is just as well, therefore, that it is not a statue of Kupi, but of one of his fellow resisters, **Musa Ulqinaku**. On the other side of La Torra, set in a little garden, is a bust – inaugurated in 2003 – of an earlier gendarmerie commander, Major Lodewijk Thomson, who died in action in Durrësi in June 1914. See the box opposite for more about Major Thomson.

The beaches If you are staying in the town centre and want a quick dip, the best option is the shore at Currilat, just to the north of the town. The Kështjella Hotel (see page 92) and several of the restaurants along this stretch have reserved sections of sandy beach.

With thanks to Charlie Nuytens

Albania declared its independence on 28 November 1912, shortly after the outbreak of the First Balkan War (see *Chapter 1*, pages 11–12). However, the armed forces of the Balkan League continued to invade and attack their newly independent neighbour. In December, a Conference of Ambassadors was hastily convened in London; its remit was to consider the organisation of the new Albanian state and its international status. It was May 1913 before the London conference concluded its deliberations and formally recognised Albania. It decided that Albania would be ruled not by the government established in November 1912 under Ismail Qemali, but by a foreign prince chosen by the Great Powers, and that its internal order would be maintained by a gendarmerie under Dutch officers.

The Dutch mission arrived in Albania in October 1913, commanded by Major Lodewijk Thomson, whose military career had included postings in Aceh, South Africa and Greece. (Tintin fans will be happy to learn that Edith Durham, who met him in June 1914, spells his surname 'Thompson'.) The Dutch officers' task was far from easy. Not only did they have to try to create a disciplined Albanian force, changing ingrained habits such as looting after a victory; they were also supposed to oversee the handing in of the weapons which practically every Albanian man held. The only real incentive at their disposal was the carrot that anyone who volunteered as a gendarme could keep his weapons.

Prince Wilhelm of Wied, Albania's appointed ruler, landed at Durrësi on 7 March 1914, and made the mistake of appointing Essad Pasha as his Minister of National Defence. Essad had been the military commander of Shkodra who surrendered the city to Montenegro in 1912; since then he had done his best to undermine the Qemali government, with encouragement and probably financial support from Serbia. Almost as soon as Wied arrived in Albania, fighting broke out between supporters of Qemali (by now in exile in Italy) and Essad.

By early June, the political and military situation was deteriorating. Insurgents were advancing on Durrësi; the Dutch-trained gendarmerie tried to contain them by firing on the crowd, killing several people. In the early hours of 15 June, Edith Durham awoke to the sound of rifle fire and rushed to find out what was happening. She soon learned that Thomson had been fatally wounded in the first hours of the battle; he died in a roadside guardhouse, in the arms of *The Times*' correspondent, Arthur Moore.

Thomson's remains were taken back to the Netherlands, where he was buried in the city of Groningen. A few weeks later World War I broke out and the Dutch mission was ordered back home. Prince Wilhelm of Wied left Albania on 3 September, never to return. Thomson, however, is still honoured with statues and street names in the countries of his birth and death. In Durrësi, the bust next to La Torra (see page 95) is a replica of the original in Groningen. Behind it is a pleasant café called (another variant of his name!) 'Tomson Garden Grill'. A little further up Rruga Naim Frashëri, a group of columns forms a memorial to Thomson and to the others who died that day; a plaque affixed to one of the columns dates the inauguration of this memorial to Independence Day 1927. The parallel street, where Alexander Moisiu's house stands, is called Rruga Koloneli Thomson.

The beaches to the **south** of Durrësi have become very built up and cannot be recommended, particularly in the peak tourist season (July and August), when huge numbers of Albanians from land-locked Kosova and Macedonia fill the hotels and holiday apartments with which the coast is lined. At this time of year you should expect to find crowded beaches covered in litter, with the sea full of empty plastic bottles and crisp packets. On the positive side, Durrësi Beach has lively nightlife during the tourist season. Out of season, the beaches at Golemi and Mali i Robit are slightly less intensively built up than the area closest to the city.

Quieter beaches, in or out of season, lie to the **north** of Durrësi, on Lalëzi Bay (Gjiri i Lalëzit) and beyond, at Cape Rodoni (Kepi i Rodonit). The road from Durrësi is asphalted as far as the Franciscan church of Shën Ndout, just before the last beach at Rodoni. A small charge is levied on cars to enter this area. From here, it is possible to **kayak** to remoter beaches and to Rodoni Castle, the medieval sea-fortress said to have been built in 1465 by Skanderbeg (see box, pages 200–1). Outdoor Albania organises one-day sea-kayaking excursions to Rodoni from Tirana; see page 31 for contact information. Samiu's restaurant (really just a hut with tables overlooking the beach; $$) serves fish and prawns pretty much straight from the sea.

DIVJAKA

The Karavastaja Lagoons to the south of Durrësi are an internationally recognised wetland area – a Ramsar site. It is the winter home of several rare bird species and is the most westerly breeding ground of the Dalmatian pelican. The main wetland area comprises a shallow inner lagoon, and a smaller outer lagoon. The large inner lagoon is an atmospheric, slightly spooky place, full of small, low islands, ideal for pelicans' nests. Between the two lagoons is a large, forested sandbar where there is a small beach resort, with fish restaurants and hotels. The forest consists mainly of maritime pine (*Pinus pinaster*) and umbrella pine (*P. pinea*).

The lagoons themselves are designated as a Strict Nature Reserve (IUCN's Category Ia), while the forested sandbar is a Category II national park. In theory, this makes Karavastaja quite well protected. The local villagers have the right to collect dead wood but not to chop down the trees. In the inner lagoon only artisanal fishery is allowed, although there are more intensive fisheries in the outer one.

The beach resort on the sandbar has so far been spared the unchecked development which is overwhelming most of the Albanian coast, and would make a pleasant overnight stop for birdwatchers or beach lovers. Divjaka's biggest drawback, reasonably enough given it is in the middle of the largest wetland in Albania, is that it is infested with huge, thirsty mosquitoes from late spring to early autumn. If you visit at these times of year, you should take strong insect repellent and, if you plan to stay overnight, mosquito coils to put outside your window – electrically powered devices will be of no use if the electricity goes off while you are asleep.

GETTING THERE AND AWAY The Karavastaja Lagoons are near the village of Divjaka, northwest of the town of Lushnja. It is clearly signposted off the main highway south, just beyond the turn-off for Elbasani and the bridge over the Shkumbini River. The village of Divjaka is about 15 minutes' drive down this minor road; to get to the lagoons, 3–4km further on, go through the village and turn right at the crossroads, following the signpost 'Plazh'. The road leads through the pine woods and ends at a cluster of small restaurants and guesthouses. Vehicles entering the national park are charged a small fee. The journey from Tirana takes about 1½ hours.

To get to Divjaka by **public transport** from Tirana (or Durrësi), you can take any bus going south beyond Kavaja – to Lushnja, Fieri or Berati, for example – and ask the driver to let you off at the roundabout. Divjaka taxis wait near the junction until at least midday (probably later in the summer). The usual system is for the driver to wait until his car is full, although obviously he will take you at once if you pay four fares. You should specify at the outset that you are going to Divjaka Beach (*Plazhi i Divjakës*), to avoid arguments about the fare when you get to the village.

✗ **WHERE TO EAT AND DRINK** There are several restaurants at Divjaka Beach, serving fresh fish and grilled meat (**$$$**).

Ali Kali The weirdest dining experience in Divjaka is at Ali Kali ('Ali the Horse'), which is hidden at the end of a track, the first right after the entrance barrier to the national park. It is not signposted and there is no indication that it is a restaurant until you are practically at the tables, which are set up outside, further concealed behind a house. There is no menu; Ali rides up to your table on a white horse (hence the name) with your food and serves it to you from horseback. Then he brings you more, and more, until you can convince him to stop. Fresh fish, meat and bread, all grilled, feature prominently, perhaps thanks to their aerodynamic qualities. Rough red wine and honey from the comb complete the meal. Further surprises await when you come to pay. The toilets are pleasantly civilised, with running water and hand wash. (*Full meal, with wine* **$$$**.)

WHAT TO SEE AND DO Apart from the long, sandy beach (and Ali Kali), the main reason to go to Divjaka is to see the pelicans and other birds. There are no restrictions on walking along the beach; birdwatchers who wish to access the western side of the sandbar, or the islands in the inner lagoon, should approach the Prefecture for this area, which is headquartered in the town of Fieri (see page 104). It may be possible to obtain informal access with the park rangers; try asking the staff at the entrance barrier to the national park area.

The Dalmatian pelican (*Pelecanus crispus*) is listed as 'vulnerable' owing to its small and declining population. The total European breeding population is only about 1,500 pairs. Commercial trade in it is prohibited; it is the only member of the Pelecanidae on any of the CITES appendices, which regulate trade in endangered species. However, conservation measures are resulting in a population increase in Europe, particularly at the world's largest breeding colony at Lesser Lake Prespa (see pages 144–5). Karavastaja is the only place in Albania where the Dalmatian pelican breeds – the colony at Prespa is on the Greek side of the lake – and in the 1990s there were between 40 and 90 resident pairs here, although the numbers seem to have declined. The breeding season runs from April to July, although the pelicans winter at Divjaka (and elsewhere in Albania) and can thus be seen at other times of year too.

The site is also important for wintering waterbirds – BirdLife International censuses recorded 45,000 individual birds in 1996 and 68,171 in 1997. These include wigeons (*Anas penelope*), northern shovelers (*A. clypeata*) and teals (*A. crecca*). Over 1,000 avocets (*Recurvirostra avosetta*) have been recorded at Karavastaja. As well as the pelicans, collared pratincoles (*Glareola pratincola*) and little terns (*Sterna albifrons*) also breed there. The 'vulnerable' spotted eagle (*Aquila clanga*) winters there and has also been observed at other times of year, although it does not breed. Cormorants (*Phalacrocorax carbo*), pygmy cormorants (*P. pygmeus*) and great egrets (*Casmerodius albus*) are all present. The site is also potentially very important for the extremely rare ('critically endangered') slender-billed curlew (*Numenius tenuirostris*). See pages 199–202 for further details of the bird species which can be observed in the Albanian wetlands.

KRUJA   Telephone code: 0511

Kruja has been fortified since ancient times – ceramics and coins from the 3rd century BC have been excavated there. The name comes from the Albanian word for the spring (*krua*) within the castle which provided its inhabitants with water. The castle of Kruja was the centre of Albanian resistance to the Ottoman invasion in the 15th century, which was led by the great national hero Gjergj Kastrioti, also known as Skanderbeg (see box, pages 200–1). The buildings and museums within the castle walls, combined with the attractively restored bazaar area just outside them, provide an excellent introduction to Albanian history and traditions. Kruja is the only town in Albania, apart from Saranda in the far south, which is really geared towards tourists and it is the best place in the country to shop for souvenirs.

Kruja was the northernmost stronghold of Bektashism (see pages 22–3) – it was the Kruja *baba* (father) who is said to have converted Ali Pasha Tepelena (see box, pages 246–7). Apart from the lovely *teqe* within the castle (see page 103), there is a link with the Sufi saint Sari Salltëk: the teqe dedicated to him in the mountains above the town and, a few kilometres downhill, beside the road which leads up to the town, a rock where his foot is supposed to have left its print in the stone as he strode up from the plain.

GETTING THERE AND AWAY Kruja is about an hour's drive from either Tirana or Durrësi. Minibuses leave Tirana throughout the morning from a street behind the Zogu i Zi roundabout; the fare is 200 lek. You should take care to board a vehicle which is going all the way up the hill to Kruja; some minibuses only go as far as Fushë-Kruja ('Kruja on the Plain'), which is the town at the junction on the main Durrësi–Shkodra highway. The drivers will keep you on the right track if you ask; if you do end up having to get off at Fushë-Kruja, it is easy enough to transfer to a local minibus for the Kruja you want. Once in Kruja, the minibuses go into the centre of town and terminate just beyond the statue of Skanderbeg. The last minibuses usually leave Kruja towards the middle of the afternoon.

Kruja is less than half an hour's drive from Rinas airport. With the new airport road, some of the minibuses to Tirana now pass the roundabout a few minutes' walk from the airport terminal, and can let passengers off there. This makes it even more attractive an option than before to spend your last night, or your last morning, in Kruja and go from there directly to the airport. A taxi from Kruja to Rinas should cost around €20.

For cyclists, bikers and those with their own 4x4 transport, an alternative route from the north is over the Shtama Pass (Qafa e Shtamës). It is about 50km to Kruja from Burreli (see pages180–1). There is no public transport on this route and the pass is closed when there is snow.

 WHERE TO STAY Map, page 102.

Most tourists visit Kruja for the day and do not stay overnight. If you miss the last bus out, or if you plan to continue the following day by the mountain road to Burreli and Peshkopia, there are a couple of hotels in the town centre and another next to the Bektashi teqe at Sarisalltëk, about 7km above Kruja. There is an asphalted road to the teqe and also a footpath; it takes about one hour to get there on foot.

⌂ Panorama (18 rooms) Rr Kala; ☎23092; m 069 20 98 528, 069 20 98 528; e hotelpanoramakruje@hotmail.com; http://hotelpanoramakruje.com. Unbeatable location at the lower end of the bazaar, with superb views of the castle from many rooms. Restaurants, terrace bar, lift, secure parking, transport to airport can be arranged. Wi-Fi throughout. All rooms en suite with AC, cable TV, hairdryer; some have balconies looking out on to the castle & bazaar. **$$$**

✗ WHERE TO EAT AND DRINK   Map, page 102.

There are a couple of restaurants within the castle walls, with seats outside from where you can admire the view. In the bazaar, several traditionally furnished restaurants serve good Albanian food.

✗ Taverna Veseli ☎24416; m 069 24 24 079. At the top of the bazaar, the closest restaurant to the castle. Traditional Albanian dishes, plus the usual pasta & pizza. Good service, non-smoking, nicely decorated with traditional agricultural implements & old photographs. **$$$–$$$$$**

WHAT TO SEE AND DO Kruja Castle stands on a crag overlooking the plain below the town, with views on a clear day out to the Adriatic (it can sometimes be seen from the plane as you approach Tirana International Airport). Within the castle walls are two very different museums, a historic Bektashi teqe and several other places of interest; you could easily spend several hours visiting these and wandering around the cobbled lanes in the residential area. The usual approach to the castle is up the cobbled street of the bazaar, which is closed to traffic. The road which runs parallel to it, around the back of the Panorama Hotel, lets you drive up to the castle entrance, but it is hard to park there. You should allow at least two hours, and preferably more, for your visit.

Historical Museum (⊕ 09.00–13.00 & 16.00–19.00 Tue–Sun; winter afternoon hrs 15.00–18.00; 200 lek) On your left as you emerge from the vaulted entranceway is the Historical Museum, a modern (1982) building designed in a sort of castle-ish style by the architects Pranvera Hoxha – daughter of the communist leader Enver – and her husband. The displays on the ground floor cover the Illyrian city-states, the Roman and Byzantine periods and the development of Albania's medieval principalities. Then comes the story of Albania's struggle against the Ottomans, told through maps, murals, books and replicas. On the upper floors, there are models of the castles at Kruja, Petrela, Rodoni and Berati (see pages 84, 98 and 123–5, respectively) and an exhibition of documents and pictures showing the links which Albania had with other European countries in Skanderbeg's time, focusing on his diplomatic efforts to rally support for the resistance. There are good views from the upper terrace over the Kruja Plain towards the sea.

The Kruja museum is sometimes criticised for its idolatry of Skanderbeg and the implied parallel with the personality cult around Enver Hoxha, and it is true that the relentless 'Skanderfest' can become a little wearing. In fairness, however, he was probably the most significant single individual in the entire history of Albania and the museum is a well-presented introduction to this period of Albanian history. Almost none of the information is translated; non-Albanian visitors are expected to use the services of one of the museum's guides, who are knowledgeable and multilingual.

Ethnographic Museum (⊕ 09.00–13.00 & 16.00–19.00 Tue–Sun; 300 lek) The Ethnographic Museum, opposite the entrance gate (from where the sign is clearly visible), is located in a house built in 1764 for the powerful Toptani family. This is

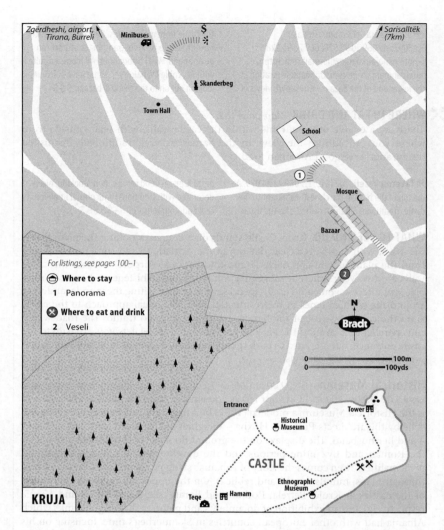

For listings, see pages 100–1

🛏 **Where to stay**
1 Panorama

❌ **Where to eat and drink**
2 Veseli

Minibuses

Zgërdheshi, airport,
Tirana, Burreli

Sarisalltëk
(7km)

Skanderbeg

Town Hall

School

Mosque

Bazaar

N

Bradt

0 ————— 100m
0 ————— 100yds

Entrance

Tower

Historical Museum

CASTLE

Ethnographic Museum

KRUJA

Teqe   **Hamam**

one of the most interesting ethnographic museums in the country, in part because the house itself was designed for such a prosperous and influential family.

The ground floor of the house is where the livestock were kept, the produce from the family's lands was processed and where the tools were made or repaired. There is a raki still (see pages 50–1 for more about Albania's national drink), an olive press and (in replica) the equipment for making felt, one of Kruja's traditional industries. The herdsman slept in the stable, with the sheep or goats; the family lived upstairs, in rooms accessed from the covered balcony which was used as the living space in summer. The doorways off the balcony have a stepped threshold, to keep out draughts once the door was closed, and an arch so that those entering had to lower their heads, thus showing respect to those within. Some of the rooms have been maintained with their original 18th-century furniture, frescoes and carved wooden panelling. The reception room, where (male) visitors would be welcomed and entertained by the men of the house,

102

has a beautifully painted ceiling and an enclosed gallery, with a couple of small windows, where the women could sit without being seen by their male relatives' visitors. The room in which the family ate and slept also has a gallery, although it is not walled; this was where the children slept and played, out from under their parents' feet. The large fireplace heated not only the room, but also the water for the house's own steam bath, or *hamam*. The museum also has a rich collection of traditional costumes and jewellery.

A walk around the citadel Ordinary families still live within Kruja Castle, although in less luxurious houses than the Toptani house. A network of cobbled alleyways spreads downhill from the open area where the museums are. Down one of these is the castle's beautiful little Bektashi **teqe**. Bektashism (see pages 22–3) is a Sufi order, founded in 1420; it was introduced to Albania in the wake of the Ottoman conquest and became widespread there in the early 19th century. The Kruja teqe was built in 1770 (1191 in the Islamic *hijri* calendar) and is one of the oldest in the country. The olive tree in its garden is said to have been planted by Skanderbeg himself, as part of his campaign to encourage the other landowners of Kruja to plant olives.

A teqe is not a mosque, but it is a holy place; visitors must remove their shoes before entering. The Kruja teqe was used for storage after religion was banned in 1967; it was restored by local Bektashis after freedom of worship was regained in 1990. It is a small, simple building, housing the tombs of past *babas* and is decorated inside with rugs, embroideries and pictures given to the teqe by Bektashis around the world. The atheism campaigners of 1967 (see pages 16–17) attempted to destroy the frescoes on the ceiling and walls, but fortunately the local people managed to convince them in time that the teqe was a Cultural Monument, and saved these beautiful paintings. The guardian will explain the building's history and the items in it to you, if you are able to establish a common language. A small donation is expected at the end of your visit.

To find the teqe from the open area between the museums, look for its dome and head down the winding paths aiming for it. It is reached up a flight of steps through a stone arch. Across from the foot of the steps is a **bathhouse** (*hamam*), five centuries old; the earthenware pipes which can be seen were installed, it is said, by Skanderbeg as a technological innovation which he had learned during his years at court in Constantinople.

At the other end of the citadel, up at the top beyond the museums, the **tower** was originally a lookout and signalling post. Skanderbeg used this castle as part of a chain of communication running the length of Albania – a beacon lit here could be seen by the garrison at Lezha Castle to the north and in Petrela, to the south of Tirana. Beside the tower, on the other side of a retaining wall, are the **remains of a medieval church**, with a couple of surviving fragments of fresco. The lack of maintenance of this church is disgraceful and the frescoes are unlikely to survive much longer.

The bazaar The bazaar was restored in the mid-1960s, but the wood-built shops and cobbled streets have a very authentically Ottoman feel. The extra-long eaves and the gutter in the middle of the road mean that rain, or wet snow, falls off the roofs and drains downhill straight away – an unusual but effective architectural device. Many of the shops sell small souvenirs such as Albanian flags, copper plates and ashtrays in the shape of bunkers. There are also traditional felt-makers, who produce slippers and the felt caps called *qeleshe*; carpet shops, in some of which you can watch the local women weaving the next batch of *qilime* (woven rugs; this is the same word as the Turkish *kilim*) with their ancient patterns; and antique dealers, where wooden butter paddles, cradles and intricately carved dowry chests pause in their journeys from highland villages to modern cities. Kruja's bazaar is a laid-back place and nobody will mind if all you want to do is window-shop.

Zgërdheshi Archaeologists think that the Illyrian ruins at Zgërdheshi may have been the city of Albanopolis, mentioned by Ptolemy (in the 2nd century AD) as the capital of Arbanon, the name from which Albania has taken its modern name. Built, like all Illyrian cities, on a hilltop, Zgërdheshi was fortified in two stages – first the acropolis, in the 6th century BC, and then a larger area, with the addition of watchtowers, in the 4th or 3rd century BC. Part of a tower, built with the huge stone blocks characteristic of Illyrian fortification, can be seen at the entrance to the site. There is no on-site interpretation, just a faint path which can be followed up to the acropolis, passing further traces of fortification on the way. Wild flowers and herbs grow all around and there are good views westwards to the Adriatic.

The turn-off for Zgërdheshi is about 5km out of Fushë-Kruja towards Kruja itself, before the road begins to climb. It is signposted at the junction, but not thereafter. Any Kruja minibus will let you off at the junction; it takes 15–20 minutes to walk up to the first line of ruined fortification.

APOLLONIA AND ARDENICA

The ancient city of Apollonia and the 18th-century monastery at Ardenica can easily be combined into a single day trip from Tirana, or indeed from Berati or Durrësi. Apollonia was founded in the 6th century BC and became one of Roman Albania's most important cities; there is a medieval monastery beside the ancient site, which houses an excellent museum. The Church of St Mary, part of the Ardenica Monastery, has frescoes painted by the Zografi brothers, who were renowned throughout the southern Balkans during their lifetimes.

GETTING THERE AND AWAY The nearest town to both Apollonia and Ardenica is Fieri, on the main highway south from Durrësi, just north of where it divides for Gjirokastra and Vlora. The turn-off for Ardenica, signposted, is about halfway between Lushnja and Fieri. Apollonia is about 12km west of Fieri, on a reasonably good, asphalted road. It is signposted from the city and at the turn-off to the site.

By **public transport**, there are frequent buses and minibuses to Fieri from all major towns in southern and central Albania. There is no onward public transport to Apollonia; the main **taxi** rank in Fieri is on the main square, where the Prefecture building is. A reasonable taxi fare, including an hour's waiting time, would be about 3,000 lek. At certain times of day, taxis also wait beside the café at the bus stop on the main road. This café is a good place to ask about public transport for your return or onward journey.

You could get to the monastery at Ardenica by alighting from an **interurban bus** at the turn-off for Ardenica village and walking up the hill. However, not only is it a long walk, but you will probably find you have to pay the full fare to the final destination. It would be a lot easier, and might work out no more expensive, to agree a price with a Fieri taxi driver to take you to both sites.

WHAT TO SEE AND DO
Ardenica The 18th-century Church of St Mary, part of the monastery at Ardenica, is decorated with frescoes by Kostandin and Athanas Zografi, famous icon-painters in the tradition known as the Korça School. There is more information about the

Zografi brothers and the Korça School on page 135. The monastery is surrounded with high walls, but it is usually possible to gain access. A church was first built on this site during the 13th century and the monastery gatehouse dates from 1474.

The existing church is a long building of creamy-coloured stone, with a cloister running along most of its length. Stones from more ancient sites were used in its building, and in the outer walls, especially at the back, you can see pieces of column capitals and Byzantine Greek inscriptions. The entrance to the church is around the side of the more recent belltower (rebuilt in 1925) and up a flight of steps. Straight ahead is a gilded wooden iconostasis, and on the walls to your right and behind you are the frescoes, paintings of various saints and of biblical scenes.

On the other side of the steps is an elegant cloister of stone arches supporting a wooden terrace, which gives shade to the monks' cells on the first floor. A plaque on the wall says that this was rebuilt in 1942; if this is the case it would indicate surprising optimism on the part of the wartime monks.

Apollonia (☉ *Oct–Mar 09.00–17.00 daily, Apr–Sep 08.00–20.00 daily; 300 lek, free on the last Sun of the month, except Jun–Aug*) The city of Apollonia was the second Greek settlement on the Illyrian mainland, after Epidamnos (now Durrësi; see pages 87–98). Founded, according to tradition, in 588BC and named after the god Apollo, it was settled first by Corinthians, who were followed by others, especially from nearby Corcyra (Corfu). At the time, Apollonia lay only a kilometre from the Aoos River (the Vjosa, in Albanian) and it became a major port. The city grew in importance and, by the time of the Roman conquest in the middle of the 2nd century BC, its coins were in wide circulation, especially in the Danube provinces where Roman coinage was not accepted. With its rival Dyrrachium (the Romans' name for Durrësi), it was one of the starting points of the Via Egnatia, the great arterial road which linked the Adriatic coast with Byzantium (see page 8).

In addition to its importance as a trading and military port, the Roman élite considered Apollonia a centre of higher learning. The young Octavian studied there before he was given the title of Augustus – indeed, he had to rush back to Rome to claim power after the Ides of March, 44BC, when his adoptive father, Julius Caesar, was assassinated. Most of the remains which can be seen at Apollonia date from the Roman period. Augustus later awarded Apollonia the status of a 'free and immune city' – immune, that is, from the obligation to pay taxes. Apollonia's status meant that – unlike Dyrrachium and other colonies – it continued to elect its local authorities, its everyday language was Greek, not Latin, and its coins had Apollonia's own symbols on them.

In late antiquity, a series of earthquakes shifted the course of the Aoos – the Vjosa River – far to the south and left Apollonia without the port which had brought its prosperity. The ancient city now stands, isolated and forlorn, on its hill overlooking the fertile Myzeqeja Plain and, a few miles to the west, the Adriatic.

Apollonia was first excavated by the French archaeologist Léon Rey, between 1924 and 1938. It was Rey and his team who uncovered the building which immediately draws the visitor's eye: the **Bouleuterion**, where the city council met. It was built in the late 2nd century AD by the brother of a military commander who had died on Rome's eastern front. Both brothers held the position of *agonothetes*, the official who presided over and judged the games, and so this building is also sometimes known as the Monument of the Agonothetes. We know all of this from the Greek inscription on the pediment above the columns. These were restored in the 1970s by Albanian archaeologists, who fortunately made it very obvious which bits are restored and which are original.

4

Behind the Bouleuterion, and built around the same time, is a little theatre known as the **Odeon**. This was not the city's public theatre (that stood on the western edge of the ancient city, and little of it can be seen today), but a venue for cultural and musical events for the élite, seating only about 300 people. The line of four marble-clad column bases, between these two buildings, is all that remains of a triumphal arch, through which all traffic into the square would have had to pass.

Leading off this civic area to the northwest is the portico known as **Stoa B**. At 75m long and 12m wide, the stoa predates the Bouleuterion and Odeon by some five centuries. Built to a Corinthian pattern, its ground floor was separated with Doric columns into two parallel walkways. Above these walkways, an upper promenade, probably with Ionic columns, allowed Apollonia's rich citizens to enjoy the marvellous views over their thriving port and the Adriatic Sea. The whole structure backed on to the slope of the hill leading up to the city's acropolis; to reinforce it, 17 niches were built into the hillside on the ground floor. The stone for these was brought, by sea, from the Karaburuni Peninsula, 70km away. During Léon Rey's excavations, several busts of famous philosophers were found around these niches; perhaps they had been placed there to inspire intellectual conversations.

A restored arch at the northwestern end of the stoa marks the site of one of the shops that once stood there. In the area around it are the remains of a cistern, in which rainwater was collected (Apollonia has no aqueduct), and a rectangular building which had a mosaic floor and which archaeologists believe may have been a cult sanctuary.

Like all Greek cities, Apollonia had a reserved area called the *temenos*. This was dedicated to a god, or to several gods, and was not in everyday use. In Apollonia, the temenos was on the hill to the east of the Bouleuterion, which Rey called Hill 104. It was surrounded by a wall, part of which can be seen by following the path uphill from the Bouleuterion, on either side of the beautiful archway which was the entrance to the temenos. Neatly cut from limestone and sandstone, some of the rectangular blocks are marked with a monogram consisting of the Greek letters D and A: 'belonging to the state of Apollonia' – in other words, the temenos wall was a public work. Further along the path, an information panel – in English and Albanian – shows the location of the city's necropolis (cemetery) and explains its excavation. One tumulus has been dated to the Iron Age, thus predating the Greek settlement.

Apollonia is a complex, multilayered site and it is estimated that only about 10% of the city has been excavated to date. Unfortunately, the visitor interpretation around the site leaves a lot to be desired; the information about the necropolis is all there is, apart from small signs at each of the main structures. A large map at the entrance to the site shows the various buildings, with a key in Albanian and French. A very helpful leaflet, which guides the visitor around the entire site, was published in 2011, but it is difficult to obtain. The souvenir kiosk at the entrance to the monastery may have copies.

Fortunately, though, the site **museum**, located on the first floor of the monastery building, is full of well-presented information about the history of Apollonia and its excavations. There are three rooms of lovely, interesting artefacts: imported and locally made Greek vases, bronzes and busts; armour, including a 4th-century shield, which was excavated in hundreds of pieces and took 27 years to restore; and a case of coins minted in Apollonia and elsewhere. You should try to allow at least 45 minutes to look around the museum. Outside, the 13th-century church and the 14th-century refectory are also well worth a look. There are beautiful frescoes in the refectory, including one of Mary Magdalen washing Christ's feet; the eyes of some of the saints were scratched out by believers, who would mix the paint and plaster from them with water and drink this potion as a miracle cure.

There are two cafés at Apollonia: one, named after Léon Rey, is at the summit of 'Hill 104' (the temenos hill) and has good views; the other is straight ahead as you enter the fenced-off area of the archaeological site. There are reasonable toilets behind this bar, which visitors to the site may use.

BYLLIS

(⊕ *Mar–Oct 08.00–18.00 daily, Nov–Feb 08.00–16.00 daily; 300 lek*) Byllis is a vast archaeological site spread over 30ha of hilltop overlooking the River Vjosa. The ancient walls which surround the site were built in the second quarter of the 4th century BC. Within them are the remains of Illyrian private houses, Roman public buildings, including an impressive theatre, and Byzantine basilicas paved with outstanding mosaics. It is easy to linger for hours in the haunting atmosphere of this remote hilltop, surrounded by the ruins of buildings which are two and a half millennia old. Good interpretative panels around the site, in Albanian and English, mean that it can be readily understood by non-specialists. A well-surfaced and fairly level path leads the visitor around the most important remains.

It was the British traveller Henry Holland who, in the early 19th century, first identified this site as the ancient Byllis, mentioned by Caesar and Cicero. Systematic excavation began in the winter of 1917/18, under the direction of the Austrian archaeologist Camillo Praschniker. Several eminent Albanian archaeologists have excavated at Byllis, among them Neritan Ceka and Skënder Muçaj, who have written a guide to the site, *Byllis: History & Monuments* (see *Appendix 2*, page 273). It is worth buying a copy of this book just for the photographs of the Byzantine mosaics, which are usually kept covered to protect them from the elements. Several interesting objects discovered at Byllis can be seen in the National Archaeological Museum in Tirana (see pages 77–8).

HISTORY Byllis was the capital of the small republic (*koinon*) of the Byllines and it was the largest city in southern Illyria. The Byllines had a sophisticated system of government, minted bronze coins and controlled an area of about 20km². Their state flourished until 229BC, when the Romans occupied Apollonia and Byllis became a battleground between Rome and Macedonia, thanks to its strategic position overlooking the River Vjosa, and the route from Apollonia to Epirus and Macedonia. The advantages of this location would later encourage Rome to make Byllis one of its colonies. The colonial period saw the city flourish again, as Roman veterans built luxurious houses and sponsored public works such as bridges and bathhouses.

Byllis was sacked by the Visigoths towards the end of the 4th century AD, and its enclosing wall was repaired using the original blocks. The sections which were repaired can be identified by the cement which was used to stick the blocks together. Between AD547 and AD551, Byllis was attacked again. It was rebuilt and it was decided a new wall should be erected, enclosing a much smaller area than the old Illyrian city. The order to construct the new fortification was given by the Emperor Justinian (AD527–65), but it was implemented by a general called Victorinus, and so it is known as Victorinus's Wall. It follows the line of the Hellenistic wall on the western and southern sides of the city, where the hillside is steeper. For the new defences to the north and east, Victorinus reused some of the old limestone blocks and built a new wall 2.2m thick, interspersed with 12m-high towers. A touching inscription on one of the blocks of his wall, now in the Archaeological Museum in Tirana, reads: 'I am no longer worried or frightened about barbarians, because I was destined to be built by the hand of great Victorinus.'

GETTING THERE AND AWAY Byllis is about half an hour's drive from the nearest town, Ballshi, which is approximately 2½ hours from Tirana. Local taxis can be hired in the centre of Ballshi, beside the war memorial. The 'Ancient City of Bylis' is signposted, in Albanian and English, off to the right on the brow of a hill a couple of kilometres south of Ballshi. It is 5km from the junction to the site; the road is well surfaced and a 4x4 is not required. A minibus operates hourly between Ballshi and the village of Hekali, about 1km short of the entrance to the site; the owner of the café at the junction is very helpful and will be able to advise on bus timings. The new Levan–Tepelena highway passes below Byllis, but there is not (yet) a road up to the site from it.

On the way up to the site, many small oil rigs and other installations can be seen. The oil field under this part of Albania stretches from Ballshi and Fieri to the district of Kuçova, north of Berati; parts of it are now being exploited with modern technology by multi-national companies.

Cars can be parked at the entrance to the site, beside the café where entry tickets are sold and where there are toilets. Admission is free on the last Sunday of the month, except in the summer, and on certain dates such as International Museums Day. The café carries a small stock of publications about archaeology in Albania.

WHAT TO SEE AND DO The walls which enclosed the Illyrian city form a rough triangle more than 2km around. On the southern edge there is a gap in the wall where the hillside drops away in a steep cliff for about 200m. The Hellenistic (Illyrian) walls were 8–9m high, built with large rectangular blocks of limestone. These were laid in two lines 3.5m apart, and the gap between the rows was then filled with small stones laid at right angles to the blocks. There were six entrance gates, each guarded by a tower, and additional towers were built at the corners of the walls, to protect and strengthen them.

Between 230bc and 167bc, Byllis's protection was enhanced with the addition of a fortified courtyard at the northern apex of the triangle of its walls. The courtyard was guarded in its turn from a round tower, nearly 9m in diameter and 9m high. The remains of this fortified courtyard are on the right of the modern road as you approach the site.

From the site entrance next to the café, follow the path to the *agora*, the area of the city which the Byllines reserved for public spaces and civic buildings. A wall divided this public area from the residential quarter, which was laid out in a grid, with the houses in blocks known as *insulae*. Covering 4ha, the agora was completed during the 3rd century bc, with buildings including the **Great Stoa** (to your east), the Stadium and the vaulted Cistern. On the southern edge of the agora, the Theatre is perhaps the most imposing of Byllis's ancient monuments.

The limestone vaults of the **Cistern** were originally covered with stone tiles to form an underground reservoir, with a capacity of about 1,200m³, which supplied the city with water. Even more remarkably, the roof of the reservoir formed the northern part of the Stadium. Limited suitable space meant that Byllis's **Stadium** had only one track, rather than the more usual oval form. The spectators stood on the steps rising up to the east of the track, which continued as far as the Theatre. The steps were made of rectangular limestone blocks; some can still be seen. Associated with the Cistern is a much later **Bathhouse**, which dates from the reconstruction of

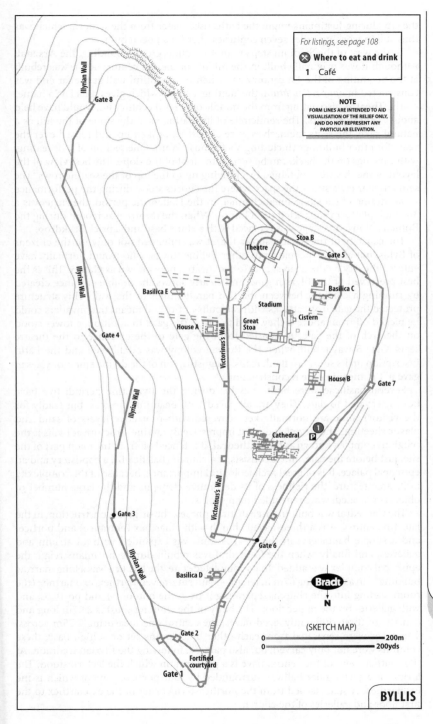

For listings, see page 108

⊗ **Where to eat and drink**
1 Café

NOTE
FORM LINES ARE INTENDED TO AID
VISUALISATION OF THE RELIEF ONLY,
AND DO NOT REPRESENT ANY
PARTICULAR ELEVATION.

Illyrian Wall
Gate 8

Illyrian Wall

Gate 4

Illyrian Wall

Gate 3

Illyrian Wall

Gate 2

Gate 1

Fortified
courtyard

Theatre
Stoa B
Gate 5

Basilica E

Basilica C

Stadium

Cistern

Great
Stoa

Victorinus's Wall

House A

House B
Gate 7

Cathedral
1
P

Victorinus's Wall

Gate 6

Basilica D

Bradt
N

(SKETCH MAP)
0 ——————— 200m
0 ——————— 200yds

BYLLIS

the city during Justinian's reign; the baths used water from the Cistern, which was thus still in working order seven centuries after it had been built.

To the west of the Stadium steps is another underground building, the **Arsenal**. Although it was originally built in the middle of the 3rd century BC, it was rebuilt at the beginning of the 1st century AD, when the beautiful wall at the far end was constructed in *opus reticulatum*, the 'netting' pattern which gives it its Latin name.

The **Theatre**, also dating from the middle of the 3rd century BC, would have held about 7,500 spectators. The semicircle of its seating used the slope of the hill as a natural rake; the seats themselves were almost all broken up and reused over the years for other buildings (including Victorinus's Wall). One section of VIP seating, with carvings on the back, can be seen at the foot of the slope. The best view of the layout of the theatre is obtained by climbing up to the top of the seating rows. The semicircular *orchestra* – the space where the chorus stood during the performance – was drained by a stone-lined channel. In the Hellenistic period, the stage was a 3m-high platform supported on columns. When the theatre was rebuilt during the Roman colony, this stage was replaced with a stone base and a brick backdrop.

The capacity of the theatre shows that it was intended not only for the citizens of Byllis, but also for people from other Bylline towns, who would normally have entered the city by the nearest gate to the theatre, now known as **Gate 5**. This is the best preserved of the Illyrian gates and clearly shows the double entrance created by running a corridor between the two parallel lines of the wall. This structure protected the gate from attacks with catapults or fire and meant that invaders could be picked off from above if they tried to storm the gate. In addition, a tower stood on the arch of the gate. A stoa led from the gate to the entrance to the theatre seats. Gate 5 was rebuilt when the Roman colony was established and the Latin inscription on its southern flank reads: 'Augustus, son of the divine emperor Caesar, gave it' ('it' meaning the reconstruction).

Several basilicae were built at Byllis during the Byzantine period; five have been excavated to date. They are all paved with beautiful mosaics, but (sadly for the visitor) these are normally kept covered with protective layers of sand and plastic sheeting. The largest and most impressive Byzantine structure at Byllis is the religious complex known as the **Cathedral**. It is fenced off from the main part of the site, just before the café, and it consists of a church (Basilica B), a baptistery and an episcopal palace. It is of great archaeological importance, because of the complexity of its architecture, the richness of its decorative elements and the large number of objects excavated, which included many coins.

The Cathedral was built in three distinct phases: the original construction, in the late 4th century, was a three-naved church with a narthex (entrance) and portico, and a simple baptistery; in the AD470s, this was expanded with an atrium and galleries; and finally, when the Cathedral was rebuilt during Justinian's reign, the episcopal complex was added. In its completed state, the basilica was a long, narrow building – an astonishing 67m in length – with side-naves, narthex, exonarthex (the room leading into the church, separating it from the outdoors) and porticos, and with galleries on the upper floor. The body of the church (*naos*) is 24.7m long and consists of three differently sized naves, the central one measuring 7.75m across. The naves were separated from each other by columns set on a high base; these columns were not only carved, but also painted, following the Illyrian tradition. At the southern end of the central nave is a platform on which the lectern stood. The atrium is a rectangular hallway surrounded by four porticos, one of which is the exonarthex. A staircase led from the northeastern corner of the exonarthex to the first floor and galleries of the church.

The floors of several sections of the church are paved with magnificent mosaics, which are usually covered to protect them from the elements. One shows a rustic scene; others depict the fishermen of Nazareth and the brothers Simon and Andrew (and an especially cute jellyfish); smaller panels bear different kinds of animals and birds. The basilica's walls were decorated with frescoes, but only a few of these remain, geometric patterns from the first phase of construction.

In AD586, Byllis was sacked and burned once again, this time by invading Slavs. After this destruction, the city was abandoned and the bishopric moved to the nearby town whose name, Ballshi, is a corruption of Byllis.

ELBASANI   *Telephone code: 054*

Elbasani's origins lie in the 2nd century BC, when a trading post called Scampa grew up at the junction of the branches of the Via Egnatia, the great Roman road running between the Albanian coast and Byzantium, whose starting points were Dyrrachium and Apollonia. By the 2nd century AD, this had developed into a sizeable way station called Mansio ad Quintum. During the upheavals and invasions of the 4th century AD, the Romans fortified the settlement and stationed a legion there to protect the Via Egnatia. The castle which they built is right in the centre of the modern town of Elbasani and covers almost a square kilometre.

The city walls were rebuilt by the Ottomans in 1466, during Mehmed II's expedition against Skanderbeg (see box, pages 200–1). Their plan was to use the fortress as a base for extending their conquest and they gave it the name 'Elbasan', which in Turkish means 'the place for raiding other people's territory'. The town flourished under the Ottomans, and by the 17th century it had become an important commercial centre, exporting its leather, fabrics and silverwork throughout the Ottoman Empire. In the 20th century, Elbasani was the home for many years of Margaret Hasluck, a British archaeologist and ethnographer who went on to direct SOE's activities in Albania (see box, pages 116–17).

The metallurgical complex called the Steel of the Party was built in 1974, with technical and financial support from China, and it employed over 8,000 people in its heyday. Now, most of the plant lies idle; it is almost impossible to bring it up to international environmental standards, and the result has been unemployment and emigration. For many people, it is the only thing they know about Elbasani and so they drive straight past the town without realising that its history goes back much, much further.

GETTING THERE AND AWAY A new highway, with tunnels blasted through the mountains, has cut the journey time between Tirana and Elbasani to under an hour. Buses leave Tirana from the northern side of the Qemal Stafa Stadium; the fare is 150 lek. There are buses to Elbasani from every other major town in central and southern Albania.

The main **bus station** in Elbasani is in the square in front of the sports centre. The Tirana buses leave from a little further down and on the opposite side of the street. Local buses and minibuses (eg: for Llixhat and Belshi) leave from a bus stop on Rruga Thoma Kalfi, beyond the market.

For those with their own transport, the old Tirana–Elbasani road is slow and precipitous, but has spectacular views over the Martanesh Mountains. The highest point of the road is almost 931m above sea level; then it hairpins back downhill, passing a series of large Socialist Realist murals on the hillside wall, until Elbasani's vast steel plant comes into view, spreading for miles at the foot of the mountain.

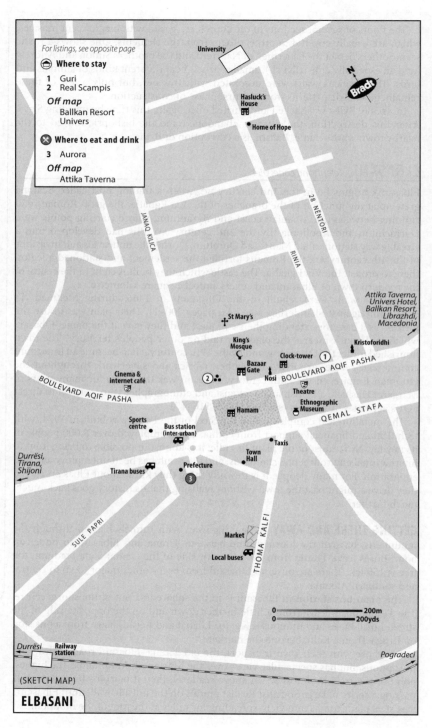

For listings, see opposite page

Where to stay
1 Guri
2 Real Scampis
Off map
   Ballkan Resort
   Univers

Where to eat and drink
3 Aurora
Off map
   Attika Taverna

University

Hasluck's House

Home of Hope

28 NENTORI

RINIA

JANAQ KILICA

Attika Taverna, Univers Hotel, Ballkan Resort, Librazhdi, Macedonia

St Mary's

King's Mosque

Bazaar Gate

Clock-tower

Kristoforidhi

Nosi

BOULEVARD AQIF PASHA

Cinema & internet café

BOULEVARD AQIF PASHA

Theatre

Ethnographic Museum

Hamam

QEMAL STAFA

Sports centre

Bus station (inter-urban)

Taxis

Durrësi, Tirana, Shijoni

Tirana buses

Prefecture

Town Hall

SULE PAPRI

THOMA KALFI

Market

Local buses

0 ———————— 200m
0 ———————— 200yds

Durrësi Railway station

Pogradeci

(SKETCH MAP)

ELBASANI

112

WHERE TO STAY *Map, opposite.*

🏠 **Ballkan Resort** (18 rooms) Miraka, Rr Elbasan-Librazhd; m 069 44 39 601; e info@resortballkan.com; Facebook: Ballkan Hotel. Country setting in hills between Labinoti & Librazhdi; modern building set in lovely gardens on the Shkumbini River; English spoken at reception. Large outdoor swimming pool, restaurant, terrace bar, contemporary cocktail bar; Wi-Fi throughout. All rooms en suite with AC, TV, minibar; some have a balcony. $$$

🏠 **Guri** (12 rooms) Bd Qemal Stafa, Lagja Kala (in the castle); m 069 20 83 089; e hotelguri@hotmail.com; www.hotel-guri.com. An old house within the castle walls, nicely renovated; has small art gallery & museum within one of the towers of the wall, with outdoor bar area at the tower's foot. Generously sized rooms, all with good en-suite bathrooms inc superb shower; AC, LCD TV, Wi-Fi, phone, fridge. Rooms on 1st floor have Juliet balcony overlooking castle walls; top floor have skylights & attic ceiling. $$$

🏠 **Real Scampis** (7 rooms) Bd Qemal Stafa, Lagja Kala (in the castle); ☎255 575; f 240 162. Fantastic location within the castle walls, with archaeological remains visible under the café & around the extensive, beautiful gardens. The best restaurant in town, with traditional Elbasani dishes & interesting chef's specials, as well as the usual grilled meat. Vehicle entrance at rear of hotel, with car park. Good-sized rooms, all en suite (some have jacuzzi) with AC, satellite TV, Wi-Fi, balcony, phone. $$$

🏠 **Univers** (14 rooms) Lagja Emin Matraxhiu; ☎256 193; m 069 40 71 278, 069 40 71 277; e univers_hotel_elbasan@yahoo.com; www.univershotel.eu. On the eastern outskirts of town (Ura e Bakallit); English spoken. Quiet, modern & comfortable, good restaurant, bar, parking, Wi-Fi throughout; outdoor swimming pool, gardens. All rooms en suite with AC, satellite TV, phone; most have balcony or terrace. $$

WHERE TO EAT AND DRINK *Map, opposite.*

✗ **Attika Taverna** Rr Kozma Naska (near Ura e Bakallit); ☎243 583; m 068 20 71 290. A range of unusual & delicious dishes, neither traditionally Albanian nor, despite the restaurant's name, noticeably Greek. Carnivores will enjoy Sofra e Pashait ('the Pasha's Table'); lots of cheese treats for vegetarians. $$$

✗ **Aurora** Around the corner from the Prefecture, has a shady terrace, set back from the road, particularly nice in the summer. $$$

WHAT TO SEE AND DO

The old town The surviving castle walls run along one side of Rruga Aqif Pasha and down the streets perpendicular to it. Within them lie Roman remains, including traces of the Via Egnatia (see page 8), one of the oldest mosques in Albania, and a fine Orthodox church. There are four entrances through the walls, one of them also the pedestrian entrance to the Real Scampis Hotel. Descending the steps here will bring you right into the archaeological excavations which were carried out while the hotel was being built. Some of the remains are actually beneath the raised terrace bar, protected by a perspex covering so that they can be seen.

On the other side of Rruga Aqif Pasha, outside the walls, is a *hamam*, an Ottoman bathhouse, whose current structure dates from the 19th century, but which has occupied this site since the 1670s. The exterior is in good condition and the tiled domes on its roof are particularly attractive. The 60m-high clocktower, set into one of the bastions of the wall, was built in 1899.

To find the **King's Mosque** (Xhamia e Mbretit), enter the old town through the **Bazaar Gate** – the archway with the lion fountains on either side. The street forks just inside the entrance; the left-hand fork will bring you straight to the King's Mosque – one of the oldest in Albania. Construction began in 1492, the year Columbus discovered the New World. The building was neglected under communism, though not deliberately damaged, and the interior has been substantially, though faithfully, renovated.

4

From the mosque, **St Mary's Church** (Kisha e Shënmërisë) is a couple of hundred metres further into the old town, bearing in the same direction. A church was first built on this site in 1486, with renovations and additions made over the centuries. In the garden, as you enter the churchyard, is the tomb of the 19th-century lexicographer and grammarian Kostandin Kristoforidhi (see box below). The church was used by the army for storage after the atheism campaign of 1967, but the fabric of the building was saved from wanton destruction by the cobbled streets of Elbasani's old town, which are too narrow for bulldozers. The interior

KOSTANDIN KRISTOFORIDHI

Kostandin Kristoforidhi was an illustrious figure in the 19th-century cultural nationalist movement, *Rilindja Kombëtare*. He was prolific as a translator of religious texts into Albanian, but his life's work was as a lexicographer and grammarian. He was born in Elbasani in 1826 and studied in Ioannina, where he assisted in the preparation of the first Albanian–German dictionary. His first translation was of the New Testament, which he published in both of the main dialects of Albanian, Gheg and Tosk. He would continue throughout his life to translate into both dialects, as a way of demonstrating their similarity to each other.

After living for a time in Istanbul, Malta and Tunis, he returned to Istanbul in 1865 as a translator for the London-based Bible Society, which retained him until 1874. In that year, the Bible Society dismissed him on the grounds that he did not believe the Bible was divinely inspired. His surviving religious translations are versions of the Four Gospels (1866), the Psalms (1868 in Tosk and 1869 in Gheg), the New Testament (1869 in Gheg and 1879 in Tosk), Genesis and Exodus (1880), Deuteronomy (1882), the Song of Solomon and the Book of Isaiah (both 1884).

Unemployed, Kristoforidhi returned to Tirana, where he scraped a living selling wood and charcoal, and opened a bar. Meanwhile, like many other Rilindja figures, he gave clandestine Albanian lessons. In 1884, he returned to Elbasani, where he continued to teach secretly. He was a member of the Commission on the Alphabet which met in the late 1860s to try to agree on a common alphabet in which to write Albanian; it would not be until 1909, 14 years after Kristoforidhi's death, that the congress held in his native town would formally adopt the Roman alphabet for this purpose. He published a Gheg ABC in 1867, and a Tosk ABC the following year. He also wrote Albanian-language textbooks for his students, and a story called *Gjahu i malësorëve* (*The Highlanders' Hunt*).

His scientific work on the Albanian language – his *Dictionary of the Albanian Language* and *Grammar of the Albanian Language* – laid the foundations for the establishment of a unified national language, and it is for this that he is generally remembered today. Kostandin Kristoforidhi died in Elbasani in 1895 and he is buried in the churchyard of St Mary's Church within the castle walls. A statue of him stands on the corner of Rruga Qemal Stafa and Rruga Rinia and a plaque depicting him giving one of his clandestine language classes can be seen on the castle wall near the Bazaar Gate. The words on the plaque read: 'Albania will never learn anything, will never be illuminated, will not be at all civilised with foreign languages, but only with its mother tongue, which is Albanian.'

walls of the church were covered in frescoes until they were whitewashed during the atheism campaign; the only ones which survive are the Pantocrator in the dome and the early 20th-century fresco on the south wall. The iconostasis, however, is the original, intricately carved in boxwood in 1870 by craftsmen from the district of Dibra, famous at the time for the skill of its woodworkers. The icons of St Michael and St Gabriel, the protective saints of all Orthodox churches, were painted in 1659 by the great Albanian artist Onufri (see page 123).

Ethnographic Museum (🕑 *09.00–15.00 Mon–Fri; 200 lek*) Elbasani was an important commercial centre in the 17th century, exporting its leather, fabrics and silverwork throughout the Ottoman Empire. Its craftsmen were organised in no fewer than 45 guilds; the Tanners' Guild had a written statute as early as 1658. The city's traditional crafts are given special attention in Elbasani's museum, in addition to the more usual displays of traditional furniture and costumes. The collection is housed in an 18th-century building where, in 1908, the city's first Albanian-medium school was opened. The following year, Elbasani would be the venue for a famous congress, at which the Roman alphabet was formally adopted as the script for the Albanian language. The Congress of Elbasani also chose the town as the site of Albania's first teacher-training college, which opened later the same year.

The ground floor of an Albanian house was traditionally used for workshops, storage, and – in rural areas – the stabling of livestock. The Ethnographic Museum has used this space to display the tools used in the various crafts practised in Elbasani, and examples of the items produced. One room is devoted to wool-working, including the making of felt. The different types of *qeleshe*, or fez, are displayed and explained.

Another room contains blacksmith's and carpenter's tools, and some of the things that these craftsmen produced. An intriguing bladed device is a tobacco-cutter, of a design still used in the countryside today – the whole leaves are bundled into the hopper and pushed through with one hand while the other works the chopper. Another interesting exhibit is a set of bells, in different sizes for different animals, including an extraordinarily heavy cow bell.

Upstairs, in what would have been the living quarters, the central area is open to a covered wooden balcony (*çardak*). In the summer, the family would have spent much of its time out here, where the breeze could circulate. The rooms leading off the central space each had their own function and they have been furnished accordingly. In the 'women's room', with its intricately carved wooden ceiling, a beautiful cradle and a tiny embroidered jacket show that this was more like a nursery. The wooden cradle has dragons carved on the ends, to keep the baby from harm. Next to the nursery is where the women spun and wove silk for their embroideries and tapestries. Some raw silk is on the spinning wheel, and some part-woven fabric is on the loom, so that you can see the process; some of the embroideries hang on the walls.

The 'men's room' has a fine plaster fireplace (*oxhak*) and is panelled in wood. Like the babies' room, there is a brazier in the middle of the floor. Finally, the 'couple's room' has beautifully embroidered bedlinen, a 250-year-old mirror and a wooden dowry chest. The traditional wedding clothes on display include the long surcoat typical of Elbasani.

The museum's rich collection has been well laid out and makes a very interesting display, taking an hour or so to look round. There are explanatory panels in Albanian and English. Access for groups can be arranged outside normal opening hours by calling ☏ 259 626.

EXCURSIONS FROM ELBASANI Top of the excursions list, for anyone with even the slightest interest in religious art, is the Church of St Nicholas (Shën Nikolla) at **Shelcani**. This 14th-century church somehow escaped the whitewashers of the atheism campaign. Its interior walls are completely covered with magnificent frescoes painted, in 1554, by the great Albanian artist Onufri (see page 123). Better still, the frescoes have recently been cleaned by specialists from the Albanian Institute of Monuments. Images of saints and scenes from the Bible, such as Lazarus rising from the grave and Christ entering Jerusalem on Palm Sunday, glow in radiant colours. Shelcani is in the Shpati Mountains to the southeast of Elbasani; the road is asphalted all the way, apart from 50m or so up to the church, and the journey takes about half an hour.

The National Historical Museum in Tirana has the original doorway, and several icons, from the church of **St Gjon Vladimir**, part of a medieval monastery about 5km from Elbasani on the old road to Tirana. According to the inscriptions on the lintel, the church was built by Karl Topia, 'lord of Arbër', in the early 1380s, after an earthquake had destroyed the church which previously stood on the site. Karl Topia was one of the powerful feudal princes, who between them ruled Albania from

MARGARET HASLUCK

The combination of archaeology, ethnography and wartime special operations is not a classic career path, yet Margaret Hasluck achieved success in all three fields. She spent 16 years in Albania, researching and publishing on topics as diverse as Roma customs, Albanian grammar and blood feud. In 1935, she settled in Elbasani, where she is remembered to this day as *anglezka*, 'the little Englishwoman'.

The 'Englishwoman' was born in northeast Scotland in 1885, the daughter of a farmer, John Hardie. Despite her humble origins, she went on to study classics at Aberdeen, one of Scotland's four ancient universities, which had opened its faculties to women in 1892. She graduated from Aberdeen in 1907 and went south, to continue her studies at Cambridge University, where (it should be recalled) women were not awarded degree titles until 1921.

This remarkable young woman then turned her attention to archaeology. She studied at the prestigious British School in Athens (known as the BSA) and took part in excavations in Turkey. In 1912, she married Frederick Hasluck, whom she had met at the BSA.

Their married life would be short, however; Frederick Hasluck died of TB in 1920. He had published research on the followers of Bektashism (see pages 22–3), and his widow used a travel grant from Aberdeen University to return to Albania and conduct her own ethnographic fieldwork there. She became an expert on the customs and traditions of the northern clans – her comprehensive study of blood feud, *The Unwritten Law in Albania*, was published posthumously; she learned the language well enough to publish *Këndime anglisht-shqip*, a collection of stories which illustrate points of Albanian grammar and vocabulary; and she conducted extensive field research in the mountain villages around Elbasani, where she became friendly with Lef Nosi, an Elbasani intellectual and politician. Over the years, they worked together investigating Albanian folklore and ethnography. In 1936, she had a house built on a plot of land which Nosi sold to her.

In April 1939, just before Italy invaded and annexed Albania, Margaret Hasluck was expelled from the country. She ended up in Cairo where, in early 1942, SOE (see boxes, pages 13–15) recruited her to explore possible ways to encourage resistance the middle of the 14th century until the Ottoman conquest (see pages 10–11). The church itself is set in a peaceful garden, with the monastic buildings to the side. They are attractive buildings, but the church has been completely restored internally, apart from a large fresco which survives in poor condition behind the altar. It is known locally (for example, by taxi drivers) as Kisha e Shijonit, the Church of Shijoni.

The best-preserved piece of Elbasani's Roman heritage is **Mansio ad Quintum**, a few minutes' drive out of town. The original trading post which grew up at the junction of the Apollonia and Dyrrachium branches of the Via Egnatia (see page 8) developed over the years into something much more substantial – an official roadhouse, or *mansio*. Every major Roman road had these; they were intended to provide accommodation and entertainment for government officials and others travelling on important business. Mansio ad Quintum had a bathhouse (how could it not?) and shops as well as accommodation; the baths' hypocausts are particularly impressive. The site is up a track just off the main road towards Durrësi, near the village of Bradasheshi. It is unattended and can be accessed at any time.

Llixhat, the Albanian word for 'spa', is an area of thermal springs about 12km from Elbasani. Over the last decade or so, several new hotels have opened there, but the

in occupied Albania. By 1943, she was the head of SOE's Albanian section. She briefed SOE operatives before they were parachuted into Albania, taught them the rudiments of the language, and provided and collated intelligence.

As SOE came to concentrate on supporting the partisans, at the expense of the non-communist resistance, Margaret Hasluck became increasingly disillusioned. She resigned from SOE in 1944, around the same time as she was diagnosed with leukaemia and told she had only a short time left to live. She was awarded the MBE for her services in 1944.

Meanwhile, Lef Nosi had agreed to participate in the Council of Regency, the Albanian quisling government set up by the Germans after Italy's capitulation. After Albania's liberation, not surprisingly, he was tried and shot. Margaret Hasluck wrote a personal letter to Enver Hoxha, pleading for clemency for her friend. Not only was her appeal unsuccessful, but the communist government put it about that she and Nosi had been lovers, in an attempt to destroy both of their reputations.

Margaret Hasluck died of her leukaemia in October 1948, and is buried with her parents, brothers and sisters in the churchyard of the Moray village of Dallas. Her published works are difficult to obtain – *The Unwritten Law in Albania* was last issued in 1981 by Hyperion Press – although the National Library in Tirana holds copies of some of them. The Marischal Museum at her *alma mater*, Aberdeen University, holds many of the ethnographic artefacts which she sent back there from Albania (the catalogue can be viewed online through the website of the University Museums in Scotland, www.umis.ac.uk). These include unusual items such as medicinal minerals and herbs, amulets and children's toys.

Her house in Elbasani, built on the land she bought from Lef Nosi, is now a state kindergarten; next door, also on her land, is a children's home which is partly funded by a British charity (see page 56 for details of how to support its work). In 2010, a plaque was placed on the wall outside the orphanage to commemorate the 125th anniversary of Margaret Hasluck's birth. A statue of her friend Lef Nosi now stands in front of the castle walls on the city's main street.

very first was **Park Nosi Spa Resort** (*Stacioni Termal Park Nosi; 78 rooms;* \ *04 235 687;* m *068 20 66 546; www.llixhat.com;* $), built in 1932, to an Austrian design, by Lef Nosi's brother Grigor. This lovely historic building requires major investment to bring the accommodation up to international standards, but the quality of the waters has been undisputed since they were first analysed scientifically in 1924. See box, page 152, for more information about this and other thermal baths in Albania. The spa has immersion pools and mud-baths in which clients are treated for a range of ailments, supervised by specialist doctors. The surrounding grounds – over 50,000m² – are partly wooded and partly laid out as gardens. There are eight en-suite rooms; others share toilets and showers on each corridor. Park Nosi is about 30 minutes' drive from Elbasani, following the road towards Gramshi. 'LLixha' buses operate from the bus stop just beyond the market in Elbasani.

Just over halfway between Elbasani and Librazhdi, near the village of Miraka, an attractive **Ottoman bridge** crosses the Shkumbini River. The structure is Ottoman, but there has been a bridge here since at least Roman times – this is the route of the Via Egnatia, which connected the Adriatic coast with Constantinople. The Biçaku restaurant ($$) in Librazhdi, with its terrace overlooking the river, is a pleasant spot for a drink or for lunch.

Two nice places for **day hikes** around Elbasani are Lake Banja, an artificial lake created in the 1980s for hydro-electric power generation, but never used; and the gently rolling hills around the (natural) lakes of Belshi, both about half an hour's drive away. There is no public transport to Lake Banja. Local minibuses to Belshi leave from near the town hall. If you have your own transport (with two or four wheels), it is possible to continue on the same road as far as Kuçova, in Berati region. The drive from Elbasani to Kuçova takes about two hours, the second half on a rough road for which a 4x4 would probably be needed in wet weather.

BERATI *Telephone code: 032*

Berati is one of the oldest cities in Albania and one of the most attractive; the view of its white houses climbing up the hillside to the citadel is one of the best-known images of Albania. The citadel walls themselves encircle the whole of the top of the hill. Within them are eight medieval churches, one of which houses an outstanding collection of icons painted by the 16th-century master Onufri. Berati also has an excellent Ethnographic Museum and several other interesting buildings, including two of the oldest mosques in Albania. Thanks to their historical value, the religious buildings in the citadel were protected from the worst ravages of the atheism campaign (see pages 16–17), and in 1976 the government designated Berati as a 'museum city', which saved the town centre from communist urban planning.

Berati has been inhabited since the Bronze Age, over 4,000 years ago. The great Tomorr Massif, which rises behind it, was a sacred mountain from very early times and it still hosts a huge Bektashi festival every August. The first traces of building on the citadel date from the second half of the 4th century BC, when the Illyrian Parthini controlled the area.

Berati thrived in the Middle Ages, thanks to its strategic location at the point where the trading routes from the south met the lowland plain. This made it an appetising conquest for successive invaders. The Bulgarian Empire took the city in AD860 and held it – barring a 40-year period during which it was reconquered by Byzantium – until 1018. Berati's second return to the Byzantine fold lasted longer, despite a determined attack by the Angevins, who besieged the citadel for seven months in 1280–81. By the mid-14th century, however, as Byzantium's power waned, Berati and much of the rest of Albania became part of Stefan Dušan's 'Empire of the Serbs and the Greeks'. (For more background to this confusing period in Albania's history, see page 10.)

After Stefan Dušan's death in 1355, the whole of what is now southeast Albania, reaching as far as Kastoria (now in northern Greece) came under the control of the Muzakaj family of Berati, one of the powerful Albanian clans which emerged as the only functioning authorities in the period before the Ottoman conquest. The citadel of Berati fell to the Ottomans in 1417 and, despite an attempt to retake it, led by Skanderbeg (see box, pages 200–1) in 1455, it remained in their hands for nearly 500 years. The mountains of the Berati region were a hotbed of partisan activity during World War II, and the city was the first seat of the Interim Government which came to power in October 1944, under the leadership of Enver Hoxha (see box, page 83).

The name of the city may come from the Turkish word *berat*, meaning an order conferring a decoration, a sort of royal warrant; or it might derive from 'Beligrad', the name the Slavs gave the town, although there is debate about whether this is philologically possible. Berati won recognition as a UNESCO World Heritage Site in July 2008.

GETTING THERE AND AWAY Berati is easy to get to from almost everywhere in central and southern Albania, having good **bus** connections with Vlora, Durrësi and Elbasani as well as Tirana. However, the condition of the road has been deteriorating for several years and at the time of writing at least three hours should be allowed for the journey from Tirana. A new road bridge, on the western outskirts of the city, now takes most traffic across the Osumi River, effectively replacing the narrow Gorica Bridge.

The buses from **Tirana** leave every 45 minutes, from 04.30 until about 14.30, from Kombinati, in the western outskirts of the city; urban buses go there from Skanderbeg Square. The journey takes about two hours and the fare is 300 lek. When minibuses are running, they leave from Sheshi Qemal Ataturk (known universally by its communist-era name of 21 Dhjetori); this is on the Unaza city bus route. In Berati, the buses terminate a kilometre or so before the city centre. There are local buses and taxis there to take passengers into town.

By bike or on foot, there are several interesting routes to and from Berati. See pages 127–8 for details.

TOUR OPERATORS The Castle Park Hotel just outside Berati (see listing below) offers **rafting** weekends (April to June) through the spectacular canyons on the Osumi River, with two nights' accommodation and a full day on the river. The hotel also organises excursions to places of interest in the Berati area, including the castle and the Çobo vineyard (*www.cobowineryonline.com*).

The Tirana-based company Outdoor Albania has qualified and experienced guides for **rafting** and, in summer, **river-hiking** trips; see page 31 for contact information. Outdoor Albania can also organise hiking, ski touring and climbing expeditions in the Tomorri Massif.

WHERE TO STAY Map, pages 120–1, unless otherwise indicated.
Reservations in several of the hotels listed below can be made online through the Tirana-based Albania Holidays (*www.albania-hotel.com*), or the usual international booking websites.

4

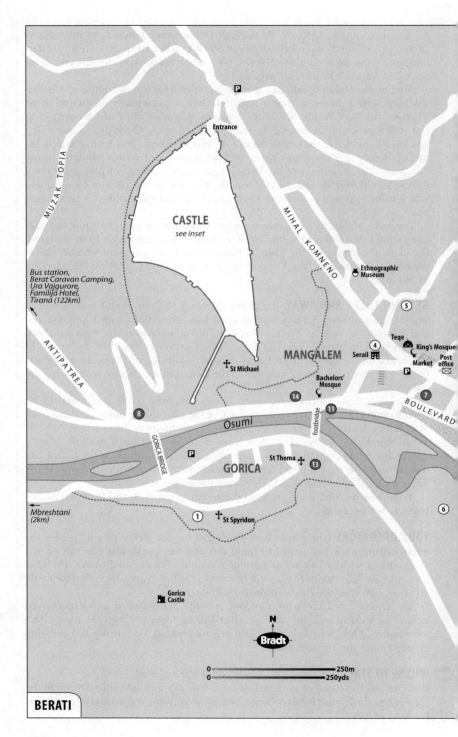

BERATI

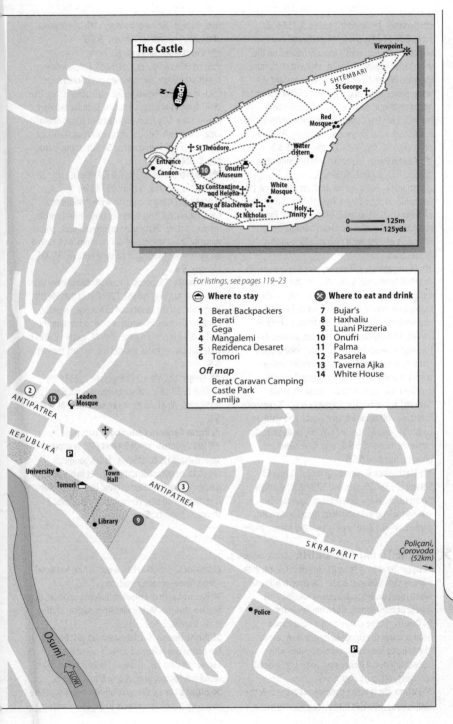

The Castle

J SHTËMBARI

Viewpoint

St George

Red Mosque

St Theodore

Water cistern

Entrance
Cannon

Onufri Museum

10

White Mosque

Sts Constantine and Helena

St Mary of Blachernae

St Nicholas

Holy Trinity

| 0 | 125m |
| 0 | 125yds |

For listings, see pages 119–23

🏠 Where to stay
1 Berat Backpackers
2 Berati
3 Gega
4 Mangalemi
5 Rezidenca Desaret
6 Tomori

Off map
Berat Caravan Camping
Castle Park
Familja

✕ Where to eat and drink
7 Bujar's
8 Haxhaliu
9 Luani Pizzeria
10 Onufri
11 Palma
12 Pasarela
13 Taverna Ajka
14 White House

② ANTIPATREA

⑫ Leaden Mosque

REPUBLIKA

P

University

Tomori

Town Hall

ANTIPATREA

③

Library ⑨

SKRAPARIT

Poliçani, Çorovoda (52km)

Police

P

Osumi

FLOW

⌂ **Tomori** (47 rooms, 3 suites) ☏234 462; m 068 20 24 225; e info@hoteltomori.com; www.hoteltomori.com. Centrally located on the town's main square. Friendly, efficient staff, some English-speaking. Lift to all floors; constant hot water & electricity in guest rooms. Good restaurant on ground floor; pizzeria on roof terrace with magnificent views; popular bar, with tables outside in summer, ideal for people-watching. All rooms en suite, with AC, CH, Wi-Fi, TV, phone. **$$$$**

⌂ **Castle Park** (8 rooms) Rr e Drobonikut; ☏f 235 385; m 067 20 06 623; e castlepark_2003@yahoo.it. On the left bank (the Gorica side) of the Osumi River, 1.3km (uphill) out of town; shuttle bus available for guests. Excellent restaurant with splendid views from the terrace. All rooms en suite with AC, cable TV, balcony, fridge. **$$$**

⌂ **Mangalemi** (20 rooms, plus 6 in annexe) Rr Mihal Komneno; ☏232 093; m 068 23 23 238; e hotel_mangalemi@yahoo.com; www. mangalemihotel.com. Named for its location & also known as Tomi's, after the friendly, helpful owner. A family-run hotel now spread over 2 traditional Berati houses; English spoken. Good restaurant with traditional specialities such as lamb's liver & homemade sausages; bar with excellent selection of rakis. Çardak (covered balcony) & roof terrace; laundry service & generous b/fast inc. All rooms en suite (some also with bathtub), with AC, cable TV, Wi-Fi, desk, safe; 'superior' rooms (**$$$$**) also have hairdryer, phone & minibar. **$$$**

⌂ **Rezidenca Desaret** (5 rooms) Lagja 13 Shtatori; ☏237 593; m 069 30 37 480; e info@ desaret.com; www.desaret.com. Spectacular setting high up in Mangalemi; good restaurant; garden; Wi-Fi. Large, well-appointed rooms, all en suite with AC, TV; large balcony with lovely views of the city towards Mt Tomorri. **$$$**

⌂ **Berat Backpackers** (22 beds) Gorica 295; m 069 78 54 219, 069 30 64 429; e info@ beratbackpackers.com; www.beratbackpackers. com. Traditional Berati house with garden, bar, free Wi-Fi & internet access, kitchen, laundry facilities, movie room. Day tours organised to surrounding area. 3 dorms & 1 dbl, sharing bathroom facilities; camping possible in garden (**$**). B/fast inc. Dorm bed **$**, dbl **$$**

⌂ **Berati** (9 rooms) Rr Veli Zaloshnja, Lagja 28 Nëntori; ☏236 953; m 069 20 74 199; e hotel_berati@yahoo.com; www.hotelberati. com. Traditional Berati house, modernised within; internet access. Restaurant on ground floor, plus more intimate traditional dining room. Dbl, twin & 4-bed rooms upstairs, all en suite with AC, TV, CH, balcony. **$$**

⌂ **Familja** (5 rooms, 1 suite) Rr Kombëtare Ura Vajgurore-Kuçova; ☏0361 22474. Just outside Ura Vajgurore, off the main road to Kuçova. Friendly, English-speaking management; good restaurant, parking. All rooms en suite with AC, cable TV, Wi-Fi; suite has corner bath, smaller rooms only shower. **$$**

⌂ **Gega** (22 rooms) Rr Kryesore; ☏234 429; m 069 20 87 181; www.hotelgega.com. Bar, restaurant, Wi-Fi. All rooms en suite with AC, TV. **$$**

⋏ **Berat Caravan Camping** [map, page 89] Ura Vajgurore; m 069 42 63 697; e info@ sarandaholidays.com; https://sites.google. com/site/beratcaravancamping. Set in beautiful garden; 12km from Berat, good bus service; bar & restaurant on site; Wi-Fi; laundry facilities; 2 showers, 2 toilets. **$**

✖ WHERE TO EAT AND DRINK *Map, pages 120–1.*

✖ **Ajka** Next to St Thoma's Church in Gorica, with a lovely view of Berati across the river. Traditional Berati meat dishes such as steak stuffed with cheese or mushrooms. Open fire in winter. **$$$**

✖ **Onufri** In the castle, on the right as you head towards the Onufri Museum. Basic menu of escalopes & so forth, supplemented with occasional special dishes such as turkey (a Berati speciality) & lamb's liver. **$$$**

✖ **Palma** Next to the pedestrian bridge over the Osumi River. Good for traditional Albanian meat dishes such as shish kebab & *qofta*. Also has hotel rooms (*www.brpalmahotel.com*). **$$$**

✖ **Pasarela** In the modern building opposite the Leaden Mosque. Meat specialities such as stuffed steak & *qofta*. **$$$**

✖ **White House** On the main road, just beyond the pedestrian bridge on the way out of Berati. Excellent Italian-based menu, the best fish in town, wood-fired pizzas, good risotto & pasta. **$$$**

✖ **Bujar's** In an alleyway off the street opposite the market which connects Rr Kryesore with the

Boulevard; ☺ lunchtime only. Very keenly priced traditional dishes such as *tavë kosi* & *turli* (see page 49). **$$**

✖ **Haxhaliu** Just beyond the Gorica Bridge on the way out of Berati. The entrance is up the stairs around the corner of the building. Friendly service,

good traditional meat dishes such as stuffed steak. **$$**

✖ **Luani Pizzeria** Rr A Qafoku, just beyond the football pitch next to the Children's Cultural Centre. Good pizzas, cold beer. **$$**

WHAT TO SEE AND DO

The castle The citadel of Berati was first fortified in the 4th century BC by the Illyrian Parthini. At the same time, they also fortified the hill opposite, on the left bank of the River Osumi; the remains of the massive walls there, known as Gorica Castle, can still be seen. The pair of fortresses ensured that the whole river valley could be controlled and defended.

To get to Berati Castle on foot, the easiest way is to walk up Rruga Mihal Komneno (also known as Rruga e Kalasë, 'Castle Street') – the steep cobbled road through Mangalemi, one of the city's protected 'museum zones'. It is also possible to drive this way, although an easier driving route leaves the main road just where it enters Berati from the north and curls around the back of the castle hill; it is signposted in Albanian and English for 'Kala, Castle'. Cars can be parked just outside the outer entrance gate. There are short cuts up the winding stone staircases through Mangalemi, and then through the trees below the citadel, but it is difficult to find the way without a guide.

On the wall by the archway, which forms the outer entrance to the castle, a cross can be seen with the initials MK. This probably dates from a refortification of the citadel undertaken in the 13th century, during the reign of Michael II Comnenus Ducas, Despot of Epirus (see page 9). Next to the vaulted inner entrance is a kiosk at which an admission charge of 100 lek is payable. Audio guides to the castle, in several languages including English, are available at this kiosk. Like Kruja Castle (see pages 101–3), this citadel is still inhabited – by several hundred people. The walls follow the contour of the hilltop in a rough triangle and a network of narrow cobbled streets connects the stone-built houses within them. The huge bust of Constantine the Great (AD306–37) near the entrance was installed in 2003, on the curious grounds that he was one of the Illyrian emperors (even though he was from Niš, hundreds of miles from Berati in what is now Serbia).

Of the 42 churches which the castle walls once contained, only eight remain and, with one exception, they were locked up after the atheism campaign of the late 1960s. The exception was the Church of the Dormition of St Mary (Kisha e Fjetjes së Shënmërisë), a three-naved basilica which was built in 1797 on the foundations of a 10th-century church and which now houses the **Onufri Museum** (☺ *09.00–16.00 Tue–Sat, 09.00–14.00 Sun; 200 lek, inc information leaflet & guided tour, in English*), signposted from the inner entrance to the castle.

Onufri was the greatest of a group of Albanian icon-painters – many of them anonymous – of the 16th century. He worked throughout the Balkans, but many of his finest icons were painted for the churches of the Berati citadel. Onufri followed and developed the Byzantine traditions of icon-painting, but his work is special because of his mastery of colour; the red paint he used has the technical name of 'Onufri red'. As well as icons by Onufri, the museum in Berati has a valuable collection of work by other Albanian icon-painters and by the craftsmen who created silver and gold Bible-covers and chalices for use in the citadel's churches.

The guided tour, which lasts about an hour, usually begins in the *naos*, the main section of the church. The ornate iconostasis (altar screen) at the far end was carved in walnut wood and decorated with gold leaf by master craftsmen from the Berati school. The three main icons were the work of Onufri and placed in the church at the time it was built; others were done in the mid-19th century by the Korçan artist Joan Katro (see page 134). The two manuscripts known as the *Codices of Berat* were discovered in 1968, buried behind the altar – the 6th-century *Purple Codex* is one of the oldest such manuscripts ever found, anywhere – and are now conserved in the State Archive in Tirana.

In the galleries around the naos are icons from churches in Berati and the surrounding area, painted by Onufri, his son Nikola and other masters. There are also examples of the beautiful work of Berati's silver- and goldsmiths, including a wrought-metal icon by the 20th-century Berati master Agathangjel Mbrica. Some of the icons combine traditional Byzantine iconography with Ottoman images – a round table, like the *sofra* which can be seen in the Ethnographic Museum, in an icon of the Last Supper (anonymous, 18th century), and the minarets of mosques peeking above the city walls in the icon called 'The Life-Giving Source'. An icon by the 19th-century artist Kristo depicts the city of Berati, complete with the Osumi River, the Gorica Bridge and the two left-bank churches (see page 126).

The Church of St Theodore (Shën Todri) has some surviving frescoes by Onufri. Other masterpieces of Albanian religious art can be seen in the National Historical Museum in Tirana (see pages 75–7) and in the National Museum of Medieval Art in Korça (see pages 133–4)

A walk around the perimeter walls to the **viewpoint** will give you a feel for the size and layout of the castle, as well as giving you great views of the city below and the mountains across the river. The 13th-century **Church of St Michael** nestles into the hill below and can be seen to good effect from the Gorica quarter across the river. A path leads up to this church from the main road, but it is usually locked. Above the viewpoint, just within the walls, is the **Church of St George** (Shën Gjergji, 14th century), which was converted into a restaurant during the communist period but has now been restored by the local people. **St Mary of Blachernae** (Shën Mëri Vllaherna) is the oldest church in the castle; local tradition holds that this church was built to celebrate the defeat of the Angevin besiegers in 1281. It was rebuilt in 1578, as the inscription about the narthex door reveals, and its frescoes were painted by Nikola, Onufri's son.

Almost as old is the beautiful **Holy Trinity** (Shën Triadha), which stands on the slope of the hill just below the inner fortification of the castle (the English text on the information board refers to this, a little confusingly, as the 'citadel'). This part of the castle was built at roughly the same time as the church, in the 13th century. Up in the corner near the entrance is an underground water cistern, dug deep into the rock on which the castle stands, and supported with brick columns and elegant arches. In the 1930s, the Italians adopted a different approach to ensuring the citadel's water supply; they piped spring water across country from Mount Shpiragu (the 'striped' mountain which faces Mount Tomorri to the west). Sections of the piping can still be seen in the area around the cistern. Information panels have been installed outside each of the churches and at some other points around the castle.

Berati fell to the Ottomans in 1417 and the conquerors wasted no time in refortifying the citadel. They also built two mosques there, the Red and White mosques. Both date from the 15th century and are among the oldest in Albania. The **White Mosque**, so called because of the beautiful white stone of which it was built, stands at the corner of the inner fortification opposite the water cistern. The **Red Mosque** lies just outside this area; it was badly damaged by German bombs during World War II and there are plans to restore it, using early 20th-century photographs as reference.

Set into an archway in the outer walls, above the first entrance gate, is a **cannon** which bears the date 1684 and which local tradition claims is English. In fact it may well have been made by the British gun founder Thomas Western (1624–1707). Western carried out contract work for export to the Republic of Venice in 1684; some of his Venetian mortars are in Corfu and one is displayed in the Tower of London. The cannon in Berati is probably a large saker, a widely used gun which fired a cast-iron solid shot of 6–9lb. The emblem engraved on it seems to be the Lion of St Mark, the symbol of the Venetian Republic. The saker may have been captured in battle from Venice (which briefly occupied nearby Vlora in 1690–91), or simply acquired through trade. (I am grateful for this information to Nicholas Hall of the Royal Armouries.)

The town Just off Rruga Mihal Komneno is a beautiful traditional house, built in the late 18th century and inhabited until it was turned into the **Ethnographic Museum** (⊕ *winter 09.00–16.00 Tue–Sat; summer 09.00–13.00 & 16.00–19.00 Tue–Sat, 09.00–14.00 Sun; 200 lek, covers a guided tour, in English*). A visit to the museum is an excellent opportunity to learn about Berati architecture and find out more about people's way of life until only a few decades ago.

Like traditional houses elsewhere in Albania, the ground floor was not used for living in, but for storage and household activities such as pressing olive oil or distilling raki. Part of the ground floor has been converted to represent a medieval bazaar, with examples of traditional costumes and displays about the crafts traditionally practised in Berati, such as metalwork. The first floor, where the family lived, is accessed by an external stone staircase which leads to the *çardak* – a vast covered balcony on which they would have spent most of their time in the hot summer months. Rooms lead off from the *çardak*, furnished with items which the inhabitants would have used in their day-to-day lives, such as looms for wool and silk, cooking utensils and dinner services. Two of the rooms have a *mafil*, a screened gallery in which the women of the household sat while their menfolk ate and drank in the room below; visitors to the museum can climb up the steep wooden steps to the women's gallery in the *oda e miqve*, the guests' room. In the centre of this room is a beautiful dinner service of engraved copper, set out on a metal *sofra* – a low, circular table around which the diners sat on the carpeted floor.

Berati's historic mosques are located fairly close together near the modern town centre. The **Bachelors' Mosque** (Xhamia e Beqarëve), on the main boulevard, was built in 1827 for the use of the city's (unmarried) shop assistants, and its external walls are beautifully decorated with wall paintings. The **Leaden Mosque** (Xhamia e Plumbit), so called from the covering of its dome, dates from 1555. The oldest of the three – and one of the oldest mosques in Albania – is the **King's Mosque** (Xhamia e Mbretit), behind the market at the foot of Rruga Mihal Komneno, the street up to the castle. It has a beautifully carved and painted wooden ceiling, and a large women's gallery. It is possible to see inside the mosque immediately after prayer times; at other times it is usually locked.

The two-storey building with the arched porch across the courtyard from the King's Mosque was a *teqe* of the Sufi order of the Khalwati (or Halveti). It has a beautifully painted ceiling surrounded with frescoes, stained-glass windows and painted wall-cupboards. The inscription above the door reveals that the teqe's construction was funded by Ahmed Kurt Pasha, who governed Berati and much of the rest of central Albania in the second half of the 18th century (see box, page 193 for more about the Albanian *pashaliks*). It is thought that he was buried in a now-empty grave behind the *mihrab*. Ahmed Kurt Pasha was also responsible for building the Gorica Bridge (see below) and the governor's palace (Serail) on the other side of Rruga Mihal Komneno. There are informative and helpful panels, in English and Albanian, next to the various historic buildings around the town.

Three neighbourhoods of Berati are designated as 'museum zones', with restrictions on the alterations which may be made to the properties in them. Mangalemi and Kalaja (the castle) are two; the third, Gorica, lies on the other side of the Osumi River. The two sides of the town are connected by the **Gorica Bridge**, a narrow stone bridge built in the 18th century to replace the wooden bridge which had been used until then. To get to the Illyrian fortifications known as Gorica Castle, turn right over the Gorica Bridge and then head left up the hillside until you reach the top.

After the Ottoman conquest, Gorica became the Christian quarter. The churches shown in the 1873 icon in the Onufri Museum are dedicated to St Spyridon and St Thoma. **St Spyridon's** is the larger of the two; it can be a little tricky to find, up the narrow paths into the heart of Gorica. The little **Church of St Thoma**, tucked into a corner of the cliff at the eastern end of Gorica, has a shrine behind it where a local saint is said to have left his footprint in the rock. A modern footbridge leads from opposite the Bachelors' Mosque to just below St Thoma's church. This is also the best end of Gorica from which to see the citadel and the houses of Mangalemi below it.

Those who are interested in Byzantine religious architecture might also visit the 12th-century church in the nearby village of **Perondia**. It is usually kept locked, but it is sometimes possible to gain entry by asking around in the village for the key-holder. The carved wooden iconostasis dates from 1786; a small amount of badly damaged fresco survives on the walls. The icon of The Birth of St Mary in the Onufri Museum came from this church. Perondia and its church are about 15km from Berati, signposted to the right, off the road to Kuçova from Ura Vajgurore.

The mountains Mount Tomorri is a long, complex massif, most of it over 2,000m high. It runs roughly north–south to Çorovoda from Lake Banja south of Elbasani, with its highest peak, Çuka e Partizanit (2,414m), pretty much halfway along it. An easy way to see some of the spectacular mountain scenery of the Berati area is by taking the good, asphalted road (about 50km) down to Çorovoda, the district capital of Skrapari. Buses leave Berati for Çorovoda at 08.20, 09.00 and 11.00 and take about 1½ hours each way; they are supplemented by minibuses which leave from beside the Tomorri Hotel.

About half an hour down the road is the little town of Poliçani, one of communist Albania's main arms production centres. The huge factory complex on the valley floor once employed 4,500 people; now the factory lies almost idle, with the only work being the production of ammunition for the Albanian police and other clients. The main source of employment in the area nowadays is the quarrying and preparation for export of the decorative stone tiles which you will see stacked by the roadsides as you drive through the area. After Poliçani, the river valley narrows and the mountains become even more dramatic. The buses from Berati stop in Çorovoda, an uninspiring modern town, but the transport hub for trips out to the stunning scenery which surrounds it. Bus services operate from Çorovoda to all the main villages (*komuna*) in the district of Skrapari, of which it is the administrative centre, and taxis can be hired in the main square. It has reasonable hotels and restaurants; there is an ATM below the Turizmi Hotel.

A couple of kilometres out of Çorovoda, along the Gjerbësi road, is a lovely little Ottoman bridge over the Çorovoda River. Once this linked trans-continental trade routes; now it's in the middle of nowhere. The village of Gjerbësi is high up on the northeastern flank of Mount Tomorri; the road to it is rough, reaching 1,200m above sea level at one point, but the scenery is spectacular, with beautiful cliffs which give way to strangely coloured mountains of an almost lunar barrenness. There are cafés in Gjerbësi which can arrange meals, given some notice.

This road continues up Mount Tomorri as far as the Kulmaka *teqe*, where the Bektashi saint **Abaz Aliu** is buried. This is said to be the oldest teqe in Albania and is one of the holiest sites of Bektashism (see pages 22–3), the focal point of a great pilgrimage every August. The scenery is wonderful, with little villages and farms clinging to the mountains on either side of the Tomorrica River. A 4x4 is needed to reach the teqe; from Çorovoda, you should allow at least four hours there and back.

The **Osumi Canyons** are several kilometres of stunning multicoloured cliffs, which drop down to the fast-flowing Osumi River below. Rafting excursions to the canyons can be arranged at the right times of year; see *Tour operators*, page 119. The Osumi Canyons are 20 minutes' drive along the road to Çepani; there is a lovely picnic spot at the top of the cliffs.

Where to stay and eat
⌂ **Osumi** (6 rooms) Main square, Çorovoda; ☎0312 22220. Generator, restaurant. All rooms en suite with TV; 2 twins have balcony overlooking the river & mountains; 2 en-suite family rooms each with 1 dbl & 1 twin room. **$$**

⌂ **Turizmi** (17 rooms) Çorovoda; m 068 20 57 424, 068 40 10 042. Also known locally as 'ish-VEFA'. Constant water & electricity, large restaurant with terrace. Good-sized dbl bedrooms, slightly smaller twins, all en suite with small TV. **$$**

Walking, hiking and cycling Mount Tomorri offers magnificent hiking opportunities, but the seriousness of this mountain should not be underestimated. There are no neatly marked footpaths, no hiking maps and no mountain rescue service. Your hotel may be able to arrange a guide for you. Appropriate footwear and clothing are essential, and you should be in reasonable physical shape. Do not assume that you will have a mobile phone signal and leave a note of your planned route with someone – perhaps the management of your hotel.

A less intimidating option is to head towards Mount Shpiragu on the left bank of the Osumi River. A minor road leads more or less westwards through Gorica, then starts to climb past some destroyed barracks and other military buildings, with tunnels into the hillside visible on the other side of a small river. After an hour or so you reach a pretty reservoir, just before the village of Mbreshtani, which is a nice spot for a picnic. An alternative walk is to the village of Droboniku, a couple of kilometres up past the Castle Park Hotel; this is especially nice in springtime when the cherry trees are in blossom.

If you have your own 4x4 or two-wheeled transport, you could approach or leave Çorovoda using the ancient trading route along the Tomorrica River, between the Tomorri and Kosnica ranges. This route connects with the town of Gramshi, at the southern end of Lake Banja (see page 118). It is only passable in dry summer weather, since it follows the river, crossing and recrossing it, and there are no bridges between Gjerbësi and Gramshi. It is important to be well equipped on this route, since there is almost no habitation and there will certainly be no other traffic. It takes the villagers about six hours to walk from the Gjerbësi Bridge to Gramshi. From Gramshi you could continue north to Elbasani, or you could head for Macedonia or northern Greece along the Devolli River. See page 140 for information about that route.

With good bikes, or on foot, another route out of Berati via Çorovoda takes you to the district of Përmeti, continuing south on the Çepani road and then on to Frashëri (see pages 152–3), or to Këlcyra via Prishta; it is about 40km from Çorovoda to Përmeti as the crow flies. Another possibility, on foot only, is to cross the Ostrovica mountain range from Çorovoda to Vithkuqi or Voskopoja, in the district of Korça. The road is reasonable as far as the village of Potomi, in Skrapari district. A minibus operates between Çorovoda and Backa (check times locally). From Backa a path leads east-northeast to Çemerica; the track to Vithkuqi goes off to the east there. For Voskopoja, continue through Marjani, a beautiful stone village, to Gjergjavica. From there it is an easy walk to Voskopoja (thanks to John Shipton for his route notes). Two days should be allowed for this hike. See the rough map at the start of the next chapter for guidance on these routes.

The Italian-built road over the 900m-high Gllava Pass to Këlcyra is, at the time of writing, impassable for any but the most rugged of 4x4 vehicles. It is fine as far as Tërpani on the Berati side and Ballabani on the Këlcyra side; the problem is the pass, where lack of maintenance has caused the road to deteriorate in recent years.

The Southeast

KORÇA   *Telephone code: 082*

Southeastern Albania is a fascinating and little-explored corner of the country, with dozens of medieval churches, a wealth of prehistoric sites, the wild Gramoz mountain range and the beautiful Ohrid and Prespa lakes. Korça, the regional capital, is an ideal base from which to visit these attractions. It is also home to the National Museum of Medieval Art. The city itself is refreshingly civilised, with streets relatively free of the litter which disfigures most of the rest of the country, traffic which recognises the existence of some sort of highway code, and clean mountain air. Its altitude (850m above sea level) and inland position make it very cold in winter and spring, and delightfully cool in summer.

The people of Korça are justifiably proud of their town's cultured and tolerant traditions. It was one of the main centres of the Albanian cultural renaissance (*Rilindja Kombëtare*), which created the sense of national identity that ultimately led to the country's independence from the Ottoman Empire. The first Albanian-medium school was opened here in 1887, with the first girls' school following four years later, and the town was one of the focal points of the movement to standardise the Albanian alphabet. The building where the first school was opened is now a museum, with an interesting display of contemporary photographs and documents.

Korça's history became rather chequered in the early 20th century. The Epirote Insurrection of 1913 saw much of southern Albania raided and terrorised by Greek irredentists, who sought its incorporation into Greece. Korça was occupied and its Albanian-medium schools closed, until the Greek government ordered its troops home in June 1914. This respite was short-lived, however, and a year later a Greek army returned to occupy Korça and Berati, laying waste to Muslim villages and farmlands and driving streams of refugees across the country to Vlora. In the military confusion which overwhelmed Albania during World War I, Korça actually became an autonomous republic, under French military protection, between 1916 and 1918. Not surprisingly, this turbulent period saw a great deal of emigration, mainly to the USA, where Korçans still make up a large proportion of the Albanian-American community.

GETTING THERE AND AWAY   From northern **Greece**, several bus companies run up to Korça from Kastoria (called Kosturi in Albanian), 70km away. There are also buses from Thessalonica (Selaniku). If you have your own transport, the small crossing at Tre Urat (called Mertzani by the Greeks), between Konitsa in Greece and Leskoviku in Albania, will take you on to the beautiful mountain road up to Korça via Erseka.

From **Macedonia**, there are two main border crossings into Albania, one at Qafa e Thanë, southwest of Struga, and the other at Tushëmishti, at the southern end of

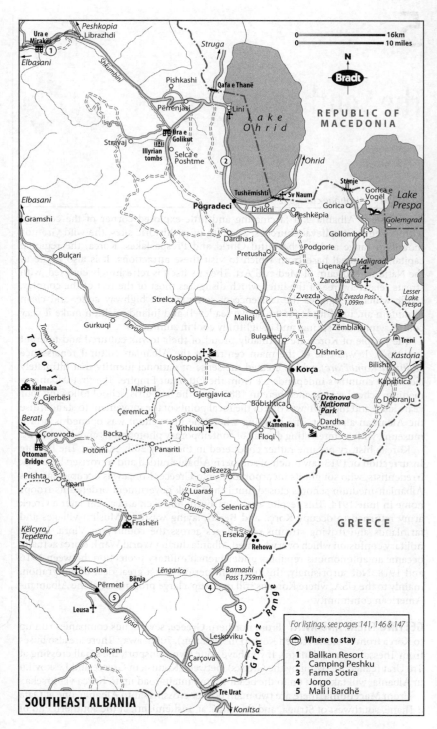

For listings, see pages 141, 146 & 147

🛏 **Where to stay**

1 Ballkan Resort
2 Camping Peshku
3 Farma Sotira
4 Jorgo
5 Mali i Bardhë

SOUTHEAST ALBANIA

Lake Ohrid. If you are travelling without your own transport via Qafa e Thanë, you will probably have to arrange for a Struga taxi to take you up to the border; during daylight there are always Albanian taxis and minibuses on the other side. See page 140 for information about crossing the border at Tushëmishti.

Within Albania, there are frequent buses to Korça from Tirana, running from early morning until early afternoon. They leave from the northern side of the Qemal Stafa Stadium (see map, page 69) and the journey takes about three hours; the fare is 600 lek. See pages 145–6 for the long but scenic route through the Gramoz Mountains and along the beautiful Vjosa River. Buses serving this route leave Gjirokastra at 07.00 every day except Sundays, and Përmeti at 07.00 every day.

For suggested routes on foot or by bike into the Korça area, see the *Walking, hiking and cycling* section at the end of the preceding chapter (pages 127–8) and the Pogradeci section (pages 139–44).

GETTING AROUND As so often in Albania, public transport to different towns leaves from completely different parts of Korça. Intercity services leave from Sheshi Korça, the junction formed by Rruga Midhi Kostani and Rruga Kiço Greco. The local bus station, for destinations such as Liqenasi and Voskopoja, but also for the bus to Gjirokastra via Erseka and Përmeti, is opposite the market. Minibuses to Erseka, however, leave from near the town hall. Taxi drivers are the only reliable guides to all the nuances of bus and minibus departures.

TOURIST INFORMATION The tourist information office (257 803; m 067 20 34 403; e info@visit-korca.com; www.visit-korca.com; 09.00–17.00 Mon–Fri, 09.00–13.00 Sat) is located just off the main square, at the start of Bulevardi Gjergj Kastrioti. Friendly, English-speaking staff can advise on where to stay and what to do, not only in the town of Korça but also in the rest of the Prefecture, which includes Pogradeci, Voskopoja, the Prespa Lakes and the Gramoz Mountains. The office stocks free maps and interesting brochures, and has further publications available for sale, as well as souvenirs made locally. Guided city tours and excursions can be arranged.

Maps of the town and the surrounding region are posted on information boards outside the Prefecture and the tourist information office.

WHERE TO STAY *Map, page 132.*

Regency (18 rooms) Rr Ismail Qemali 7; 243 868, (in USA) +516 520 5227; m 068 20 30 070; e RegencyAlb@aol.com; www. regencyalbania.com. Built & owned by Albanian-Americans originally from Korça; English spoken; professional service. Restaurant, bar, lift, Wi-Fi; conference rooms, private dining room, office facilities. All rooms en suite with AC, CH, cable TV, minibar & phone. **$$$$**

Behar Koçibelli (30 rooms) Main square; 243 532, 230 925; m 069 20 75 539; reservations through www.albania-hotel.com. Great location overlooking the main square. Some English spoken at reception; parking for clients. Lift; good restaurant with some Korça specialities (**$$**); Wi-Fi; fitness centre. All rooms en suite, with

shower screen & hairdryer (some also bathtub), AC, CH & cable TV. 3 luxury rooms (**$$$$$**) have jacuzzi & excellent shower. **$$$**

George (37 rooms) Rr e Mborjës; 243 794; m 069 20 83 112; e hotel.george@hotmail. com; www.hotelgeorge.info. 1.2km from town centre (walking distance, though uphill on the way back!), quiet & set in attractive grounds; terrace bar, formal restaurant & bar; Wi-Fi. All rooms en suite with CH, TV, bedside lights & phone; some have balcony with mountain views. **$$$**

Grand Palace (84 rooms) Main square; 243 168, 244 339; e grandhotelko@hotmail. com; www.grandhotelpalacekorca.com. Great location overlooking the main square. English spoken at reception; lift; good restaurant; Wi-Fi on

For listings, see pages 131–3

🛏 **Where to stay**
1 Behar Koçibelli
2 Grand
3 Regency

Off map
George
Kristal

✖ **Where to eat and drink**
4 Mësonjëtorja
5 Shtëpia Voskopojare
6 Taverna Vasili

Off map
Birra Korça

Kristal hotel,
Prespa (c 30km),
Kapshtica (37km)

Skënderbeu Stadium

Bunker   Skanderbeg

Pogradeci,
Tirana (180km)

I MAJI

DHIMITER DENASI

BVD GJERGJ KASTRIOTI

NUÇI GOGO

Minibuses

KONFERENCA E LABINOTIT

DHIMITËR RËMBECI

Kristal Hotel

MIDHI KOSTANI

LLAZI PULLUQI   K GAÇE

VANGJEL QAFEZEZI

BVD REPUBLIKA

SHËTITORJA FAN NOLI

VANGJEL E LLAZO PENDAVINJI

QEMAL STAFA

NOLI

GURI DOLANI

KONGRESI I LUSHNJËS

DHORI LUARASI

VETERANEVE   PANDI QELESHI

VANGJEL E LLAZO PENDAVINJI

RAQI QIRINXHI

4 SHKURTI

FAN NOLI

MBLEDHJA E BERATIT

Tourist
Information
Office

KRISTO GRABOCKA

QEMAL STAFA

29 NENTORI

FRASHËRI

NENTORI

Martyrs'
Cemetery (steps)

Buses

Albtelecom/
post office

KOÇO ÇAMCE

VASIL

TROMARA

DHJETORI

Hani i
Elbasanit

SH LIRIA   E DURHAM

MJEDA

N DODONA

KRISTOFORIDHI

E DVORANI KOSTURI

ABDYL

JOVAN VRETO

REPUBLIKA

Cinema

SOTIR GURRA

FAN NOLI

SOTIR GURRA

Voskopoja
(23km)

NDRE
ISMAIL
QEMALI

M MAME

BVD SHËN GJERGJI

10

S PECI

ELBASANI

PETRO NINI

LUARASI

XH DISHNICA

KONF E PEZËS

Museum of
Education

Vila
Themistokli

BVD

Prefecture

KRYEPISKOP
ANASTAS

National
Museum of
Medieval Art

ALQI KONDI

THIMI MITKO

Mirahori
Mosque

Erseka

Patriotic Warrior

Cathedral

SHPRESA PALLA

Naim
Frashëri

N FRASHËRI

V Mio
Museum

Archaeological
Museum

S LUARASI

Police

Town Hall

SOTIR POJANI

L REMBECI

G KOROVESHI

MIHAL GRAMENO

BAJRAM CURRI

28 NENTORI

SHËTITORJA FAN NOLI

G PEPA

6 DËSHMORËT

Radio Korça

P BOGDANI

AVNI RUSTEMI

0   500m
0   500yds

Bratko
Museum

Birra Korça,
George Hotel,
Mborja (1.7km)

28 NENTORI

N

Bradt

REXHEP TELHA

10 KORRIKU

BVD
PARTIZANI

TODI VOGLI

KORÇA

Boboshtica, Kamenica (8km),
Dardha (20km), Vithkuqi (26km), Erseka

Drenova

ground floor; parking for clients. All rooms en suite (some with bathtub), with CH, small TV, bedside light & direct-dial phone. **$$$**

⌂ **Kristal** (82 rooms) Rr Konferenca e Labinotit; ☎ 248 993; m 069 20 98 321, 068 58 88 555; e info@hotelkristal.al; www.hotelkristal.al. On the hillside above the town, the former Workers' Camp (Kampi i Punëtorëve) has been well modernised

& is comfortable. Wonderful views – city to the front & pine forest to the rear – & a long way from town centre but just about within walking distance for the fit & energetic. Large restaurant; parking. A range of room types, inc apts (**$$$$**), 1 dbl & 1 twin bedroom, living room with fireplace, bathroom. All rooms en suite. Standard dbl **$$**

✗ WHERE (AND WHAT) TO EAT *Map, opposite.*

Korça specialities include *kërnaca*, small cylindrical meatballs, and *lakror*, a sort of *byrek* or filo-pastry pie. A good place to try these traditional dishes is the village of Boboshtica, a few kilometres south of Korça – it is signposted at the turn-off from the main road to Erseka – and one of the places where Korça families go for lunch at weekends. Another is Dardha, in a lovely alpine setting (1,344m above sea level) and with a good hotel (*Hotel Dardha*; m *068 20 60 362; www.hoteldardha.com*; **$$$$**).

Apart from beer (Birra Korça) and wine, the Korça area is renowned for its speciality raki, distilled from mulberries (*mani*). **Mësonjëtorja**, next to the Museum of Education (its name means school – see page 135) has a pleasant atmosphere and a good range of different types of raki, including mulberry.

✗ **Shtëpia Voskopojare** Rr Gavril Pepa (near the cathedral); ☎ 242 784. Fairly formal restaurant in restored historic house, informal dining in garden. Italian & Albanian dishes, inc *kërnaca*; grilled veal & chicken dishes; salads, pasta & risotto; friendly service, although not English-speaking. **$$$**

✗ **Taverna Antoneta** Boboshtica; m 068 22 64 963. Lovely garden with tables set around a

fountain. Serves roast lamb & other traditional specialities, inc *lakror*. **$$$**

✗ **Taverna Vasili** Rr Kostandina Gaçe (near the stadium); m 069 21 48 583. Formal dining; interesting photographs of the town displayed in restaurant. Excellent local specialities, good service. **$$$**

WHAT TO SEE AND DO

National Museum of Medieval Art (*Muzeu Kombëtar i Artit Mesjetar; Rr Sotir Peçi;* m *069 32 75 022, 068 31 71 925;* ⊕ *08.30–14.00 & 17.00–19.00 Mon–Fri, 09.00– 12.00 & 17.00–19.00 Sat–Sun; 200 lek*) The Museum of Medieval Art has the largest collection of icons in Albania, with 7,500 objects spanning seven centuries. It also has a fine collection of other religious art, such as hammered silver Bible covers as well as crosses. The earliest works held here were painted by anonymous artists in the 13th and 14th centuries; they include a 13th-century icon of St Nicholas from one of the churches in Vithkuqi (see page 138), icons from the church on Maligrad Island in Lake Prespa (see pages 144–5), and the stunning icon of St Michael from St Mary's Church in Mborja (see pages 136–7).

In the 16th century, a school of artists began to emerge in Berati, a powerful diocese and an economic centre. The best known of the icon painters there was called Onufri; many of his works can be seen in the eponymous museum in Berati Castle (see pages 123–4), but some are displayed here. They include a set of Royal Doors (the main doors in the iconostasis, through which the priest enters) and several beautiful, complex icons which tell stories such as the Raising of Lazarus, the Baptism of Christ and the Transfiguration.

Starting from the middle of the 17th century, new iconographical themes and European Enlightenment influences gradually creep into Albanian iconography. An example of this is the *Akathistos Hymn* of the 18th-century artist Kostandin

Shpataraku, with its portrayal of the Western image of the Coronation of St Mary. Taking his inspiration from the other direction, Kostandin Jeromonaku (Constantine the Chief Monk), in his *Christ Pantocrator*, has Christ seated on a throne decorated with motifs from Islamic art.

Two icon-painting families dominated the 19th century: the Zografi brothers and their sons, and the Katro family. Kostandin and Athanas Zografi worked all over the Balkans and many of their frescoes have survived in the churches of Voskopoja (see pages 137–8). Their work shows clear Venetian influence, with careful brushwork and a more realistic portrayal of the human figure than had been seen before. Their sons worked with the family of Joan Katro (also known as Johannes Çetiri). Many beautiful Zografi and Katro icons are exhibited in the museum. These were the last artists of the old style of Albanian icon painting. Early 20th-century work, such as the icons on display from Dardha, saw a complete break with the post-Byzantine tradition.

The National Museum of Medieval Art is housed in what was once Korça's cathedral, built in the 1930s to replace the original cathedral (destroyed in an earthquake) and then, in the 1960s, shrouded in cement by the atheism campaigners (see pages 16–17). The iconostasis from the medieval cathedral was saved and can be seen in the new church next door, complete with some of its original Zografi icons which are good examples of the Korça School's realistic tendency. The iconostasis in the museum was taken from the Church of St Nicholas in Rehova. Most of the exhibits are labelled, and the museum has high-quality publications for sale about Albanian religious art.

Archaeological Museum *(Rr Mihal Grameno; ⊕ (in theory) 08.00–16.00 Mon–Fri, 08.00–14.00 Sat–Sun; 200 lek)* The items displayed in Korça's Archaeological Museum come from sites all over the southwest region, including the neighbouring districts of Devolli, Kolonja and Pogradeci. This area is a prehistorian's paradise, with many very large tumuli (raised barrows) excavated – one of these, Kamenica, is open to the public and has an excellent site museum (see pages 138–9). Although the most significant artefacts are displayed in the Archaeological Museum in Tirana, the curators of the Korça museum have created a very informative and useful exhibition in the traditional Korçan house which is their headquarters. Unfortunately, staffing problems have meant it is not usually open to the public except by prior arrangement.

The people in the Korça region traded with other cultures throughout most of their prehistory. Late Neolithic ceramics and other items from central Europe have been excavated, while Mycenaean weapons have been found in Bronze Age sites. In the Iron Age, imports began to appear from the Greek colonies to the west – Butrint, Apollonia and Dyrrachium – and it is in this period that it becomes possible to differentiate Illyrian culture from the neighbouring Hellenic and Thracian cultures.

The exhibition begins with a display of examples of the different types of tools used by Neolithic people, and the bones and horns of some of the animals they hunted or domesticated. The display proceeds chronologically and is enhanced by scale models: a barrow with concentric burials radiating out from the clan chief's grave; examples of the different shapes of lake-dwellings found at Maliqi, just north of Korça; and a fortified acropolis showing the multiple walls which reinforced its defences. There are photographs of the excavations which revealed these fascinating structures and uncovered the artefacts on display. The curators have assembled replica graves, in which they have arranged examples of grave goods just as they would have been placed 4,000 years ago.

The house in which the museum is located dates from the early 19th century, and is in two separate parts. The main building, where the museum's offices and workshops are, was the family residence, with the traditional covered balcony (*çardak*) on the first floor. The archaeological exhibition is in the *han i mysafirëve*, the guest quarters, where visitors to the family were received and accommodated. The Neolithic section is in what used to be a kind of drawing room, where weddings and other parties were held – the band used to play on the little stage behind the stairwell.

Museum of Education (*Bd Shën Gjergji;* ☉ *08.00–14.00 & 17.00–19.00 Mon–Fri, 09.00–12.00 & 17.00–19.00 Sat–Sun; small charge*) The very first school anywhere in which subjects were taught in the Albanian language opened in Korça on 7 March 1887. This was a triumph for the *Rilindja* campaigners who had focused on the language as the key to building an Albanian national consciousness. The *Rilindja's* polemicist, Sami Frashëri, wrote:

The sign of nationhood is language; every nation supports itself on its language. Those who forget their language, and leave it behind, and speak another tongue, in time become people of that other nation whose language they speak, and they abandon their own nationality.

The Korça school went through ups and downs over the years, getting closed down intermittently whenever the country's Ottoman rulers noticed its existence, but the movement it began proved unstoppable. A girls' school was opened in Korça in 1891 – the first girls' school in Albania of any kind, never mind the first to teach in Albanian – and teachers travelled around the country giving lessons in impromptu classrooms or even the open air. The first Albanian-medium teacher-training college (Shkolla Normale) opened in Elbasani in December 1909.

The Korça school is now a Museum of Education, with photographs of the first pupils and teachers of both the boys' and the girls' schools, and an interesting collection of early textbooks. None of the material is labelled in English, and your visit will be greatly enhanced if you can find someone to interpret for you. A room on the ground floor is set up as one of those first classrooms, with a blackboard and uncomfortable-looking benches. The upstairs section, an exhibition of facsimiles of letters from *Rilindja* leaders, together with rather faded photographs of these illustrious figures, is likely to be of interest only to those who are especially keen on Albanian history.

The Museum of Education is easily identifiable from the 'ABC' sculpture in its garden. If the building appears to be closed during opening hours, try rattling the gate.

Bratko Museum of Asian Art (*Bd Fan Noli;* **m** *069 21 56 561;* ☉ *10.00–13.00 & 17.00–18.00 daily; 100 lek, inc guided tour*) The most unexpected museum in Korça – perhaps in all of Albania – is the private collection of Oriental art donated to his home town by Dhimitër Borja, who made his fortune in the USA from film and photograph laboratories. The collection is housed in a purpose-built museum, an attractive modern building, on Fan Noli Boulevard just beyond the new court buildings. It includes one whole room of lovely Oriental carpets and another of objects from the Far East, India and Africa, all collected by Mr Borja or given to him during his travels around the world. Chinese and Japanese prints and paintings hang on the walls. A third room contains a display of signed photographs of famous Americans and other memorabilia.

The Bratko museum is very much a collector's museum; those who find modern museums too thematic and interactive will love it. Many of the items on display are quite beautiful and the whole collection is fascinating. It takes about an hour to look carefully at everything.

A walk around the town centre The modern Orthodox Cathedral dominates the junction of the two boulevards, Shën Gjergji and Republika, dwarfing the statue of the kilted **Patriotic Warrior** (cast by Odhisë Paskali, the sculptor of imposing statues in several other Albanian towns and cities). In the warren of streets behind it lies a whole neighbourhood of 19th-century houses, built of local stone, slaked with lime and roofed with small, curved tiles. The historic centre of Korça has been badly neglected for 20 years, and many of these lovely old houses are in poor repair. However, some have now been restored, often because they have been turned into bars or restaurants in which you can pause during your explorations. The Archaeological Museum is a beautiful example of a traditional house of this period. Another which is open to the public, in theory (✎ 244 332 for access), is the former house and studio of the Albanian Impressionist painter, **Vangjush Mio** (1891–1957). Many of his paintings are exhibited here; others hang in the National Art Gallery in Tirana (see page 78).

Along Bulevardi Republika, and in the cobbled side streets on either side of it, the buildings are a little later and generally in better condition. These houses, with their columns and wrought-iron gates, have a more European feel than the fortress-like houses of Gjirokastra or Berati – a sign of the French influence on Korça in the early 20th century. At the end of the boulevard is the town's football stadium, with a **bust of Skanderbeg** (after whom the local team is named) and a solitary **bunker**. There are good views of the town and the surrounding countryside from the Kristal Hotel and from the **Martyrs' Cemetery** (Varreza e Dëshmorëve; access by steps is signposted from Bulevardi Republika).

A meander back through the side streets between the Republika and Gjergj Kastrioti boulevards (perhaps with a pause at Taverna Vasili) will bring you out at the main square, where the tourist information office and post office are. Rruga Miss Edith Durham (see box, pages 178–9), diagonally across the square from you, leads to the Ottoman bazaar and the oldest surviving part of the town centre. The bazaar is still used as a market, but many of the buildings are in very poor condition indeed. The **Hani i Elbasanit** is a traditional Ottoman guesthouse, with the rooms arranged around a gallery which overlooks a central courtyard with a well (the courtyard now acts as an extension of the market). Some restoration and conservation was supposed to be done in the bazaar, but all that seems to have happened is that a new supermarket has been built in the middle of it.

A few minutes' walk south from the market is the **Mirahori Mosque**, built in 1484 and thus one of the oldest mosques in Albania, although it was rebuilt in the late 18th century. Crossing the little park behind it will lead you out on to Shëtitorja Fan Noli, an attractive tree-lined boulevard which runs along the southern edge of the old quarter behind the cathedral. If you have any energy left, turn right on to this boulevard and head uphill, past the Bratko museum, to the **Birra Korça brewery**, founded in 1928. Guided tours of the brewery can be arranged when staff time permits; ask the security officers at the gatehouse.

St Mary's Church (Kisha e Ristozit), Mborja The village of Mborja, up beyond the brewery in the southern outskirts of Korça, was once the market town for the whole area, including Voskopoja and Vithkuqi – its name comes from the Greek *emporion*, meaning 'market'. Its little 14th-century church, known locally as Kisha e Ristozit ('Church of the Resurrection'), is a dignified and attractive building of local stone roofed with slates, like so many historic Orthodox churches in southern Albania. Unlike most of them, however, its marvellous frescoes have survived the ravages of time and of the atheism campaign.

The outer section of the church, the narthex, has a particularly enchanting series of frescoes, which begins with a disembodied hand holding a balance in which people are being weighed and found wanting. The unhappy-looking sinners are then whooshed down a chute into the jaws of a dragon, raped, or attacked by serpents. The inner part of the church (the *naos*) is tiny, with a beautiful dome; this is the original, cross-in-square church. It can be rather dark and a torch will be useful. The frescoes on the walls here show the Resurrection and assorted saints, but they have survived less well and the colours are not as vivid. The original icons, such as the breathtakingly beautiful St Michael, are in the National Museum of Medieval Art (see pages 133–4).

To reach the church, bear left into the village, following the small sign for 'Ristozi 200m', and continue up the hill until you see the church on the left. The villagers are used to foreign tourists and will help you to locate the key-holder. It takes about half an hour to walk from the town centre.

VOSKOPOJA

In the early 18th century, when the Industrial Revolution was just getting under way in Britain, Voskopoja was the largest city in the Balkans, bigger even than Athens or Sofia, with a population of about 35,000. It had the first printing press in the region, and an academy where artists were trained to create frescoes and icons for the churches in Voskopoja and elsewhere. Voskopoja itself had no fewer than 24 churches, two in each neighbourhood of the town, plus a basilica in each quarter. This past glory is remarkable. Towards the end of the 18th century the city was plundered and burned several times, and it was completely supplanted in importance by the rapidly growing Korça. Today Voskopoja is a remote village, with a population of just a few hundred peasant farmers, mostly Vlach (see page 19). Only seven churches have survived and some of these are in such disrepair that they are not open to the public.

One of the four basilicas was the Church of St Nicholas, or Shënkoll, which was built in 1726 at the height of Voskopoja's wealth and power. To find it, follow the sign up to the left as you enter the village from Korça, past the commune council office. The church is usually kept locked, but the neighbours are used to foreigners trying to visit it and will go and look for the priest if you ask them. While you are waiting for him, you can admire the patterned brickwork of the exonarthex (portico) and the frescoes within it. These were painted by the brothers Kostandin and Athanas Zografi (see page 134), whose work was in great demand throughout the Balkans. The belltower was added later – originally there was another church, to the left as you look from the fence by the belltower, which joined St Nicholas's to form a U-shape.

The interior frescoes, painted by David Selenicasi (from Vithkuqi), are in better repair than those outside, with beautiful rich colours. The iconostasis is original – the fire damage which can be seen on part of it was caused during World War II – but the icons which were once set in it are now in the National Museum of Medieval Art in Korça. The ornately carved throne was given to the faithful of Voskopoja from the episcopate of Durrësi in 1758, as can be seen from the inscription.

The basilica of St Thanas (Shën Athanas), built in 1724, is down the hill on the other side of the village; you will see its pale stone belltower before you see the shingled roof of the church, tucked into the lee of a hillock. This technique of 'hiding' the church was more common in the 17th century, when it was a condition imposed by the Ottomans (this is also why the belltower is often of more recent date than the body of the church). St Thanas's has a beautiful arcaded exonarthex with frescoes depicting scenes from the Apocalypse, painted by the Zografi brothers. Within, extending right around the walls of the naos, is an extended cycle of the martyrdoms of the saints, with lots of grisly detail.

St Mary of the Dormition (Shën Maria e Fjetjes) is one of the largest basilicas in Albania, holding up to a thousand worshippers; its size demonstrates how wealthy and powerful Voskopoja was at the time it was built (1699). The astonishing frescoes around its three-naved naos include a beautiful Pantocrator surrounded by saints, with the four evangelists at the four corners of the dome. There are more frescoes behind the iconostasis. There is a charge of 200 lek per person to visit these two churches.

High up in the forests above the village is the Monastery of St Prodhromi, the oldest building in Voskopoja. The church was built in 1632, with various wings of the monastery added later and now mostly ruined apart from a 20th-century section where the caretaker lives. The church is small, with a beautiful iconostasis; the entrance hall, or narthex, is reminiscent of a Bektashi *teqe* in its layout and furnishings. The monastery is signposted from the centre as 'St John the Forerunner'. The road up to it is in reasonable condition as far as the Akademia Hotel; unless you are in a 4x4 vehicle you should park there and walk the remaining few hundred metres.

Those with a particular interest in Byzantine religious architecture will also want to visit **Vithkuqi**, which once rivalled Voskopoja in the level of its development. Like Voskopoja, it was destroyed several times before it was finally supplanted by Korça.

GETTING THERE AND AWAY Both Voskopoja and Vithkuqi are about 25km from Korça; the drive takes about an hour each way. There are buses, but it is unlikely you will get there and back in the same day. If you do not want to stay overnight, you could agree a fare with a taxi driver to take you up there, wait, and bring you back to Korça.

 WHERE TO STAY AND EAT There are several small guesthouses in both villages, in addition to the Akademia Hotel listed here. The tourist office in Korça will be able to advise on these. The hotel is very popular in the summer and it would be advisable to book accommodation there before making the journey up to Voskopoja.

⌂ **Akademia** (29 rooms, 11 chalets) Voskopoja; m 069 20 23 047; e hotelakademia@hotmail.com; www.akademia.al. The former 'Pioneers' Camp' above the village of Voskopoja, fully modernised; 2,286m above sea level; set in lovely gardens. English spoken. Good restaurant with traditional dishes; bar, recreation centre, conference room, laundry service; hiking guides, horseriding and skiing can be arranged. All rooms en suite with CH & TV. **$$**

PREHISTORIC SITES

The **Tumulus of Kamenica** (*www.kamenicatumulus.org*; m 069 29 08 193; ⊕ 08.00–14.00 Mon–Thu, 08.00–12.00 Fri; *200 lek*) is one of the most significant prehistoric burial sites in the western Balkans. Three groups of graves have been excavated to date, with the remains of 420 humans in total. The earliest group dates from the late Bronze Age, the 12th century BC. The bodies were arranged within a circle

13m in diameter and covered by a tumulus (or barrow) which, in its final shape five centuries later, was 3m high. By the end of the 7th century, the people of Kamenica stopped using this tumulus and began to bury their dead in new sites around it. These graves seem to have been family burials; DNA analysis of the skeletons in this group has shown that they were related to each other, whereas in the earlier tumulus there is no genetic connection. One of those buried was a woman who was at the start of the ninth month of her pregnancy – the skeleton of the foetus was still in her womb, meaning that she did not die in childbirth but of some illness. This is the only example of such a case found anywhere in Europe.

Unlike most prehistoric sites in Albania, Kamenica is very accessible to non-specialist visitors. The three excavated grave-groups can be viewed and part of the tumulus has been built back up, with earth, to its original height. The site museum has an excellent exhibition, in English and Albanian, which explains the history of the tumulus and the archaeological research which has been done there. Replicas of some of the human remains and items found during excavation are also displayed. The site is easy to get to – it is only 8km from Korça, just off the main Korça–Erseka road. The turn-off is signposted for 'Tuma e Kamenicës', just before the village of Kamenica, and the minor road (less than 1km) is asphalted all the way to the site entrance. Photographs of, and information about, the site can be found at www.kamenicatumulus.org.

The tumulus at **Rehova**, near Erseka, is the largest ever discovered in Albania, with nearly 300 graves. As well as the human remains, 700 pottery objects were excavated, including elegant double-handled jugs and rare double-cupped vessels. The findings have been published, in Albanian with English translation and full illustrations (*Tuma e Rehovës*, Skënder Aliu, Korça, 2012). The museum in Rehova has recently reopened with an exhibition about this important site.

Another significant prehistoric site, more difficult to get to, is the **Treni Cave** at the western tip of Lesser Lake Prespa (see pages 144–5). Excavations within the cave have revealed evidence that it was inhabited in the Neolithic period and then throughout the Bronze Age and into the Iron Age. On the cliff face opposite the cave, overhanging the lake, there is prehistoric rock art depicting a hunting scene. The entrance to the cave is protected by a gate; anyone who is especially keen to see inside should ask the tourist information office in Korça (see page 131) to arrange access. A reproduction of the rock art is displayed at the National Historical Museum in Tirana (see pages 75–7).

POGRADECI   *Telephone code: 083*

Pogradeci lies on the southwestern shore of Lake Ohrid (called Ohër or Ohri in Albanian), a large (358km²), deep lake bisected by the international border between Albania and Macedonia. Ohrid is a tectonic lake, formed by movements in the earth's crust, and it has unique species of fish. It is fed by underground streams from Lake Prespa, about 10km away (see pages 144–5). These streams bubble up in places to form attractive pools and backwaters – one of these is at Driloni, on the way to Macedonia, and another can be visited at Sveti Naum, just across the border (and, indeed, part of Albania until 1925). Lake Ohrid's only outlet is the Black Drini River, which leaves it at Struga, on its northern tip, and flows through a corner of Macedonia before re-entering Albania. (See page 176 for information about the ravishingly beautiful Black Drini Valley between Peshkopia and Kukësi, where the river joins the White Drini and the vast hydro-electric system of northern Albania.)

The deepest parts of Lake Ohrid are nearly 300m, and below about 100m its temperature is a constant 6°C. Closer to the shore, however, the water warms up in summer to a very pleasant 20–21°C, and there are places to swim on both sides of the lake. The Macedonian side tends to be built up and busier, while the Albanian shore is quieter, although in high summer Pogradeci becomes quite lively.

Several of the restaurants on the Albanian side have built jetties out over the lake so that people can swim off them. Pogradeci's waste water is properly treated, not released straight into the lake, and so it is safe to swim there. There is a long stretch of sandy beach on the eastern side of town, towards the border. Further on in the same direction is Driloni, where the underground streams from Lake Prespa bubble to the surface. The restaurant at Driloni, surrounded by weeping willows, has tables and chairs set out by the pools formed by these springs, where you can sit with your drink and watch the swans go by.

The attractions of Pogradeci itself are pretty much limited to strolling around in the sunshine and eating fish, but it is also a good base for several interesting excursions (see pages 142–4). The park along the lakeside has benches looking out on the water, and several attractive statues, including one of the poet Lasgush Poradeci. The author Mitrush Kuteli, extracts from whose stories are translated in this book, was also from Pogradeci.

GETTING THERE AND AWAY Pogradeci is only 4km from the Tushëmishti border crossing at the southern end of Lake Ohrid; it is about an hour's drive from Qafa e Thanë, southwest of Struga at the northern end of the lake. Qafa e Thanë is the main crossing between Albania and Macedonia; during daylight there are always **taxis and minibuses** waiting on the Albanian side. The Tushëmishti crossing can be reached on foot from the resort and hotel at Sveti Naum on the Macedonian side, by means of a path along the lakeshore. Transport on the Albanian side is not quite as reliable as at Qafa e Thanë; the earlier in the morning you get there the more chance you will have of finding a taxi waiting. If you plan to stay overnight in Pogradeci, you could telephone your hotel in advance and ask the management to send a taxi to come and meet you at the border. There are a couple of small hotels within walking distance of the border post on the Albanian side.

Frequent **buses** run between Tirana and Pogradeci, from early morning until early afternoon (later in the summer). They leave from the northern side of the Qemal Stafa Stadium (see map, page 69) and take less than three hours. From Korça, the journey takes about 45 minutes and the fare is 150 lek.

A passenger-only **ferry** across the lake between Ohrid and Pogradeci was piloted in the summer of 2014 and, if successful, will no doubt continue to operate. From May to September 2014, it ran once a week and the return fare was 3,000 lek or €30.

Pogradeci is well situated for several interesting cycle (or motorbike or 4x4) routes. From Maliqi, between Pogradeci and Korça, a minor road goes off to the west and follows the Devolli River until it flows into Lake Banja (see page 118), just northwest of the small town of Gramshi (about 95km). From Gramshi, you could either continue north to Elbasani, or double back southwards, this time along the River Tomorrica. An ancient track follows the Tomorrica upstream before curling around the base of the Tomorri Massif to Çorovoda, south of Berati (see pages 126–7). Another interesting route, starting from either Pogradeci or Elbasani, is the road which links Librazhdi and Peshkopia (about 100km), which runs through very remote mountains and along the border with Macedonia. See pages 177–80 for more information about Peshkopia.

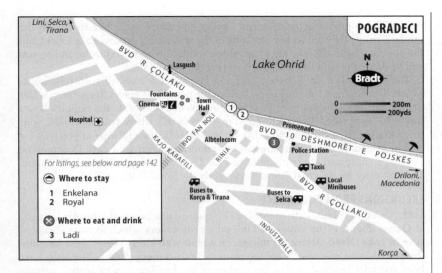

For listings, see below and page 142

Where to stay
1 Enkelana
2 Royal

Where to eat and drink
3 Ladi

TOURIST INFORMATION The tourist information office (⊕ *09.00–17.00 Wed–Mon*) is in the piazza with the fountains, where the town hall is. It stocks a range of information leaflets and sells books, postcards and souvenirs. A useful street plan is posted outside the town hall. The municipality's website (*www.bashkiapogradec. gov.al*) has information, in Albanian only, about Pogradeci and nearby attractions.

WHERE TO STAY *Map, above, unless otherwise indicated.*

Enkelana (100 rooms) Bd Rreshit Çollaku; ☏222 010; m 069 20 94 646, 069 40 52 956; e info@enkelanahotel.com; www.enkelana.com. Right on the lakeside, fully modernised. 2 lifts, powerful generator; restaurant, large terrace bar overlooking lake; free Wi-Fi throughout; souvenir shop. Direct access to beach; pedalos for hire; outdoor pool with separate section for children; sauna; conference room with simultaneous translation facilities. All rooms en suite with AC, LCD TV & small balcony, some with stunning views over the lake. **$$**

Royal (25 rooms) Bd Rreshit Çollaku; ☏223 158, 223 159; m 067 40 68 700/701/702; e hotel_royal08@yahoo.com; Facebook: Hotel royal pogradec. Right on the lakeside, fully modernised. Panoramic lift (lake views) to all floors; rooftop bar & restaurant with spectacular views; free Wi-Fi throughout; friendly, helpful staff,

some English spoken. All rooms non-smoking, with nice en-suite bathroom, shower screens, hairdryer, some have bathtub; CH, AC, TV, bedside lights; most have lake view, some have good-sized balcony, furnished in summer. **$$**

Camping Peshku [map, page 130] Hudënishta 40° 58′01″ N 20° 38′ 34″ E; ☏086 880 102; m 068 36 47 956, 068 23 61 701; e campingpeshku@gmail. com; www.campingpeshku.com; ⊕ year-round. 7km north of Pogradeci, on the lakeshore; English spoken; reserved section of sandy beach; local guides can be arranged. Good restaurant (**$$$**) overlooking lake; Wi-Fi in restaurant. 30 pitches for mobile homes; separate area for tents; washing machine; extra blankets available if required. Solar-heated water; expansion of toilet & shower facilities under way summer 2014. Mobile home pitch €10, tent pitch €4.

WHERE (AND WHAT) TO EAT AND DRINK *Map, above.*

Lakes caused by plate tectonics are often home to species which do not occur elsewhere (Loch Ness is a tectonic lake, for example) and Lake Ohrid is no exception. Notably, it has two unique species of trout, both of which taste excellent. *Salmo letnica*, called *koran* in Albanian, has a delicate taste similar to that of sea trout; *Salmo ohridanus* (*belushkë*) is smaller and tastes more like its cousin the rainbow trout. They are widely available in the restaurants around Lake Ohrid, but the populations in the lake are vulnerable to pollution and overfishing and so you will be doing the wild fish a favour if you eat the farmed ones.

The whole lakeshore between Lini and Pogradeci is studded with restaurants which all serve fresh fish, including *koran*. One of the best places to eat *koran* is just before you get to Driloni from Pogradeci: a gravelled road off to the right leads to a fish farm (signposted 'Rritja e Koranit', ie: 'trout farm'), where you can choose your trout straight from the net and drink the restaurant's draught wine as you wait for it to be grilled. In town, there are several restaurants along Bulevardi Dëshmorët e Pojskës; a cheap and cheerful option is Fish Taverna Ladi, just beyond the square. The best place for a formal dinner is currently the Royal Hotel (**$$$**).

EXCURSIONS FROM POGRADECI

Lini About 15 minutes' drive north of Pogradeci, just before the border crossing at Qafa e Thanë, is the village of Lini, on a promontory which forms a sheltered cove in Lake Ohrid. Above the village, on a bluff with lovely views of the lake and the Macedonian mountains, are the ruins of a 6th-century church. The walls have been partially restored so that the outline of the building can be seen – a single nave with an apse and two conches on either side, giving it a kind of five-leafed clover shape. Other buildings surround the church, including a deep cistern, brick-built and sealed with cement. The church and some other buildings are paved with fine mosaics. As usual in Albania, these are kept covered to protect them from the elements; at Lini, however, a small mosaic has been left covered with a tarpaulin which can be lifted up so that it can be seen. It shows two peacocks (or rather peahens) eating grapes which spring from a *kantharos*, a wine jug: wine is the symbol of the blood of Christ, while peacocks symbolise Paradise and everlasting life. It is a privilege to be able to see this beautiful mosaic; please do not forget to cover it up again before you leave the site.

Getting there and away To get to the church from the village, you can either climb the steps which begin opposite the mosque, or you can drive or cycle up the rough track which begins near the (modern) church. It takes about 20 minutes to walk; the last 50–100m are not drivable.

 Where to stay and eat

Motel B&B Lin (3 rooms) **m** 069 45 04 577. Near the church; nicely furnished en-suite rooms, all slightly different; two dbls, one twin; shared terrace overlooking lake. Boat trips can be arranged. **$$**

Illyrian royal tombs The magnificent rock-hewn tombs at Selca, in the mountains to the west of Lake Ohrid, offer a rare insight into the funeral rites of Illyrian kings. Selca was first settled in the Bronze Age and became a royal residence in the 4th century BC. This was the territory of the Dassaretes, whose capital was the modern town of Ohrid, on the other side of the lake. They cut three tombs into the rock face for their kings, the earliest in the second half of the 4th century. It measures 6.5m by 4m, with an antechamber leading into the burial chamber, where a stone bed held the body of the deceased king. The other tombs are from the 3rd century. It is thought that one of these, a two-level tomb with Ionian 'columns' carved above the actual grave, may have held the remains of King Monun (see page 87). This is because the bas-relief of a helmet which decorates the entrance is just like a real helmet, discovered in the

Ohrid area during World War I and now in Berlin, which is inscribed with Monun's name. A little theatre beside the tombs, also carved out of the rock, may have been used during the funeral rites. The third tomb, which also has carved 'columns' at its entrance, is set a little apart; there are steps up to it and it is linked to the other two by a path. A fourth tomb, below the others, was built with stone blocks, some of them with chiselled decoration. The royal palace must have been on the summit of the hill above the tombs; excavation in this area continues. It is worth climbing at least part of the way up for the views. The Dassaretes chose a beautiful spot to lay their kings to rest.

Until a few years ago, getting to the Illyrian tombs (*varrat ilire*) required dedication and a 4x4. Now, the road is asphalted all the way to the village of Selca e

BUNKER STRATEGY

As soon as you cross the border into any part of Albania, you can scarcely avoid noticing the bunkers. Hundreds of thousands of these pillboxes were sunk into the fields and hillsides, most of them during the 1970s, after Albania had left the Warsaw Pact. The most frequent type is the small, single-person bunker with two slits above ground. They are set 1–1.5m into the ground and are therefore difficult to remove; they are now sometimes used as outhouses or to store animal feed.

It is commonplace to sneer at the bunkers, but the military strategy which inspired them is solid. During World War II, the Albanian resistance fighters were generally best at mountain-based guerrilla warfare. They spent most of their time in the hills and came down to the plain only to carry out attacks. This *modus operandi* proved highly successful and it therefore made considerable sense to try to adapt it to the post-war situation in which Albania found itself.

The idea behind the bunkers is that they enable this kind of mountain warfare to be conducted down on the plain. The small bunkers are laid out in lines radiating down from a large command bunker and have a line of sight to it. The large bunkers were permanently manned; the small ones were not. In the event of an invasion, every able-bodied male was expected to collect a gun and take up position in his assigned pillbox until ordered to leave it.

The commanders in the large bunkers had radio contact with their superiors, and from their positions high up on the hill they could control the road or valley along which the invaders would be coming. The men further down the hill could receive visual orders by looking through the slit on one side of their pillbox, and shoot the invaders through the other.

Those who consider it paranoid to think that your country is about to be invaded should remember that between 1947 and 1953 Britain and the USA did in fact attempt to infiltrate anti-communist agents into Albania. These attempts failed dismally; all the agents were captured almost as soon as they landed, and were either killed on the spot or executed after being tried as spies.

There are fewer bunkers around now than there used to be; as Albania's cities have grown and its roads have been widened, many pillboxes have been removed during construction work. However, arrays of bunkers showing the strategy that lay behind their positioning can still be seen, especially in border areas. There is a particularly clear example a few kilometres south of Peshkopia, on the hillsides just beyond Maqellara. The area around the junction for the border crossing at Qafa e Thanë, at the northern end of Lake Ohrid, is another good place to study bunker layout.

The Southeast POGRADECI

5

Poshtme, leaving the highway at Uraka, just east of Prrënjasi; the last few kilometres beyond the village, up to the entrance to the site, are paved and can be tackled in any reasonably sturdy car. A path leads across a field and up to the tombs; it can be slippery in wet weather. There is a lovely Ottoman bridge (Ura e Golikut) on the way from Uraka to Selca, one of many built on the sites of much older bridges that formed part of the trade route which, in the 2nd century BC, became the Romans' Via Egnatia. Asphalting of the southern section of this road, via Dardhasi, is foreseen, which would create a very attractive alternative route between Korça and central Albania. A bus serves Selca e Poshtme from Pogradeci, a journey of just over an hour. The bus leaves Pogradeci around lunchtime and does not return until the following morning, but it would be a good option for those with tents.

THE PRESPA LAKES

The water which bubbles up so prettily at Drilon and Sveti Naum has travelled through about 10km of subterranean channels from another tectonic lake. Greater Lake Prespa is separated from Lake Ohrid by the Mali i Thatë Mountains. 'Mali i Thatë' means 'the dry mountain', and it is so called because the limestone which forms it sucks Lake Prespa's water underground, leaving no visible rivers (this geological formation is called karst). The larger of the two Prespa Lakes, usually called simply 'Lake Prespa', has a surface area of 273km² and straddles the borders between Albania, Greece and Macedonia. The smaller, Lesser Lake Prespa, is only 45km², all but 6km² of which are in Greece. In 2000, the whole Prespa basin was designated as a Transboundary Park, the first cross-border protected area in the Balkans. The lakes are rich in wildlife and, in particular, are home to the largest population of Dalmatian pelicans (*Pelecanus crispus*) in the world.

Although it is quite close to Korça, the Albanian part of Greater Lake Prespa was, until recently, rather remote and difficult to reach, which means that the economy of the villages around the lakeshore is still based almost entirely on small-scale farming and fishing. The recent improvement of the road over the hills from the highway has started to bring them some welcome income from tourism. Prespa is an ideal base for a few days of gentle hiking, birdwatching or just relaxing in the peaceful atmosphere; it is less than an hour's drive from Korça and so a day trip is perfectly feasible for those with their own (motorised) transport.

The main attraction is the island of Maligrad (meaning 'little town' in Macedonian, the native language of the villagers of the Prespa area). This small, uninhabited island rises steeply from the turquoise water of the lake. In the 14th century, people built a church here, within a natural rock shelter, and beautified it with frescoes outside and in. The church was too remote to attract the attention of the atheism campaigners (see pages 16–17) and so both it and its frescoes have survived, although the latter have been badly damaged by modern graffiti. As well as visiting the church, it is fairly straightforward to climb up to the summit of the island, a tranquil spot covered with wild flowers and the remains of another, ruined, church. From the summit, there are good views of the snowy mountains on the western shore and of Lake Prespa's second island, Golemgrad ('big town'), which lies in Macedonian waters. A low spit of land at Maligrad's northwest has tiny beaches where you can swim when the weather is warm enough: Lake Prespa is 850m above sea level and the water is noticeably colder than Lake Ohrid, 150m lower. The boat trip out to the island is a good opportunity to see pelicans and pygmy cormorants (*Phalacrocorax pygmeus*) up close.

The point at which Lake Prespa drains into the karst is up at the northernmost corner of Albania's part of the lake, near the village of Gorica e Vogël. The cliffs around it are riddled with caves and sink-holes; broken reeds and other lake debris cluster around the outflow, providing sustenance to fish of all sizes. On the other side of the lake, the road ends just beyond Zaroshka, but there is a footpath beyond the (modern) church along the lakeshore and past a tiny chapel built into the rock face. Another, larger, cave church lies just across the border in Greece.

GETTING THERE AND AWAY The village best geared to visitors is Zaroshka, with hotels and restaurants. It is about 45 minutes' drive from Korça; the road is asphalted all the way. The administrative centre of the Prespa area is Liqenasi, served by a daily bus from Korça; it leaves Liqenasi at 07.00 and returns, from the local bus station in Korça, at 13.00. Otherwise, any **bus** or **minibus** from Korça to Bilishti will drop you at the petrol station (*karburanti*) just before the village of Zëmblaku. Informal **taxis** wait at the petrol station for passengers to Liqenasi, Zaroshka or any of the other villages around the lake; the going rate is 1,000 lek. It is a very steep 17km from the petrol station to Liqenasi.

Zaroshka is about 30 minutes' drive from the Macedonian border at Stenje; the border crossing closes at night. Liqenasi has a health centre but there are no ATMs; bring sufficient cash from Korça or Bilishti.

 WHERE TO STAY AND EAT

⌂ **Aleksandar** (4 rooms) Zaroshka; m 068 25 49 759. Simple but comfortable hotel in village; under same ownership as large restaurant (**$$$**) at entrance to village, where hotel rooms will also be available as construction proceeds. Owners exceptionally kind & helpful; boat trips & other excursions can be arranged. All rooms en suite with lake-view balcony. **$**

⌂ **Ilo** (6 rooms) Zaroshka; m 068 26 04 383 (Albanian number), +389 7666 7035 (Macedonian number). Boat trips can be arranged. All rooms en suite; 3 have balcony with lake view. **$**

Both hotels have good, popular restaurants offering fresh fish, grilled meat, salads, and Macedonian wine at very reasonable prices. Ilo is in the village, very close to the lakeshore; Aleksandar is just before the start of the village, in a stunning location overlooking the lake, with tables outside in a garden with views of the lake and Maligrad Island.

THE GRAMOZ MOUNTAINS

The Gramoz range rises like a wall between Albania and Greece, with some of its summits over 2,500m high. These are serious mountains, with harsh weather conditions and a tough life for the people who live among them. Luckily for the visitor, a well-surfaced road runs along the Albanian side of the range, which allows the spectacular scenery to be enjoyed in relative comfort. It is a good route for cyclists, although the narrow road means that you have to keep your wits about you. The gradients are much easier southbound, from Korça to Përmeti.

About 40km south of Korça is Erseka which, at 900m above sea level, is the highest town in Albania. Erseka is a well-organised little place, with restaurants and hotels, and the mountains which surround it give it a very alpine feel. It has a small Ethnographic Museum in the main square; fans of Socialist Realist art will like the monument outside the museum, with its partisan peasants learning to read in between battles. A couple of kilometres from Erseka, the village of Rehova has a small museum with information about the highly significant Rehova tumulus (see page 139). Frequent minibuses run all day between Erseka and Korça.

Beyond Erseka the road begins to climb, up startling hairpin bends, and the scenery becomes more and more dramatic. The highest point, 1,259m above sea level, is just beyond the village of Barmashi and its fine partisan statue. The road continues through dense conifer and beech forests which open out from time to time to reveal the towering mountains on either side. About 45km from Erseka, a turn-off leads to the little town of Leskoviku.

From here, the border crossing into Greece at Tre Urat is about 15 minutes' drive away. The main road between Leskoviku and Çarçova is narrow and in poor condition; but if you are approaching Tre Urat from Përmeti, there is a second road to Tre Urat from Çarçova, along part of the Vjosa River. The border crossing closes overnight, at 19.00 Albanian time (20.00 Greek time). If you get to Leskoviku too late to cross the border, simple accommodation (**$**) is available above the two restaurants on the street that becomes the road to the border: Jorgo (m *068 37 91 134*) and Leskoviku (m *069 27 30 716*). Jorgo serves huge portions of roast lamb or kid and salads and sweet local wine (**$$**). At the Çarçova junction is a shop and restaurant; a bus to Athens, via Tre Urat, passes Çarçova around 07.00 on Mondays and Fridays (it leaves Përmeti at 06.30; m *069 81 87 559, 068 23 86 048*). For details of the buses between Gjirokastra and Korça, see page 131.

 WHERE TO STAY AND EAT *Map, page 130.*

🏠 **Farma Sotira** (5 chalets) m 069 23 42 529; e info@farmasotira.com; www.farmasotira.com. 15km (30mins' drive) from Leskoviku on the way to Erseka, set in meadows fringed with fir & hazel woods; 1,100m above sea level. A working farm, with sheep, cattle, chickens & horses; also trout nursery; water from the farm's own spring. Guided hiking & riding excursions can be arranged; outdoor pool with separate shallow section for children; laundry facilities. Excellent restaurant with open fire: home-reared lamb cooked in *saç* (Dutch oven), trout, *lakror* & other traditional dishes, all genuinely organic. Campsite (**$**) with 3 charging points for mobile homes & space for tents; good, modern toilets & showers (1 of each for each sex). Each chalet sleeps up to 4 ppl in 2 rooms with nice bathrooms; heating, power points. **$$$**

🏠 **Jorgo** (6 rooms) m 069 24 09 641. Just beyond Gërmenji turn-off, 24km from Erseka on the main road. Has water, electricity, restaurant & lovely scenery, up amid the forest in the mountains. Dbl & trpl rooms, all en suite. **$$**

PËRMETI *Telephone code: 0813*

Përmeti is a pleasant, clean little town in a lovely setting, surrounded by mountains and flanked by the river Vjosa. The journey to it, from both north and south, runs along the valley of this beautiful river, past dramatic gorges and waterfalls. The Vjosa rises in northern Greece as the Aoos, and is one of the loveliest rivers in Albania, with crystalline, greenish-blue waters. Hill farmers lead their laden donkeys home across precarious wooden bridges and large birds of prey can be seen quite close at hand.

Përmeti was settled in prehistoric times, but the earliest traces of habitation are the remains of a medieval castle on the City Rock, which overlooks the gorge through which the Vjosa flows out of the town. In the course of World War II, Përmeti was burnt down no fewer than four times, by Italians and Germans; the 6th Partisan Brigade, led by Enver Hoxha and Mehmet Shehu (see box, page 83), was mustered here in 1943, and a large **memorial** to its fallen stands at the entrance to the town.

In 1944, the Congress of Përmeti elected the provisional government which took power following liberation later that year. It consolidated the exclusion of the non-communist forces from the country's future, annulled various decisions and agreements made by the pre-war monarchist government, and specifically banned King Zog from returning to Albania. The congress is commemorated with a fine Socialist Realist statue of a partisan, cast by the Përmeti sculptor Odhisë Paskali, which stands at the side of the main square. Përmeti is famous for its roses, which can be admired from late spring throughout the summer, and for its raki, which can be sampled at any time of year. It is also the home of *gliko*, a way of preserving fruit or walnuts in syrup, and of a budding Slow Food Consortium.

GETTING THERE AND AWAY There are buses and minibuses to Përmeti from **Gjirokastra** (55km) until lunchtime; they leave from the terminus on the highway at the northern edge of the city and take about 1½ hours. The route goes through the pretty, wooded Drinos Valley and then along the magnificent Këlcyra Gorge. It continues along the Vjosa, with mountains on either side of the river, before coming into Përmeti. Another option is to take a bus to Këlcyra and change there on to a minibus for Përmeti. There are also minibuses to Këlcyra and Përmeti from Tepelena.

There is a daily bus service between Përmeti and **Korça**; it leaves Përmeti at 07.00. The Gjirokastra–Korça service (daily except Sundays) can be boarded at the end of the bridge into Përmeti, where it passes between 08.00 and 08.30. The journey to Korça from Përmeti takes about four hours and the fare is 600 lek. It is a spectacular trip, starting with the gorges and rapids of the Vjosa, then climbing through forests to Gërmenji, and finishing with a run through the imposing Gramoz Mountains. There is also a Përmeti–Leskoviku bus daily at 12.30.

The border crossing at Tre Urat – called Mertzani by the Greeks – is about two hours' drive from Përmeti. See page 129 for details.

TOURIST INFORMATION The tourist information office (☎ 23725) is on Odhisë Paskali Boulevard, opposite the police station. Friendly, English-speaking staff can advise on where to stay and what to do. The office stocks free maps of the town and brochures; a small museum highlights some of the traditions of the area. Hiking maps of Bredhi i Hotovës (see page 152) are also available. Staff can contact the key-holders of St Paraskevi and the cinema (see page 150), to open them up for you; visits to *gliko* producers and to vineyards can also be arranged.

The website www.visitpermet.org has information about the town in English and Albanian.

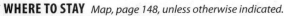

WHERE TO STAY *Map, page 148, unless otherwise indicated.*

🏠 **Alvero** (16 rooms) ☎23514; m 068 23 39 508, 068 20 81 334; e vnikolla@yahoo.fr; www. visitpermet.org. Modern & comfortable; panoramic lift; friendly, helpful owners speak English, French & German; tours & fishing trips in the area can be arranged. Large restaurant with terrace overlooking river; fresh, local food; conference room, rooftop bar. All rooms have good, well-equipped en-suite bathroom, AC, LED TV, direct-dial phone, Wi-Fi, fridge; some have balcony. **$$**

🏠 **Ana** (10 rooms, 2 suites) m 069 23 98 174; e info@hotelanapermet.com; www. hotelanapermet.com. Entrance behind grocery shop on main street. Bar/b/fast room with French windows opening on to balcony; Wi-Fi throughout. All rooms en suite with AC, TV, fridge; most have balcony. **$$**

🏠 **Mali i Bardhë** [map, page 130] (9 rooms) 1km from main road on way to Bënja; m 068 21 63 964; e taseapostol@yahoo.com. Good restaurant with traditional menu; tables on terrace, fringed with 400-year-old plane trees; open fire indoors. Hiking & climbing tours can be arranged. All rooms en suite with CH, TV, balcony with view of either mountains or forest & stream; HB possible. **$$**

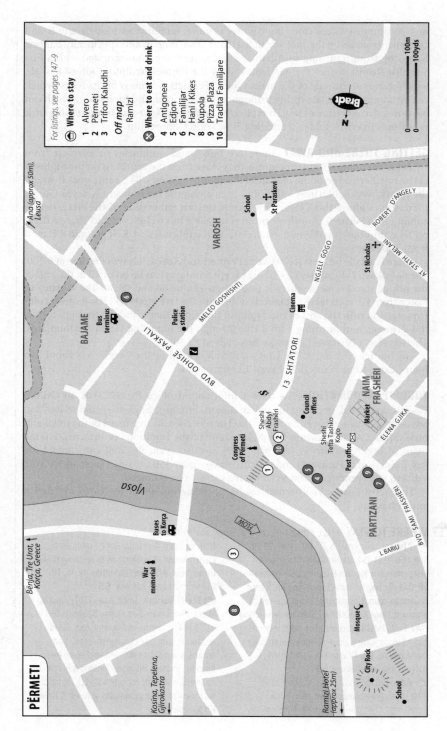

PËRMETI

Bënja, Tre Urat, Korça, Greece

Kosina, Tepelena, Gjirokastra

VAROSH

BAJAME

Ana (approx 50m), Leusa

Vjosa

Bus terminus

Buses to Korça

War memorial

Police station

Sheshi Abdyl Frashëri

Congress of Përmeti

BVD ODHISE PASKALI

MELEO GOSNISHTI

13 SHTATORI

NGJELI GOGO

Cinema

Council offices

Sheshi Tefta Tashko Koço

Post office

Market

NAIM FRASHERI

ELENA GJIKA

St Paraskevi

School

St Nicholas

ROBERT D'ANGELY

AT STATH MELANI

PARTIZANI

L BARIU

BVD SAMI FRASHERI

Mosque

City Rock

School

Ramizi Hotel (approx 25m)

FLOW

N

Bradt

0 ───── 100m
0 ───── 100yds

☗ **Përmeti** (30 rooms) ✆22611; m 069 78 34 572. The former 'Turizmi'; fully renovated & upgraded. Lift; bar on main square, good for people-watching; Wi-Fi in public areas & lower floors; some English spoken. All rooms en suite with AC, TV, good-sized dbl or twin beds, views of either City Rock or main square. **$$**

☗ **Ramizi** (18 rooms) Just beyond the City Rock; ✆23858; m 068 20 73 826; hotelramizi@yahoo. com. Restaurant; wine & raki made on site; hiking & kayaking trips & visits to *gliko* producers can be arranged. Free Wi-Fi throughout; computer with fast internet access for guests' use. All rooms en suite with AC, TV, bedside light, shutters; 4 on top floor are wood-panelled attic rooms. **$$**

☗ **Trifon Kaludhi** (4 rooms) m 068 23 10 079. Modern building, with generator, across the river from the main square. Restaurant & bar on ground floor. 2 rooms overlook the river, 2 have views of the mountains. All are en suite with AC, TV & private balcony. **$$**

✗ **WHERE TO EAT AND DRINK** *Map, opposite.*
For snacks, there are *byrek* and *sufllaqë* shops ($) around Sheshi Tefta Tashko Koço, behind the Përmeti Hotel.

✗ **Antigonea** Excellent meat, river fish, game dishes such as rabbit & partridge. Good, professional service, English spoken. **$$$**

✗ **Edjon** Good range of meat dishes, professional service. **$$$**

✗ **Tradita Familjare** Large indoor restaurant, tables outside on main square; fairly standard menu of escalopes, chops & salads, some fish & game. **$$$**

✗ **Familjar** The standard menu of grilled meat & salads, nice interior with traditionally carved wood; handy for bus station. **$$**

✗ **Hani i Kikes** Friendly, welcoming atmosphere; traditional southern Albanian meals; good selection of wines. **$$**

✗ **Pizza Plaza** A lovely garden is hidden behind the unpromising café-like exterior on the street. Good pizza, traditional Albanian dishes such as lamb's liver, English-speaking owner. **$$**

WHAT TO SEE AND DO Përmeti's setting is really beautiful. Behind the town rises the Dhëmbel mountain range, 2,050m high at its peak, and all around are other imposing mountains. The road access to the town is over the river Vjosa, which rushes through a dramatic gorge right next to the pavement. In summer, the local children swim and sunbathe on the shingle riverbanks. A huge boulder – the City Rock – sits by the gorge and can be climbed to enjoy the view of the river from the top; a metal staircase leads up the western face of the rock.

Most of Përmeti's buildings are modern, having been rebuilt after liberation in 1944. Two attractive old churches remain. **St Paraskevi** is a Greek saint, who was martyred by decapitation; she is often shown in icons with one head on her shoulders and another in a bowl. Her name is the Greek word for Friday; in Albania she and her churches are usually referred to as *Shënepremtë*, 'St Friday'. This St Friday was built in 1776, a long, low building with an attractive whitewashed exonarthex (a colonnaded porch). The roof is unusual: normally the roof of the narthex is lower than that over the nave, but here it is on a single level. Another interesting architectural feature is a channel, under the paved floor, which took water from the font out into the rainwater drain outside. The frescoes were painted in 1808, by Tërpo Zografi (see page 134); they are lovely, but in sore need of conservation. Flooding in 1963 damaged the women's gallery so badly that, ever since, women have worshipped in the nave, although they sit separately from the men. The entrance door is modern, carved by a local craftsman to replace the original door which was destroyed during the atheism campaign.

St Nicholas (*Shën Koll*) is slightly older, built in 1757, and set in a peaceful garden, surrounded by cypresses and flowers. It is not usually possible to get inside, but in any case its walls were whitewashed in 1967.

Another interesting building is the **cinema**, built in the 1980s. It is possible to visit the projection box (ask at the tourist information office) and inspect the impressive projectors, made in China to a Soviet model, and other equipment. The walls are covered with stills from well-known Albanian films of the 1960s and 1970s; see page 24 for more about Albanian cinema in the communist period.

Every June, Përmeti hosts a **folk festival** in which traditional musicians come together from all over the Balkans. There is also a wine festival in the last week of May.

EXCURSIONS FROM PËRMETI

Historic churches The churches at Leusa and Kosina have outstanding frescoes and should be visited by anyone who is interested in Byzantine religious art. **Leusa** is only a couple of kilometres from Përmeti, a stiff uphill walk; the road is often in poor repair and a normal hire car is unlikely to be adequate. It is a large church, 23m long, built at the end of the 18th century. The paintings on the wall

THE FRASHËRI BROTHERS

Abdyl, the oldest of the three famous Frashëri brothers, was born in 1839 and became a fairly senior civil servant in the Ottoman administration. In 1877, he was elected to represent Ioannina in the Ottoman parliament. By this time, he was already actively involved in the movement for Albanian autonomy. He set up a secret Albanian Committee, which submitted a memorandum to the Ottoman government in the spring of 1877; it called for the unification of the four Ottoman provinces (*vilayets*) into which the Albanian-speaking lands were divided, and for the establishment of Albanian schools. The memorandum met with no response.

Abdyl Frashëri gave the opening address at a meeting of Albanian nationalist leaders held in Prizreni in June 1878, which soon became known as the Prizren League. Most of the delegates at Prizreni were from Kosova or the Albanian highlands; Frashëri was one of only two from southern Albania. The meeting was timed to coincide with the Congress of Berlin, which had been convened by the European Powers – Britain, France, Austria-Hungary, Russia, Germany and Italy – to try to find a solution to the imminent disintegration of the Ottoman Empire and Russia's eagerness to fill the void left by it.

The 'solution', in the end, was the Treaty of Berlin, which returned Macedonia to Ottoman control, kept Serbia out of Kosova, handed Bosnia-Herzegovina over to Austrian administration, and gave part of Kosova to Montenegro. This last concession caused great resentment in Kosova, and radicalised the Prizren League. Abdyl Frashëri, who was Bektashi (see pages 22–3), used the network of the Bektashi order to rally support for Albanian autonomy among the Muslims of southern Albania, who were not affected by the Treaty of Berlin. As the Albanians' demands developed and became more radical, Abdyl Frashëri travelled around the capitals of Europe, lobbying on their behalf.

In early 1881, the Prizren League began to organise real resistance to Ottoman authority, capturing Prishtina and expelling the Ottoman administrators from the whole of Kosova. The empire belatedly realised the danger the League posed, and moved swiftly to suppress it. Abdyl Frashëri was captured and imprisoned, but the national awareness which the League had awakened could not be crushed so easily. He was released in 1886 on condition that he lived in Istanbul and took no part in political activity. His health was broken by his imprisonment and he died in 1892.

of the exonarthex have been damaged with graffiti, but there are some charming compositions among them, including a cute pelican. Inside, the frescoes on the narthex walls include gruesome scenes of sinners being tortured in various ways. A wooden staircase leads up to a screened gallery, with more frescoes. From here there is a good view of the ceiling frescoes in the body of the church (the *naos*). Further frescoes decorate the walls of the naos; bats live in the vaults above it. The key is held by the family in the first house on the right off the track opposite the church gate.

Kosina Church is just off, and visible from, the main road towards Këlcyra, about halfway between the two towns. This beautiful little cross-in-square church, with its patterned brickwork, is typical of palaeochristian buildings of the 12th and 13th centuries. The fresco in the dome, of Christ Pantocrator surrounded by his saints, has survived reasonably well, but the whole church urgently needs conservation work. You can park in the village and walk the final 45m or so up to the church; ask locally for the key-holder.

The youngest of the three brothers, Sami Frashëri (1850–1904), edited an influential daily newspaper in Istanbul, which in 1878 published an article by Abdyl Frashëri outlining the demands of the Prizren League – a single *vilayet*, Albanian-speaking officials, elected local authorities and Albanian-language schools. Sami led the Albanian Committee of Istanbul, and went on to become the nationalist movement's chief propagandist. His essay entitled *What Albania has been, what it is, and what it will become* was effectively its manifesto. On the Albanian language, he wrote:

How can it be that Albanians do not have the right to write and read their language, when every nation has this right and nobody forbids it? Why are Albanians deprived of a right which every nation on earth has? Not to be able to write and learn their language, but to have foreign nations coming and opening schools in their languages?

After the crushing of the Prizren League, the emphasis of the nationalist movement shifted to cultural and linguistic demands. Cultural societies in Istanbul and Bucharest printed and distributed books in Albanian and raised funds for Albanian-medium schools (see page 135). Naim Frashëri (1843–1900) was active in the Albanian Committee of Istanbul, but more importantly became one of the Albanian language's greatest poets. He wrote allegorical nationalistic works, such as *The Candle's Words* (*Fjalët e Qiririt*), and a paean of homesickness, *Livestock & Agriculture* (*Bagëti e Bujqësi*):

O Albania, my mother, while I am in exile
my heart has never forgotten your love.
When the lamb, wandering from the flock, hears its mother's soft voice,
it bleats two or three times and rushes off;
even if twenty or thirty people block its way
and frighten it, the lamb does not turn back, but goes through them like an arrow.
In the same way, my heart too leaves me here, where I am,
and hurries with longing to your lands.

Frashëri The village of Frashëri, where the illustrious brothers Abdyl, Naim and Sami Frashëri came from, is about 40km from Përmeti, high in the mountains beyond the Bredhi i Hotovës (Hotova Firs) National Park. It is a lovely drive (or cycle, for those with good leg muscles) through forests of fir and spruce which open up from time to time to reveal towering mountains on all sides. The road is not asphalted, but it is in reasonable condition and a 4x4 is not required. There is no public transport; the turning off the main Përmeti–Këlcyra road, between Kosina and Piskova, is signposted for 'Bredhi i Hotovës' and the Bektashi *teqe* of Alipostivan. Note that some commercial maps of Albania show a completely fictitious route.

In the 19th century, Frashëri was a sizeable place, with 22 distinct neighbourhoods. The village's most famous sons were the three brothers who contributed in different ways to Albania's *Rilindja Kombëtare*, the cultural movement which led

THERMAL BATHS

Albania's thermal baths have been enjoyed since Roman times. In the 20th century, some of them were developed into spas – they are known generically by the Albanian word *Llixhat* (the indefinite form is *Llixhe*). The first to have its waters scientifically tested was Park Nosi, in Llixhat e Elbasanit (see page 118). The water here was first analysed in 1924, and the spa was built in 1932 by a businessman from Elbasani, Grigor Nosi (a brother of the politician Lef Nosi; see pages 116–17). Detailed research into the chemical components of the water was conducted by a Czech scientist between 1932 and 1936; the main elements are sodium, magnesium, calcium and potassium. The spa treats a range of ailments, including rheumatism, circulatory problems and skin complaints such as eczema. The water is said also to aid fertility. The springs at Park Nosi rise from 13,000m below the surface and emerge at 56°C; the current administrator remembers, as a child, his grandfather Grigor Nosi boiling an egg for him in the thermal water. Nowadays, many other spa hotels have been built at Llixhat e Elbasanit, although some of them pump their water from underground, rather than allowing it to emerge naturally, as is supposed to be better for the conservation of its medicinal properties.

Another spa hotel, built during the communist period, is near Peshkopia (see page 180). The water here emerges at between 35° and 43°C; its principal minerals are potassium and sulphur. People come to this spa from Macedonia and Kosova, as well as from other parts of Albania; the waters are said to be of great benefit in the treatment of rheumatism and arthritis.

The prices for treatment at these spas are astonishingly low by northern European standards. A two-week course of treatment at the municipally run hotel at Peshkopia, with full board, costs about €200. At Park Nosi, a single bath, with the obligatory medical examination, costs 100 lek (less than €1) and a session of mud therapy is 1,000 lek.

Spas can also be found near Fushë-Kruja and Leskoviku, and there are free thermal baths, open to the elements, in various places around the Albanian mountains. One of these is at Bënja, near Përmeti, and is a large pool fed by several thermal springs. See opposite for details of how to get there. Finally, there are numerous drinking water springs, which are also said to have beneficial medical effects; these are often known as *Uji i Ftohtë*, the Albanian for 'cold water'.

top   Saranda's little harbour, with Lëkurësi castle in the background (SS) pages 215–18

right   The azure Valbona River is renowned for its dramatic gorges and spectacular waterfalls (A/D) pages 164–7

below   The Albanian shores of Lake Ohrid, on the border between Albania and Macedonia, are mostly quiet and studded with fish restaurants (M/S) pages 4–5

above left   Albanian independence was declared in Vlora on 28 November 1912, and is commemorated with both this monument and a museum (GG) pages 252–9

above right   Gjirokastra's brooding castle was built from the 5th century onwards to control the Drinos Valley and the passes through the Lunxhëria Mountains (SS) pages 235–7

below   Kruja's attractively restored bazaar and buildings, including the Ethnographic Museum built in 1764, make the city an excellent place to get a feel for Albanian history and traditions (P/D and DD) pages 100–4

above   Berati is one of the oldest cities in Albania, and one of the most attractive (P/S) pages 118–28

right   The galleries around Durrësi's Roman amphitheatre contain a Byzantine chapel with a number of wall mosaics, the only examples of their kind ever to be found in Albania (SS) pages 93–4

below   Korça's new cathedral towers over the statue of a kilted patriotic warrior (IL/S) page 134

above   The Albanian Orthodox Church is independent from other Orthodox authority and ordains its own bishops (SS) pages 21–2

above left   A Bektashi cleric reading the Koran: Albania has been the world headquarters of the Bektashi order since 1925 (SS) pages 21–2

below left   Traditional *qilime* — woven rugs — on sale at the bazaar in Kruja (WB/AWL) pages 100–1

below   A weaver at work in her house in Jagodini, near Elbasani (AL)

above   A shepherd leading his flock to pasture over a wooden bridge near Butrint (O/S) pages 222–3

right   The artisans' cooperative in Gjirokastra includes a stonemason's workshop (AL) page 233

below   Men playing dominoes in Berati (SS) pages 118–28

above	Bunkers in the Vjosa Valley — pillboxes like these were part of the Communist regime's military strategy against possible invasion (SS) page 143
below	The Vjosa River is spanned by precarious wooden bridges that provide picturesque crossing points for hikers (SS) page 146
bottom left	The spectacular Mesi Bridge near Drishti is the longest Ottoman bridge in Albania, at 108m (AL) page 195
bottom right	The ancient city of Apollonia was a major port for many centuries, until the course of the Vjosa River shifted (WB/AWL) pages 104–7

above   The view from Rozafa Castle, overlooking the ravishingly beautiful River Drini (DD) page 189

below left   The 13th-century Church of St Michael backs onto the steep cliff-face below Berati's citadel
             (NDC/D) page 124

below right   The 'lock-in tower' in Thethi was used as a safe house when a family was involved in a blood-feud
             (GG) pages 204–7

bottom right   Lezha was where the national hero Skanderbeg united the clan chieftains against the Ottomans
             (SS) pages 196–9

above The beautiful Albanian Alps lie in the far north of the country and are one of the richest remaining corners of Europe for wild flora (LM/S) pages 202–14

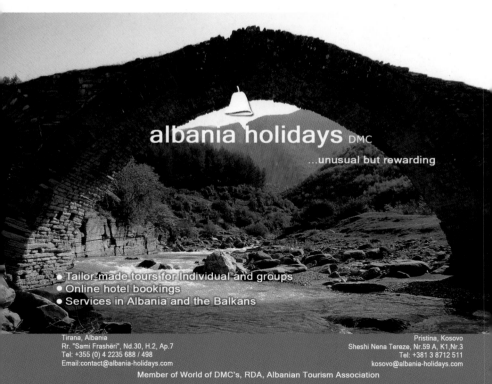

ultimately to the country's independence. See the box on pages 150–1 for more about the Frashëri brothers. Their family home is now a museum, with interesting photographs and maps of the village and surrounding district as it was in the past. There are displays about the family and each of the three brothers, and paintings representing various events in which they played a part.

Frashëri is a largely Bektashi village (see pages 22–3) – indeed, the three famous brothers were Bektashi. The local *teqe*, built in 1781, was used as a school in the communist period. It is a single-storey, whitewashed building, with a *tyrbe* on the hillside above. It is indicative of the religious harmony which generally prevails in Albania that the caretaker of the teqe is a Christian.

There is no hotel in Frashëri; accommodation could probably be arranged with a local family. A campsite is being planned in Bredhi i Hotovës; wild camping would certainly be possible. The tourist information office in Përmeti can supply hiking maps of the trails around the national park. The road onward to Erseka is not suitable for cars, but it can be cycled. It takes the villagers eight to ten hours to walk. Hikers might alternatively head northwest to Çepani, in the district of Skrapari, and on to Çorovoda and Berati; see page 127.

Bënja The thermal baths at Bënja are a popular day trip for the people of Përmeti. Below an elegant Ottoman bridge over the Lengarica River, the water from several thermal springs collects in a large pool, wide and deep enough to swim in. The water temperature of the springs is 23–32°C. The 3.7km canyon above the bridge is excellent for kayaking, at least until the Lengarica is dammed for hydro-electric power; Outdoor Albania (see page 31) can organise tailor-made tours here.

A minibus between Përmeti and Bënja operates in the summer, starting when enough local people want to go there (sometime in June) and continuing until summer turns to autumn. There is a café just before the bridge, where coffee, water and other drinks can be bought and which has a toilet for customers' use.

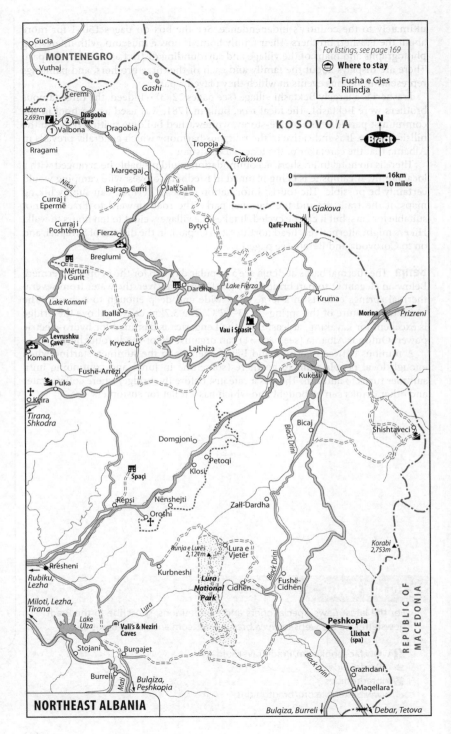

For listings, see page 169

Where to stay
1 Fusha e Gjes
2 Rilindja

MONTENEGRO

Gucia
Vuthaj
Çeremi
Jezerca
2,693m
Rragami
Valbona
Dragobia
Cave
Dragobia

Gashi

KOSOVO/A

N

Bradt

Tropoja

Gjakova

0 _____ 16km
0 _____ 10 miles

Margegaj
Bajram Curri
Jah Salih
Nikal
Curraj i
Epermë
Curraj i
Poshtëm
Fierza
Breglumi
Mërturi
i Gurit
Lake Komani
Iballa
Komani
Levrushku
Cave
Kryeziu
Fushë-Arrëzi
Puka
Kçira
*Tirana,
Shkodra*

Dardha
Lake Fierza
Vau i Spasit
Lajthiza

Bytyçi

Gjakova
Qafë-Prushi

Kruma

Morina   *Prizreni*

Kukësi

Bicaj

Shishtaveci

Domgjoni
Petoqi
Spaçi
Klosi
Rëpsi
Nënshejti
Oroshi

Zall-Dardha

Black Drini

Korabi
2,753m

Rrësheni
*Rubiku,
Lezha*
*Miloti, Lezha,
Tirana*
*Lake
Ulza*
Stojani
Burreli

Kurbneshi

Runja e Lurës
2,121m
*Lura
National
Park*

Lura e
Vjetër

Cidhën

Black Drini

Fushë-
Cidhën

Lura

Vali's & Neziri
Caves
Burgajet

Mati

*Bulqiza,
Peshkopia*

Peshkopia
Llixhat
(spa)

Grazhdani

Maqellara

REPUBLIC OF MACEDONIA

NORTHEAST ALBANIA

Bulqiza, Burreli ↓   Debar, Tetova

The Northeast

MIRDITA   *Telephone code (Rrësheni): 0216*

Mirdita is an enchanting blend of wild mountain scenery and centuries of unique religious and cultural history. The first of these unique features is the institution called the Captaincy, or Kapedania, a hereditary position which combined the roles of judiciary and head of state. The chiefs of all of Mirdita's clans accepted the authority of the Captain, not as first among equals, like the *bajraktarë* of the rest of highland Albania, but as their judicial authority and their head of state. Edith Durham (see box, pages 178–9) attended a council of the Mirdita clans in 1908 and took a famous photograph of the highlanders gathered, all armed to the teeth, on the lawns of St Paul's Church. The Captain resolved legal disputes according to the traditional Code, or Kanun (see box, pages 174–5) – the version used in Mirdita was the Code of Skanderbeg – and represented the region to the Ottoman authorities and, eventually, those of independent Albania. The Captaincy's palaces were in Mirdita's ancient capital, Oroshi.

Also in Oroshi was the seat of the Abbacy of Mirdita, with special *Nullius* status (the only one in Albania) which made it directly dependent on the Vatican, not on any of the archbishoprics covering the rest of Albania. Mirdita has always been fiercely independent and it managed to keep the Ottomans from establishing their authority over it, dealing with them instead as practically an autonomous state. Because of this resistance, almost the entire population of Mirdita is still Catholic. Most of its churches, including the Abbey at Oroshi, were burned to the ground during the atheism campaign of 1967 (see pages 16–17) and have been rebuilt since freedom of worship was restored in 1990.

There was some industrialisation during the communist period, most of it linked to the copper mines in the area. At its peak, the copper industry employed 5,000 people in Mirdita alone; there were small copper-processing plants all over the district, feeding into the main plant at Rubiku. From there, the copper was sent on to Shkodra to be further processed into wire and other industrial materials. The mines are now closed and the plants which processed the minerals lie idle. Mirdita experienced very high emigration as a consequence of the lack of local employment but, thanks in part to the job opportunities provided by the construction of the Durrësi–Morina highway, which cuts straight through Mirdita, people have recently begun to return to their ancestral homes.

Until very recently, most of the district was difficult to get to; but the inauguration of the new highway, in 2010, and improvements to minor roads have meant that access to wild and beautiful parts of Mirdita is now much easier. Hotel accommodation is limited, but it would be perfectly feasible for hikers or cyclists to base themselves in Rubiku or Rrësheni and explore the district from there. Those with tents could, of course, base themselves in whichever remote corner took their fancy; see page 45 for advice on wild camping in Albania.

GETTING THERE AND AWAY The new **highway** connecting Kukësi (and Kosova) with the Adriatic port of Durrësi has transformed travel to and from northeastern Albania. It begins at the Miloti roundabout on the main north–south highway, about halfway between Tirana and Shkodra, and cuts pretty much due northeast, straight through Mirdita, with state-of-the-art tunnels blasted through any inconveniently located mountains. Cyclists can avoid almost all of the highway, as far as Oroshi, by crossing the Fani River just after the Miloti junction and then using the old roads which run more or less parallel to it.

There is good **public transport** to the district capital, Rrësheni, from Tirana and Lezha. In **Tirana**, buses and minibuses leave from the Zogu i Zi roundabout; the journey takes about 1½ hours. From **Kukësi** (130km), any bus heading for Tirana could drop passengers at the turn-off for Rrësheni or Rubiku. See page 160 for information about public transport from Rrësheni to the Lura National Park.

With **bikes** or a **4x4** vehicle, an alternative route is the old road south from the district of Puka (see page 161), following the Fani i Madh River. Until the Durrësi–Morina highway was constructed, this was the shortest, although not the quickest, way from Rrësheni to Kukësi; now all the traffic whizzes up and down the new dual carriageway and this old road is almost deserted. The road surface is reasonable; it is a beautiful run of about 60km to Rrësheni from Fushë-Arrëzi, in Puka. This would make a very attractive little circuit around a fascinating part of highland Albania for those who do not have the time or inclination to venture further north. It is also possible to cross into Mirdita through the Lura National Park from Peshkopia; see pages 160 and 177 for more information about this option.

🏠 **WHERE TO STAY**

🏠 **Marub** (19 rooms) Katundi i Vjetër, Rubiku; m 068 20 77 424, 068 24 64 009; e info@ hotelmarub.com, hotelmarub@yahoo.com; www. hotelmarub.com. 2km from Rubiku, set in forested hills on the (asphalted) road to the village of Katundi i Vjetër. Modern alpine-style building, designed to be environmentally sustainable; beautiful views, ample car parking; CH throughout. Restaurant & bar; Wi-Fi. Guides & horses can be arranged for excursions in the area. All rooms en suite with AC, satellite TV, balcony with mountain view. **$$**

🏠 **Arbëri** (7 rooms) Rrësheni; ✆23376; m 069 21 83 887. Opposite the cathedral, convenient for buses. Friendly management; excellent restaurant; bar with terrace above street. En-suite rooms. **$**

🏠 **Kaçorri** (23 rooms) Rrësheni; m 069 23 40 986. Conveniently located in the main square. Pleasant, helpful management; reliable water & electricity. Most rooms share the toilets & showers installed on each corridor; dbls have small balcony & wash/hand basin; trpls have TV & reasonable en-suite bathroom. **$**

✖ **WHERE TO EAT AND DRINK**

✖ **Eksklusiv** Rrësheni; ✆23375. Just off the main square, on the opposite side from the Kaçorri. Standard menu of *qofta* or steak with chips & salad; if given prior notice, it can also prepare locally caught trout; excellent local wine, made from the indigenous Kallmet grape. **$$**

✖ **Europa** Rubiku. On the main street, on the right if coming from Tirana. Exceptionally good food inc, astonishingly, vegetarian dishes other than salad. Carnivores should (also) try the grilled pork. Excellent, locally produced, Kallmet Arbëri wine. **$$**

WHAT TO SEE AND DO

Rubiku Rubiku is a pleasant little town, with well-maintained public spaces and a commendable absence of litter. Above it stands a beautiful old church, which survived the atheism campaign (see pages 16–17) thanks to its age and the frescoes behind its altar. There has been a church on this site since the 13th century; in the 19th century, a monastery was built beside it. Both the church and the monastic buildings suffered great damage during World War II, because the hill on which they stand controlled the road. The monastery is still in ruins; the church, however, was re-roofed and repaired in the 1990s. More recently, the road up the hill has been asphalted and the Stations of the Cross have been installed along it. The church is dedicated to St Anthony (Shën Ndout), to whom there is also a little shrine near the church.

Rrësheni The district capital, about 20 minutes' drive beyond Rubiku, is the only other town of any size in Mirdita. Rrësheni has a small museum and a fascinating collection of the traditional costumes of Mirdita. It is also worth visiting the cathedral – new in ecclesiastical terms as well as architectural because, before World War II, Mirdita's cathedral had been the Abbey at Oroshi. It was only in December 1996 that Rrësheni was made the seat of the diocese, covering not only Mirdita but also the neighbouring districts of Mati, Bulqiza and Dibra. Construction began almost immediately and continued in defiance of the destructive civil unrest which overwhelmed Albania at the beginning of 1997. The new cathedral was consecrated in 2001.

Mirdita costumes are instantly recognisable because of the preponderance of red rather than the range of colours used elsewhere in highland Albania. The costume display is in the Cultural Centre, just off the main square; it also has a collection of traditional musical instruments. The museum is at the other end of town, beside the Europa café. The displays are themed to illustrate the development of Mirdita as a state, the importance of Catholicism and the region's ethnological heritage.

Rrësheni has a couple of good internet cafés and, for those heading for the Lura Lakes, the last ATMs before Peshkopia. It is the main hub for public transport out to the rest of the district and for intercity buses or minibuses to Lezha, Tirana and Shkodra. The bus terminus is on Rruga Shën Vinçenci i Paulit (St Vincent de Paul Street), near the cathedral.

Oroshi The traditional capital of Mirdita, Oroshi was the seat of both its ecclesiastical and temporal powers: the Abbacy (Abacia), first mentioned in Vatican documents of 1703; and the Captaincy (Kapedania), Mirdita's unique system of government. The Captain was recognised by all other clan chiefs as the leader who could negotiate on Mirdita's behalf with foreign powers, such as the Ottoman authorities, and who was the last court of appeal in legal disputes, which were resolved according to the traditional Code (see box, pages 174–5). The Captaincy was a hereditary position, although it did not automatically pass to the eldest son (of course it was always a man; Mirdita was not *that* different from the rest of Albania!). The Captain and his household had two palaces at Oroshi, one of them right next to the Abbey.

The importance of Oroshi as a symbol of Mirdita's unity and resistance meant that aspiring oppressors have completely destroyed it no fewer than three times. The first was during a sustained assault by the Ottomans in the 1870s, described by Edith Durham (see box, pages 178–9) in *High Albania*. The church was rebuilt by the energetic abbot Prend Doçi, who also successfully negotiated with the Vatican to be brought under the direct jurisdiction of the pope (as a 'territorial prelate' or 'prelate *nullius*'). This meant that, from now on, the abbots of Oroshi would report directly to the Vatican, rather than via an archbishop – Oroshi was the only diocese in Albania which had this special *Nullius* status. The church and palace were burned down again during the Second Balkan War, then demolished by the Albanian government in 1967 (see pages 16–17). The church which now stands on its historic site in Oroshi was built in 1994–95, using old photographs to create an exact replica of the building destroyed by the atheism campaigners. The individuals who represented Mirdita's traditional institutions were also eliminated by the communist government: Gjon Markgjonaj, the last Captain of Mirdita, led an insurrection against it and was killed in 1946; the Abbot of Oroshi, Monsignor Frano Gjini, was shot in 1948, one of dozens of Catholics executed in northern Albania who are now commemorated in Shkodra Cathedral.

The village of Oroshi, scattered across the hillside across from the church and the ruins of the palace, is now home to 20 families. It is served by two minibuses a day from **Repsi**, 7–8km away. Further up in the mountains is **Nënshejti**, a beautiful village with a 500-year-old church, set in magnificent scenery. It is 23km from Repsi, but the road is so bad that it takes at least two hours to get there. There is no public transport and a 4x4 vehicle is essential. There is no accommodation in Nënshejti at the time of writing, but it would be a wonderful place to camp.

Spaçi In 1967, the Albanian government decided to use the copper mine at Spaçi as a forced-labour camp for political prisoners. Over the next 24 years, thousands of men were imprisoned at Spaçi, behind three rings of barbed-wire fence which enclosed the whole 12ha of the mine. An unknown number died, sometimes of exhaustion and malnutrition, sometimes shot. Not all the bodies were returned to their families – the guards would take corpses across the river and bury them in unmarked graves on the hillside opposite. The author Fatos Lubonja, who spent 11 years in Spaçi, survived (just) and has written about his experience in a book translated into English as *Second Sentence* (I B Tauris, 2009). Spaçi was not the only forced-labour camp in Albania, but it was the only one which used exclusively political prisoners. There were also a few non-prisoners employed at Spaçi. Their job was to handle the explosives, which for obvious reasons were not made available to the prisoners. At any one time there was an average of 800 prisoners in the camp; when it closed, in 1991, 830 men were freed. They were kept, 30 to a room, in cells measuring 5m by 6m. The slightest breach of discipline could mean a stay in the isolation cell, where prisoners were left for days with no food or blankets; the temperature at Spaçi falls to –5°C in winter.

A plan has been developed to restore this chilling place, in its bleak setting amid bare, harsh mountains, so that it can be opened to the public as a museum, along the lines of Robben Island in South Africa. It is 14km from the highway; at the time of writing, a 4x4 vehicle is needed, although the road will be asphalted once the museum is opened. The camp is up the road signposted for Gurth-Spaç, not Kodër-Spaç.

Caves and *kulla* The easiest of Mirdita's **caves** to visit is the Vali's Cave (Shpella e Valit), near the district boundary with Mati (see pages 180–1). (A *vali* was a provincial governor in the Ottoman administration.) The cave is 3–4km from the road and has stalagmites and stalactites. To its south, in Mati, is the Neziri Cave. The caves have not been properly explored by speleologists, but it is thought that they may be connected by an underground passage. They are also linked by an overground track across the pass between them, so that both caves can easily be visited in the same trip, approaching them from either Mati or Mirdita. The Marub Hotel near Rubiku (see page 156) and the Vila Bruçi in Burreli (see page 181) can organise excursions to these caves.

There are also caves in the commune of Fani, in the far northeast of Mirdita. Fani is the most traditional part of Mirdita, because it is completely surrounded by high mountains (nearly 2,000m above sea level). Until recently, it was almost impossible to get to. Now, though, the main village, **Klosi**, is right next to the new highway and slip-roads have been built along it to provide access for the villagers. These include exits on either side at the entrance to the Kalimashi Tunnel, which is 5.6km long and cuts through the mountains to Kukësi district. Fani has 17 villages, many in spectacular settings, with traditional fortified houses (*kulla*; see page 180) still occupied. One which can be reached in an ordinary car is **Petoqi**, 800m above sea level. The village of **Domgjoni** is less accessible, but has a 4th-century aqueduct system, a very unusual structure which provided water to the ancient settlement of Sukbukëra.

THE LURA LAKES

The Lura National Park covers 1,280ha of mountainous terrain around the Crown of Lura (Kurora e Lurës) Massif, which rises at its peak to 2,121m. The area was designated as a national park because of the beautiful lakes which lie within it, and a road into the park was constructed to give access to the seven largest. These lie in cirques 1,600–1,720m above sea level, surrounded by pine trees and wild flowers, with the mountains rising high above them. Each of the seven main lakes has a subtly different atmosphere. Several of them are covered in white and yellow water lilies, and huge dragonflies dart around them. Others have no flowers in them; the stillness of their water is dappled with the reflection of the surrounding trees.

The Lura Lakes were a popular destination for Albanian holidaymakers during the communist period and visitor numbers are now starting to pick up again. They are still rather difficult to get to; over the past ten years or so, illegal logging within the park has reached calamitous levels, and the logging companies' trucks have destroyed the roads. Even worse, the loggers have also destroyed large swathes of pine forest and their clear-felling on the hillsides is causing serious erosion.

Despite the logging companies' efforts, however, there is still quite a lot of forest left, and the lakes are still lovely, tranquil places. The closest lakes to the village of Lura e Vjetër, about 1½ hours' drive from it, are Liqeni i Rrasave (Slate Lake) and Liqeni i Lopëve (Cattle Lake). Slate Lake is a pretty little tarn, with water lilies and reeds in the water, and beech trees growing around it. Cattle Lake is larger, and is overlooked by an impressively craggy hill. Around it are the remains of concrete steps and patios, which must have been built when Lura was a holiday resort. There is a path leading off the road to the right just before Slate Lake; it used to lead to another lake, but this was exploited for irrigation during the communist era and is now dry.

The next lake in the chain is Liqeni i Madh (Great Lake), which is divided into two sections by an artificial dyke. The main section is a large lake, surrounded by hills and trees, although these are marred by deforestation. Local children swim in this lake; less hardy adults might find the water a bit too cold. Great Lake is the highest of the main lakes, at 1,720m above sea level. Behind the dyke is a beautiful little lake, covered in water lilies, with a shady clearing under a couple of trees, which is an ideal spot for a picnic. Huge, electric-blue dragonflies live around this lake, which is considered as part of Great Lake.

The next two lakes along the road are Liqeni i Hotit (Hoti Lake) and Liqeni i Zi (Black Lake), so called because it is very deep. Black Lake is also very steep, and its sides are thickly forested with pines, although there is some deforestation further up the slopes.

It is 8.8km from Slate Lake to the last of the seven lakes, Liqeni i Lulëve i Vogël (Little Flower Lake). The two Flower lakes (Liqeni i Lulëve i Madh, Great Flower Lake, is the other) are in a part of the park where clear-felling has caused especially

6

ugly scarring on the hillside and around the lakes themselves. They are remarkably beautiful lakes, particularly Little Flower Lake, whose surface is carpeted with yellow and white water lilies, but it is hard not to feel depressed – or outraged – by the environmental damage which surrounds them.

Most of the trees which are being felled are mountain pines (*Pinus mugo*), although the national park is also recorded as having Macedonian pine (*P. peuce*), which is only found in this part of the Balkans. Its limited range gives it 'near-threatened' status. At lower levels are beech (*Fagus sylvatica*) and silver fir (*Abies alba*). There are roe deer, red squirrels, European brown hare, red foxes and polecats in the national park. Wolves, lynx, wild cats and brown bears used to live in the forests, although nowadays they have probably moved away to a quieter neighbourhood with fewer chainsaws. Golden eagles (*Aquila chrysaetos*) are readily spotted, from as low down as the hotel. Capercaillie (*Tetrao urogallus*) and rock partridge (*Alectoris graeca*) were formerly reported as breeding in the park, although no recent data are available.

GETTING THERE AND AWAY The administrative centre of the Lura commune, in which the national park lies, is the village called **Lura e Vjetër**. The best way to get there, at the time of writing, is from Rrësheni in the neighbouring district of Mirdita (see page 157), 60km away. The road is reasonable as far as Kurbneshi and then deteriorates. The journey takes at least two hours. Once a day – possibly more in the summer, if there is demand – a **minibus** runs between Lura e Vjetër and Rrësheni. This is currently the only way to reach the Lura Lakes by public transport.

The road from Peshkopia (see pages 177–80) to Lura e Vjetër is at present even rougher than the road from Rrësheni. It is theoretically possible to drive into Lura from Burreli, to the southwest of the park, but this is the worst of the three roads. In 2014, work began on a new road which, if the original plans are followed, will cross below the southern end of the national park between Peshkopia and Burreli. Once it is finished, this will become the easiest way to get to the Lura Lakes.

GETTING AROUND THE PARK The road which runs roughly north–south through the Lura National Park is very bad – parts of it are more like a dry riverbed, with large stones and deeply rutted sections – and it is sometimes blocked completely with felled trees. A resilient and high-axled 4x4 vehicle is essential, unless you plan to move around on foot or on two wheels. A jeep with driver can be hired in Rrësheni (try asking at your hotel there), but not in Lura itself. The road is not passable in winter or after heavy rain.

If you are walking, there are short cuts up through the trees, although it is easy to lose the path and end up battling through the forest. You might consider hiring a local guide in the village – ask the hotel staff or the family you are staying with to find someone to show you the quickest way to the lakes.

However, the start of the route is straightforward. From the Turizmi Lurë Hotel, head roughly southwest straight uphill. The walking is considerably more pleasant than along the stones and boulders of the road, over rough grass and past thickets of wild fruit – raspberries, blackberries, strawberries and blaeberries. The track rejoins the road at a flat, open area which would be a good place to camp overnight. It takes 30–40 minutes to reach this point from the hotel.

It is best to follow the road for the next stretch, until you come to a waterfall which runs under the road. A few metres after the waterfall, a clear path leaves the road to the right, and then rejoins it a couple of hundred metres before Cattle Lake. There are also large pipes leading downhill, and where these meet the road, their line can be followed as shortcuts.

Other possible campsites are around the main section of Great Lake and on the far side of Little Flower Lake. Caution should be exercised when logging is under way, as the trees are simply rolled down to the road from wherever they are felled. They are big logs and would have no difficulty whatsoever in sweeping a tent downhill with them.

WHERE TO STAY AND EAT There are a couple of small hotels in Lura, one in the village of Lura e Vjetër, the other beside the road up to the lakes. This road is steep and (at the time of writing) in very bad condition; only resilient 4x4 vehicles or trucks can negotiate it. Either of the two hotel proprietors can arrange transport for their guests from Rrësheni or from Tirana. It is also possible to find accommodation with local families in the village.

There are several places in the park where a tent could be pitched, in clearings in the steep, forested terrain; see above for some suggestions. If you plan to camp, you should bring adequate supplies of food and water with you. There are no shops in Lura e Vjetër, although it ought to be possible to buy basic foodstuffs such as bread and cheese from local families.

Lura (15 rooms) m 068 21 87 497 (the owner, Hasan Hoti). In the village of Lura e Vjetër. FB also possible. All rooms en suite with TV & AC. B/fast inc. **$**

Turizmi Lurë (10 rooms) m 068 53 17 082 (the owner, Faik Buçi). About half an hour's walk from the village (& probably only slightly less by car). In a magnificent setting at the entrance to the park, surrounded by trees & with wonderful views across the valley & the village below. Restaurant & bar. FB also possible. All rooms en suite with TV & AC. B/fast inc. **$**

PUKA *Telephone code (Puka town): 0212*

The district of Puka nestles in the corner formed by the spectacular lakes created by the hydro-electric damming of the Drini River. The old road from Shkodra to Kukësi, which more or less bisects Puka, follows much of the line of an ancient trade route along which the Romans built one of their great arterial roads, the Via Publica. This connected the Adriatic ports of Dyrrachium (now Durrësi) and Apollonia with Prizreni, Niš and, eventually, Odessa on the Black Sea. Traces of the Roman road can still be seen in Puka district. In the Ottoman period, the route became even more important: there was a customs post at **Vau i Spasit**, the ford by which travellers crossed the Drini from Puka to Hasi (see page 172). Fortifications were built to protect the road at Qafa e Malit and at Vau i Spasit.

Thanks to the road, Puka was a commercial centre for hundreds of years. Its rich history is reflected in the variety of its textiles as well as its castles, bridges and fortified houses. Thanks to the mountains and fjord-like lakes which ring it, Puka also has magnificent scenery; and thanks to its good infrastructure, this scenery can be enjoyed in winter as well as summer. The town of Puka is 838m above sea level and, at the time of writing, it is the best place to ski in Albania; see page 164 for further information.

GETTING THERE AND AWAY The main road which cuts across the district of Puka makes much of its territory surprisingly accessible; and, happily for cyclists, the heavy traffic which used to congest it has now transferred on to the new Durrësi–Morina highway to the south.

There are **buses** to the town of Puka from Tirana and Lezha, and **minibuses** from Tirana and Shkodra. The first minibus from Tirana leaves from the Zogu i Zi roundabout at about 07.00 and takes about 3½ hours. From the central square in

Shkodra, the journey takes 1½–2 hours, depending on how often the minibus stops and for how long.

With **bikes** or **4x4** vehicles, an alternative route into Puka is by the old road up from Mirdita (see pages 155–9), following the Fani i Madhë River. The road is almost deserted, now that all the traffic uses the new highway, and the surface is reasonable; it is a beautiful run of about 60km from Rrësheni in Mirdita to Fushë-Arrëzi in Puka. This would make a very attractive little circuit around a fascinating part of highland Albania for those who do not have the time or the inclination to venture further north.

 WHERE TO STAY AND EAT

Puka town

⌂ **Hani i Përparim Laçit** (11 rooms) Lagja Laçaj, Puka; m 068 20 56 472; e perparim65@ yahoo.com. Hotel & guesthouse complex a few mins' drive outside the town, near the ski piste also operated by the Laçi family. Welcoming & friendly; wonderful home cooking with local specialities; some English spoken; hiking, climbing & jeep excursions around the district can be arranged. 5 en-suite rooms in hotel above restaurant; guesthouse has 1 room en suite, others share showers & toilets. FB available. **$$**

⌂ **Hotel Turizëm Puka (HTP)** (33 rooms) Puka Qendër; ☎ 22586; m 067 20 70 304/306; e info@hotel-puka.com; www.hotel-puka.com. The former 'Turizmi' hotel, privatised & completely refurbished; great location right in the town centre. Good restaurant with award-winning chef; popular bar serving Puka beer, brewed next door; lift; ample parking. Excursion guides can be arranged. All rooms with good en-suite facilities, hairdryer, TV, CH, phone; some have balcony. **$$**

Dardha

⌂ **Alpin** (6 rooms) On main road above Dardha village; m 068 55 09 598. Sympathetically designed modern chalet-style building; beautiful setting on edge of forest with views of Lake Fierza; landscaped gardens with trout pond & water features; restaurant offering local specialities. Motorboat available for lake excursions. All rooms en suite; 1 has balcony. **$$**

⌂ **Kunora** (4 rooms) On main road above Dardha village; m 068 23 13 943; e Albano-Uka@ hotmail.com. Beautiful location overlooking Lake Fierza, views on clear days to Bajram Curri & Kukësi. Renowned restaurant with traditional specialities, menus available in English & Italian; popular bar with selection of local drinks, inc cornelian cherry raki; private dining room with *sofra* (low, circular table), *oxhaku* (hearth) & balcony. Boats available for lake excursions & fishing trips. Campsite planned. Simple twin rooms, shared toilet & basic shower. **$**

WHAT TO SEE AND DO A good way to begin a visit to Puka district is by looking round the small **museum** in the town centre. It has an excellent exhibition of traditional costumes and other local textiles, richly embroidered with ancient designs. There is a small display of locally made musical instruments, *lahuta* and *sharki*, while the historical section gives an overview of the archaeology of the area, from prehistory through the Roman and Byzantine periods to the Middle Ages.

Most of Puka's historic churches were demolished in the late 1960s (see pages 16–17 for more about the atheism campaign of those years). Some have been rebuilt since the restoration of freedom of worship; one of these is at **Kçira**, where the foundations of the destroyed church have been lovingly walled around and planted with herbs and flowers. The Catholic community of Kçira runs an interesting agricultural improvement programme, with experimental plantations of cereals, fruit and herbs. They are testing different kinds of crops, to see which do best in the local soil, and dry herbs for use as medicinal infusions (see box, pages 6–7 for information about medicinal plants in Albania). They also keep pigs, which end up being turned into sausages, prosciutto and salami in the project's kitchens, and breed sheepdogs. Kçira is on the main road, 15 minutes' drive from Puka town;

coming from there, the church is visible down a track to the right just after the village of Kçira, indicated with a large cross at the junction. The community plans to sell some of its produce from a stall at this junction.

Puka is famous for the quality and quantity of its ceps (*porçini*) and other fungi. Most of these are exported fresh to Italy; **Agropuka**, in Puka town, is spearheading an attempt to add value locally to these and other sought-after products. In modern dryers, they prepare ceps, fruit such as apple and persimmon, and herbal teas, which are then packaged in-house and sold locally and in Tirana. The factory outlet is an excellent place to stock up on these treats, whose great advantage for the traveller is that they are very light and unbreakable. Agropuka also sells fruit conserves and local honey. Finally, no visit to Puka town would be complete without sampling a beer from the town's very own brewery, next to the Hotel Turizëm Puka and with the same owners. The brewery produces an unfiltered version as well as the standard filtered beer.

A nice spot for a picnic, once you have bought all these goodies, is **Mrizi i Memajve**, signposted up a reasonable track off the main road between Puka and Fushë-Arrëzi. A *mriz* is a shady grove where livestock can shelter from the heat of the afternoon; Mrizi i Memajve is now used by the people of Puka for barbecues in summer. There are beautiful views of the surrounding mountains. It is also possible to camp here.

Puka district has many surviving fortified houses, or *kulla* (see page 180). Some fine examples can be seen on the way to one of Puka's most exciting attractions: the Levrushku Cave (Shpella e Levrushkut). This cave was used as a hermitage and it has a tiny chapel at the entrance, built into the rock; for this reason, it is also known as **'the Christian's Cave'** (Shpella e Kaurrit). The exciting thing about it is that it can only be accessed from the lake; you clamber up the rock face from a small boat, as the hermits would have done, a 5–10m climb depending on the water level in the lake. At the entrance to the cave, in front of the rock chapel, the hermits built a wall with an embrasure, just like a fortified house. The interior of the main cave – 20m long – is divided into two levels, each with a balcony from which the inhabitants could keep an eye out for intruders. The Christian's Cave can be reached by boat from the dam at Komani, but a more interesting option is to hike (with a guide) from Qelëzi, an hour or so drive up rough roads from Puka town. From Qelëzi, a path leads down to and then along the river which you will follow almost to the point where it joins Lake Komani. The path rises high above the river and provides lovely views of the mountains and of *kulla*, in clusters or standing alone. Two abandoned *kulla* can be explored just beyond the village of Levrushku, on either side of a smaller river (which you have to ford). Finally, you reach the place where the boatman will meet you and take you across the river and around into the lake, where the entrance to the Christian's Cave is marked by a high, tumbling waterfall. A whole day should be set aside for this excursion; it is one for which a guide is advisable, even for travellers who like to be very independent, because co-ordination with the boatman is essential and the path is not always clear.

Right on the other side of the district, on Lake Fierza, is **Dardha**. With two hotels above the village (see *Where to stay*, opposite), this is an ideal base for a couple of days' hiking or boat trips on the lake. It is about 55km from Puka town, on the road to Fierza from where one can continue up to Tropoja (see pages 164–71) or take the passenger-ferry down Lake Komani (see page 186) and back to the coast. The descent from here down to Fierza is very steep, with many hairpin bends; cycling in the opposite direction would be very hard work, possibly more than 2,000m ascent in total. There are old fortified houses in Dardha, one said to be 300 years old, right down on the lakeside. Near the top of the hill which leads down to the lake from the main road is a three-storey *kullë* whose owners can show you around. From the outside you can see the niche built into the wall of the guests' room; coffee and the implements to make it were kept here, so the head of the household could reach them easily from where he sat, to prepare and serve coffee for his guests. Below it is a *frëngji*, the embrasure from which unwanted visitors could be shot; the owners of the house have bricked it up to keep out draughts, but its shape is still clear. The owners do their best to maintain this fascinating old house, but the upkeep costs are very high and they would appreciate a small donation towards this.

In the dry weather of a normal summer, it would also be possible to get to Mërturi i Gurit, which has more than a dozen fortified houses, although only two of them are inhabited. A good base for hiking and exploring in summer, including to Mërturi, is **Iballa**, tucked into the centre of a ring of high mountains. There are no hotels or guesthouses in Iballa at the time of writing; local families may be able to offer simple accommodation.

WINTER SPORTS Puka is the best place to ski in Albania. It is easy to get to, it has good accommodation (see page 162) and, in most years, there is snow from October to March, with over 1m in the winter months. Përparim Laçi (m *068 20 56 472*; e *perparim65@yahoo.com*), who is a registered ski instructor with the Albanian Ski Federation, runs the small ski resort a few minutes' drive from the town centre. A piste has been cut through the forest, with a charming stone-built restaurant and small hotel at its foot. Skis can be hired and training can be provided for children aged five or over and adults. Ice skates are also available, for use on the nearby reservoir.

Përparim is also a mountaineer – he has climbed in the Himalayas – and can offer advice and guiding to climbers who wish to explore some of the peaks in Puka district or beyond.

TROPOJA

The district of Tropoja nestles in the top right-hand corner of Albania, cut off physically from the rest of the country by huge lakes and towering mountains. These geographical features, inconvenient though they are for the local people, offer the visitor the chance to see spectacular scenery in unspoiled surroundings rare in Europe. The highlights of any visit to Tropoja are the approach by boat up Lake Komani and excursions in the valley of the Valbona River. There are many mountain tracks for hillwalkers to enjoy, although you should exercise the same caution as you would in any other remote high mountain area – don't go alone, leave your planned route with someone you trust, don't assume your mobile phone will work, and so on.

Tropoja district takes its name from a village in its northeastern corner, which gives some indication of the disastrous effect on it of the Great Powers' decision (see page 12) to deprive the newly independent Albania of what is now western Kosova. The district is very far – and difficult to reach – from Tirana, but very close and accessible to the Kosovar towns of Gjakova, Peja and Prizreni. There can scarcely be a single family in Tropoja which does not have relatives on the other side of the border: in Kosova, in Montenegro or in both. Yet during the communist period it was completely cut off from these trading centres, while for most of the first decade of democracy, sanctions against Yugoslavia closed the border once again. At the same time, the district was sidelined and starved of resources by successive governments, even when the president of Albania was Sali Berisha, a native of Tropoja village.

In these circumstances, smuggling and criminality flourished during the 1990s, and Tropoja gained a reputation for being violent and unsafe. In a kind of vicious circle, this meant it got even less money from central government and none at all from foreign donors, who were afraid to go there. However, the security situation improved dramatically during 2001–02, after a clampdown by central government, and ordinary, law-abiding Tropojans are anxious to welcome visitors to their beautiful district.

GETTING THERE AND AWAY By far the best way to approach Tropoja from the south is on the **ferry** up Lake Komani, a world-class journey through outstanding fjord-like scenery. Details of this route to or from Shkodra and Tirana can be found below.

There are no roads into Tropoja from the west or the north. The best **road** route is from Gjakova (Đakovica) in neighbouring Kosova. The whole road has been upgraded and is now in excellent condition; formalities at the border are minimal for holders of most passports (indeed, practically non-existent for Albanian adults). **Minibuses** from Gjakova to Bajram Curri, the administrative capital of Tropoja, leave frequently during the day and the journey takes about one hour. The one-way fare is 300 lek; if the driver is Kosovar, it will probably be necessary to pay in euros.

Between Bajram Curri and Tirana, almost all minibuses now go via Gjakova, Prizreni and Kukësi. The fare for the whole journey is 1,000 lek; it takes about five hours. The first departure from Tirana is at 05.00 and minibuses then run hourly until 14.00. In the other direction, the first minibus leaves Bajram Curri for Tirana at 08.00 and departures continue until 14.00. Passengers can alight anywhere along the route; from Bajram Curri, it takes about 2½ hours to Kukësi and the fare is 500 lek. Those travelling in their own **cars** will be required to buy a minimum of 15 days' car insurance for Kosova, which at the time of writing costs €30. The only other feasible route, apart from the Komani ferry, is the old road through Puka and across the bridge at Fierza (see page 163). For transport between Bajram Curri and Valbona, see page 169.

Properly equipped and prepared **hikers** can walk into Tropoja across the Valbona Pass (1,817m) from Thethi; see pages 207–11 for further information about this splendid hike. There are no official border crossing points between Vermoshi (see pages 211–14) and the main road from Gjakova. It is possible to obtain permits to cross the international border on foot between Albania, Kosova and Montenegro; the forms and instructions to apply for these can be downloaded from the Peaks of the Balkans website (*www.peaksofthebalkans.com*) or the Balkans Peace Park website (*www. balkanspeacepark.org*). However, it is practically impossible for individual travellers to surmount the bureaucratic obstacles which will confront them. The Thethi-based hiking company Zbulo (*www.zbulo.org*; see page 31) can submit your paperwork and chase up its approval, for a small fee. The locals apparently do the journey from Çeremi (see page 170) to Plava in one hour, but then they are pretty fast walkers.

WHERE TO STAY AND EAT In the district capital, Bajram Curri, there are a couple of reasonably good hotels and restaurants; see pages 167–8 for details. Most visitors head quickly for Valbona, where there is a wide choice of accommodation, from boutique hotels to the family homes known as *hans*. See pages 169–70 for accommodation in Valbona and page 45 for general advice on wild camping in Albania.

LAKE KOMANI The journey along Lake Komani deserves to be one of the world's classic boat trips, up there with the *Hurtigrut* along the Norwegian coast or the ferry from Puerto Montt to Puerto Natales in Chile. Lake Komani is narrow and twisting, with sheer cliffs right down to the water in some stretches, complete with breathtakingly high waterfalls. It is part of a huge hydro-electric system constructed in the 1970s and 1980s but, unlike Lake Fierza further upstream, its topography was not much altered by flooding. In some places, the slopes are gentler and small clusters of houses can be seen. Here the people have terraced what little land is available, to pasture their livestock and grow their maize and other crops. It must be a desperately harsh existence in these lakeside villages, where the only form of transport is a boat and where in bad weather you can be cut off completely from any shops, schools or medical care. Incredibly, some people apparently choose to live in even more remote spots, in the houses which can be spotted from time to time high up above the lake. Some of these houses are now abandoned, but others are still occupied, at least in the summertime, by hardy souls who work their land and build their haystacks as their ancestors did before them.

Thoughts of the hardship of these people's lives need not deter you from marvelling at the magnificent scenery. Because the lake follows the twisting line of the river on which it is based, the boat at times appears to be heading for an unbroken cliff face. At the last moment, as it begins to turn, the break in the rock appears and the continuation of the lake can be seen through the gorge ahead. In these narrow stretches, the steep rocks on either side of you seem even higher than they really are. The water is a deep jade colour, and the cliffs and trees climbing up above it are reflected in its intensity. In the less steep stretches, you can see the far-off summits of the Dinaric Alps, more than 2,500m high. Herons (*Ardea cinerea*) and pygmy cormorants (*Phalacrocorax pygmeus*) live around the lake, and golden eagles (*Aquila chrysaetos*) and chamois (*Rupicapra rupicapra*) can sometimes be seen up in the surrounding peaks.

Getting there and away Since the opening of the Durrësi–Morina highway in 2010, the Lake Komani car-ferry has ceased operations. It is no longer economically viable now that all freight and most other vehicles go through Kosova. Pedestrians or cyclists, however, have a choice of passenger ferries; there is usually also space for one or two motorbikes. The traditional option, the *Dragobia* (m *068 52 70 934, 068 57 91 007, 068 23 62 798, 068 64 58 255, 069 68 00 748*, leaves Fierza at 06.00, takes about two hours, and begins the return trip from Komani at 09.00. The one-way fare is 700 lek per person. A summer-only service, operated by **Mario Molla** (☏ *026 373003*; m *068 20 22 686, 068 52 63 884, 068 63 74 712*; e *mariomolla@ outlook.com; www.komanilake.com; Facebook: KomaniLake*), leaves Komani around 09.00, docks at Fierza around 12.00 and leaves again at about 13.00. This boat takes longer because it is more of an excursion, with a swimming stop on the way back. The one-way fare is €10; English spoken. Mechanical problems are a common occurrence with both of these boats; they are not a good option for anyone whose time is tight. Mario also charters boats for day trips on and around the lake.

To get to Komani, the main road as far as Vau i Dejës is good; after the Komani turn-off, it is rather slow going, for 22 mountainous kilometres, and you should allow at least two hours in a **car** from Shkodra. Cars can be parked for the day or overnight beside the jetty at Komani. There is a small, basic hotel at the Komani jetty (**Natyra**; **$**) and a campsite beyond the tunnel. **Cyclists** should note that the tunnel leading to and from the jetty at Komani is badly lit and badly surfaced.

A **minibus** operates daily from Shkodra to connect with the 09.00 departure from Komani; it leaves Shkodra around 06.30, but you should check locally for departure times (m *068 39 58 101*). There is no longer public transport from Tirana, because the Tirana–Bajram Curri minibuses use the new highway to Kukësi and then go through Kosova. Mario Molla (see opposite) can arrange to collect you from Tirana or Shkodra, or from Rinas airport, and get you to Komani in time for his boat's departure. In the other direction, minibuses run between Bajram Curri and Fierza in the mornings; the journey takes about half an hour. The boats leave Fierza not from the old ferry terminal, 3km beyond the town, but from a jetty on the other side of the bridge, called Breglumi ('The Riverbank').

The most reliable and up-to-date source of information about the permutations of boats and buses, and all other aspects of travelling to or from Tropoja, is www. journeytovalbona.com.

BAJRAM CURRI *Telephone code: 0213*

The administrative centre of Tropoja district, Bajram Curri was purpose-built under communism and named after one of the key figures in the liberation of Albania from Ottoman rule. Bajram Curri was in fact Kosovar, which brought him into conflict with Ahmet Zogu (later King Zog; see page 12), for whom reunification with Kosova was not a priority. After two decades in and out of the leadership of Albania, he died in a cave near Dragobia in 1925, probably assassinated on Zog's orders. A large Socialist Realist statue of him looks down over the main square of the town named after him. The museum behind the statue was looted in 1997 and has been closed ever since.

 Where to stay and eat *Map, below.*

Vllaznimi (19 rooms) 068 20 79 060, 068 36 19 177. English spoken by some staff. Owners also run hotel in Dragobia. Restaurant

($$) & lively, though very smoky, bar. All rooms en suite with TV, AC & constant hot water; 5 'superior' rooms have small balcony; nice, good-

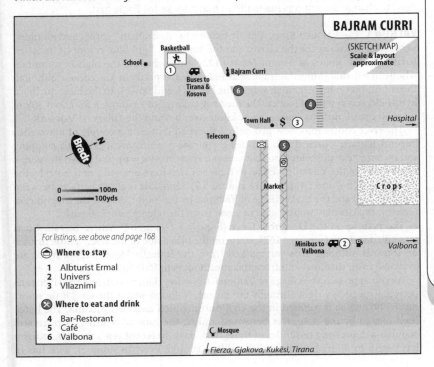

BAJRAM CURRI

(SKETCH MAP)
Scale & layout
approximate

School
Basketball
1
Buses to
Tirana &
Kosova
Bajram Curri
6
4
Town Hall $
3
Telecom
5
Market
Crops
Hospital

0 — 100m
0 — 100yds

For listings, see above and page 168

Where to stay
1 Albturist Ermal
2 Univers
3 Vllaznimi

Where to eat and drink
4 Bar-Restorant
5 Café
6 Valbona

Minibus to
Valbona 2
Valbona

Mosque

Fierza, Gjakova, Kukësi, Tirana

The Northeast TROPOJA

6

sized bathroom with shower; good-sized dbl bed or twins. **$$**

⌂ **Shkëlzen** (23 rooms) m 068 35 97 178. The former 'Turizmi' hotel, now upgraded to a reasonable standard; staff friendly & helpful. Good restaurant (**$$$**) & bar, a popular local meeting

place. 9 rooms en suite with shower, TV, AC & fridge; 14 basic rooms with shared facilities. **$**

⌂ **Univers** (5 rooms) m 067 25 96 335, 067 25 96 366, 068 56 88 189. Above restaurant, Wi-Fi in public area. Twin rooms, all with basic en-suite bathroom, AC, TV. **$**

✗ Where to eat and drink *Map, page 167.*

✗ **Bar-Restorant** (so called on sign above door) behind the Vllaznimi Hotel. Serves good home-cooked Albanian dishes. **$$**

✗ **Valbona** Convenient for the minibuses to Gjakova & Tirana. Range of grilled & roast meat dishes at lunchtimes, salads & light meals at other times. **$$**

Other practicalities The town has the usual things you find in Albanian towns, such as grocery stores, ATMs, a post office, internet cafés, a hospital and large new mosques. Travellers heading onward to Valbona should note that there are no cash machines, Accident and Emergency facilities, or petrol stations beyond Bajram Curri. Nor are there any shops in the Valbona Valley; there is no shortage of food or drink, but hikers should stock up here on snacks, fruit, cigarettes, batteries, plasters and anything else which might be required. There is a small hardware store where the minibus for Valbona waits (see *Getting there and away*, opposite).

There are no fixed-line telephones in the Valbona Valley. Once you are about ten minutes out of Bajram Curri, the only mobile phone provider whose signal is reasonably reliable is Eagle Mobile (numbers beginning with 067). Vodafone (069) can be picked up in some places; at the time of writing, there is no AMC (068) signal at all in the valley. If you are using roaming on your home phone, you may need to change the settings manually so that it looks for Eagle first.

VALBONA The Valbona River is justly famous for its dramatic gorges and plunging waterfalls, as well as for the clarity and the beautiful, light blue colour of its water. It rises on the slopes of Mount Jezerca (2,694m), which is the highest mountain wholly in Albania (Mount Korabi, near Peshkopia, is partly in Macedonia, although the summit is on the Albanian side of the border), and flows into the huge northern hydro-electric system at Fierza. The road runs alongside or above it for about 30km, up to Rragami, near its source, a few kilometres beyond the village of Valbona.

The river comes into view just before the road crosses it a couple of kilometres beyond Bajram Curri; if you are using your own transport it is worth stopping somewhere near the bridge, so that you can enjoy the view up and down the gorge. The owners of the Vllaznimi Hotel in Bajram Curri have opened a new hotel by the roadside just beyond Dragobia (18 rooms; **$$**). Dragobia is about halfway between Bajram Curri and the main village of Valbona; by this point, despite the magnificent scenery, cyclists may well be glad of a rest from the relentless uphill paths.

The path up to the **Dragobia Cave** (Shpella e Dragobisë), where Bajram Curri was killed in 1925 (see page 167), starts on the other side of the river, a little further on towards Valbona. It is waymarked from the Rilindja Hotel; hiking maps are available from the hotel and from the guesthouses in Valbona.

As you approach the village of Valbona, the valley flattens out, and the river runs between meadows right through the village. Valbona was a thriving little resort until 1997, when it suffered in the civil unrest which engulfed Albania. The hotel, then owned by the state, was destroyed and, at the time of writing, its ruins still stand as a depressing reminder of those dark days. In recent years though, tourism has begun to flourish again and the village is quite lively in summer, with lots of visitors who come from Kosova for the day or the weekend, as well as a smaller number of foreign hikers.

The local authority operates a tourist information centre (Qendra e Turizmit Valbonë) from the modern wooden building in the main village (Valbona Qendër). It stocks maps, brochures, books by local writers and locally made souvenirs; paintings by local artists are exhibited and are for sale; and performances of live traditional music take place in summer. Hotel rooms and camping are also available here; see the hotel listings below for details.

Getting there and away A minibus operates from Valbona down to Bajram Curri in the mornings and back again in the afternoons; the one-way fare is 300 lek. It leaves Valbona punctually at 07.00, from the western end of the village, just down the hill from the Lamthi and Çardaku guesthouses (see *Where to stay*, below); barring delays, it should be possible to connect with the Tirana minibus which leaves Bajram Curri at 08.00. The Valbona minibus usually leaves Bajram Curri again at about 14.30; it picks up passengers outside a little shop just before the last petrol stations on the road out to Margegaj and Valbona (see town map on page 167). The road has been surfaced and widened as far as the main village of Valbona, although it tends to disintegrate in the winter. Beyond the main village, a drivable road goes as far as Rragami, bridging the river just beyond Fusha e Gjes.

 Where to stay and eat

Hotels

⌂ **Margjeka** (9 rooms, more planned), Ziçi; m 067 33 82 162, 067 37 92 003, 069 21 18 206; e hotel@hotelmargjeka.com; www. hotelmargjeka.com. More or less directly above Fusha e Gjes, 500m uphill from the main road to Rragami. Restaurant with large terrace, beautiful views over the valley; German spoken. All rooms en suite with TV, CH; 2 family rooms with 1 dbl bed, 2 bunks & cot; 7 twin or dbl. **$$$**

⌂ **Fusha e Gjes** (3 chalets, 28 rooms) m 067 20 18 005. Beyond the main village of Valbona, on the way to the new bridge; lovely setting; restaurant & bar; a popular stopping-off point for hikers coming from Thethi. Rooms & chalets all with 1 dbl & 1 sgl bed, en-suite toilet & shower, wardrobe, heater in bathroom. **$$**

⌂ **Jezerca** (8 rooms) Valbona Qendër; m 067 30 93 406. Traditional house, trpl & dbl rooms, shared bathroom with shower, restaurant. Camping also possible. **$$**

⌂ **Rezidenca** (11 rooms) Quku i Valbonës; m 067 30 14 637/8; e catherine@ journeytovalbona.com; www.journeytovalbona. com. In village (also known as Quku i Dunishës) 3km before the centre of Valbona; luxury rooms in a traditional setting; same owners as Rilindja, English spoken. All rooms have 1 dbl & 1 sgl bed, CH, wardrobe with hangers, en-suite bathroom

with good shower, balcony with table & chairs. Sitting room with fireplace, self-service kitchen with espresso machine. **$$**

⌂ **Rilindja** (4 rooms) Quku i Valbonës; m 067 30 14 637/8; e catherine@journeytovalbona.com; www.journeytovalbona.com. Just off the main road on way up to Valbona; attractive wooden building set in landscaped garden & surrounded by magnificent mountains; large covered balcony looking on to the garden; English spoken. Excellent restaurant & bar on ground floor; information centre with maps, brochures & advice on hiking routes. The friendly, dynamic Albanian-American couple who run both Rilindja & Rezidenca can arrange hiking guides, with or without horses; qualified naturalist available to lead walks. Campsite (**$**); dedicated bathhouse for campers under construction (2014) with toilets, showers & bathtub. 4 twin rooms share good bathroom; 2 have large balconies with table & chairs. **$$**

⌂ **Qendra e Turizmit Valbonë** (6 rooms) Valbona Qendër; m 067 34 07 776, 067 34 26 658; e florian.selimaj@yahoo.com. A new, wooden building, part of the tourist information centre; restaurant serving traditional cuisine; traditionally furnished *oda* on 1st floor where groups can eat; live traditional music on some evenings. German spoken. Generator; 24hr satellite internet access; 3 computers available for use by guests; hiking guides can be arranged. Car park; camping also possible, €2 per tent. Room facilities vary: 2 have 1 dbl & 1 sgl bed, 2 dbl, 1 trpl, 1 with 4 bunk beds; most have en-suite shower but share toilet with other rooms or with campers. B&B pp **$**

⌂ **Tradita** (5 chalets, 6 rooms) Valbona Qendër; m 067 33 80 014, 067 30 14 567. Restaurant. Chalets (**$$**) newly built in 2013, each with 1 dbl & 1 sgl plus 1 fold-up bed; AC; wardrobe with hangers; nice en-suite bathroom with shower. Rooms in traditional farmhouse (**$**), sharing shower & toilet; 2 dbl, 4 twin. **$–$$**

Guesthouses (han)

All prices are per person with b/fast (**$**); FB and HB options are also available.

⌂ **Ilirjan Lamthi** (12 beds) Rragami; m 069 25 22 486. 1 dorm, shared bathroom; home-cooked food, inc honey from Ilirjan's own bees.

⌂ **Kol Gjoni** (20 beds) Valbona, just beyond the main village; m 069 26 40 836. Some English spoken; 1 member of the family is the English teacher at the village school. 2 rooms sharing bathroom; home-cooked food.

⌂ **Lazër Çardaku** (8 beds) Rragami; m 067 28 86 309, 069 23 11 499. Some English spoken; Lazër is a teacher at the village school. 2 rooms sharing modern bathroom; traditional, home-cooked food & homemade raki & wine; picnic lunches can be provided.

⌂ **Mark Lamthi** (16 beds) Rragami; m 069 25 03 941, 067 30 14 524. 1 twin room with beautiful carved wooden ceiling, 3 dorms, 2 shared bathrooms; camping also possible; home-cooked food.

What to see and do There are plenty of short **hikes** in the Valbona area, to lovely alpine meadows, mountain lakes and spectacular waterfalls. Hiking information is available at guesthouses in the village and at the Rilindja Hotel. The trout fishing in the Valbona River is generally excellent, and permits are not usually required for light, non-commercial fishing; the hotels and guesthouses may be able to provide rods. The path over the Valbona Pass, from Rragami to Thethi, has been waymarked and a guide is not necessary; see pages 210–11 for more about this increasingly popular hike. Waymarking has also been done around the Rilindja Hotel; for example, to the Dragobia Cave (see page 168) and to Liqeni i Xhemës, a beautiful little lake hidden away among beech trees only a couple of hundred metres from the main road. The waymarking around Valbona is more discreet than the Rragami–Thethi markings and, some would say, more in keeping with the wilderness environment here.

A longer waymarked hike – 2.4km from the main road – goes through the forests to **Çeremi**, a tiny traditional village right up on the border with Montenegro. There is also an asphalted road up to the village. For those who have hiked into Albania across the border (see page 165), Çeremi is a good place to stop for lunch or for the night. **Berti's** (*4 beds*; m *067 22 74 913 (use SMS, no mobile signal in village);* **$**) offers a single dorm room with four single mattresses on the floor. Some English is spoken. Solar panels provide electricity and hot water, and there are a toilet and shower in separate cubicles. Camping is possible in a field behind the family house. Berti's mum prepares huge traditional lunches of home-produced ingredients. Some English is spoken.

For other hikes, and certainly for longer expeditions, a local guide should be hired. The families in all the guesthouses will be able to recommend a knowledgeable guide; for short hikes, the going rate is around 1,000 lek. These guides are unlikely to speak much English. The Rilindja Hotel has a pool of guides who can lead all-day or multi-day treks and can communicate in assorted languages; they charge €50 per day. The Rilindja can also provide horses for longer expeditions. Outdoor Albania in Tirana (see page 31 for contact details) can also organise hiking and climbing expeditions in the Valbona and Thethi areas.

Beyond the main village, the road turns into a bulldozed track across rough, stony ground – a (usually) dry riverbed, in fact. Just after the surfaced road ends is the beginning of the village-cluster of **Rragami**. There are several guesthouses here and a small hotel with a bar and restaurant. Beyond the hotel, a new bridge has been built where before there was only a ford; however, to drive this section of the road requires a 4x4 vehicle. Users of less rugged cars can park at the hotel and walk the rest of the way to the Gjelaj settlement, where the drivable track ends – at least, where it ends at the time of writing; surveying was conducted in 2010 for a new road over the mountains to Thethi.

Gjelaj i Rragamit is a beautiful place, nestled right in the angle where the mountains meet, but it is a harsh environment to live in, with 2m of snow every winter and no community facilities at all. The village school closed in 2007, and so families with school-age children had no option but to move away or board their children with friends or relatives. No families live in Gjelaj all year round; apart from a couple of ne'er-do-wells, everyone now leaves before the first snow and comes back home in the spring. In the summertime, though, when most visitors are here, there are plenty of people working their fields and tending their livestock. There are no shops or bars, but bread, cheese and raki can be bought from the villagers. One of the local families might be able to provide accommodation; as for camping, the challenge will be to find enough relatively flat space which is not covered in rocks. There is a lovely mossy spring about half an hour's walk beyond the village, which might be one possibility; in any case, it is a fine spot for a picnic. A scramble up through the woods above Gjelaj leads to a spectacular waterfall; the route is not obvious and it would be wise to hire a local guide.

From Gjelaj, an ancient path leads over the Valbona Pass to Thethi. This hike requires a good level of fitness and should not be attempted without adequate footwear and clothing. There is usually snow on the pass until the first week of June. The track has been waymarked and route-finding is now straightforward. Less experienced hillwalkers may still prefer to hire a local guide, so that they can relax and enjoy the stupendous views and the rich flora and fauna, instead of having to concentrate on navigation. Horses or mules can be hired on either side of the pass to carry rucksacks or other equipment; ask at your guesthouse or hotel. See pages 210–11 for further information about this hike, the box on pages 208–9 for details of the plants, animals and birds which are present in these mountains, and pages 204–5 for information about the (limited) transport options once you reach Thethi.

For those who find the Valbona Pass a little too well trodden, an alternative route between Thethi and Valbona goes through the beautiful, wild country of the Nikaj Valley. Cut off from the rest of Tropoja by walls of mountains, the remote village of Curraj i Epermë is now uninhabited apart from three or four families who return for the summers. From Valbona, the easiest pass into the valley is Qafa e Kolshit, which can be reached by road from Bajram Curri; then you walk down to Bëtosha and up the river to Curraj i Epermë. There are also passes from Dragobia and Rragami, but they are more difficult. If you are coming to Tropoja by boat, you could get off at Lekbibaj and walk up to Peraj i Nikajt, from where a good, clear path leads over Qafa e Mrrethit (about two hours) and down to Curraj i Epermë. From there, it is a stiff hike over another gigantically high pass to Nderlysaj, down the Shala River from Thethi. *Journey to Valbona* has created the first reliable hiking map of these routes; see page 41 for details. There is no accommodation in Nikaj, although the families in Curraj i Epermë will look after you *in extremis*; wild camping is possible everywhere. Take enough food with you; there is plenty of wonderful spring water.

KUKËSI *Telephone code: 024*

The town of Kukësi is a pleasant but unremarkable town in a dramatic setting, surrounded by mountains and overlooking the vast Lake Fierza. This is the largest in a chain of three interconnecting lakes which generate most of Albania's electricity. The damming of Lake Fierza in 1978 created the Light of the Party hydro-electric plant but inundated several settlements, including the old town of Kukësi. The existing town was built to rehouse the people whose homes are now underwater and so it is entirely modern. In very dry years, when the water level in the lake is exceptionally low, the roofs of the old town appear above the surface and the old people go down to the lakeside to sit and look at their former homes.

While Kukësi is not a top tourist destination in itself, it is a convenient base from which to explore further afield: north to Tropoja, south along the Black Drini River to Peshkopia, west to Puka or Mirdita, or east to Prizreni and the rest of Kosova.

GETTING THERE AND AWAY

From Kosova Kukësi is only 42km from Prizreni, in southwestern Kosova, and **buses** and **minibuses** ply frequently across the border, with the journey taking about half an hour. An alternative route from Kosova is from Gjakova (Đakovica, in Serbian) by the border crossing at Qafë-Prushi and via the district of Hasi. This takes about two hours by car; using public transport would require a change of minibuses in Kruma (the district capital, usually also referred to as Hasi). There are several minibuses a day between Hasi and Kukësi; the fare is 150 lek. This is a very interesting route with wonderful scenery – wild, desolate country, with traditional fortified houses (*kulla*) and beautiful views over Lake Fierza.

The **Jupa Hotel** in Kruma offers simple accommodation (**$**) – three rooms, sharing a toilet and shower – and serves good fish and traditional Albanian food. Just off the main road at the junction for the village of Gjinaj, a simple wooden restaurant serves fresh zander (pike-perch) and grilled meat dishes. There are wonderful views from here of the confluence of the two Drini rivers.

From Tirana and the rest of Albania A highway connecting Kukësi with the Adriatic port of Durrësi was inaugurated in 2010, and has transformed travel to and from northeastern Albania. The new road cuts southwest from Kukësi, through brand-new tunnels and state-of-the-art highway engineering, to join the main north–south highway at Miloti. The journey between Tirana and Kukësi now takes less than three hours, even on a bus. In Tirana, the buses for Kukësi leave from the Zogu i Zi roundabout. There are also minibuses to Kukësi from Rrësheni in Mirdita (see page 156).

From Bajram Curri (see pages 167–8), the buses to Kukësi (and Tirana) now go through Gjakova/Đakovica and Prizreni. The journey to Kukësi takes about 2½ hours; the through buses to Tirana drop passengers for Kukësi on the highway below the town, from where slightly rickety metal stairs lead up to town level. Negotiating these stairs with a large rucksack in heavy rain is an interesting experience.

A civilian airport has been constructed just outside Kukësi, but it is not operational at the time of writing.

 WHERE TO STAY AND EAT *Map, opposite.*

Amerika (42 rooms) \223 278; m 068 20 37 874; e office@baramerika.com; www.baramerika. com. For many years the nicest place to stay in

Kukësi, the Amerika is now a fully fledged boutique hotel. Expanded & rebuilt, it has inevitably lost some of its quirky charm, but the improved facilities are

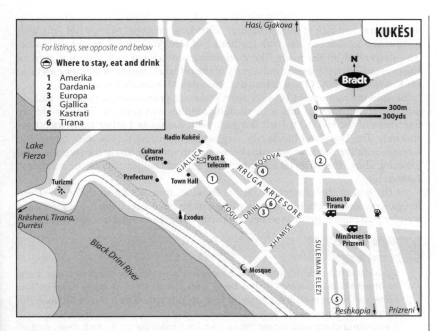

a compensation. English spoken. Secure lift to all floors, operated with guest's key-card. Function suite, conference rooms. Excellent restaurant (**$$$**; menu inc game & other specialities) & bar on ground floor; cocktail bar with picture windows on 6th floor, accessed by panoramic lift; stairs to roof terrace with hot tubs, telescope & binoculars. Good, friendly service; free Wi-Fi throughout, plus a desktop computer with internet connection & printer on every guest floor. All rooms have well-finished en-suite bathrooms, cable TV, AC, direct-dial phone, free minibar; suites also have enclosed balcony & spa-shower. Rooms, **$$$**; suites, **$$$$**

⌂ **Dardania** (7 rooms) ✆ 224 343; m 069 39 38 223. Quiet location opposite park. All rooms en suite with TV & balcony. Restaurant on ground floor. **$$**

⌂ **Gjallica** (22 rooms) ✆ 222 327, 222 527; m 068 20 23 098/096; e savepashpk@gmail.com, savepa-shpk@hotmail.com; www.savepashpk. com. Right in the town centre & can be rather noisy.

English spoken by some reception staff; parking; boat trips on lake can be arranged. Excellent restaurant (**$$$**), with traditional dishes, friendly service, nice table decoration & some enforcement of smoking ban; popular bar, separate from restaurant. Good-sized rooms, all en suite with Wi-Fi, TV, CH & AC; good heating & hot water. **$$**

⌂ **Europa** (4 rooms) m 069 22 93 391. Spacious rooms with twin beds; a 3rd bed can be added if required. 1 room has en-suite shower & toilet, the others share bathroom facilities. **$**

⌂ **Kastrati** (28 rooms) ✆ 222 719; m 068 20 64 315. Conveniently located for buses & minibuses. Restaurant. Some dbl, mostly twin rooms, all en suite with AC & TV. **$**

⌂ **Tirana** (14 rooms) ✆ 224 819; m 069 20 44 280. On the corner of the main street (Rruga Kryesore); might be a bit noisy. Good salads in restaurant (**$$**), some tables on terrace overlooking city centre bustle. Rooms with basic en-suite facilities. **$**

WHAT TO SEE AND DO

The town A walk around Kukësi takes an hour or so. The main square, with the administrative buildings for the town and region, is as good a place to begin as any. At the southern corner of the square, overlooking the lake, is an imposing monument to the **exodus** from Kosova during the 1998–99 war. Most of the 500,000 refugees who fled Kosova entered Albania at Kukësi, which – despite its own poverty and lack of infrastructure – somehow managed to cope not only with its Kosovar cousins but also with the hordes of foreign aid workers and journalists who descended on the town. The monument was erected by a group of grateful Kosovars in 2009, the tenth anniversary of the refugees' return to their homes (also via Kukësi) after NATO had driven out Slobodan Milošević's forces.

Beyond the monument runs the town's lakeside promenade, a pleasant walk on a fine evening, when it fills with strolling families and couples. To the right are fine views of the lake; to the left is a park, with swings and other amusements for children. The Durrësi–Morina highway, which connects Kukësi and, beyond it, Kosova, with the Adriatic Sea, runs below the promenade, along the lakeside. And towering above the town, lake and highway, Mount Gjallica rises to the southeast, 2,486m high.

At the end of the promenade, at the mosque, turn left up to the main street, Rruga Kryesore. Just to the right as you meet the main street, the buses for Tirana wait for passengers; 100m or so beyond them, parked around a triangular car park,

BLOOD FEUD

Blood feud is an ancient mechanism for resolving serious conflicts between clans or other social groupings. It has been (and still is) used in many cultures, but rarely has it achieved the degree of formal codification as it did in Albania. The codes which govern blood feud and other matters of clan administration were transmitted orally until recent times, and are known by the Turkish (from Arabic) word for 'law', *Kanun*. There were several versions of these codes in different parts of highland Albania; the best known are those of Lekë Dukagjin and of Skanderbeg. The latter, of course, is Albania's national hero, the chieftain who united all the northern clans against the Ottoman invaders in the 15th century (see box, pages 200–1 for more about Skanderbeg). The Dukagjins were another of the powerful clans of medieval Albania, and the Lekë concerned is thought to have been the clan chief in the 15th century, although many of the laws in his *Kanun* must date from earlier times.

The *Kanun* regulated all aspects of life in the northern clans, including marriage, property and taxes. It also attempted to regulate the practice of revenge killing, or *gjakmarrja* ('blood-taking'), by setting out ways in which feuds between clans could be reconciled. In a society governed by revenge, if a member of your clan is killed by a member of a rival clan, you are duty bound to avenge that killing. The family of the man you kill (in such societies, women and children do not count) is then obliged to kill either you or – if that proves impossible – one of your close male relatives. It is perfectly obvious that if no mechanism is found for stopping this cycle, your clan and that of your enemy will both die out.

The *Kanun* way to end a blood feud was *besa*, an Albanian word which means many things ranging from 'word of honour' (its usual modern meaning), through 'sacred oath', to its *Kanun* meaning of a truce between clans. *Besa* could be cemented with a marriage between the two families concerned, or by the payment of a tribute, or not at all, since the word itself was enough – but it was not necessarily permanent and, if the feud revived, the male members of the families involved would begin the cycle again. The lock-in tower in Thethi (see page 204) is a reminder of the devastating effect which blood feud had on northern Albanian families.

The communist government managed to suppress blood feud fairly thoroughly, presumably through the same mechanisms of fear and suspicion are the minibuses which go to Kosova and Peshkopia. The best chance of obtaining information of any reliability about minibus departure times is to ask in the cafés here. Keeping straight on across Rruga Kryesore will lead you to a little wooded park; you can walk through it or around it to meet Rruga Kosova. There is a bunker (see box, page 143) half-hidden among trees at this junction. A left turn here will bring you back to the main street, just beside the Gjallica Hotel.

To return to the administrative square, turn right along Rruga Kryesore. The Radio Kukësi building stands at its northern end, with a wonderful Socialist Realist bas-relief above its door. At the other end of this street (Rruga Gjallica) is the square, with the Cultural Centre, town hall and regional government building, or Prefecture. There is also a minor road up to the right, beside the Cultural Centre. Through trees and above fields, this leads to the ruined shell of the former 'Turizmi' hotel, used as offices by international organisations during the war in Kosova and, since then, left to decay and crumble. From the other side of the ruins, however, there are marvellous views of Lake Fierza, the Black

which it used to suppress activities such as listening to the BBC World Service. In the 1990s, however, blood feud re-emerged and has once more become a serious problem, although foreigners are extremely unlikely to be even tangentially affected. Feuds have been revived from several generations back, and because there is now freedom of movement, the young men who are at risk have left their mountain villages for Albanian cities, for Italy or Greece, or for further-flung destinations. Unfortunately, freedom of movement also means that the feud can follow them, thus spreading the problem from the highlands into the poor suburbs of the big cities.

Shkodra has been particularly badly affected by blood feud, with certain streets in the city functioning effectively as a 'lock-in neighbourhood', populated by people who have fled their villages and who allow no stranger to enter, lest he bring death to one of the families there. Having an enclave like this means that the men need not be confined to their houses, but can at least walk up and down the street and drink coffee with their neighbours. The women, of course, fulfil the same role as they would in the village, except they can buy food in the market instead of ploughing the fields on their own. There is even a 'lock-in apartment building' in the centre of Tirana.

The traditional codes exclude women and children from revenge killing. However, because they were maintained orally, by the elders of each clan or village, when it was revived after 50 years of suppression, there was nobody left to interpret them according to the ancient custom when they were revived after 50 years of suppression. Since the resurgence of blood feud in the 1990s, therefore, it has taken on quite anarchic aspects. Young boys are prevented from attending school because they might be the target of a blood feud, and the old *besa* systems of feud reconciliation have almost completely broken down. The botched land privatisation of the early 1990s has not helped; the majority of revenge killing cycles nowadays are started over disputes about property or water rights.

One group which offers advice to families involved in blood feud and helps with reconciliation, when this is possible, is the Diocesan Commission in Albania of the Catholic organisation Justice & Peace (*Sh. Papa Gjon Pali II;* ✆ *022 248 795;* e *p&dshkod@albnet.net; www.juspax-eu.org*).

Drini coming into it from the south and the confluence of the White Drini just visible to the north. The White Drini rises near the Kosova–Montenegro border and flows down to Albania through Kosova; the Black Drini begins its overland life at the northern end of Lake Ohrid and flows through Macedonia before entering Albania to the south of Peshkopia. See below for details of the trip between Kukësi and Peshkopia along the course of the Black Drini: one of the most beautiful mountain roads in this country. From here there is also a good view of the new bridge over the Black Drini and the highway which continues to Rrësheni, Durrësi and Tirana.

Shishtaveci Shishtaveci is the largest of a group of eight villages on the Shishtaveci Plateau, 31km southeast of Kukësi right on the border with Kosova. The plateau is over 2,000m above sea level at its highest point and, in the communist period, Shishtaveci, with its natural ski-slope, was one of the country's ski resorts. In the summer, the countryside is beautiful, but the road is in atrocious condition and it is very difficult to get to without a 4x4 vehicle; it might be possible, in dry weather, on motorbikes or really rugged mountain bikes. A minibus leaves the village for Kukësi first thing in the morning and returns to Shishtaveci in the early afternoon; there is no accommodation there, although wild camping would be possible.

Hikers should exercise caution in this part of Albania and avoid straying off beaten tracks. This is because there may still be some unexploded ordnance remaining in the border areas of the northeast from the 1999 war in Kosova. The mines were laid by Kosovar fighters to stop the Serbs following them into Albanian territory; it is thought that all of them have now been cleared, but it is impossible to be certain that none have been missed. The northeastern border is the only part of Albania where landmines present any risk at all.

The Black Drini (Drini i Zi) The Black Drini runs through spectacular gorges, wild rocky mountains and pretty hillside villages, making for a magnificent drive or bike run. A new road, further to the east, is now the main route between Kukësi and Peshkopia and there is no longer any public transport on the Black Drini road. The old road was widened and asphalted in 2011 and, in dry weather, it should be transitable in any reasonably sturdy car. Rain can cause flooding where the road crosses streams and, in such conditions, it is easy to get stuck.

From Kukësi, the road runs first through pretty woodland, with good views behind of the town and the lake – and the unused airport. After about 20km the scenery becomes more dramatic; for the next 20km or so, the views are really quite breathtaking, with the river far below and tributaries tumbling down towards it through willows and alders. There are clusters of houses fortified in the traditional style, using the slope of the hill to protect the back of the building, with small windows on the upper floors and none at all at ground level. Along the way, birds of prey hang on the thermals and spectacular white cliffs tower on the other side of the river.

Around Sllova, half an hour or so before Peshkopia, the countryside becomes slightly tamer and more inhabited. The road goes past terraced orchards (the district of Dibra is renowned for its apples) and wooden watermills. High up in the mountains to the right are the Lura Lakes, although this is not the best way to reach them (see pages 159–61). The local government office of the Kastrioti commune marks the (signposted) junction for Peshkopia, now only five or ten minutes' drive away; a trout farm where the road crosses the river again is a good place to stop for lunch.

PESHKOPIA *Telephone code: 0218*

Peshkopia is set amid spectacular mountains which make it rather isolated from the rest of Albania. Like Tropoja, it was cut off from its natural hinterland by the border drawn in 1913, and it suffered further from many years of neglect by central government. In recent years, though, foreign aid and local enterprise have begun to turn the town into a thriving and pleasant place. The district of which it is the administrative centre is called Dibër (or Dibra), and the town itself is also sometimes referred to by that name. This can lead to confusion, since the nearest town on the other side of the border is also called Dibër (or, in Macedonian, Debar). The key is to remember that only 100 years ago, before the drawing of the lines which have caused so much turmoil in the Balkans, it was all the same district.

GETTING THERE AND AWAY
By public transport From Tirana, the **minibuses** for Peshkopia leave in the early morning, from the Zogu i Zi roundabout. In Peshkopia, they terminate in and leave from the main square. The journey takes about four hours, or slightly longer if the traffic is bad in the outskirts of Tirana; the road is showing its age, especially compared with the new highways elsewhere in the north, but it is very scenic, running along the lovely green Mati River (see pages 180–1 for more information about the district of Mati) and then through pretty wooded countryside, with views of fortified houses and interesting arrays of bunkers (see box on page 143).

Getting to Peshkopia from neighbouring Macedonia by public transport is a bit complicated; try taking a Tirana bus from Tetova or Gostivari, and getting off in Maqellara, a bustling little transport hub about 13km from Peshkopia. There are very frequent minibuses from here to Peshkopia, taking about 30 minutes. A new road is under construction which will connect Macedonia with the Adriatic. If the original plans are followed, this will swing north of the existing road and no doubt improve Peshkopia's own transport links with Macedonia, as well as with Tirana and the coast.

By bike The new road between Kukësi and Peshkopia is very hard going on a bicycle. It has a good surface all the way, but the gradients are very tough – 15–20% in places. You should allow up to eight hours on this route. An alternative is the 'old' road which runs above the Black Drini; see opposite for details.

Another route to and from Peshkopia for cyclists, bikers, or those with the use of a 4x4 vehicle, is the unasphalted road to Librazhdi, about halfway between Elbasani and Lake Ohrid. This turns off the main Peshkopia–Bulqiza road, just after the village of Shupenza, and continues south for about 80km through remote mountain terrain, along the border with Macedonia.

 WHERE TO STAY *Map, page 180.*

Brazil (9 rooms) pranë Gjykatës, Peshkopia; 23934; m 069 26 30 141, 068 35 87 876; e hotelbrazili@yahoo.com. Friendly management; bar & restaurant on ground floor; treatment at nearby spa & hiking trips can be arranged. Rooms nicely furnished (with bedside lights!), all en suite. **$$**

Korabi (60 rooms) Rr Elez Isuf Ndreu, Peshkopia; f 22481; m 069 20 70 106/7, 068 20 70 107; e hotelkorabi@yahoo.com. The former 'Turizmi' hotel, refurbished. Good restaurant (**$$–$$$**) with separate entrance; in the summer, tables outside on lovely raised terrace; Wi-Fi. Rooms all en suite with AC, TV, balcony. **$$**

Veri (30 rooms) Peshkopia; 25090; m 069 20 98 172, 069 20 98 182; f 25222. Popular with Tirana-based NGOs, for seminars & meetings; room

The Northeast PESHKOPIA 6

rates negotiable for groups; Wi-Fi throughout; good restaurant (**$$$**). 12 rooms have enclosed balcony & mountain view, others face street, all rooms en suite with CH & TV. **$$**
🏠 **Peshkopia Hostel** (5 rooms); m 068 27 76 848; e info@peshkopiahostel.com; www. peshkopiahostel.com. Renovated villa once used as accommodation for visiting communist leaders. Overlooking the town; huge garden with trees & hammocks; ample parking; 2 common rooms, 1 with fireplace; fully equipped kitchen; 2 bathrooms on each floor. Tours organised, inc. to Lura & Mt Korabi. 1 dbl, 1 twin, **$$**; 3 dorms, **$**

✗ **WHERE TO EAT AND DRINK** *Map, page 180.*
Apart from the hotel restaurants, the **trout farm** by the side of the road out towards Kukësi serves the freshest possible fish in simple surroundings (**$$**). The **Taverna**

EDITH DURHAM

Edith Durham, like many other travellers to the Balkans, came to the region almost by accident. She was born in London in 1863, into a comfortably off professional family. Her father was a distinguished surgeon, and her seven brothers and sisters later became eminent in their various professions. She herself studied fine art and exhibited twice at the Royal Academy. However, when her mother became ill in the 1890s, it fell to Edith, as the eldest daughter in the family, to abandon her artistic career and devote herself to her mother's care.

Understandably enough, she became depressed and ill herself – 'The future stretched before me in endless years of grey monotony, and escape seemed hopeless,' she wrote – and, in 1900, she was advised by her doctor to take two months' holiday every year, as a complete break from her duties as a carer. She decided to take a cruise, with a friend, down the Dalmatian coast from Trieste to Kotor, in Montenegro. From there, she followed Baedeker's advice to drive up to Cetinje, then the Montenegrin capital, in order to 'be able to say ever afterwards, "I have travelled in Montenegro"'. Durham was struck both by the picturesqueness of this tiny, mountainous princedom and by what she described as its 'impossibly feudal views'.

That first short trip to Cetinje and Podgorica, where she saw Albanians for the first time, had sown the seeds of a lifelong engagement with the Balkans. When she returned to London, she learned the Serbian language and studied Balkan history. In subsequent years, her travels grew increasingly adventurous; she visited Montenegro four times, travelled extensively in Serbia, and ventured into the Ottoman province of Kosova. In 1904, she published an account of these journeys, *Through the Lands of the Serb*. She hoped that her ethnographic studies of the region might help to solve the vexed question of Balkan borders, which continued to give rise to so much diplomatic intrigue and military skirmishes.

In 1903, she visited Albania, the least known of all the Balkan provinces and the only one without a sponsor in one of the Great Powers. She discovered a growing feeling of national unity among Albanians which belied their religious and cultural differences, and realised that Albanian national aspirations would need to be taken into account if the problems caused by the decline of the Ottoman Empire were to be adequately addressed. She returned to Albania in 1908 and embarked on a remarkable journey through the northern highlands. Very few foreign men had ever travelled in this remote and mountainous region; for a foreign woman to undertake such a journey was completely unprecedented. Edith Durham recorded it in her book *High Albania*, a combination of travelogue, café ($$), at the western end of the main square (closed in the evenings), offers traditional Albanian dishes, including the local speciality, *jufra*, a kind of fine pasta; the Veri Hotel restaurant (see above) also has *jufra* on its menu.

WHAT TO SEE AND DO Towards the end of October each year, Peshkopia hosts an important **festival of traditional music** from all over the Albanian-speaking world (Oda Dibrane). It is difficult, although not impossible, to get tickets for Oda Dibrane, and it is essential to book accommodation in advance while it is on.

The local **museum** is set a little back off Rruga Elez Isuf Ndreu, just along from the Hotel Korabi. Its permanent exhibition includes finds from and information about prehistoric sites in the district, as well as displays about the town and district's

ethnographical observations and political reporting of the historical events which affected Albania during her stay.

In 1911, the Catholic clans of northern Albania, encouraged and armed by Montenegro, rebelled against Ottoman rule. The uprising did not last long – the clans were obliged to make terms with the Ottomans when Montenegro withdrew its support – but during and after it Edith Durham organised the provision of humanitarian aid from her base in Scutari (the Italian name for Shkodra). She distributed flour, roofing materials and money, and gave medical treatment to sick highlanders who would often travel for days to find her. She remained in Montenegro and Shkodra during the two Balkan Wars of 1912 and 1913, and described the events of the wars and her own experiences in *The Struggle for Scutari*.

Edith Durham was in Vlora when Greek troops occupied southern Albania in October 1914, and in Korça when it was taken the following year. She and a friend tried to save Korça by pleading on its behalf with the Council of Ambassadors in London; this involved their walking for three days across the mountains to Berati, the nearest place from where a telegram could be sent. After the war, she became the Secretary of the Anglo-Albanian Society, a pressure group of Members of Parliament and other promoters of Albanian interests. Her final visit to the country, in 1921, was cut short by illness, but during her stay she was greeted by cheering crowds and fêted by Albanian politicians. In Shkodra, delegations of clansmen came down from the mountains to welcome her.

Although she did not return to Albania after her 1921 trip, she continued to write about the Balkans. She was a council member of the Royal Anthropological Institute and wrote an ethnological study entitled *Some Tribal Origins, Laws & Customs of the Balkans* (published in 1928), as well as political-historical accounts of her travels such as *Twenty Years of Balkan Tangle* (1920). King Zog awarded her the Order of Skanderbeg and offered her a home in Albania. However, she remained in London, where she died in 1944.

Edith Durham is still revered in Albania, where she is sometimes referred to as 'The Highlanders' Queen' (Krajlica e Malësorëve; '*krajlica*' is an archaic word used in folk epics, and so the Albanian expression has a kind of fairy-tale sound to it). Streets still bear her name – sometimes they are the only streets which have signs – as do schools.

It is now very much easier to obtain copies of Edith Durham's books than it was before the advent of print-on-demand OCR reproductions. See *Appendix 2, Further Information*, pages 271–4, for further details.

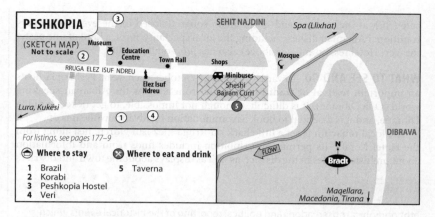

PESHKOPIA

(SKETCH MAP)
Not to scale

SEHIT NAJDINI

Spa (Llixhat)

Museum

Education
Centre

Town Hall

Shops

Mosque

RRUGA ELEZ ISUF NDREU

Elez Isuf
Ndreu

Minibuses
Sheshi
Bajram Curri

Lura, Kukësi

DIBRAVA

FLOW

N

Bradt

Maqellara,
Macedonia, Tirana

For listings, see pages 177–9

Where to stay

1 Brazil
2 Korabi
3 Peshkopia Hostel
4 Veri

Where to eat and drink

5 Taverna

contribution to the Albanian Renaissance (*Rilindja*; see page 23) and other historical events. Fans of Socialist Realist art should visit the restaurant of the Hotel Korabi, where one of the walls has a wonderful mural of a highland wedding.

Peshkopia is a good size for walking around, although the hill up behind the mosque is quite steep. Bear left up here for the old quarter, Lagja Sehit Najdini, with a few surviving Ottoman houses and, from the top, marvellous views over the town and of the mountains to the east, on the border with Macedonia.

Just outside the town is a well-known **spa complex**, known by the generic Albanian word for thermal springs: *Llixhat*. See box, page 152 for more about thermal baths in Albania. Although a two-week course of treatment is said to be the most beneficial, it is also possible to turn up and pay a small entrance fee – you will need to bring your own towel. You will be assigned a private cubicle where an attendant will fill the tub with the warm, sulphurous water from the springs, and then leave you to soak for half an hour or so. The spa is at its busiest in the summer, but the *cognoscenti* say that it is better to go in autumn when the days are cooler. Llixhat is a long walk or a short taxi ride from the town; the Brazil Hotel in Peshkopia can arrange transport and treatment.

MATI *Telephone code (Burreli): 0217*

Mati was the home district of Ahmed Zogu, who became King Zog (see page 12), and it is full of history: fortified houses, ancient bridges, caves and castles. The district capital, Burreli, is only 45km from the Miloti junction on the main Tirana–Shkodra highway. It is worth the detour, or a stop on the way to or from Peshkopia.

The traditional family houses of northern Albania were highly defensible stone buildings, usually two storeys high, called *kulla*, whose literal meaning is 'tower'. The word is often translated into English as 'tower house', which is quite confusing because these houses are not towers at all. *Kulla* are big enough for a traditional extended family to live in; the living quarters are usually on the first floor, accessed with an external staircase; where there is a third storey, this will have been used for bedrooms. The windows are small – hard to fire into and easy to shoot out of – and are often protected with stone embrasures, called *frëngji*, instead of wooden shutters. Mati has several well-preserved *kulla*, some built as recently as the 1930s – these later buildings have windows of a more normal size, because by then security was better. The imposing cluster of *kulla* where the Zogu family lived, in Burgajet just across the river from Burreli, was razed to the ground after World War II. The site can be seen from the terrace of the Vila Bruçi Hotel.

The best places to see fortified houses in Mati are in the villages of Macukullu and Guri i Bardhë. However, the roads to these villages are very rough and a 4x4 vehicle is needed. Easier to access are the *kulla* near the town of Klosi. The beautiful white stone bridge called the Maiden's Bridge (Ura e Vashës), is also near Klosi and can be reached in a normal car. As for the caves, they are in the north of the district, on the border with Mirdita. Excavations in the Neziri Cave (Shpella e Neziri) have revealed evidence that it was inhabited in Hellenistic times. The Vila Bruçi Hotel can arrange transport to all these sites, given a few days' notice. The caves and the *kulla* at Macukullu can also be reached from Mirdita; there is another interesting cave across the district boundary, in Mirdita, which is thought to be connected to the Neziri Cave by an underground passage. See page 158 for this option.

GETTING THERE AND AWAY From **Tirana**, minibuses to Burreli leave from a side street off to the north of the Zogu i Zi roundabout. The journey takes about 2½ hours, depending on the traffic in the outskirts of Tirana. From **Peshkopia**, the minibuses to Tirana go through Burreli, taking about 2½ hours or, if there is a meal stop, a bit longer. This is a very scenic route, through pretty woodlands and then along the beautiful Mati River, with fortified houses visible from the road. The fare for either of these journeys is 400 lek. From **Macedonia**, the buses from Debar (Dibra e Madhe) to Tirana could also drop passengers in Burreli. All these timings will change if the new highway connecting Macedonia with the Adriatic – Rruga e Arbërit – is ever built.

For cyclists, bikers and those with their own 4x4 transport, an alternative route is from Kruja (see page 100) over the Shtama Pass (Qafa e Shtamës), about 50km. There is no public transport on this route and the pass is closed when there is snow.

 WHERE TO STAY AND EAT

Vila Bruçi (14 rooms) Lagja Drita, pranë Spitalit Poliklinik (near the hospital); 23266, 22387; m 069 40 57 776, 068 21 59 926; e vila-bruci@hotmail.com; Facebook: Vila Bruci Burreli. English spoken, attentive service. Excellent restaurant ($$$), fresh trout & local wine, wonderful views over Mati River to mountains; lounge area for guests; Wi-Fi in public areas & some bedrooms. Tours of surrounding area & beyond can be arranged. Most rooms have balcony with mountain views; those on top floor have wooden beams. All rooms comfortable, good-sized, with good en-suite bathroom, AC, TV. Substantial b/fast inc. $$

Orkidea (5 rooms) On the road out towards Tirana; 22454. Friendly management. Restaurant on ground floor, b/fast available at small extra charge. Good-sized rooms with basic en-suite facilities, AC, TV. $

WHAT TO SEE IN BURRELI Burreli's main attraction is as a base for exploring the rest of Mati. The small museum is worth a visit; the gunpowder machine is particularly interesting. Gunpowder was produced in Mati from Ottoman times until 1939, when Italy annexed Albania. The occupying forces closed down the gunpowder factories because they thought, probably quite correctly, that the Albanians might use the product to blow up Italian soldiers or strategic targets such as bridges. Aficionados of Socialist Realist art will like the murals in the main hall, one of them painted by Fatmir Haxhiu (1927–2001). The museum is open only on weekday mornings; the entrance is at the side of the building, not through the main gates where the local minibuses wait.

The other interesting sight in Burreli is the large statue of King Zog, just off to the side of the main square. The statue is modern, of course, since during the communist period it would have been completely out of the question to erect even a small bust of the exiled king.

For listings, see pages 169, 188 & 197–8

🛏 **Where to stay**
1 Camping Albania
2 Fusha e Gjes
3 Lake Shkodra Resort
4 Rilindja

✖ **Where to eat and drink**
5 Mrizi i Zanave

MONTENEGRO

Vermoshi

MONTENEGRO

Plava

Gucia

Vuthaj

Lepusha

Ceremi

Gashi

Tamara

Nikçi

Jezerca
2,693m ▲

Dragobia
Cave

MONTENEGRO

Radohima
2,569m ▲

Thethi
National
Park

Valbona

Dragobia

Rrapsha

Boga

Thethi

Rragami

Margegaj

Bajram Curri

Hoti

Rrazma

Ndërlysaj

Nikaj

Hani i Hotit

Podgorica ◄

Dedaj

Curraj i
Epermë

Tropoja,
Gjakova

Currai i
Poshtëm

Fierza

Kiri

Mërturi
i Gurit

Breglumi

Kopliku

Lake Komani

Iballa

Kukësi

Ura e
Shtrejtë

Levrushku
Cave

Kryeziu

Kukësi

Mesi
Bridge

Drishti

Lake
Vau i Dejës

Komani

Fushë-Arrëzi

Shkodra

Zogaj

Drini

Puka

Ulqini ◄

Muriqani

Kçira

Buna

Vau i Dejes

Spaçi

Bushati

Repsi

Blinishti

Kallmeti

Oroshi

Velipoja

Shëngjini

Rubiku

Kurbneshi

Ishulli i Lezhës

Lezha

Rrësheni

Lura

Adriatic Sea

N

Bradt

Lake
Ulza

Vali's & Neziri
Caves

0 ————————— 16km
0 ————————— 10 miles

Fushë-Kuqja

Miloti

Stojani

Burgajet

NORTHWEST ALBANIA

Laçi

Patoku

Durrësi,
Tirana

Burreli, Kruja, Peshkopia

182

7

The Northwest

SHKODRA   *Telephone code: 022*

Shkodra has been a highly significant city during most of its long history. It was the capital of the Illyrian state of the Ardiaeans from the 3rd century BC until the Roman conquest in 168BC. During the Ottoman occupation it was the seat of a semi-autonomous *pashalik* (see box, page 193) under the Bushati family, which at one point stretched east into what is now Kosova, and south as far as Berati. Shkodrans were prominent in the Albanian cultural and political renaissance (*Rilindja Kombëtare*) which led ultimately to independence from the Ottomans.

Italian influence has always been strong in Shkodra – the city was part of the Venetian Republic from 1396 until it was surrendered to the Ottomans, after a long siege, in 1479 (see page 10). Almost all Shkodrans speak Italian, and donations from across the Adriatic fund much of the city's cultural, environmental and social welfare activity. Since the end of communist rule, though, there has been considerable immigration into the city from the surrounding highlands, and this has led to some friction between Shkodra's urban intellectuals and the highly conservative traditions of the mountain incomers.

Shkodra has two outstanding museums which should not be missed: the archaeological display in the Historical Museum, and the huge collection of 19th- and 20th-century photographs in the Marubi Photothèque. The museums' collections, together with a visit to Rozafa Castle, provide a good overview of the different phases of the city's development. Those interested in traditional domestic architecture should also allow time to walk around the Dugajtë e Reja (the New Shops) area, whose Ottoman-era houses have now been smartened up to some extent. See later in this chapter for further details of all these attractions.

Shkodra is a good base for excursions into the wild and beautiful Albanian Alps. On the coast, there are two nature reserves at Velipoja and Kune-Vaini, which are important wetland habitats, and where many rare and attractive waterfowl and other birds can be observed. See pages 199–202 for further information about birdwatching in these reserves.

GETTING THERE AND AWAY   From **Montenegro**, buses run between Ulqini (called Ulcinj in Serbo-Croat) and Shkodra all year round. It takes 1½ hours; the one-way fare is €4. Helpfully, the Montenegrin and Albanian authorities operate a joint border post at Muriqani, 14km from Shkodra, which saves time. In Shkodra, the buses leave from outside the Rozafa Hotel; in Ulqini, from the bus station. There are departures from Ulqini at 06.00, 12.30 and 16.30; buses leave Shkodra at 09.00, 14.15 and 16.00. Taxis also do this run; they charge €8 per person, or €25 for the whole car. In Shkodra, the drivers tout for passengers outside the Rozafa Hotel.

SHKODRA

Montenegro
(freight only)

Mesi (7km),
Drishti (10km)

Bregu i Ranës
(2km)

Kopliku (17km),
Hani i Hotit (35km),
Podgorica, Montenegro

UNAZA

Venice Art

SKËNDERBEG

General
Hospital

LIN DELIA

BADRA

LUDOVIK SARAÇI

3 HERONJTË

FUSHË FIREJ

FUSHË F

GJUHADOL

JUSTIN GODARD

ZONA INDUSTRIALE

LEVIZJA E POSTRIBËS

GOLEMIT

DOBRAÇ

DOBRAÇIT

KOPLIKUT

Minibuses to
Kopliku &
Albanian Alps

RUS MAXHAR

EUROPA

Sheshi Rus
i Madh

BASHKIMI

RUS I MADH

SHIHOKA

KARDINAL MIKEL KOLIQI

JERONIM DE RADA

GJUHADOL

AT GJ FISHTA

EDITH DURHAM

SERREQ

ARRA MADHE

VASO KADIA

FUSHË ÇELE

F NOPCA

BVD SKËNDERBEU

DOM BOSKO

28 NËNTORI

13 DHJETORI

D

BORIÇI

DASHO SHKRELI

RAMADANI

DERGUT

FAHRI

DERVISHEJ

KIRAS

UNAZA

ZOOTEKNIKË

UNAZA

KARVANEJ

DUDAS

BUJAR BISHANAKU

Sports centre

OBAJKA

NDOCAJ

ISUF SOKOLI

VËLLEZËRIT FRASHËRI

RUS I
VOGËL

SHYQYRI
HAXHA

NAZMI KRYEZIU

MARTIN ÇAMAJ

A BALLAÇI

ZDRALE

LEKË DUKAGJINI

PARRUÇË

ENJLA
ÇELEBIU

QEMAL KUKA

Sheshi
Demokracia

see page 187

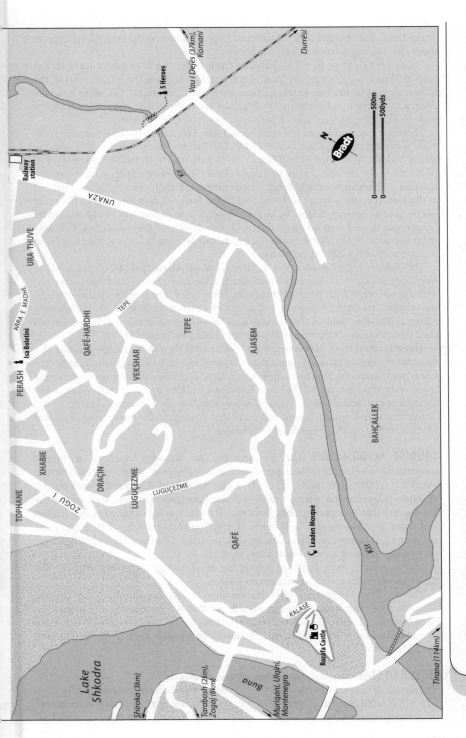

The Northwest SHKODRA

There are no direct buses to Shkodra from Podgorica, nor, at the time of writing, are there any passenger trains across the border.

There are two ways to get to Shkodra from **Italy**: one is to take a **ferry** to Bar (called Tivari in Albanian) in Montenegro, and then drive the 30km or so to the border, or pick up the bus which operates from Budva to Tirana. The other is to take a ferry to Durrësi and come up the highway from there. The road is good all the way; in a car, the journey takes just over an hour, by bus a little more.

There are frequent buses and minibuses from **Tirana** to Shkodra, running from early morning until the last bus at 17.00. The journey takes about two hours; the fare is 300 lek. The buses leave Tirana from a side street just beyond the Zogu i Zi roundabout. In Shkodra, buses to Tirana depart from Sheshi Demokracia, outside the Radio Shkodra building. From Tirana **airport**, a right turn at the roundabout at the exit from the airport will lead you to the Fushë–Kruja junction of the main north–south highway, 2.8km from the airport; a taxi all the way to Shkodra from the airport should cost no more than €50. The drivers of the minibuses to Tirana from Shkodra, or anywhere else in the north, can drop passengers at the airport, on request and with a 200-lek surcharge.

The outstandingly beautiful journey down **Lake Komani** from Fierza is one of the world's great boat trips, through breathtaking mountain scenery and narrow gorges. There is no longer a car ferry on this route, but it is the best way for cyclists or those using public transport to approach Shkodra or Lezha from Kosova or northeastern Albania. It is described in *Chapter 6* (pages 163–4). The alternative is to use the old road from Kukësi, via the beautiful district of Puka (see pages 161–4).

Those coming from **Montenegro** on foot or with their own transport could also consider the border crossing, open all year round, between Gucia (Gusinje, in Serbo-Croat) and Vermoshi, high up in the Dinaric Alps. There are minibuses every morning from Vermoshi (see pages 211–14) to Kopliku and Shkodra. See Bradt's *Montenegro* for information about Gucia, Vuthaj (Vusanje) and the district capital, Plava.

Minibuses to Kopliku, Thethi and other destinations to the north leave from Rus Maxhar, in the northern outskirts of Shkodra.

TOURIST INFORMATION The Municipality of Shkodra operates a tourist information kiosk across the square from the main post office, near the Rozafa Hotel (⏱ *07.00–21.00 Mon–Fri, 07.00–13.00 Sat, closed Sun; shorter opening hrs in winter*). During the summer, well-informed, English-speaking staff attend the kiosk every day, except for public holidays. The kiosk stocks a range of free leaflets and maps, guidebooks and souvenirs. The staff are less reliable when it comes to advising on transport to, and accommodation in, the Albanian Alps, although they may be able to book a guesthouse there for you.

Many agencies now organise hiking in the Albanian Alps; see page 31 for information about specialist hiking companies.

The local authorities in Shkodra rename streets constantly. Most people, when they use any street names at all, still use the old, communist-era names. As elsewhere in Albania, Shkodrans are more likely to give directions with reference to neighbourhoods and landmarks. The **municipal police** are friendly and helpful to lost tourists.

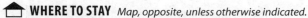

WHERE TO STAY *Map, opposite, unless otherwise indicated.*

🏠 **Colosseo** (41 rooms) Rr Kolë Idromeno; ☎ 247 513/4; **m** 068 20 60 130; **e** info@ colosseohotel.com; www.colosseohotel.com.

Completely remodelled & extended in 2010; English spoken. Good, long-established restaurant offering Albanian & Italian dishes; bar on 5th floor

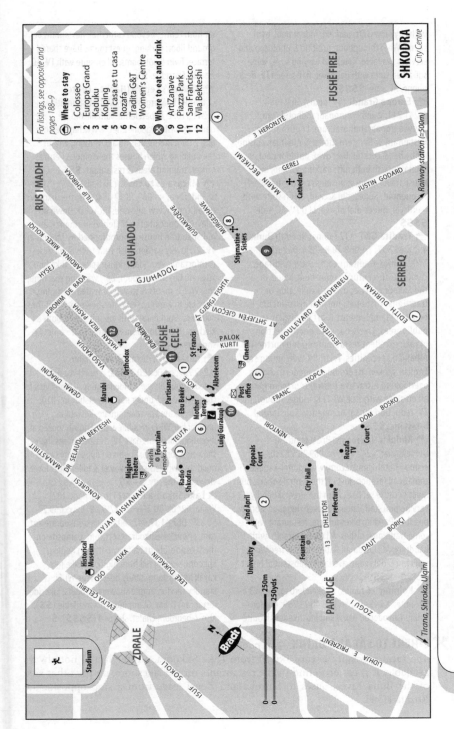

For listings, see opposite and
pages 188–9

Where to stay
1 Colosseo
2 Europa Grand
3 Kaduku
4 Kolping
5 Mi casa es tu casa
6 Rozafa
7 Tradita G&T
8 Women's Centre

Where to eat and drink
9   ArtiZanave
10 Piazza Park
11 San Francisco
12 Vila Bekteshi

FUSHË FIREJ

3 HERONJTË

GEREJ

MARIN BEÇIKEMI

Cathedral

JUSTIN GODARD

Railway station (=500m)

RUS I MADH

FILIP SHIROKA

GJUHADOL

KARDINAL MIKEL KOLIQI

HYSEH

JERONIM DE RADA

GJUHADOL

IDROMENO

GURAKUQEVE

MUNGESHAVE

Stigmatine
Sisters

8

9

SERREQ

EDITH DURHAM

AT GJERGJ FISHTA

AT SHTJEFEN GJEÇOVI

BOULEVARD SKENDERBEU

JESUITËVE

QEMAL DRAÇINI

VASO KADIJA

HASAN RIZA PASHA

12

Orthodox

FUSHË
ÇELË

St Francis

11

1

PALOK
KURTI

Cinema

Albtelecom

Post
office

5

FRANC NOPCA

DOM BOSKO

Rozafa
TV

Court

28 NENTORI

Marubi

Partisans

Ebu Bekër

Mother
Teresa

KOLE

10

Luigi Gurakuqi

6

TEUTA

3

Shëtri
@ Fountain
Demokracia

Radio
Shkodra

Migjeni
Theatre

Appeals
Court

2nd April

2

City Hall

Prefecture

13 DHJETORI

DAUT BORIÇI

Fountain

DR SELAUDIN BEKTESHI

IRG MANASTIRIT

KONGRESI

BYJAR BISHANAKU

LEKE DUKAGJIN

OSO KUKA

Historical
Museum

EVLIYA ÇELEBIU

University

PARRUÇE

ZOGU I

LIDHJA E PRIZRENIT

Tirana, Shiroka, Ulqini

ZDRALE

ISUF SOKOLI

Stadium

250m

250yds

Bradt

N

with city views; lift; parking; indoor pool, gym, sauna. Wi-Fi throughout; printing & photocopying services available. Rooms of varying sizes, some sgl, all en suite with hairdryer, flat-screen TV, desk, phone, AC, safe. **$$$$**

⌂ **Europa Grand** (50 rooms) Sh 2 Prilli; ✆241 211; e info@europagrandhotel.com; www.europagrandhotel.com. English spoken. Restaurant with international & Albanian cuisine; lobby bar & cocktail bar; gym, outdoor pool, sauna, Turkish bath; lift; parking; casino; in-house travel agency; business centre; free Wi-Fi throughout. Suites, dbl & twin, all en suite with hairdryer, direct-dial phone, LCD TV, AC, safe. **$$$$**

⌂ **Tradita G&T** (12 rooms) Rr Edith Durham 4; ✆240 537; m 068 20 86 056, 068 62 63 770; e info@traditagt.com; www.traditagt. com. A 17th-century, stone-built house in the Shkodran style; owner's collection of traditional costumes, musical instruments, household implements & art on display in all public areas. Lively bar with good selection of raki; excellent restaurant serving northern Albanian specialities. Friendly, welcoming staff; English spoken. Bedrooms in modern annexe overlooking attractive central courtyard garden, all en suite with free Wi-Fi & fridge, though no TV; reduction for sgl occupancy. Substantial b/fast inc. **$$$**

⌂ **Kaduku** (15 rooms) Rr Studenti, Sh Demokracia; ✆242 216; m 069 25 51 230; e info@hotel-kaduku.com; www.hotel-kaduku. com. Good location, just off the central square, but quiet because set back from the street. Friendly, very helpful staff; English spoken; luggage storage possible. Parking; bikes for hire; restaurant with some traditional dishes. All rooms en suite with hairdryer, AC, CH, small flat-screen TV, free Wi-Fi; sgl, twin & dbl rooms available. Substantial b/fast inc. **$$–$$$**

⌂ **Kolping** (6 rooms) Rr Skënderbeg, Lagja 3 Heronjtë; ✆245 492; m 068 40 21 759; e info@ kolpingshkoder.al; www.kolpingshkoder.al. Quite

far from centre, beyond cathedral. Restaurant on ground floor; parking; guest rooms have shared terrace. Twin & sgl rooms, all en suite with TV, AC, free Wi-Fi, fridge. **$$**

⌂ **Women's Centre (Hapat e Lehte)** (2 rooms) Rr Murgeshave (Motrat Stigmatine); ✆241 316; e hapatelehte@gmail.com, qendragruashk@adanet.net; www.hapatelehte. org. 2 twin rooms sharing a bathroom, within the building which houses the Women's Centre's offices, training areas & restaurant. **$$**

⌂ **Mi casa es tu casa** (30 beds) Bd Skënderbeu; m 069 38 12 054; e hostelshkoder@ gmail.com; www.micasaestucasa.it. Down an alleyway opposite the Millennium cinema, an old Shkodran house (photographed by Marubi in 1912), lovely garden with fruit trees & tortoises, comfortable veranda; English spoken. Bike hire; kitchen; big sitting room; bar; washing machine; free Wi-Fi; sheets & towels provided. Camping possible in garden; separate shower & toilet for campers. Studio apt with en-suite bathroom & kitchen (**$$**). Dbl room & dorms share toilets & showers. **$–$$**

⌂ **Rozafa** (68 rooms) Rr Vasil Shanto; ✆242 767; m 068 20 33 122; e Hotel-rozafa@ uldedajgroup.al; www.uldedajgroup.al/hotel-rozafa. com. Renovated, under new ownership, in 2010; centrally located on main square. Restaurant, popular bar, Wi-Fi in public areas; English spoken at reception. All rooms have TV, cheaper rooms share showers &/or toilets. Rooms on upper floors are a good size, with en-suite shower & toilet, AC & lovely views over the city. **$–$$**

⋏ **Lake Shkodra Resort** [map, page 182] Vraka, 42° 08' 30.2" N 19° 27' 93.8" E; m 069 27 50 337, 067 41 17 947; e faye@lakeshkodraresort. com; www.lakeshkodraresort.com. Campsite on the lakeside, about halfway between Kopliku & Shkodra; signposted from highway. Bike hire, kayak hire, fishing, sandy beach. Free Wi-Fi; laundry service; ample showers & toilets; lakeside restaurant & bar. Glamping tents available (**$$**); also 2-bedroom chalet, sleeps 4 (**$$$$**). **$**

✗ WHERE TO EAT AND DRINK *Map, page 187.*

The local speciality is carp (*krap*) from Lake Shkodra, although it is not always available. It is easier to find in the restaurants on the lakeshore, on the other side of the Buna River; buses to Shiroka and Zogaj leave from a stop opposite the Rozafa Hotel.

✕ Piazza Park Sh Nënë Tereza. Upmarket pizza, pasta, salads, etc. Tables outside on large terrace in summer. $$$

✕ San Francisco Rr Kolë Idromeno. English spoken, English menu; big terrace on 1st floor, overlooking pedestrian street. Meat, seafood, carp, pasta, good pizza. $$$

✕ Tradita G&T Rr Edith Durham 4; ☎240 537; m 068 20 86 056. It is well worth eating here even if you are not staying at the hotel. Restaurant in 17th-century stone-built house, open hearth where meat is grilled, excellent menu with local specialities inc game, wild fungi & forest fruits in season. Some English

spoken; service can be rather slow. Interesting exhibition of traditional costumes & other items at entrance. $$$

✕ Vila Bekteshi Rr Hasan Riza Pasha; ☎240 799; m 069 28 67 445. Near the Orthodox church; also known as 'Çoçja'. Tables outside in internal courtyard & upstairs in formal dining room. Good service, some English spoken. Italian-inspired menu, excellent meat dishes, pizzas good even by high Albanian standards. Locally brewed beer on draught. $$–$$$

✕ ArtiZanave Gjuhadol. Community-run restaurant; simple, tasty salads & grilled meat. $$

WHAT TO SEE AND DO

Rozafa Castle (09.00–14.00 Tue–Sun; 200 lek) Shkodra's castle stands above the confluence of its three rivers, the Drini, the Kiri and the Buna, and thus controls all but the northern approach to the city. It is an excellent place for a castle and has been fortified since Illyrian times, when the Ardiaean queen Teuta launched her attacks on the Romans from it (see page 8). Traces of the Illyrian walls, constructed of large stones with no mortar, can still be seen at the entrance to the castle.

Most of what remains is Venetian and Ottoman. The outer walls follow the line of the hill; within, successive lines of fortification create three distinct areas, of which the most secure and easily defensible is the section at the narrowest part. The views from the citadel are wonderful, across Lake Shkodra to Montenegro, out to the Adriatic, and down towards Lezha.

Rozafa Castle was twice besieged by Ottoman armies; when it finally surrendered in January 1479, it was only after a lengthy blockade, supervised for a time by Sultan Mehmed II in person, had brought Venice to the realisation

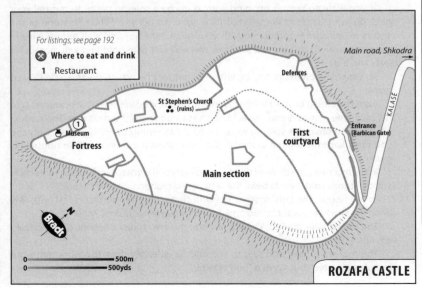

For listings, see page 192
⊗ Where to eat and drink
1 Restaurant

Main road, Shkodra

Defences

St Stephen's Church (ruins)

Museum
Fortress

First courtyard

Entrance (Barbican Gate)

KALASE

Main section

0 — 500m
0 — 500yds

ROZAFA CASTLE

that it had no choice but to make peace. Rozafa was the last fortress in Albania to fall to the Ottomans. Two and a half thousand Shkodrans chose to leave under the terms of the surrender and were granted pensions by Venice. The new rulers continued to use the castle as a military and administrative centre; it was the vizier's residence and, from 1840, was the capital of the whole northern Albanian province (*vilayet*). It was last used for military purposes in 1913, when it operated as the Ottoman command centre during yet another siege, this time by Montenegrins.

You enter through the vaulted barbican gate to the first courtyard, where you can see the defensive system very clearly. The second section is the largest and is where the barracks, stores and prison were built; the prison was in use until the early 20th century. The **ruined church** on your right was once Shkodra's cathedral, a 14th-century building which – as the stump of the minaret shows – was converted into a mosque after the Ottoman occupation. The circular, chimney-like structures here

ROZAFA CASTLE   *From Mitrush Kuteli's* Old Albanian Tales

On top of Valdanuz Hill, three brothers were working. They were building a castle. The wall which they built by day collapsed by night, so they were never able to get it any higher.

Along there came a good old man. 'May your work go well, you three brothers!'

'May you go well, too, good old man. But where do you see anything going well with us? By day we work, by night it falls down. Might you be able to give us some advice? What can we do to keep the walls standing?'

'I know,' said the old man, 'but it would be impious to tell you.'

'On our heads be it, because we want this castle to stay standing.'

The good old man pondered and said, 'Are you married, my brave lads? Do all three of you have girls?'

'We are married,' they replied. 'All three of us have our girls. So tell us, then, what to do to keep this castle standing.'

'If you want to keep it up, bind yourselves by a solemn oath; do not tell your girls, do not discuss at home what I am about to tell you. Whichever one of the sisters-in-law comes tomorrow with your meal, take her and wall her up alive in the castle wall. Then you will see how the wall will take hold and will remain for ever and a day.'

So spoke the old man, and he left: one moment he was there, the next he was gone.

Alas! The eldest brother broke his solemn word. He discussed it at home, he told his own wife just as it was, he told her not to go there the next day. The middle brother also broke his solemn word: he told everything to his own wife. Only the youngest kept his solemn word: he did not discuss it at home, he did not tell his own wife.

In the morning, the three of them got up early and went to work. Sledgehammers struck, stones split, hearts beat, the walls grew higher.

In the house, the lads' mother knew nothing. She said to the eldest wife, 'My dear, the workmen want bread and water; they want a flask of wine.'

The eldest wife replied, 'On my honour, mother, today I cannot go, because I am ill.'

The mother turned and said to the middle wife: 'My dear, the workmen want bread and water; they want a flask of wine.'

and there on the ground open into water cisterns, constructed in the 15th century and fed by pipes running into them from all over the castle.

The third section was a real fortress, with underground stairways and tunnels connecting to different parts of the citadel. Some of the entrances to these secret passageways can still be seen, although the tunnels themselves are not open. The well is original; it was stolen in the civil unrest of 1997 and reappeared mysteriously ten years later. The three-storey Venetian building at the end of the third courtyard was the garrison commander's residence in the 14th and 15th centuries and now houses the **museum** (*150 lek*). This covers not only the history of the castle but also of the surrounding area. In 2011, it was completely reorganised on modern museological lines; it is perhaps the only museum in Albania which is designed to be accessible to disabled visitors, including information in Braille (in Albanian and English) and tactile displays. The exhibition includes a 3rd- or 4th-century mosaic, discovered at the foot of the castle hill; this is the only mosaic ever found in northern Albania.

'On my honour, mother, today I cannot go, because I am going to visit my parents.'

The lads' mother turned to the youngest wife. 'My dear...'

The youngest wife leapt to her feet: 'Honoured mother, what is your command?'

'The workmen want bread and water; they want a flask of wine.'

'On my honour, mother, as for myself, I have my little son. I am afraid he will want my breast and he will cry.'

'On you go, we will take care of the boy, we won't let him cry,' said her sisters-in-law.

The young wife, the good wife, got up, she took bread and water, she took the flask of wine, she kissed her son on both cheeks and set off. She climbed up Valdanuz Hill, towards the place where her husband and her two brothers-in-law were working.

'May your work go well, workmen!'

But what was this? Their sledgehammers stopped striking, but their hearts beat harder and harder. Their faces grew pale. When the youngest saw his wife, he cast the hammer from his hand, he cursed the stone and the wall. His wife said, 'What is the matter, my lord? Why do you curse the stone and the wall?'

The oldest brother broke in: 'It was a black day when you were born, sister-in-law. We have given our word to wall you up alive in the castle wall.'

'Oh my brothers-in-law, may you prosper! But I have one request for you: when you wall me up, leave my right eye free, leave my right hand free, leave my right foot free, leave my right breast free. For my son is little. When he starts to cry, with one eye I shall look at him, with one hand I shall caress him, with one foot I shall rock his cradle, and with one breast I will feed him. May my breast turn to stone, may the castle endure, may my son grow up brave and strong, may he become king and rule!'

They took the young wife and walled her up in the foundations of the castle. And the walls grew higher, they did not collapse as before. But at their foot, the stones are damp and mossy to this day, because the mother's tears still fall for her son.

There is stonework from Rozafa Castle – including a Venetian lion which may once have been over the entrance gate – and from the nearby castle of Drishti (see pages 195–6); coins from various periods, including some minted in Shkodra by the Nemanjić dynasty of medieval Montenegro, and others with the symbol of the Balsha family, the feudal power in northern Albania in the 13th to 15th centuries; and copies of documents including a map from 1600, the Statute of the city of Shkodra, written – in Latin and Dalmatian – in 1346 and discovered in Venice in 2002, and interesting political cartoons from the early 20th century. Next to the museum is an atmospheric **restaurant**, which has excellent views from the balcony to its rear.

From the castle walls, you can see the **Leaden Mosque** on the floodplain below, an 18th-century building with an attractive arched courtyard. It is a long way to the castle from the centre of town, and a stiff climb up from the main road; if you do not have your own transport, you could take a taxi up and walk back down to catch a bus back into town.

Historical Museum   (*Rr Oso Kuka 12;* ☏ *243 213;* ⊕ *09.00–15.00 Mon–Fri, groups at other times by arrangement 1 day ahead; 150 lek*) The house of Oso Kuka, who died defending Shkodra against Montenegrin attackers in 1861, is now home to the town's Historical Museum, and provides an opportunity to see traditional domestic architecture. From the street, a Shkodran house is just a windowless wall with a thick wooden door; once through this door, you find yourself either in a narrow entrance hall or, as in the case of Oso Kuka's house, in a courtyard, with the house in the centre, far away from the surrounding walls. The courtyard always had a well and this one has two; the original, from when the house was built in 1840, and a Venetian well from the 15th century. Various large items recovered from the castle or found elsewhere in the area are displayed in the courtyard and in the garden behind the house. One of the most interesting is an Ottoman coat of arms, intricately carved in stone, which dates from the late 19th century and was found in the castle.

The archaeological collection is exhibited on the ground floor of the house, which – like traditional houses all over Albania – was originally used for storage or workshops. The archaeological display could do with better labelling, but there are some interesting items. The prehistory section includes finds from the Mesolithic site at the Gajtan Cave; Bronze Age goods from Mycenae and the Celtic world, which demonstrate the extent to which Shkodra was then trading with other civilisations; and a cute 'family' of terracotta figurines, discovered in a burial mound. The museum has a good collection of coins and medals, including a *denarius* bearing the head of Brutus, Julius Caesar's rival, and coins struck in Shkodra in the 2nd century BC, during the reign of the last Illyrian king, Genthios; these bear on their reverse a *liburnis* – a small, fast ship – like that on the modern 20-lek coin.

In the days when this house was lived in, the living quarters were on the first floor, reached by a flight of wooden stairs up to a large wooden landing, with doors leading off it to the rooms within. One of these rooms, the *oda e miqve* or guest room, now houses the museum's ethnography collection. Beautifully carved wood decorates the walls, and the room is overlooked by a gallery, where the women of the house could sit while their menfolk were entertaining guests. The hosts and their guests sat on either side of the huge stucco chimney, made in a style unique to Shkodra. Traditional costumes are displayed in glass cases in this room: those worn by Muslim and Catholic men and women in the city, alongside the outfits characteristic of Shkodra's mountainous hinterland.

The last communist President of Albania, Ramiz Alia, was born in this house while his parents were renting it, and so taxi drivers and other Shkodrans sometimes refer to it as 'Ramiz Alia's house'.

The Marubi Photothèque (*Rr Vaso Kadija (formerly Muhamet Gjollesha);* ☉ *08.00–16.00 Mon–Fri; 100 lek*) The Marubi Photothèque (*Fototeka*) is a marvellous photographic record of historical events and ordinary people in northern Albania. The exhibition consists of a selection of photographs taken by the Marubi 'dynasty', whose founder, Pietro Marubbi, came to Shkodra as a political refugee from Italy, after the defeat of Garibaldi in 1836, and albanicised his name to become Pjetër Marubi. The Photothèque's archives hold 150,000 glass-plate negatives taken by Pjetër, his apprentice Kel, who took his mentor's surname after his death, and Kel's son Gegë, who conserved the photos after the Marubi *atelier* closed in the 1940s and ultimately donated them to the Albanian state. The very first photograph ever taken in Albania is here, a portrait of a Shkodran man made by Pjetër Marubi in 1858. Also displayed are fascinating images of people and places in the northern highlands, views of the cities of Durrësi and Shkodra in Ottoman times, inter-war

THE BUSHATI DYNASTY

By the 17th century, the gradual weakening of Ottoman authority over the empire's peripheral areas led, in Albania, to the rise of feudal lords known as *beys* or *pashas*, all anxious to control as much territory (and therefore revenues) as possible – the territory controlled by each pasha was called a *pashalik*. The rivalry between the pashas gave rise to wars and, ultimately, to a period of anarchy. This was brought to an end, in the middle of the 18th century, by the emergence of two powerful pashas, one in northern Albania and one in the south, who managed to gain control of almost all the small pashaliks and merge them into two huge ones. The southern pashalik was ruled by Ali Pasha Tepelena, about whom there is more information in the box on pages 246–7.

The northern pashalik was created in 1757 by Mehmet Bey Bushati (the surname is alternatively spelt 'Bushatlli'). His ambitious son, Kara Mahmoud Bushati, extended the territory of the pashalik of Shkodra east to what is now Kosova and south as far as Berati, the border with Ali Pasha Tepelena's territory. In 1785, Kara Mahmoud invaded Montenegro and captured the pirate stronghold of Ulqini. The Ottoman authorities besieged his troops in Rozafa Castle for three months in 1787, but Kara Mahmoud managed to secure an imperial pardon by threatening to switch his allegiance to Austria-Hungary. Like his southern counterpart Ali Pasha, however, he ended up overstretching Ottoman tolerance. When he launched a second attack on Montenegro in 1796, he was defeated and – again, like Ali Pasha – beheaded. The Ottoman authorities appointed his brother Ibrahim Pasha as the governor of Shkodra, which, thanks to Kara Mahmoud's policies, had become an important trading centre.

The pashalik remained under the control of the Bushati family, effectively autonomous until 1830, when Sultan Mahmoud II determined to break the independence of the Albanians. Another siege of Rozafa ended in the surrender of the Bushatis and the end of the pashalik of Shkodra. This did not mean the end of the family's influence, though, and nor did it do much to improve the porte's control of its restless Albanian subjects.

portraits of men and women from Shkodra's prominent families and of ordinary Shkodrans going about their business, and historic events such as the arrival of Wilhelm of Wied in Durrësi, in 1914, and the wedding of King Zog in 1938.

The photographs displayed in the Photothèque are all labelled in Italian and some also in an apparently random combination of French, English and Spanish. Reproductions of some of them are on sale as postcards. Work is in progress to scan all the plates on to CD-ROMs and thus make the archive more accessible. The Photothèque is signposted, with brown 'tourist information' signs reading 'Marubi', at each end of the street on which it is located; however, it is then down an alleyway and behind a gate, which makes it a little tricky to find. The people around on the street, such as the money changers, are used to foreigners hunting for this elusive building and will point you the right way. Its advertised opening hours are more of a statement of intent than a reliable indication.

Venice Art Mask Factory (*Rr Lin Delia;* m *068 20 47 291;* e *edmondangoni@ gmail.com;* ⊕ *Mon–Sat by arrangement*) In an intriguing twist on the historic links between the two cities (see page 183), many of the masks worn by revellers at the Venice Carnival are produced in a factory on the outskirts of Shkodra. They are handmade with papier mâché ('cartapesta', in Italian): sheets of paper are soaked in glue and layered over a mould to make the basis of the mask. Once it is dry, it is then painted, decorated with sequins, gold leaf, lace and feathers, and finally varnished to give it an antique look – the whole process has 15 stages. Visitors can watch the masks being made and admire the finished products in the factory showroom.

A walk around town Although Shkodra is a large and rather straggly town, the historic centre is quite compact and easy to walk around. The circuit described here should not take much more than an hour, excluding time to look around. Alternatively, do as the Shkodrans do, and cycle.

The Ebu Bekër, or El Zamil, **Mosque** is as good a place to start as any, since it occupies practically a whole block of the town centre and is impossible to miss. It was rebuilt with Saudi money in the 1990s on the site and as a replica of the historic mosque which was completely demolished in the late 1960s. Its beautifully engraved minarets and copper roofs were not enough to save it from the atheism campaigners (see pages 16–17). Behind the mosque, in the large garden which surrounds it, is a rather weather-beaten and neglected partisan monument.

Leaving the mosque grounds, turn left out of the gate and then left again towards the road junction called Mother Teresa Square, with a recent statue of the nun herself, outside the Telekom building. Albania claims **Mother Teresa** (1910–97) as its own – although she was born in Macedonia – thanks to her father's Mirdita origin. Shkodra, with its large Catholic community, is especially proud of her; on Mother Teresa Day in October, the people decorate the statue with flowers. Across the junction, with his hands in his pockets, is **Luigj Gurakuqi** (1879–1925), one of Shkodra's most illustrious sons, who served Albania in various capacities including as Minister of Education in the independent country's first government.

The statue of Gurakuqi stands at the corner of what used to be a park but is now a jumble of restaurants, hotels and building works. Following the street to Gurakuqi's right will lead you past some of these to the **2nd of April Monument**. This commemorates the date in 1991 when Shkodran students and others demonstrated in protest against the result of the elections two days earlier, which had been won by the Albanian Party of Labour (PPSH, the Communist Party, which had governed Albania since 1944). Security forces opened fire on the demonstrators and four students were killed.

From the 2nd of April Monument, a short cut across the grounds of the Europa Grand Hotel will bring you to the other side of the erstwhile park, where there are some attractive 19th-century governmental buildings: the Prefecture pretty much straight ahead of you, and the City Hall round to the left. Following this street beyond the City Hall will bring you back to Mother Teresa Square; and across the main road, up the street between the mosque and the Colosseo Hotel, is **Dugajtë e Reja**, or 'the New Shops'. This area, roughly defined by the streets called Kolë Idromeno and Gjuhadol, has the highest concentration in Shkodra of Ottoman-era buildings. Rruga Kolë Idromeno has been pedestrianised and the houses have been restored and repainted. A stroll down Rruga Gjuhadol brings you out almost at the Catholic **cathedral**. Unlike the El Zamil Mosque, this building was not demolished by the atheism campaigners; instead, it was converted into a sports hall and used for basketball and volleyball matches. Its construction began in 1858, with special permission from the Ottoman authorities; the wooden ceiling was designed by the Shkodran painter Kolë Idromeno (1860–1939). The cathedral was reconsecrated in 1991 at a mass attended by, among many others, Mother Teresa. To the left of the altar is a display of photographs commemorating the dozens of Albanian Catholics – priests and lay people – who were executed during the communist regime.

Returning to the centre by a slightly different route, turning off Rruga Gjuhadol on to Rruga At Gjergj Fishta, will take you past the Franciscan convent and church, with its lovely vaulted ceiling, and back to the Colosseo Hotel.

Drishti and the Mesi Bridge

About 7km upstream from Shkodra, on the Kiri River which rises away up in the mountains which surround Thethi, is a spectacular Ottoman bridge called Ura e Mesit, or the **Mesi Bridge**. There are lots of old bridges in Albania called Ura e Mesit, which just means 'the Bridge in the Middle' – that is, the place where people from communities on opposite sides of the river met and traded. This particular bridge was built in 1868 by Mehmet Pasha Bushati, a member of the family which administered northwestern Albania on behalf of the Ottoman authorities. At 108m long, it is the longest Ottoman bridge in Albania, with 13 arches, and it is the only one with a curve. It was built for the transport of timber down from the mountains to the Buna River and on to Ulqini, which at the time was Shkodra's main port. Until 1965, when the modern bridge next to it was built, it was the only substantial bridge across the Kiri upriver of Shkodra itself. But Mehmet Pasha built his bridge at a crossing which had been used for many centuries before him, a link in a much older route connecting Shkodra with Drishti.

Drishti – or, as it was known at the height of its power, Drivasto – had an importance in the past which is hard to imagine nowadays. A fortress was built there in late antiquity; it was the seat of a bishopric until the end of the 9th century, and the citadel whose ruins can still be seen dates from the 14th century. Rozafa Castle outside Shkodra is clearly visible from the citadel; Drishti and Rozafa were both important links in the chain of communication by beacon, used by Skanderbeg (see box, pages 200–1) and no doubt by earlier lords. In 1396, Drivasto was acquired by the Venetian Republic; the well which can still be seen, surrounded by a ramshackle wall, is thought to be Venetian, from the mid-15th century. By then, around 100 families lived in the town. But in 1478, during the final siege of Shkodra, the houses within the castle walls and the fields below it were destroyed by Ottoman troops, as part of their strategy of starving out the city's defenders. Edith Durham (see box. pages 178–9) visited Drishti in 1908 and was entertained in the imposing house of the head of the village, the one with the covered balcony (*çardak*), on your right as you come through the castle walls from the main road.

The house had two entrances, each with its own flight of stone stairs, one for men and the other for women; the front steps are ruined now, but the back flight is still visible. There is now a small museum in the castle.

The road is in reasonable condition as far as the castle entrance, although a 4x4 would probably be needed in wet weather. Minibuses ply several times a day between Shkodra and Mesi, where the bridge is. From Mesi, a minibus runs early every schoolday morning and then again at lunchtime to the school in the modern village of Drishti, below the castle; it takes the schoolteachers to work and brings them back again, but they will probably be prepared to squeeze up and make room for one or two foreign tourists, if necessary. It is quite a long way from the village up to the castle, but if you are on foot you can use the cobbled path which leads up to the main gate – the entrance on the other side of the castle from the gate where the asphalt road passes.

LEZHA   *Telephone code: 0215*

Albanians are always very keen for foreigners to visit Lezha, because it is where their national hero Skanderbeg, or Gjergj Kastrioti, brought the Albanian clan chieftains together to swallow their differences and unite against the Ottoman threat. When Skanderbeg died in 1468, after 24 years successfully resisting the Ottomans, he was buried in Lezha's cathedral.

Lezha has Illyrian fortifications, including the citadel above the town, which can be visited. During the Roman period, it was called Lissus and was an important river port. In 48BC, Mark Antony landed at what is now Shëngjini (then called Nymphaeum) on his way to link up with Julius Caesar in their campaign against Pompey. Lezha was part of the Venetian Republic for most of the 15th century, and in this period the town – by then called Alessio – and its port thrived. In the Ottoman period Lezha, like Durrësi and other Adriatic-facing Albanian towns, fell into decline, and it did not really begin to recover until Italy's economic and political influence began to grow in the 1930s.

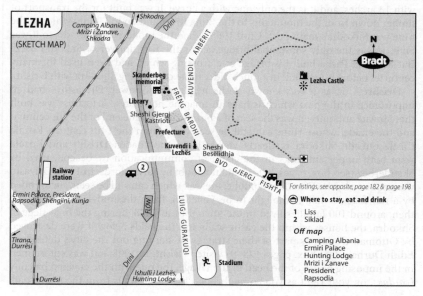

Shëngjini, known in Italian as San Giovanni di Medua, is the second-largest port in Albania, after Durrësi. To the south of the port, a beautiful sandy beach stretches for several miles to the Merxhani Lagoon, part of the wetlands which make up the Kune-Vaini Nature Reserve. In the summer months, this resort is a very popular destination for Albanian-speaking tourists, and it can become rather busy, although it is less crowded than the beaches further south at Durrësi.

The Kune-Vaini reserve straddles both sides of the Drini River, and offers magnificent birdwatching opportunities (see pages 199–202). It is within easy reach of both Shëngjini and Lezha, either of which would make an ideal base for day trips into the reserve.

GETTING THERE AND AWAY The highway between Lezha and Shkodra has been fully upgraded, and the two towns are now less than an hour's drive apart. **Minibuses and buses** ply the route constantly until at least the early afternoon; if there is no transport specifically for Lezha at the time you want to travel, you can catch a bus for Tirana or Durrësi, and get off at the Lezha junction on the highway; from there, it is a five-minute walk across the bridge into the centre of Lezha. It is also perfectly feasible to visit Lezha on a day trip from Tirana, which is less than 1½ hours away by bus. The northbound buses leave Tirana from the Zogu i Zi roundabout; in Lezha, the bus station is on Bulevardi Gjergj Fishta.

In the tourist season, many Shkodra minibuses go directly to Shëngjini, leaving in the morning and returning in the afternoon. There are also frequent minibuses to Shëngjini from Lezha, especially in the summer. There is no public transport to the Vaini area of the nature reserve, but a 4x4 is not required and any Lezha taxi driver would take you.

 WHERE TO STAY *Map, opposite.*
The room rates in Shëngjini increase substantially in the peak summer months, when all the hotels there are likely to be fully booked several weeks in advance. If you are visiting the area solely to watch birds, there are also hotels in Kunja.

⌂ **Liss** (12 rooms) Sheshi Besëlidhja, Lezha; 🔌24700; m 067 20 22 047; e info@hotel-liss.com, hotel-liss@uldedajgroup.al; http://hotel-liss.com. The former 'Turizmi', right in the centre of town, completely renovated. Comfortable, well run, some English spoken. Excellent restaurant & popular bar. Sgl, twin & dbl rooms available, all en suite with TV, AC, Wi-Fi, phone, minibar. **$$$$**

⌂ **Ermiri Palace** (29 rooms) Shëngjini; 🔌0281 22444; m 068 20 67 974; e info@ermiripalace. com; www.ermiripalace.com. Restaurant, bar, terrace; Wi-Fi; yacht hire. All rooms en suite with AC, phone & TV; also 2- & 3-room apts. **$$**

⌂ **President** (51 rooms) Shëngjini; 🔌0281 22626; m 069 20 72 161; e hotel.president@ yahoo.com; www.hotel-president-al.com. Lift, Wi-Fi; restaurant, bar, large terrace with tables outside in the summer. All rooms en suite with AC, phone & TV. **$$**

⌂ **Siklad** (14 rooms) Pranë urës së Drinit, Lezha; 🔌22333; m 068 20 33 445, 069 25 91 848. At the bridge from the highway into town; restaurant on ground floor; friendly management. All rooms en suite with good shower, Wi-Fi, TV, AC. **$$**

⋀ **Camping Albania** Barbullushi (41° 55′ 25.9″ N 19° 32′ 30.7″ E); m 067 38 07 207, 067 38 18 092; e info@camping-albania.eu; www.camping-albania.eu. Just beyond Bushati; signposted off the highway, roughly halfway between Lezha & Shkodra. Dutch-run, western European standards, English spoken; pitches for up to 50 mobile homes & tents; ample showers & toilets; laundry service. A few simple guest rooms, some en suite (**$–$$**) are also available. On-site restaurant, large outdoor pool with spring water, free Wi-Fi throughout site. **$**

✗ WHERE TO EAT AND DRINK   *Map, page 196.*

The restaurant at the Liss Hotel is the best place to eat in Lezha itself, with the usual Italian-inspired menu of pasta, pizza, escalopes and chops (**$$–$$$**). Weather permitting, the peaceful sunken garden outside the restaurant is a very pleasant place to eat or drink, with the tables arranged around a fountain. In Shëngjini, there are good, cheap fish restaurants (**$$$**) near the entrance to the port.

The wider Lezha area has several excellent restaurants and is becoming a bit of a culinary destination in its own right. Visitors who are interested in gastronomy should try to sample at least one of the restaurants listed here.

✗ **Rapsodia** On the Shëngjini road, about 4km out of Lezha; m 068 29 47 771; info@hotelrapsodia. com; www.hotelrapsodia.com. A fairly formal restaurant with excellent antipasti & fish, as well as Italian-influenced meat dishes. Once a month, the chef prepares a special gastronomic menu, sometimes cooking with flowers, sometimes reversing the order of courses; phone for details. 9 en-suite guest rooms available (**$$**). **$$$$$**

✗ **Hunting Lodge** (Hoteli e Gjuetisë) Ishulli i Lezhës; m 069 21 70 898. Built in the 1930s by Mussolini's son-in-law, Count Galeazzo Ciano, who also served as Fascist Italy's foreign minister; used by party functionaries during the communist period & ransacked by rioters in 1997; reopened after refurbishment in 2003. Specialises in traditional Albanian cuisine, inc excellent fresh fish; a good choice for a leisurely lunch after a long

morning's birdwatching in the Vaini marshlands. Also has basic guest rooms (**$**), but the hotel part of the building is in rather poor repair. **$$$**

✗ **Mrizi i Zanave** Fishta, Blinishti; m 069 21 08 032; e altinprenga@hotmail.it; www.mrizizanave. com. Beautiful setting in the countryside northeast of Lezha, in the birthplace of the priest & Gheg poet Gjergj Fishta (the restaurant takes its name from the title of his masterpiece). Associated with the Slow Food Movement, uses local ingredients to prepare perfectly grilled meat, exquisite salads, unusual side dishes & desserts. The good house wine is also locally produced. In summer, tables outside on shady terraces. English spoken. Blinishti is signposted off the main Lezha–Shkodra highway; homemade signs direct you to Mrizi i Zanave; phone the restaurant if lost. **$$$**

WHAT TO SEE AND DO   Lezha's main claim to fame is as the place where Albania's national hero, Skanderbeg (see box on pages 200–1), united the country's feuding clan chiefs against Ottoman attack, and where he was buried after 24 years of resistance. There is a monument to the gathering of the clan chiefs – known in Albanian as Kuvendi i Lezhës, the Assembly of Lezha – at the corner of Besëlidhja ('Oath-taking') Square, as you enter Lezha over the bridge from the highway.

When Skanderbeg died, in January 1468, he was buried in St Nicholas's Cathedral in Lezha. His death marked the beginning of the end for the Albanian resistance, and when the Ottomans occupied Lezha, they ransacked Skanderbeg's tomb and converted the cathedral into a mosque. Between 1880 and 1905, the site was used by the local Bektashi community (see pages 22–3) as a *tyrbe*, or shrine; Bektashis believe that the young Gjergj Kastrioti converted to Bektashism while he was in Constantinople. For the quincentenary of Skanderbeg's death, shortly after Albania had been declared the world's first atheist state, the mosque was requisitioned, its minaret was removed and Lezha's former cathedral became a shrine to Skanderbeg.

The **Skanderbeg Memorial** (⊕ *09.00–13.00 & 15.00–18.00 Tue–Sun; 100 lek*) is protected by a modern pillared structure which surrounds and roofs the ruined cathedral. As you pass through the carved wooden doors into the cathedral, there is a bronze bust of the hero directly ahead of you. Behind it, on a red mosaic background, is the double-headed eagle which was Skanderbeg's flag and is now the national flag of Albania. Below the bust are replicas of his sword and his helmet topped with a roebuck's head; the 15th-century originals are in the New Imperial Palace (Neue Burg) in Vienna, part of the Kunsthistorisches Museum's Arms and Armour Collection. On each of the side walls hang shields, each representing one of the battles he waged against the invaders. Skanderbeg lost only two battles against the Ottomans in all his years of resistance: at Svetigrad in 1448 and at Berati in 1455. On the back wall of the cathedral, a fragment of fresco has survived from the 15th century. A selection of publications about Lezha, in English and Albanian, is on sale at the memorial.

Recent excavations have revealed a 12th-century baptistery just next to the memorial, which shows that there was a church on this site long before the cathedral was built. In the surrounding park, remains of Illyrian and Roman fortifications can be seen, which once extended all the way up the hill to the citadel.

Lezha was one of the links in the chain of castles used by Skanderbeg to communicate information up and down the country; a beacon lit here can be seen from Rozafa Castle, 45km to the north, and at Kruja, 54km south. In dry weather it is possible to drive up to the **castle** (⊕ *08.00–15.00 Mon–Fri, in theory*) in any reasonably robust car; when the track is wet, a 4x4 will be needed. It is a pleasant, though steepish, walk of 30–45 minutes, with good views of the Drini Delta on the way and, of course, from the castle itself, at the top. There is another well-preserved section of the ancient wall about halfway up.

The interior of the citadel is very interesting, especially if you have previously visited Rozafa. Like its bigger and better-preserved neighbour, Lezha Castle has a church which was converted into a mosque, a cistern for storing rainwater, and a dungeon, complete with air hole so that the unfortunate prisoners could breathe. The citadel was first fortified in the 4th century BC; the surviving buildings and the watchtowers are medieval, built between the 15th and 17th centuries.

Beaches The beach at Shëngjini is lovely to walk along, but the water is often rather murky, probably because the port is so close. It becomes very crowded in the peak summer months. The water is cleaner and the beach quieter further along the bay towards the nature reserve at Kunja.

To the northwest, almost at the border with Montenegro, is another popular beach resort, Velipoja. There are many hotels at Velipoja (**$$–$$$**), although not all of them stay open throughout the year. Minibuses go to Velipoja from Shkodra.

BIRDWATCHING IN THE NORTHERN ALBANIAN WETLANDS The wetlands surrounding the mouths of the Buna and Drini rivers are of international importance to waterfowl. Some 700ha at Velipoja, on the left bank of the Buna's outlet to the sea, and 2,300ha around the Drini Delta – the Kune-Vaini Nature Reserve – have been designated as protected, mostly under IUCN Category IV ('a protected area managed mainly for conservation through management intervention'). Both reserves are easy to get to and have good accommodation nearby, making them ideal destinations for ornithologists. It should be noted, however, that the development of beach tourism in Velipoja and Shëngjini has already begun to affect the protected areas. This is a particular problem in the Kunja area, to the north of the river Drini, where the beach extends from Shëngjini all the way to the island of Kunja e Vogël, at the end of the Merxhani Lagoon. There are now several restaurants and a small hotel within the nature reserve itself. The Vaini part of the reserve is less developed, and is likely to be a more fruitful destination for birdwatchers.

The habitats The Velipoja area begins on the Albanian side of the river Buna, where a large expanse of inland marshes and reed-beds make up the Dumi Marsh (Këneta e Dumit). A forest of broad-leaved deciduous woodland stretches along to a sandy beach, with dunes and small pools. At the eastern end of the beach is a large, shallow coastal lagoon – the Viluni Lagoon (Laguna e Vilunit), about 300ha – at the foot of rocky and forested mountains. These hills continue down the coast to Shëngjini and the start of the Drini Delta.

The Drini is Albania's longest river, and where it meets the sea it has created a complex of relatively intact coastal lakes, marshes and forests covering many square kilometres. Brackish lagoons, sandbars and beaches, marshes, reed-beds and woodland areas combine to make a very varied environment, which extends south to the mouth of the River Mati and beyond. Some of the woodland is broad-leaved, while some is planted pine; much of the forest has been destroyed by indiscriminate tree-felling. The surrounding area is cultivated (Lezha is famous

SKANDERBEG

Albania's national hero was born Gjergj (George) Kastrioti, the son of a powerful Albanian chieftain who controlled a large swathe of what is now northern Albania from his citadel at Kruja. When the Ottomans advanced towards Kruja in 1433, Gjergj's father struck a deal with them to be allowed to continue ruling his lands as a vassal – this was not untypical of the decentralised way in which the Ottoman Empire administered Albania in later years too. As part of the deal, Gjergj was sent to be brought up in the sultan's court, where he was trained as a soldier and given the name Skënder (Alexander), with the honorific ending 'beg' (or 'bey').

In 1443, the Ottomans suffered a serious defeat at Niš, in Serbia. Skanderbeg seized the moment and raised his family's standard – the double-headed eagle on a red background which is the national flag of modern Albania – from the castle at Kruja. The exact circumstances in which he did so are unclear, but the traditional version is that he and his men deserted the Ottoman army at Niš and rode from there to Kruja, where Skanderbeg tricked the Ottoman guards into letting him into the citadel.

He then achieved the feat which has given him his place in history. The Albanian clans, like their Scottish counterparts of the same period, spent most of their time fighting each other, which made them easy prey for better-organised invaders. Skanderbeg managed to gather all the clan chiefs together, in Lezha, on 2 March 1444, and made them undertake to put their differences aside. A solemn undertaking of this sort is known in Albanian as *besa*, an expression which is still widely used in modern times to mean something like 'word of honour'. The swearing of the oath at Lezha is called *besëlidhja* in Albanian, and has given its name to the town's main square.

The Lezha *besa* allowed the clans to concentrate on fighting the invaders, and they held them at bay for an astonishing 34 years. Kruja came under siege in 1449–50, and many died before the Ottoman forces withdrew. The sultan, Murad II, died soon after the retreat from Kruja. His successor Mehmed II turned his attention to Constantinople, and it was not until he had conquered that city that he returned to Albania. Meanwhile, Skanderbeg tried to rally support for his beleaguered country from other European nations, but his diplomatic initiatives brought little success. In 1466, the Ottoman army returned to Kruja; Skanderbeg sought military assistance from Naples, which enabled him to break the siege the following year.

Skanderbeg died of malaria in Lezha in 1468, leaving only a son who was too young to take over his father's command; yet the *besa* held and the clans stayed for its watermelons) and is networked with an extensive system of dykes, dams, ditches and channels, although since the fall of communism these have not been well maintained and the marshes are beginning to reclaim the land in some places.

The birds Velipoja and Kune-Vaini are important sites for wintering waterfowl and for migratory waterbirds. No fewer than 8,000 individuals were recorded in a 1993 census at Velipoja, and 17,000 individuals at Kune-Vaini in January 1995. Species which nest in the Drini Delta area include spoonbills (*Platalea leucorodia*), cormorants (*Phalacrocorax carbo* and *P. pygmeus*), various herons and egrets, and grebes (Podicipedidae). Among the waterfowl which winter there are the red-crested pochard (*Netta rufina*), goldeneye (*Bucephala clangula*), shelduck (*Tadorna*

united against the Ottomans. Kruja finally fell in 1478. The last citadel to be lost was Rozafa Castle in Shkodra (see pages 189–92), the following year. Folk legend has it that Skanderbeg's son led a group of Albanians across the Adriatic to settle in southern Italy. To this day there are villages there in which an archaic form of Albanian is spoken; the dialect, and the people who speak it, are called Arbëresh.

The year after the Ottomans had taken Shkodra, they crossed the Adriatic and captured the castle of Otranto. They were unable to hold it for more than a few months, thanks in part to a revolt in Albania which occupied their troops there, and under the next sultan, Bayezid II, they gave up on their plans to expand their conquests westwards beyond the Balkans. It is often said that had it not been for János Hunyadi, the Turks would have taken Vienna and the political fault-lines of Europe would have been hundreds of miles further north than they are. Less attention has been given to the possibility that without Skanderbeg and the Albanian resistance, much of what is now Italy would have fallen, and the fault-lines would have been several hundred miles further west.

THE DEATH OF SKANDERBEG

They brought [Skanderbeg] his son – small and tender, with long golden hair. Skanderbeg took him in his arms and said: 'Oh, my little flower, who has bloomed amid the surge of battle; oh, flower of my broken heart! When I die, my comrades will continue the war. And if it turns out that you are not big enough to hold and wield a sword, take care that the Turks do not imprison you alive and lock the door. I know the Turks well. They try to distort a man's spirit, to turn him against himself and his clan, to make him an oppressor of his own land. And then honour is blanketed in disgrace.

And so, if you see that you are in trouble, take your mother and three ships, the best we have, and set off across the sea. Then, when you grow up, come back to your land and carry on my struggle. I say this to you not to save you from death, but to save the clan from defilement; because defilement is worse than death.

When you reach that pebbly beach over there, you will see a shady, mournful cypress. There, to the trunk of that cypress, tie my horse; and above the horse, raise my flag so that it ripples; and under the flag, tie my sword. When the sea breeze blows, my horse will whinny, the flag will flutter and my sword will resound under the shady cypress. The Turks will hear it. They will be afraid of the death which my sword brings, and they will not dare to throw themselves into battle.

From Mitrush Kuteli's Old Albanian Tales

The Northwest   LEZHA

7

tadorna), teal (*Anas crecca*), wigeon (*A. penelope*) and pintail (*A. acuta*). The 'near-threatened' ferruginous duck or white-eyed pochard (*Aythya nyroca*) may also visit.

Herons, spoonbills and pygmy cormorants used to breed inside the Velipoja reserve, close to the mouth of the Buna, but they moved across to an island on the Montenegrin side of the river in the 1990s, probably because they were being disturbed by illegal activities such as poaching and wood-cutting. They still feed on the Albanian side and if the park's protected status is properly enforced it may be possible for the breeding colony to re-establish.

Around the Mati Delta is a third nature reserve, Fushë-Kuqe–Patoku. It is also an important site for migratory and wintering waders, including the slender-billed curlew (*Numenius tenuirostris*), which is globally endangered and very rarely seen in Europe. Pied avocets (*Recurvirostra avosetta*) winter at Patoku and there was formerly a small breeding colony of Dalmatian pelicans (*Pelecanus crispus*) on one of the islands.

THE ALBANIAN ALPS

The mountain range which forms the border between Albania and Montenegro is known variously as the Albanian Alps, the Dinaric Alps, the Accursed Mountains

BIRD SPECIES IN THE WETLANDS

PHALACROCORAX CARBO The **great cormorant** is a black, long-bodied, long-necked waterbird. It swims and dives for fish, and may perch on rocks and in dead trees. It characteristically stands with its wings outstretched, to dry them. In spring it has white feathers on its head and neck, and bold white patches on its flanks.

PHALACROCORAX PYGMEUS The 'near-threatened' **pygmy cormorant** is about half the size of *P. carbo*, but otherwise looks similar. It nests in trees, preferably willow (*Salix*), and feeds in reed-beds and in the transition zones between reed-beds and open waters. Pygmy cormorants occasionally forage together in flocks. It is thought that they may drive shoals of fish towards the edge of reed-beds, in order to catch them more easily.

ARDEOLA RALLOIDES The **squacco heron** is a beautiful small heron and, like the other herons described here, most winter in Africa. The breeding plumage is mainly golden, with long brown streaked nape plumes and a greenish-blue bill, but in flight it is surprisingly white. It is rather shy and often solitary, feeding either by 'standing and waiting' or walking slowly along.

EGRETTA GARZETTA **Little egrets** are white, medium-sized herons, with black legs and bright yellow feet, and in the breeding season have long white nape plumes. They are sociable, often boisterous, birds and nest with other herons in trees. They feed mostly on fish and small shore-dwelling animals.

NYCTICORAX NYCTICORAX The black-crowned **night heron** is the size of the little egret, but stockier. Adults are a soft grey colour, with a black back and crown, and white head plumes in spring. Young birds are brown-buff and spotted. The legs are raspberry-pink at the start of the breeding period and yellowish the rest of the or, more usually in everyday Albanian parlance, just 'the Highlands' (Malësia). The eastern part of the highlands is covered in *Chapter 6*, pages 164–71. The western part, Malësia e Madhe or 'the Big Highlands', is usually accessed from Kopliku, a small town 17km north of Shkodra. Minibuses to Kopliku leave from Rus Maxhar, on the northern outskirts of Shkodra (see the map on pages 184–5 for the departure point). From Kopliku, minibuses run to all the main villages in Malësia e Madhe and to Thethi; sometimes they can also be picked up at Rus Maxhar, but this is a less reliable option. The usual schedule for these minibuses is that the driver leaves his home village in the early morning and brings the minibus back from Kopliku (or Shkodra) in the early afternoon, after his passengers have transacted whatever business they have travelled to town for. The shopkeepers around the street in Kopliku where the minibuses wait are very helpful and will try to find out for you what time the bus you want is likely to depart.

Kopliku has the last ATMs that you will see before your return from the highlands. It is essential to carry sufficient cash for your trip; credit cards cannot be used anywhere in the Albanian Alps. Nor are there any land-line telephones beyond Kopliku.

The best map of this area – *Vermoshi: Tamarë, Razma, Thethi* – is produced by Huber Kartographie GmBH; see pages 41–2 for details. It is one of the companion

year. It rests by day in clumps of trees or bushes and is easiest to see at dusk, when it flies around and feeds.

PLATALEA LEUCORODIA **Spoonbills** are white, but much larger than little egrets. They have long, broad, spatulate bills, which make them unmistakable. They feed with a graceful side-to-side sweeping action, catching small aquatic animals. In the breeding season, adults have a yellow patch round their necks and a bushy crest at the back of the neck.

PLEGADIS FALCINELLUS The **glossy ibis** is the size of a little egret but very dark, and with a long, down-curved bill. The rich chestnut plumage has beautiful green and purple highlights. It is quite common in southeastern Europe, although its numbers are declining. Glossy ibis eat small water-dwelling animals and, like spoonbills, they fly with their necks stretched out, often in single file.

AQUILA CLANGA The **spotted eagle** is a medium-sized eagle (wingspan 1.53–1.77m), with dark brown plumage and slightly paler flight feathers. Juveniles have rows of white spots along the upper wing. It occurs in lowland forests near wetlands, where it nests in tall trees, and feeds on small mammals, waterbirds, frogs and snakes. Its global population is decreasing as a result of extensive habitat loss and persistent persecution, and it is classified as 'vulnerable'. BirdLife International estimates that there are no more than 900 pairs remaining in Europe, with only small numbers wintering in southern Europe.

HALIAEETUS ALBICILLA **White-tailed eagles**, also known as sea eagles, are huge birds (wingspan 1.90–2.40m), classified as 'near-threatened'. The adults are easily identified from their white tails and large yellow bills. However, it takes about five years for adult plumage to be acquired and immature birds can be confused with other eagles.

maps to a useful little guidebook, written by two Swiss hikers. The *Hiking Guide Northern Albania: Thethi & Kelmendi* has detailed maps and route descriptions, with GPS waypoint references. See *Appendix 2, Further information*, page 274, for bibliographical details.

THETHI About 50km northeast of Kopliku, at the head of the Shala River, lies the national park named after its largest settlement, the charming village of Thethi. The area was a tourist resort during (and, indeed, before) the communist period and its attractive, traditional features were accordingly maintained, while in other parts of highland Albania they were destroyed either deliberately or through neglect. Edith Durham (see box, pages 178–9) visited Thethi in 1908, and described her stay there in her book *High Albania*. 'Life at Thethi was of absorbing interest,' she wrote. 'I forgot all about the rest of the world, and … there seemed no reason why I should ever return.' The modern visitor's reaction is likely to be similar – Thethi seems to have changed little, except that it now has electricity, running water and Western-style toilets.

There are 200 houses scattered across the valley, although only a handful of families live there all year round. Most people who have not left for good spend the winter in either Shkodra or Kopliku, and return to Thethi in May to work their fields; they leave again in October, after the harvest and before the harsh winter weather sets in. The houses are built of the local grey stone, and roofed with shingles (wooden tiles). They are designed to be easily defensible – these mountains were once the heart of blood-feud territory and every family needed to be able to defend its menfolk against revenge. Of especial interest is the 'lock-in tower' (*kulla e ngujimit*), the only one remaining of its kind which is easily accessible to visitors. The tower was used when a family was 'in blood'– that is, when it was involved in a vendetta (see box, pages 174–5). The men of the household locked themselves in and lived in the tower until some other unfortunate relative had been killed or the blood feud had been reconciled. Women were not in danger of being killed in a blood feud, which is just as well since the men would otherwise have had nothing to eat.

The village is predominantly Catholic; the area is so remote that the Ottomans left it largely to its own devices and the villagers had no reason to convert to Islam. The shingled church, in the centre of the main village, was there when Edith Durham stayed in Thethi (it dates from 1892). There are several other traditional buildings which can be visited during a day trip. A longer stay in Thethi will allow you to explore further afield and see the many beautiful natural phenomena in the park. There are also many longer treks for the fit and well equipped, including the popular hike across the Valbona Pass to Tropoja.

Getting there and away The main road to Thethi, from Kopliku, goes through the villages of Dedaj (the administrative centre of the Shkreli commune, with a couple of nice cafés and a tourist information office; *www.kelmend-shkrel.org*) and Boga, which was photographed by Marubi in the late 19th century, and looks almost identical today. The photograph is on display at the Photothèque in Shkodra (see pages 193–4); it is a lovely photograph in its own right, but it is even more interesting once you have seen the real thing.

After Boga, the road begins to climb. It is now asphalted as far as the main settlement in Thethi, although this does not make the gradients any easier. A series of increasingly steep and alarming hairpin bends up to Qafa e Tërthorës, or 'Twisting Pass' (1,630m), is followed by no less alarming hairpin bends descending towards Thethi. A 4x4 vehicle is preferable, although in summer the trip can be made, with caution and in dry weather, in any reasonably robust car. The views on the way are outstanding on a clear day, with the forbidding peaks of the Accursed Mountains (Bjeshkët e Namuna in Albanian, Prokletija in Serbo-Croat) ahead and the valley of the Dry Burn (Përroi i Thatë) behind. As you get higher, you can see peaceful alpine meadows here and there. There is a memorial to Edith Durham (see box, pages 178–9) at the pass.

There are several ways to tackle this journey if you do not have your own vehicle. The most comfortable, and most expensive, option is to hire a **jeep** with a driver in Shkodra. Your hotel in Shkodra may be able to help you to contact an experienced driver with a reliable 4x4. You should expect to pay about €100 for the return trip to Thethi, plus the driver's food and – if an overnight stay is involved – his accommodation there. The journey in a 4x4 vehicle should take no more than three hours each way, which makes a day trip to Thethi possible if you do not have time to stay overnight.

In the summer, a **minibus** runs up to Thethi from Rus Maxhar, in the northern outskirts of Shkodra (see the town map on pages 184–5). It is supposed to leave at around 07.00, although there is no guarantee that it will definitely operate every day; the fare is €5 each way. The Thethi bus driver will sometimes collect foreign tourists from their hotels; ask the receptionist where you are staying. The **taxi** drivers in Shkodra are usually quite reluctant to go to Thethi, because they are worried that their cars will be damaged. You might have better luck with a taxi driver in Boga.

The 25km from Boga to Thethi are very steep indeed, with gradients averaging about 10%. **Cyclists** might want to put themselves and their bikes on the back of one of the lorries which run supplies up to Thethi from Shkodra. These trucks are known in Albania as 'IFA', after the East German make which was once ubiquitous in the country, although nowadays they are as likely to be manufactured by Iveco or Mercedes. Travelling by IFA is a dusty, bone-shaking experience; it is also an option for non-cyclists, although probably only suitable for those who are not dead set on comfort. The trip takes about four hours from Shkodra and should cost about 800 lek per person – less, obviously, from Boga.

In the peak summer months, even if the minibus is not running for some reason, it ought to be possible to hitchhike back to Kopliku from Thethi, although not necessarily on the exact day you had hoped to leave. Outside July and August, though, so little traffic leaves Thethi that you might be stuck there for several days before finding someone who could take you even as far as Boga. If you can hike to Boga, you will be able to pick up a bus or minibus from there to Kopliku or Shkodra. The footpath called the Sheep Track (see page 210) is a much shorter route than the road; it takes the locals six hours. There are guesthouses in Boga where you could spend the night.

Snow and ice close Qafa e Tërthorës for between four and six months every year. The only way out of Thethi then is south, along the Shala and Kiri rivers, to approach Shkodra from Drishti and Mesi (see pages 210–11). This road is in even worse condition than the Boga road, and the local people rarely use it except in emergencies. They stock up on essentials in Shkodra before winter sets in, and hope they don't run out of flour or cigarettes before the thaw. However, if you are travelling in a 4x4 vehicle or by bike, you could return from Thethi by this route, by way of variety. It is about 130km back to Shkodra.

For information about walking into or out of Thethi, see *Hiking in the national park*, pages 207–8.

Where to stay and other practicalities

There is plenty of accommodation in Thethi. A comprehensive list – and suggestions for hikes – can be found on a website funded by Italian and German development agencies: www.albanian-mountains. com. The houses which take in paying guests are used to the requirements of western European tourists, and have modern bathroom facilities and warm, comfortable beds. There is always constant running water, usually from the house's own spring.

The sole village shop stocks only the bare essentials, such as cigarettes; campers should bring their own food, although basic foodstuffs such as bread and cheese can be purchased from the villagers. Packed lunches can easily be arranged if you are staying with a family. Anyone concerned about their health should note that there are no medical facilities of any sort in the valley. There is mobile phone coverage in the village, but not everywhere in the national park.

Hotel

🏠 **ALPE-AL** (14 rooms) Gjeçaj; ☎022 248 467 (in Shkodra); m 069 20 99 753; e f.frash@hotmail. com; http://alpealtheth.com; ☺ May–Sep. Transport to & from Tirana or Podgorica airports can be arranged. Restaurant with Albanian & Italian dishes. Twin & trpl rooms, all en suite; camping also possible (**$**). Some English spoken. B/fast inc. **$$**

Hans (family guesthouses)

There are many family-run guesthouses in Thethi, providing twin, trpl or dormitory rooms sharing toilet and shower facilities. The daily rate is around €25 pp, which inc FB: a generous b/fast, normally 100% home produced apart from the coffee; a lunch of traditional Albanian dishes, with raki or beer for those who wish it; & a lighter evening meal. Packed lunches can be provided as an alternative to eating at the house. You will be expected to remove your outdoor shoes before entering the guesthouse (as you would in all houses in Albania); cheap flip-flops or plastic sandals can be bought in the street markets in Shkodra.

🏠 **Mëhill Çarku** (19 beds) Gjeçaj; m 069 31 64 211. Right at the top of the village, before the hotel, on the right-hand side of the road as you come into Thethi from Boga. When it is not too hot, lunch or dinner can be taken on the terrace in front of the house, from which there are beautiful views across the Shala Valley to the mountains. The downside of these lovely views is that the Çarku

house is a long way from the tourist attractions in the valley.

🏠 **Gjon Deda** (9 beds) Okoli; m 068 21 91 405. A magnificent stone house in Okoli, the settlement to the north of the main village; interesting display of traditional kitchen equipment. Rose Wilder Lane is said to have stayed here when she visited Thethi in the 1920s.

🏠 **Prek Harusha** (25 beds) Qendër; m 069 27 70 294. In the centre of the main village of Thethi, close to church; camping also possible; a lively place to stay.

🏠 **Mirash Kometa** (15 beds) Okoli; m 068 24 72 458. Slightly simpler & cheaper accommodation than the other *hans* listed, very welcoming hosts.

🏠 **Dedë Nika** (20 beds) Ndërlysa; m 069 33 46 423. Handy if approaching Thethi from the south or from Curraj i Epermë.

🏠 **Prek Tërthorja** (26 beds) Gjeçaj; m 069 28 31 287. A little difficult to find – ask the family to give you directions or perhaps meet you somewhere more central. Wonderful views.

Camping

There are several places where rough camping would be possible, although you should always enquire at the nearest house to ensure that the inhabitants do not mind you pitching your tent on their property. They will probably offer you a bed; if you prefer to sleep outside, they may well invite you to pitch your tent in their own garden, which would be a safe & courteous compromise. If they refuse payment, it is a nice gesture to put a few hundred lek into the hand of the oldest child of the family.

What to see and do

The road into Thethi winds down the hill through beech forest, passing meadows, farmhouses and the lovely Gjeçaj Waterfall, which tumbles from its cliff only metres from the road. A kilometre or so further downhill is the main village, with its fascinating traditional buildings. The first of these is the **church**, originally built in 1892 and rebuilt and re-roofed in 2005 by the parishioners. Crossing the stile roughly opposite the church entrance will take you across a field to the traditional tower house which is, according to the sign on its wall, the **Dukagjin Ethnographic Museum**. This was the house of Lulash Keqi, which Rose Wilder Lane (Laura Ingalls Wilder's daughter) visited in 1921 and which she describes in *The Peaks of Shala*. The architecture of the building is particularly interesting because it is built into the natural rock on which it stands, as a way of enhancing its defensive structure. The entrance to the living quarters was up a narrow staircase with a right-hand turn just before the door as an extra defence. Unfortunately, the building is in such poor condition, due to earthquake damage and neglect, that it can only be viewed from the outside.

It is now possible, however, to gain access to another of Thethi's historic buildings: the **lock-in tower**. Apart from the huge, heavy door there are no openings at all on the ground floor. The first floor is accessed by a ladder, and is also windowless. The men who locked themselves into the tower to hide from their avengers pulled the ladder up behind them, and used it to climb to the second floor. There they would live, sometimes for months at a time, until a *besa* (see box, pages 174–5) freed them from the obligations of blood feud. Each wall on the second floor has three tiny vertical slits in it for surveillance and to let in a few rays of light, with two horizontal openings beneath them, angled downwards so that any approaching stranger could be shot. These slits are further protected on the outside of the walls by a kind of stone cage. The men locked in this tower must have had a truly dreadful existence.

In the past such towers were relatively common in northern Albania. King Zog (see page 12) had many of them destroyed as part of his campaign to modernise the country (and, incidentally, to punish the Catholic clans who opposed him). During communism, those which remained were used as silos or barns until they fell apart from lack of maintenance, or were dismantled so that the stone could be used for other buildings. Only a few now remain, in very remote parts of the high mountains. They are all designated as Cultural Monuments now, but it is thanks to the area's status as a tourist resort that the one in Thethi has been preserved in reasonably good condition.

Below the lock-in tower is one of Thethi's **watermills**, where the villagers bring their maize for grinding. The mills are owned communally by the families who live around them. When access can be gained, the old mill-wheel can still be seen; at other times, you can clamber round to the side and look at the outer mechanism.

It is a short drive or an easy walk along the road from here to the Grunas Canyon, a spectacular gorge 2km long and 60m deep. Above it is the Gërla Bridge, more than 30m above the river. Below the bridge is an excellent spot for trout fishing, although you would need to bring your own rod, as there are none for hire locally. In 2007, archaeologists from the interdisciplinary Shala Valley Project discovered a large Bronze Age site near the Grunas Canyon; walls made of huge stones can be seen at the site.

Three or four kilometres further along the road, at the settlement of Ndërlysaj, the force of the river has carved spectacular formations out of the rocks. A wooden bridge enables visitors to get a good look at these falls. There are natural pools which are good for swimming, although the water is very cold even in summer.

Hiking in the national park Longer hikes in the national park should not be attempted alone or without suitable footwear. The most popular hiking routes around Thethi have now been waymarked – some would say excessively so.

One of the objections to waymarking is that it encourages inexperienced or ill-equipped walkers to embark on hikes which are beyond their abilities. It is essential to bear in mind that, away from the scattering of settlements which make up Thethi, the area is very sparsely populated and there are no friendly mountain rescue helicopters. Minor accidents such as sprained ankles acquire much greater significance when the nearest help is four hours' limp away, and although there is mobile phone coverage in the village of Thethi, it cannot be relied upon anywhere else in the park.

Local guides can be hired in the village; the family running your guesthouse will be able to find one for you. For a full day's guiding, you should expect to pay around €50.

Anyone who likes waterfalls and can manage a little scrambling should visit the **Grunas Waterfall**. It plunges 25m into a deep pool, whose water is so cold

FLORA AND FAUNA IN THE ALBANIAN ALPS   *Catherine Bohne*

The Malësia is a naturalist's dream. The convergence of the central European alpine climate with the Mediterranean produces the richest flora in Europe, with an estimated *minimum* of 3,200 naturally occurring species of higher plants (compare this with the 1,500 native species of the British Isles). With 14 species of wild thyme, six different mints, lavender and rosemary and 16 different members of the Sage genus, a walk in the highlands simply *smells* good.

Begin with staring at what's under your feet: the limestone rock from which the mountains are formed. Some 50–100 million years old, the mountains were forced upwards when Africa hit Europe (in summary) and so everything around you is formed of sedimentary limestone, which was originally coral, on the bottom of a large shallow inland sea. This same limestone and its tendency to dissolve in strange patterns both above and below ground gives rise to the karst geology, characterised by underground rivers, excellent drainage (not so exciting to you perhaps, but thrilling to the plants) and many, many caves. There should also, of course, be many fossils.

As you stand and stare across a valley, the further peaks and rocky outcrops may appear barren, but closer inspection reveals them to be a riot of tiny gem-like plants, such as alpine succulents, *Saxifrage*, *Sempervivums*, *Silenes* and *Sedums* (to mention only things beginning with 's'). Moving down from the peaks, you find the grassy meadows of the Bjeshkët ('alps'), an absolutely dizzy fit of flowers from May to July. Here you will find the endemic Albanian lily (*Lilium albanicum*), as well as fritillaries, several species of orchids, and some of the 32 species of *campanula* (bellflowers) on record. Dianthus (22 species of pinks), flowering peas and Lathyrus (up to 26 species), Geranium (also a possible 26) and let's not forget the up to 60 species of clover. And these are just a handful of the things it's *easy* to see.

If you can tear your eyes away from all this, you might look up to spot a golden eagle (*Aquila chrysaetos*) soaring majestically (or dropping a baby goat from a great height to stun it for lunch). Luckily for the eagles, the heights are also hopping with a large population of chamois (*Rupicapra rupicapra*); watching one casually run straight down a seemingly vertical cliff is a heart-stopping thrill not to be missed.

Descending further, these frequently vertical meadows and rock faces will intersect with marginally more gentle slopes formed by millennia of piled rock debris, now blanketed most often with beech forest (*Fagus sylvatica*). Besides being absolutely straight out of *Grimms' Fairy Tales*, these forests also shelter that any thoughts of a swim will be dispelled round about the moment it reaches your ankles. From this pool, smaller waterfalls and rapids bring the river down a further 20m without much delay. This beautiful spot is marred by the litter left by Albanians who have visited it before you; if you have room in your daysack you might wish to remove some, since nobody else seems to do it. The path is waymarked from the school; alternatively you can walk up to it from the Grunas Canyon or from just below the lock-in tower, following a footpath until you see the waterfall up on the left.

The Shala River rises high up above Thethi, in the karst of Mount Arapi (2,217m), the cliff which towers over the Thethi Valley from the north, and it flows pretty much north to south until it meets Lake Komani (see pages 165–7). It emerges above ground just before the settlement of **Okoli**, in a number of little springs surrounded by beech trees, and there are several nice picnic spots in the vicinity.

what may well be the largest population of *Ursus arctos* – brown bear – left in Europe. Although they will avoid you assiduously, sightings are still frequent and signs of them are easy to spot. Other large animals you might see signs of include wild boar (*Sus scrofa*) and, of course, no fairy-tale woods would be complete without … wolves (*Canis lupus*). There are an estimated 400 wolves in these mountains, making this the largest population in Europe. While hard to spot in the summer, when they move up to the meadows to follow the flocks of sheep and goats, in winter they are extremely prevalent, their tracks are easy to follow (particularly as they circle the houses at night) and an enthusiastic observer can begin to recognise the tracks of individual wolves. Things you are almost guaranteed not to see a sign of (but might like to know are around) include the wild cat (*Felis sylvestris*) and the very rare Balkan lynx (*Lynx lynx*). The Balkan Lynx Recovery Programme, which involves Albanian and international biologists, has been using camera traps since 2008, in an effort to monitor the movements of lynx and other wildlife in the Valbona area.

Also lurking in the forest are another plethora of rare (elsewhere) and beautiful plants of which the most notable is the *Ramonda serbica*, a sort of Balkan version of an African violet. Badgers (*Meles meles*) make a racket snuffling through the undergrowth, and a rainy day will bring out hordes of fire salamanders (*Salamandra salamandra*). Once down by the riverbanks, strolling through stands of silvery willows, you can look for the round webbed tracks of the common otter (*Lutra lutra*) and peer into eddy pools for the highly prized local trout. Smaller animals you might encounter without ever straying from your hotel or guesthouse include such pleasures as red foxes (*Vulpes vulpes*), the incredibly cute fat dormouse (*Glis glis*) and the noble eastern hedgehog (*Erinaceus concolor*).

All of this of course only touches on a fraction of what's actually here to be seen. Not mentioned yet are such joys as beetles, butterflies, the oddly friendly grasshoppers (pink ones as well as green!), snakes, vipers, cuckoos, woodpeckers – the list goes on and on.

Finally, a word of encouragement. One of the main reasons for this richness is the historical isolation and economic neglect of the area. As this changes, these precious populations will come under threat. The interest and enthusiasm of visitors will be invaluable to the future survival of this last remaining corner of wild Europe.

To get to Okoli from the main village of Thethi, turn left instead of right after you have crossed the bridge near the school, and keep going along the road. If you are staying up the hill, for example with the Çarku family, you can cut across the hillside, through woods and meadows, and come down to Okoli from the west. As you approach the village from this direction, you pass some unusual bunkers which have a design quite different from those found elsewhere in the country.

Climbing up the eastern flank of Mount Arapi, the path continues up to **Qafa e Pejës** (the Peja Pass), 1,700m high, which used to link Thethi with the Montenegrin towns of Gusinje (Gucia, in Albanian) and Plava. It is possible, in theory, to obtain permits to cross the international border on foot between Albania, Kosova and Montenegro; see page 165 for advice. There are interesting caves on Mount Arapi, pretty much due north from Okoli, and others above the alpine meadows called Fusha e Dënellit, on the other side of Thethi. Details of these routes can be found in the *Hiking Guide: Northern Albania, Thethi & Kelmendi* (see page 274). The paths are not always easy to identify, however, and the use of a guide is highly recommended.

Further up the main road out of Thethi, a footpath called Shtegu i Dhenve ('the Sheep Track') leads up to a pass at 1,830m and onward to Boga (at least six hours' walk). On a clear day there are excellent views from here over the Boga Valley as well as back down across the Shala Valley. Before the road over Qafa e Tërthorës was built in the 1930s, this was the only way for the people of Thethi to get to Boga; instead, their natural links were with Shkodra, using the route along the Shala and Kiri rivers, and with the village of Rragami in the neighbouring district of Tropoja.

An ancient track runs between Thethi and Rragami across the Valbona Pass, over 1,800m above sea level; the pass is usually snowbound until early June. The track has been waymarked and, in summer, route finding is now relatively straightforward. However, this hike requires a reasonable level of fitness and should not be attempted without adequate footwear and clothing. Less experienced hillwalkers may still prefer to hire a local guide, so that they can relax and enjoy the stupendous views and the rich flora and fauna, instead of having to concentrate on navigation. Horses or mules can be hired on either side of the pass to carry rucksacks or other equipment; ask at your guesthouse. The going rate for a mule is €50. Depending on how fit you are and how heavy your rucksack is, it takes three to four hours to reach the Valbona Pass, and then another two or three down to Rragami.

The path out of Thethi begins at a wooden bridge called the Gjeçaj Bridge, where the Shala River is fringed with willows and alders, and bubbles photogenically across rocks and stones. The track climbs very steeply through the settlement of **Gjelaj**, and then through beech forest to a beautiful alpine meadow, carpeted with lavender, clover of different colours and little orchids. In the forest, and around the stream, are patches of what might well be the most delicious wild strawberries in the world. There is a slow spring at the top of the meadow where water bottles can be replenished. In the fairly recent past, Thethi families used to live in the village in winter and move up to alps like this during the summer. This tradition has now been abandoned; these days, the only inhabitants of the meadows and forests are foxes, weasels, badgers, brown hares and squirrels. Ornithologists should look out for the beautiful and graceful bee-eater (*Merops apiaster*), the green and great-spotted woodpeckers (*Picus viridis* and *Dendrocopus major*), the rock partridge (*Alectoris graeca*), the hoopoe (*Upupa epops*), with its exotic-looking crest, the capercaillie (*Tetrao urogallus*), and the *balkanica* race of the shore lark (*Eremophila alpestris*), which has a warm pink nape and pale yellow facial markings, as well as its characteristic black horns.

Several very rare butterflies can be seen in the Thethi area, including the 'vulnerable' apollo (*Parnassius apollo*) and the large blue and Alcon large blue

(*Maculinea arion* and *M. alcon*). Little herpetological mapping has been done in Albania, but snakes which definitely occur in Thethi are the venomous nose-horned viper (*Vipera ammodytes*) and the harmless smooth snake (*Coronella austriaca*). There are fire salamanders (*Salamandra salamandra*) and alpine salamanders (*S. atra*), which like to come out when it rains; the nose-horned vipers like eating them, so they come out when it rains too. There are yellow-bellied toads (*Bombina variegata*), tree frogs (*Hyla arborea*) and agile frogs (*Rana dalmatina*). Hermann's tortoise (*Testudo hermanii*) is also present in the area. (Thanks to Joost Smets for this information.)

As the track approaches the Valbona Pass, there are magnificent views across the valley to Qafa e Tërthorës and Qafa e Pejës, and down into Thethi and towards the source of the Shala. There are informal cafés on both sides of the pass. See pages 168–71 for information about Rragami and onward travel to Valbona and Bajram Curri.

RRAZMA Like Thethi, Rrazma became a tourist destination in the 1930s. It never took off in quite the same way, however, and has only recently begun to redevelop its tourism potential. It would be a good base for hiking, especially for those who do not have the time or the inclination to venture further into the mountains to Thethi or Vermoshi. Rrazma is much closer to Shkodra and the road is good all the way. There is a range of accommodation and a good choice of places to eat, although the village does close down to some extent outside the peak summer months. In the winter, cross-country skiing is possible, although there is no piste.

Where to stay and eat

⌂ Natyral Rrazma Resort (26 rooms) m 068 60 45 457, 068 60 45 455; e info@natyralrazmaresort.com; www.natyralrazmaresort.com. Modern building in traditional style; English spoken at reception; indifferent restaurant ($$$$); bar; 25m indoor, heated swimming pool, sauna, cinema, computer in lounge with internet for guests' use; skis available. All rooms non-smoking, nicely decorated, with flat-screen TV; minibar; CH; well-equipped but rather small en-suite bathroom, some have bathtub, others only shower. 3 rooms have balcony, 1 suite has large terrace, all with mountain views. Cash only. **$$$$**

⌂ Tigri m 068 30 11 010. Clean & friendly. Rooms en suite with TV. **$$**

There are several restaurants around Rrazma, serving everything from traditional northern Albanian dishes to pizza. They are a better, and less expensive, option than the restaurant in the Natyral Rrazma Resort, which – although beautifully designed, with traditional open fireplace and attractive art on the walls – offers very average Italian cuisine, imported wine only and slow, erratic service.

KELMENDI The district of Kelmendi is Albania's northernmost extreme, a finger of territory poking up into Montenegro. The main villages are Tamara (the administrative capital), Lepusha and Vermoshi – each of them a scattering of stone-built houses surrounded by magnificent mountains. Some of these houses have been kitted out as guesthouses, from where day hikes and longer expeditions can be undertaken. The local produce is delicious – fish from the rivers, lamb and pork from the families' own livestock, cream cheese and yoghurt, fruit conserves and syrups, and plum raki.

Tamara has shops, a post office and cafés; the *Prodhimë të Kelmendit* shop stocks a range of local foodstuffs, including honey, raki, different kinds of jam and fruit syrup and *çaj mali*. The tourist information office also sells local produce. In Vermoshi, there is a café and a little shop which sells household goods, fruit and groceries, beer and cigarettes. There is no Albanian mobile phone signal much beyond Tamara; a Montenegrin signal can be picked up in some spots. However, Lepusha and Vermoshi both have an internet connection.

Getting there and away The sole road linking Kelmendi with the rest of Albania runs up the spectacular, rugged valley of the Cemi River; it is asphalted as far as

---

THE BALKANS PEACE PARK PROJECT
With thanks to Antonia Young

Since 1999, a group of international and local organisations and individuals have been working within the Balkans Peace Park Project (B3P) to establish a cross-border park which would straddle the highlands of northern Albania, southern Montenegro and western Kosova. There are more than 600 environmentally protected areas in the world which straddle international boundaries; one of them can be found at the other end of Albania, encompassing the two Prespa Lakes which are shared by Albania, Greece and Macedonia. About 25 of these cross-border parks are specifically dedicated as 'Peace Parks', symbols of peace and co-operation between countries where sometimes there has been serious conflict. One of the first was the Morokulien Peace Park between Norway and Sweden, set up in 1914. B3P is one of about 400 cross-border projects in the European Green Belt, a conservation initiative which runs the length of the old 'Iron Curtain', from Finland to the southeastern Balkans.

The mountains and valleys in the area proposed for the Balkans Peace Park, or BPP, are home to people who have retained their traditional lifestyles to an extent that is unusual in Europe, and are a habitat for exceptional flora and fauna. But the lack of economic opportunity has led to environmental threats, such as illegal logging, and the cultural threat of depopulation as people move to the cities for work. B3P's vision is that a Peace Park here would see communities from all three countries working together to protect their environment, stimulate local employment and promote sustainable tourism in the region. In Albania, the BPP boundaries would cover Kelmendi, the Valbona Valley and Shala, the area which includes Thethi. Its partner organisation, B3P-Albania, is registered as a nonprofit organisation in Shkodra.

B3P's earliest initiatives were to support walking, bike and horse treks, researching old and new routes in the proposed BPP area and working to help open up cross-border tracks. It has sponsored and organised international conferences, facilitated several significant academic studies in the region, and established regular exchange visits between the communities in the BPP area and the Yorkshire Dales National Park in England. Since 2008, it has run an annual summer programme in the former village school in Thethi, which no longer functions during the rest of the year. Albanian teachers and foreign volunteers come together in the summer programme, which has recently expanded to Kelmendi, Valbona and Plava. Adults as well as schoolchildren have the opportunity to learn skills which will help their community to survive: English, so that they can communicate with foreign tourists; marketable arts and crafts; and agricultural techniques such as permaculture.

More information about the summer programme and B3P's other activities, in Albania, Montenegro and Kosova, can be found on its website: www.balkanspeacepark.org.

Tamara, then very rough indeed until the turn-off for the border with Montenegro. Then the asphalt restarts for the few kilometres until Vermoshi. This means that it is very easy and quick to get to Vermoshi from Plava, and rather difficult and slow to get from Vermoshi or Lepusha to Shkodra.

From Montenegro, a road leads up to the border crossing from the village of Gucia (called Gusinje in Serbo-Croat), in the district of Plava. See Bradt's *Montenegro* for further information about the national parks, accommodation and transport options in the country. From Shkodra, a minibus runs up the valley to Vermoshi, through Tamara and the Bordoleçi Pass (Qafa e Bordoleçit), on the main road above Lepusha, every day except Sundays. It leaves from behind the Malësia e Madhe restaurant at Rus Maxhar at about 13.30; however, you should check in the morning whether or not the driver has definitely come down that day. The journey takes about four hours; the fare to Vermoshi is 700 lek. The minibus can also be picked up in Kopliku. On the way back, the minibus leaves Vermoshi at 04.00 and gets into Shkodra at about 08.00. Another minibus travels the route between Shkodra and Tamara. It also leaves around 13.30; the fare to Tamara is 400 lek.

In summer, it is possible to hike to Lepusha from Thethi (see pages 207–11), a two-day trip; there is a guesthouse in Nikçi (*Prekë Isufi;* m *069 52 85 003*) where the journey can be broken. The *Hiking Guide: Northern Albania, Thethi & Kelmendi* (see *Appendix 2, Further information*, page 274) gives details of this route, and other suggested hikes. The passes are usually blocked with snow until early June. The border crossing is kept clear throughout the winter and the main road is not usually closed for long.

Tourist information (m *069 47 24 658;* e *info@kelmend-shkrel.org; www. kelmend-shkrel.org;* ⊕ *09.00–18.00*) The Italian-funded tourist information office in Tamara stocks a range of useful leaflets and maps, sells guidebooks (including the hiking guide mentioned above) and local foodstuffs. The helpful, enthusiastic staff can advise on accommodation throughout Kelmendi.

 Where to stay and eat There are family-run guesthouses throughout Kelmendi, providing simple accommodation with shared toilet and shower facilities. The website www.kelmend-shkrel.org has information about several of them; to ask the tourist information staff to make a reservation for you, you should contact them via the website (see above). The daily rate for full board is around €25 per person; some guesthouses also offer half-board or bed and breakfast.

Some of the houses in Vermoshi are across the river from the main road; when the river is low you can ford it in a car, but otherwise there is only a footbridge. The family you are staying with will help you with your luggage if required.

🏠 **Gjergj Froni** (20 beds) Vermoshi; m +382 69 53 06 03 (Montenegrin number). Up a track off main road just before Vermoshi; 10 rooms of varying sizes; kitchen; dining room; washing machine; large covered terrace; garden with gazebos. Hiking guides with English & other languages can be arranged.

🏠 **Kafe Natyra** (30 beds) Vermoshi; m +382 69 52 61 18. Just off main road; 5 rooms in family house, large dorm & 1 twin in new wood-panelled building. Restaurant in tree house in huge cherry tree; all food home produced; outdoor pool with shallow section for children; orchard. Wi-Fi. Camping also possible.

🏠 **Leonard Lumaj** (7 beds) Vermoshi; m 069 30 30 733. Guesthouse separate from family home, across the river from the road. Modern bathroom, fully equipped kitchen, large sitting room. Wi-Fi in family home. Mr Lumaj operates the minibus to Shkodra, making this a convenient option if that is how you are getting to Vermoshi. Ground floor dorm with 4 beds, 1 dbl & 1 dbl & sgl upstairs.

🏠 **Lepusha** (8 beds) Lepusha; m +382 69 27 79 72 (Montenegrin number); e zef.nilaj@gmail.com; Facebook: Bujtina Lepushe. Signposted from the main road, asphalted to gate & beyond; landscaped garden; campsite on raised terrace among fruit trees; Wi-Fi. 3 rooms (1 wood-panelled dorm, 1 sgl, 1 twin) sharing large modern bathroom.

🏠 **Maja e Trojanit** (9 beds) Budaçi; m 069 45 19 116. About halfway between border turn-off & Qafa e Bordoleçit. 3 rooms (2 dorms, 1 dbl) sharing 1 shower & toilet; kitchen.

🏠 **Prelë & Mariana Vuktilaj** (28 beds) Vermoshi; m +382 69 55 24 35 (Montenegrin number); e antonjo_vuktilaj@hotmail.com; www. vuktilaj-guest-house.al. Across the river from the road. 7 rooms, 3 dorms & 4 dbls, sharing 5 modern bathrooms; dining room with TV; balcony running the length of the house; mini-museum of traditional implements & costumes; courtyard with seating & views out across valley. Horseriding can be arranged; Mr Vuktilaj can lead hiking & climbing trips.

8

The Southwest

SARANDA *Telephone code: 0852*

Southwestern Albania has many unmissable attractions: the wonderful archaeological site and national park at Butrint; the imposing Ottoman city of Gjirokastra; the beautiful beaches and crystalline waters of the Riviera. Sadly, though, Saranda – the point of entry to Albania for many foreign visitors – is no longer the attractive little port it once was. Thousands of people make the trip across the Corfu Channel every summer, most of them taking advantage of the day trips to Butrint organised by tour operators and the ferry companies on Corfu. It is a pity that their first encounter with Albania is the unappealing concrete jungle which Saranda has become. Nonetheless, it is still the most practicable base from which to visit the beautiful and interesting places in its vicinity.

Saranda has an excellent climate, averaging around 290 sunny days a year, with pleasantly warm temperatures rarely exceeding 30°C. Some of the hotels have outdoor pools, generally open only in the peak summer months, while some are linked to one or other of the beach resorts along the coast towards Butrint. The beach in the town is a pleasant enough place to catch a few rays in between sightseeing. If a day at the beach is what you are after, though, it is better to head south to Ksamili (see page 227) or north to the Albanian Riviera (see pages 245–52).

The Greek name for the town – Ayia Saranda, 'forty saints', from which the Albanian name comes – springs from a legend of 40 Christian legionaries who were put to death here in AD320. A pilgrimage church dedicated to the 40 saints was built on a hill behind modern Saranda in the 5th century, rebuilt in the early 9th century and, unfortunately, used as a base by German troops during the Battle for the Liberation of Saranda in 1944 – unfortunate, because it led to the church's destruction by British bombers. The neighbouring hill of Lëkurësi is the site of an early 19th-century castle, one of many built by Ali Pasha Tepelena (see box, pages 246–7), which has been converted into a popular restaurant and bar. From the terraces of the restaurant there are magnificent views over the Ksamili Peninsula to the Butrint Lagoon and across to Corfu. Some damaged frescoes can still be seen in the remains of the garrison church.

GETTING THERE AND AWAY

By sea Daily hydrofoils and ferries connect the towns of Saranda and Corfu all year round. The ferry journey takes about 90 minutes and the hydrofoil takes about 45 minutes. The one-way fare is €19 off-season, €23.80 in July and August. The hydrofoil leaves Corfu at 09.00 and returns from Saranda at 10.30; the ferry leaves Saranda at 16.00 and returns from Corfu at 18.30. These services are operated by **Finikas Lines** (☎ +355 852 26057; m 069 20 73 711, 067 20 22004; e info@finikas-

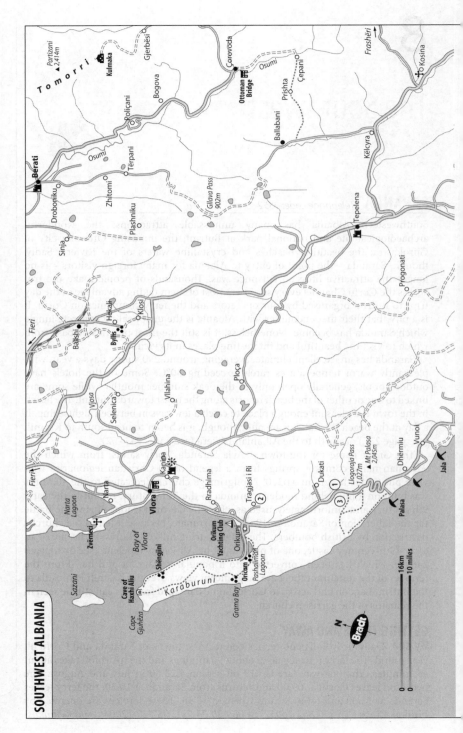

SOUTHWEST ALBANIA

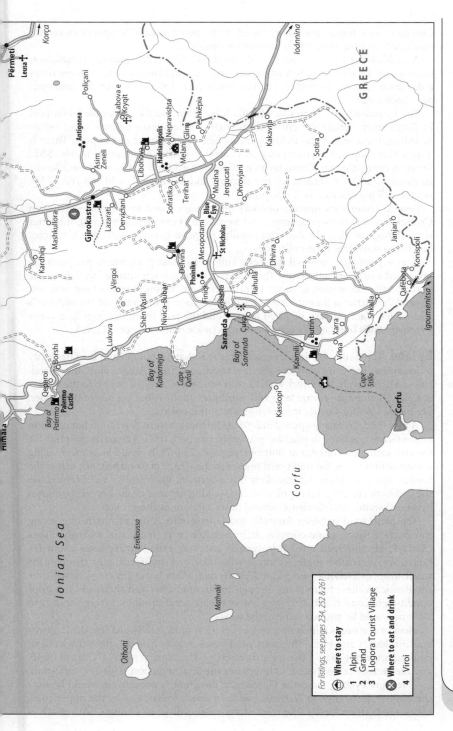

lines.com; www.finikas-lines.com), based in Saranda. Finikas also operates a service on Fridays to Parga; consult its website for details.

An additional ferry service (✆ +355 69 20 91 699; e pilo.gllava@hotmail.com) operates on Tuesdays and Saturdays, carrying cars and freight vehicles three times a day from June to November. The rest of the year, it does not take cars and runs only once a day.

The hydrofoils and ferries to Albania leave from the far end of the main port in Corfu town, where the cruise ships berth. Tickets must be purchased before boarding, from one of the ticket agencies near the entrance to the port. There is a duty-free shop just beyond passport control in Corfu. Economical hotels (**$$$**) for an overnight stay in Corfu include Atlantis (✆ +30 266 103 5560; www.atlantis-hotel-corfu.com), convenient for the seaport, and Bretagne (✆ +30 266 103 0724), within walking distance of the airport.

Several companies operate one-day and longer tours to Albania, eg: Ionian Cruises (www.ionian-cruises.com) and Sipa Tours (www.sipatours.com), the latter also offering car hire. The day trips usually comprise a visit to Butrint, a restaurant lunch and some free time in Saranda.

A new passenger terminal has been built at Saranda port, where passports are processed swiftly and efficiently. The centre of Saranda is ten minutes' walk from the port and the bus station is about 15 minutes away. Yellow, licensed taxis wait just beyond the barrier at the entrance to the port for passengers coming off the hydrofoils and ferries. Cars can also be hired just beyond the port terminal, from Sipa Tours (www.sipatours.com) and Tirana Car Rentals (www.tirana-car-rentals.com).

By land The traditional border crossing is at **Kakavija**, 60km from the Greek city of Ioannina. There are daily bus services to Saranda from Athens and other Greek cities. Alternatively, the Greek KTEL buses run several times a day up to the border at Kakavija; there are always taxis and minibuses on the Albanian side of the border. See pages 33–4 for further information about this option.

A new border crossing opened in 2005 at **Qafëbota**, a short drive from Igoumenitsa on the Greek mainland. If you have your own transport, this is a convenient option for the archaeological complex at Butrint (see pages 224–7). It would be worth making a short detour to see the traditional houses in the village of Konispoli, just across the border. By public transport, the daily buses between Igoumenitsa and Saranda use the Qafëbota crossing. Konispoli is within walking distance of the border; buses run between Saranda and Konispoli several times a day, until about 14.00.

The main road between Saranda and **Gjirokastra** is the southern one, along the Bistrica River; some commercially available maps mark this wrongly. Buses (300 lek) ply this road until at least early afternoon; the journey takes about 1½ hours. An alternative route, for those with their own transport, goes through the small town of Delvina (see pages 228–9), and offers beautiful views down over the Bistrica Valley; there is no through public transport and the road is in poor condition beyond Delvina. Taking one of the frequent minibuses from Saranda to Delvina would let you see some of the views.

Most of the buses which operate between Saranda and Tirana use the highway via Gjirokastra and Fieri. The **coast road** buses usually have a sign in the window reading Bregdeti ('coast'); there are three every day, the first leaving Vlora at 06.45, and the journey takes about four hours. See the Riviera section, page 245, for details.

If you are **cycling** from the Gjirokastra direction, a good route would be over the Mali i Gjerë range to Delvina, and then down to Saranda by the upper road, above the Bistrica Valley. The track starts at the village of Lazarati, 5km south of

Gjirokastra on the main highway to Greece; unfortunately it is not possible to access this track by bike from Gjirokastra, although you could do it on foot.

TOURIST INFORMATION The **tourist information office** (m *068 90 44 180;* ☺ *08.00–24.00 in high summer, earlier closing out of peak season, Dec–Feb closed on Wed & Thu*) on the promenade is an excellent source of information about Saranda and the surrounding area. Enthusiastic, English-speaking staff have a database of information about hotels, restaurants, bus times and so forth. Car hire, bike hire and boat trips can be arranged. There are free town plans of Saranda, brochures and leaflets. The kiosk doubles as a bookshop, with a wide selection of publications – including (usually) this guidebook – in Albanian, English and other languages. There are also children's books and games. In summer foreign newspapers are available from 09.00. Postcards and stamps can be bought and the cards can be posted on the spot. Credit cards are accepted during the summer.

The **post office** (☺ *08.00–20.00 daily*), just up from the little harbour, provides free internet access at a reasonable speed.

 WHERE TO STAY *Map, page 220.*

Saranda has more hotels per square foot than anywhere else in Albania, with the possible exception of the coast between Durrësi and Kavaja. The accommodation on offer ranges from the luxurious to the basic, with a good choice of hotels in between, and more are built every year. There are several backpackers' hostels, but they open only in the summer. Room rates are always higher in the summer; when the town is at its busiest many hoteliers will charge whatever they think they can get away with, so it is worth trying to haggle.

Saranda bus station is – so far – the only place in Albania which suffers from the problem, common in many other countries, of touts who meet the buses and attempt to convince foreign-looking travellers to stay in their 'hotels'. They are usually very reluctant to be precise about how much they charge for their accommodation; however, it is essential to agree the exact and final price of the room before going off with these people, otherwise you may well find yourself paying more, for less, than you would have in a real, licensed hotel.

🏠 **Butrinti** (78 rooms, 24 suites) Rr e Butrintit; ☎25593/4/5/6; e Hotelbutrinti.Reservation@HotelButrinti.com; www.hotelbutrinti.com. 5 stars, very well appointed, lovely views over the bay to Corfu. Restaurants, bars, large outdoor swimming pool, fitness centre, sauna. English spoken. All rooms en suite with AC, satellite TV, phone, minibar, internet access & safe. **$$$$$**

🏠 **Brilant** (18 rooms, 2 suites) Lagja 1; ☎26262; m 069 20 53 533, 069 20 57 354; e info@brilanthotel.com; www.brilanthotel.com. Just beyond Hotel Butrint, magnificent views from upper floors. Lift, bar, Wi-Fi, restaurant for b/fast only; English spoken. 18 rooms with sea view; dbl; twin & 3-bed; all good-sized, en suite, with TV, AC, minibar, balcony. **$$$–$$$$**

🏠 **Andon Lapa i Parë** (36 rooms) Rr Mit'hat Hoxha, Lagja Kodër; ☎23804; m 069 22 88

876; e info@hotelandonlapa.com; www.hotelandonlapa.com. Out of town, beyond the port, with small private beach & good-sized swimming pool. Car park, indoor restaurant & poolside bar. All rooms en suite with AC, TV, phone, minibar, balcony. **$$$**

🏠 **Kaonia** (24 rooms) Rr Jonianët; ☎22600; m 067 20 54 944; e kaoniahotel@yahoo.com, dgjoni@bkt.com.al; Facebook: Hotel Kaonia. On the promenade a few mins' walk from the town centre. Bar, lift, internet access for guests; generator. All rooms en suite with AC, TV & balconies, some with sea view. **$$$**

🏠 **Livia** (11 rooms, 1 suite) Butrint; ☎0891 22040; m 069 20 51 263; e info@hotel-livia.com; www.hotel-livia.com. 90m from the entrance to the Butrint site. Restaurant serving fresh fish (**$$$$**), tables in garden overlooking Vivari

SARANDA

N

Bradt

0 _____ 200m
0 _____ 200yds

For listings, see pages 219–21

Where to stay
1 Backpackers S R
2 Brilant
3 Butrinti
4 Kaonia
5 Myrtaj
6 Palma
7 Porto Eda
8 Sunny Side Up

Off map
Andon Lapa i Parë
Hairy Lemon Hostel

Where to eat and drink
9   Agimi
10 Demi
11 Gërthëla
12 Paradise
13 Pizzeria Limani

Off map
Kalaja e Lëkurësit

Ionian Sea

Promenade

Harbour

Harbour

Beach

Beach

Beach

Beach

Cinema

Town Hall

JONIANET Turret

Synagogue site

Parku Miqësia

PANDI

Butrint

Delvina

CONAD

Main bus station

Taxi rank

Market

Internet café

Ferry Terminal

Finikas

Museum of Tradition

Archaeological Museum

Post office

BVD HASAN TAHSINI

ABEDIN DINO

FLAMURIT

SKENDERBEU

LEFTER TALO

ONHEZMI

LEFTER TALO

VANGJEL

MIT HAT HOXHA

Mesopotami, Girokastra, The Riviera, Lëkurësit, Kalaja e Lëkurësit

Butrint

Corfu

Hairy Lemon, Andon Lapai Parë

Channel. All rooms en suite with AC, TV, hairdryer; 1 suite with a huge private terrace. **$$$**

🏠 **Palma** (40 rooms) Rr Mit'hat Hoxha; ✆22929; m 069 65 28 336; e hotelpalma@gmail. com; can be reserved through www.booking. com. Right next to the port terminal, 10mins' walk from the town centre. Restaurant & bar with lovely terraces looking across the Bay of Saranda; separate b/fast room also with sea view; large swimming pool overlooking beach; friendly, helpful staff; English spoken. Wi-Fi in public areas; lift. All rooms have good-sized en-suite bathroom with good shower; AC, TV, balcony (some have sea view), fridge, & bedside light. Dbl, twin, 3-bed rooms; suites with 2 bedrooms, sitting room & jacuzzi. **$$$**

🏠 **Porto Eda** (24 rooms) Rr Jonianët; m 069 20 63 480, 069 72 33 180; e info@portoeda. com; www.portoeda.com. Central location on the promenade opposite the little harbour. Lift; bar; free parking; English spoken at reception. All rooms en suite with AC, TV, internet access & small balcony with view over the harbour. Well-designed bathrooms with hairdryers & shower screens. **$$$**

🏠 **Myrtaj** (14 rooms) Rr Onhezmi; ✆24411; m 069 20 93 990. Opposite the taxi rank & intercity buses; can be rather noisy early in the morning. All rooms en suite with AC & TV; some have balcony with sea view. **$$**

🏠 **Backpackers SR** (14 beds) Rr Mit'hat Hoxha 10; m 069 43 45 426; www.backpackerssr.hostel. com. Good location near port terminal. Kitchen, washing machine, lift. Free Wi-Fi & bedlinen. Dorm beds; all rooms have balcony with sea view. B/fast inc. **$**

🏠 **Hairy Lemon Hostel** (18 beds) Lagja Kodër; m 069 88 99 196; e saranda@hairylemonhostel. com; www.hairylemonhostel.com. Quite far from the town centre. Kitchen, washing machine, lift, luggage storage. Free Wi-Fi & bedlinen. B/fast inc. **$**

🏠 **Sunny Side Up** Rr Lefter Talo; m 069 87 09 976; e info@sunnysideuphostel.com; www. sunnysideuphostel.com. Kitchen, laundry facilities, luggage storage; balcony with sea view; free Wi-Fi. Dorms & dbls. **$**

✖ WHERE TO EAT AND DRINK *Map, opposite.*

Almost all of Saranda's restaurants serve pretty much the same things at roughly the same prices: fish, seafood, pastas, risottos and wood-fired pizzas. Sea bream and sea bass will be farmed unless the menu specifies otherwise. Mussels, the local speciality, have been farmed in the Butrint Lagoon since the 1960s. The promenade restaurants are, as one would expect, more expensive than those in the town centre. Out of season, many restaurants tend to close quite early in the evening.

✖ **Paradise** Rr e Butrintit. At the far eastern end of the promenade, suspended over the water on stilts; also known as Ylli's. A bit pricier than elsewhere, but lots of ppl think the view is worth it. Good range of fish & seafood, professional service. **$$$$$**

✖ **Demi** Rr e Butrintit. Big covered terrace built out over the sea, just beyond the Hotel Butrinti on the way out of town. Fresh fish, various mussel dishes, seafood risotto & pasta. **$$$$**

✖ **Gërthëla** Rr Jonianët. An exclusively fish menu, mostly wild, inc less well-known varieties as well as the usual sea bass & sea bream. Nice sea-themed décor; good service; pleasant atmosphere. **$$$$**

✖ **Kalaja e Lëkurësit** Behind Saranda just off the main road (signposted); ✆25533. Built on the ruins of an Ottoman castle; fabulous views right down the Butrint Lagoon & up the coast to the north of Saranda. Traditional southern Albanian dishes. Open-air concerts in summer. **$$$$**

✖ **Agimi** Halfway up the steps from the promenade to the square. Meat & fish dishes, plus the usual salads. Pleasant, shady garden. **$$$**

✖ **Pizzeria Limani** Bd Hasan Tahsini. A lovely setting on the town harbour, in among the little boats & looking out across the bay. The usual menu, inc fish, not only pizza. **$$$**

WHAT TO SEE AND DO Saranda is an ancient town, first settled in the 4th century BC by the Chaonians (see *Phoinike*, page 228), who called it Onchesmus. Cicero mentions it as a convenient harbour with a favourable prevailing wind. It was never a Roman colony, but it must have been reasonably prosperous in the 2nd and 3rd centuries AD, since mosaics from that period have been found at various sites in the town.

In the 4th century AD, Onchesmus was fortified with a roughly semicircular wall, about 850m long and 6m high. These fortifications were further strengthened with turrets and, in one of these, coins were found which date the tower's useful life to the period from AD334 to AD578. The remains of one of the **turrets** can be seen in the sea on the town beach. The waterfront itself was not fortified, presumably because it could be defended from the sea, so this tower marks where the wall ended. The British artist and poet Edward Lear sketched the city walls in 1857, when they were practically intact. Even into the 1990s, it was still possible to see stretches of the fortifications. The relentless pace of new building in Saranda since then has destroyed almost all of them and only a couple of small sections remain.

The **Museum of Tradition** (*Muzeu i Traditës*, ⊕ *09.00–14.00 & 16.00–21.00 Mon–Fri, 16.00–21.00 Sat*) is an excellent place to learn about Saranda's history. The museum staff are very knowledgeable and enthusiastic. The exhibition begins with a reproduction of Lear's sketch and a 1930 photograph from roughly the same vantage point, by which time only eight of the 20 original watchtowers survived. More photographs from the 1930s show the Forty Saints Church before its destruction in World War II. Nothing of the original church remains above ground, although it is possible to visit the crypt (enquire at the tourist information office) which has some surviving frescoes.

The exhibition continues with very interesting photographs of Saranda between the wars. The town was built on a grid system in the 1930s; the buildings were deliberately kept low-rise so that the whole town could be seen from the sea, rising like the seats of a theatre. A collection of ethnographic objects illustrates everyday life during this period. Upstairs, textiles and musical instruments are displayed alongside photographs of people producing and playing them. The final room of the exhibition gives a fascinating glimpse into life in the 1960s and 1970s, in the town and the surrounding area, through more photographs and household utensils.

A whole corner opposite the main square has been excavated to reveal the remains of a 5th-century **synagogue complex**, with a mosaic floor depicting Jewish symbols such as a menorah (candelabrum) and a ram's horn. Earlier mosaics on the same site appear to have formed the floor of a Roman villa. Towards the end of its life in the last quarter of the 6th century, part of the synagogue was converted into a Christian church and a third layer of mosaics was laid. The panel at the entrance to the site is very informative, with a helpful map; photographs are displayed of the menorah mosaic, which is usually kept covered to protect it from the elements.

Another of Saranda's mosaics can be seen in the **Archaeological Museum** (⊕ *summer 09.00–14.00 & 16.00–21.00 daily*). This mosaic was discovered in the 1960s, during building work at the neighbouring post office, and the museum was built specifically to protect it. It has been dated to the 6th century AD and is thought to have been the floor of a basilica. The museum also has a small display of photographs and information about the archaeological and historical sites in the Saranda area, including Butrint, of course, but also Phoinike and the Islamic buildings around Delvina (see pages 228–9).

BUTRINT

The ancient city of Butrint, one of UNESCO's World Heritage Sites, is far and away the most visited archaeological site in Albania, with visible remains spanning two and a half millennia – from the first settlers in the late 6th or early 5th century BC to

Ali Pasha Tepelena (see box, pages 246–7) at the beginning of the 19th century AD. Then the site became overgrown and half-forgotten, visited only by the occasional artist (including the British nonsense poet Edward Lear), until 1928, when the Italian Archaeological Mission, led until his death by Luigi Maria Ugolini, began to uncover the city's hidden treasures. After World War II, Butrint was once again abandoned and forgotten until the Albanian Centre for Archaeology began excavating there in 1956. Archaeological research has continued at the site ever since.

Informative and well-presented panels guide the visitor through the city; the small museum, on what was once the acropolis, illustrates Butrint's history through beautiful artefacts; further interesting sites lie across the Vivari Channel, which connects Lake Butrint with the sea, and can be visited on foot or by boat. There is so much to see in and around Butrint that anyone with more than a fleeting interest in history or archaeology could easily spend a whole day (or more) there. Anything less than three hours is likely to feel rather rushed and unsatisfactory.

An information leaflet, with a map of the site, is available at the ticket office at the entrance to the site; it can also be downloaded in advance from the Butrint National Park's excellent website (*www.butrint.org*). Butrint National Park is supported, financially and scientifically, by the Butrint Foundation, a charitable trust set up in 1993 to save the Butrint site from the decay and looting which threatened its survival at the time. More academic information about the site can be found on the foundation's website (*www.butrintfoundation.co.uk*) and its publications can be ordered online.

GETTING THERE AND AWAY The ancient city of Butrint is about half an hour's drive from Saranda, 24km on a good asphalted road which runs alongside Lake Butrint and through the village of Ksamili. Cyclists might prefer to use the back road, along the eastern shore of the Butrint Lagoon, which has much less traffic. **Buses** between Saranda and Butrint leave at half past every hour in each direction, until 18.30 in summer. In Saranda, the bus stop is opposite the synagogue and basilica site; you can also board or alight outside the Butrinti Hotel. Any Saranda **taxi** will do the run; you should agree the fare before setting off. Either you could negotiate a charge for extra waiting time with the driver or, if you have a mobile phone, you could arrange to call him when you are ready to be collected. The town's main taxi rank is on the corner of the central park in Saranda, opposite the CONAD supermarket.

Butrint can also be reached from the other direction, the border crossing from Greece at Qafëbota; see page 218 for details of this route.

GETTING AROUND AND OTHER PRACTICALITIES A reasonably surfaced path leads around the site. It is fairly flat apart from a slight climb up to the viewpoint for the aqueduct (see pages 226–7) and back down to the Lake and Lion gates. However, the museum is on the city's acropolis, on the summit of the hill above the monumental centre. The usual access to it is through the Lion Gate and up several flights of steps, with intermittent handrails. Visitors with limited mobility may find it easier to use the steps to the west of the theatre. The only toilets on the site are also on the acropolis.

The Livia Hotel, a few minutes' walk from the site entrance, serves meals (**\$\$\$\$**) and drinks, and obviously has toilets for customer use; see *Where to stay*, pages 219–20, for further information. You should be sure to have enough drinking water with you, especially in high summer when it can become extremely hot. There is nowhere to buy water within the site. You may also wish to stock up on insect repellent; Butrint is low-lying and surrounded by water, ideal territory for mosquitoes and other biting insects.

A bookstall outside the museum sells publications, in a range of languages, about Butrint and other archaeological sites in Albania. Craft stalls near the ticket office sell souvenirs such as handmade mosaic decorations, wood-carvings, textiles and jewellery. These stalls are run by people from the villages on the Vrina Plain, the items they sell are all made locally, and the profits go to the craftspeople themselves.

For boat trips to Diaporit and Ali Pasha's Castle, see page 226. Plays are staged in the Butrint theatre, notably during an international drama festival which is held every summer. The tourist information office in Saranda should be able to provide details, since these are readily available on the festival's website (*www.butrinti2000.com*).

THE CITY (🕗 *08.00–sunset daily, year round, museum* 🕗 *08.00–16.00; 700 lek for non-Albanians, inc museum admission*)

Butrint is first mentioned in the 6th century BC as a harbour; its location at almost the narrowest point of the Straits of Corfu made it a strategic crossroads between the Ionian islands, particularly Corfu itself, and the wealthy trading cities of Epirus. Pottery from the 7th and 6th centuries BC has been found on the acropolis hill, but any traces of such an early settlement were built over in antiquity.

In the 5th century and into the 4th century, Butrint was effectively part of Corcyra (Corfu), the Corinthian colony across the Straits. Later, the city became integrated into the Epirote Alliance, as part of the Chaonian territory whose capital was Phoinike (see page 228). In 167BC, Rome's wars with Macedonia came to an end with the final victory for Rome, and Butrint, like the rest of Epirus, became part of a Roman-administered province.

The earliest building below the acropolis was a **sanctuary** to the god of medicine, Asclepius, in what developed into the city's monumental centre. In the 4th century BC, or slightly later, a **defensive wall**, with imposing gates at regular intervals, was built around the expanding lower city – a stretch of this, with large irregularly shaped blocks, can still be seen as you enter this area. Worshippers came to the sanctuary to be healed and, to meet their other needs, various other buildings were erected: a temple, in front of the shrine; a hostel for pilgrims or priests to stay – the so-called Peristyle Building; and, between them, a **theatre**, built with donations made to the god. An inscription on the theatre seats dates its construction to the early 2nd century BC, although this was almost certainly an extension of an earlier, simpler theatre. To the side of the walkway leading into the theatre, inscribed blocks form part of the wall; these record the freeing of slaves, more than 500 of them, between 163BC and 44BC. Behind the Peristyle Building, a long portico (a *stoa*) once ran, with a well set into the hillside within it; the ropes which hauled water from this well over the centuries have worn deep grooves into its marble door.

Wealthy Romans – including Cicero's friend Atticus – had been buying up land at Butrint throughout the 1st century, and in 44BC the city became a Roman colony. The official language became Latin and Butrint began to mint coins. In the city centre, the old Hellenistic *agora* (market) was remodelled and turned into a Roman forum. During Ugolini's excavation of the theatre, several statues were found within it, including three portrait heads of the emperor Augustus, his wife Livia and his general Agrippa, which have been dated to 27–12BC. Agrippa is in the National Archaeological Museum in Tirana; Augustus and his wife are displayed in the Butrint Museum (the head of Livia, looted in the 1990s, was recovered in 2000). Shops sprang up around the forum and a bathhouse was built next to it, paved with a black-and-white mosaic. The mosaic, like all the mosaics at Butrint, is kept covered to protect it; the hypocaust with which the baths were heated has been partly reconstructed. To feed the baths and fountains with water, Roman engineers constructed an **aqueduct**

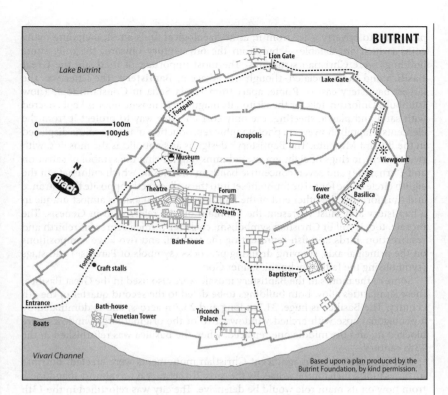

Lake Butrint

Lion Gate

Lake Gate

Footpath

0 ————100m
0 ————100yds

Acropolis

Viewpoint

Museum

N
Bradt

Theatre

Forum

Tower
Gate

Basilica

Footpath

Bath-house

Footpath

Craft stalls

Baptistery

Entrance

Bath-house

Boats

Venetian Tower

Triconch
Palace

Vivari Channel

Based upon a plan produced by the
Butrint Foundation, by kind permission.

to bring water from springs 4km away across the Vrina Plain, near the modern village
of Xarra. Some of the piers which carried the aqueduct can still be seen, looking across
the water towards Xarra from a viewpoint on the path around the site. The aqueduct
was extended into the city in the 1st century AD and piers from that extension survive
near the Great Basilica (see page 226).

In the first century AD, the city spread across the Vivari Channel and a whole
new suburb began to develop on the Vrina Plain. In the old lower city, the theatre
was expanded, with a new stage and seating for 2,000 or so spectators, and more
bathhouses were built. The city continued to grow and its wealthiest citizens
commissioned prestigious villas on both sides of the Channel. One of these, at
Diaporit on the eastern shore of Lake Butrint, can be visited by boat (see page
227 for details). Another lies southwest of the monumental centre; when it was
first constructed, it was a traditional Roman villa, with elegant, mosaic-floored
rooms arranged around a central courtyard. It is known as the **Triconch Palace**
because, around AD420, it was expanded into a much more substantial building
which included a dining room (*triclinium*) with three scalloped niches. The palace
even had its own water gate, by which visitors arriving by boat could enter the
building straight from the water's edge. Strangely, in view of all the work which
had been done to create this beautiful residence, it was abandoned shortly before it
was completed; carved window-frames had been installed but the floors were never
paved and the walls were left unpainted. The most likely reason is that the rising
water table brought construction to a halt.

Perhaps as a way of coping with seasonal changes in the water table, the people
of Butrint now began to build their houses of perishable timber. The city was not

The Southwest   BUTRINT

8

plunged into poverty – far from it, as archaeological finds attest, including many coins (which are datable) – but from the 6th century onward, the only stone buildings were Christian structures. The most important of these are the **Great Basilica** and the associated, though not adjacent, **Baptistery**. The latter was the largest baptistery east of Rome, apart from Hagia Sofia in Constantinople (now Istanbul). Unfortunately for the visitor, its magnificent mosaic floor is kept covered with sand and plastic sheeting, the only cost-effective way to protect it from the elements. Happily, however, a photographic reproduction of the mosaic is displayed in the Butrint Museum. The Baptistery's design is as symbolic as the mosaic's, with two concentric rings of eight granite columns (eight being the symbol of salvation and eternal life) and seven concentric bands in the mosaic which culminate in the eighth circle of the font. The fountain set into the wall, directly opposite the entrance and thus forming the other end of the building's principal axis, is almost unique in a baptistery and must represent the Fountain of Life referred to in Genesis. The mosaic, too, is full of Christian symbolism: cockerels, which represent rebirth and resurrection; birds and fish representing the faithful; and two large compositions on the principal axis, showing drinking peacocks (symbols of Paradise) and stags (symbolising the faithful who thirst after God).

Some of the motifs in the Baptistery mosaic were also used in the Great Basilica; these similarities allow both buildings to be dated to the second quarter of the 6th century. The Basilica is huge, 31.7m long and 23.7m across, and is dominated by a pentagonal apse with arched windows; two of the original large windows were blocked in, and the middle one replaced, when the Basilica was refurbished in the 13th century.

Not long after these magnificent Christian monuments were erected, Butrint's fortunes took a turn for the worse. By the early 7th century it was almost abandoned; from now on its main role would be defensive. The city was refortified in the 13th century and a new castle was built on the acropolis; reconstructed in the 1930s, this castle now houses the Butrint Museum. The Venetian Republic purchased Butrint, along with Corfu, in 1386 and built the tower at the entrance to the site, the triangular fortress on the other side of the Vivari Channel and, probably, the fortress at the mouth of the channel which is known as **Ali Pasha's Castle**. All these fortifications hark back to the first defensive wall, built in the 4th century BC. The path around the site and up to the museum passes three of the gates in this wall: the main entrance to the city, Tower Gate, near the Baptistery; the Lake Gate, which Ugolini called the Scaean Gate, after the *Aeneid*; and the Lion Gate, so called from the carved lintel of a lion sinking its teeth into a bull's neck, which was placed there long after the gate was first constructed. The carving is typical of Greek archaic art of the 6th century; it is thought that this relief may have come from a building associated with the sanctuary on the acropolis.

BEYOND THE CITY The triangular fortress and the remains of the aqueduct, across the Vivari Channel, are easy to visit on foot. A cable ferry plies across the channel whenever a vehicle wants to cross. Foot passengers travel free, and so they have to wait for a (paying) car or bus to turn up. The gate into the triangular fortress is in the wall furthest from the ferry jetty – the southern side. Within the walls is a courtyard, in the centre of which is a circular building (perhaps a *hamam*, or steam bath, added later by the Ottomans). The western wall contains several small vaulted chambers, probably originally used as gunpowder magazines, workshops or stores. In the southwestern corner is an unusually shaped tower; there are good views of the city of Butrint from its upper floor and from the fortress battlements.

To reach the piers of the Roman aqueduct, continue along the edge of the Vivari Channel until you reach the fish traps and the building beside them, where there are beehives. Cross the little bridge there, and head slightly inland along a track which leads to an excavated area of the Roman suburb on the Vrina Plain. By the 2nd century AD, this included villas and a public bathhouse, with a large cistern which was supplied with water from the aqueduct. If you look along the wall of the cistern, you will see the bases of the aqueduct piers in a line running towards Xarra, the village on the hill. It is about 15 minutes' walk from here back to the cable ferry.

As well as the Vrina Plain, the expansion of Butrint in the 1st century AD also meant new building at Diaporit, on the eastern shore of Lake Butrint. A large villa has been excavated here, with a bath complex, a peristyle and a mosaic-floored *triclinium*. This site, and Ali Pasha's fortress, can only be reached by boat. Vessels can be hired opposite the ticket office at the entrance to the city.

In 2000, as part of the Albanian government's efforts to protect Butrint, the archaeological site and the surrounding area were given national park status. The park now extends for 86km² and, in addition to its archaeological significance, has a wide variety of animal habitats and great biodiversity. It is listed as a Wetlands Site of International Importance, under the Ramsar Convention. Several trails have been marked around the park, of varying distances and levels of difficulty. Details of these can be found on the Butrint National Park's website (*www.butrint.org*), from where a leaflet with a map of the routes can be downloaded. The leaflet and other publications about hiking in the park can also be obtained at the ticket office at the entrance to the archaeological site.

There are clear views from the Saranda–Corfu ferry of the entrance to the Vivari Channel – with Ali Pasha's Castle, the triangular fortress and the reconstructed Butrint Castle – which give a very good idea of the geography of the channel and the city.

AROUND SARANDA

KSAMILI Until recently, Ksamili, 17km south of Saranda on the road to Butrint, was a charming hamlet, with a few dozen houses, a lovely little sandy beach and one restaurant. Now, like many other formerly idyllic spots on the Albanian coast, it has become a construction site. If you can find your way through the half-built or half-demolished apartment blocks, there is a string of little bays, each with a restaurant or hotel, a car park and sun-loungers for hire. The sea is clean and clear, with the rich blue colour of the Ionian, and Ksamili is a nice place to stop for a swim or a meal on the way to or from Butrint, especially outside the peak tourist season.

As well as fresh fish and seafood, the **Rilinda Restaurant** (**$$$**) has the best location, opposite one of the islands which close off and protect Ksamili Bay; the restaurant runs a bar on the island during the summer, to which you can swim or take a pedalo or rowing boat. To find the Rilinda using public transport from Saranda, get off the bus at the first of the two stops in Ksamili and head right until you reach the sea.

ST NICHOLAS'S CHURCH, MESOPOTAMI The Church of St Nicholas (Kisha e Shënkollit) stands, surrounded by poplars, on a hillock just outside the village of Mesopotami. It was built in the 11th century on the site of an earlier church – indeed, some of the limestone blocks used in its construction came from an even older building, perhaps in the nearby city of Phoinike (see page 228). Some of these blocks, which make up part of the rear wall of the church, bear curious carvings which are thought to predate the arrival of Christianity here: an eagle, a lion, a dragon and an even weirder mythical creature, apparently strangling itself with its own tail. Inside the church, the central pillar is constructed around a stone column. Some frescoes survive behind the altar.

It is easy to get to St Nicholas's by public transport, using one of the many buses and minibuses which run between Saranda and Gjirokastra. Coming from Saranda, you should alight just beyond Mesopotami, where a sign reading '300m, Manastir' (Albanian for 'monastery') indicates a rough track up to the right. Alternatively, the return taxi fare from Saranda is around 1,000 lek, including a short wait while you look at the church. It is usually locked, but the tourist information office in Saranda can arrange for the church caretaker to meet you there and let you in.

PHOINIKE The ancient city of Phoinike was the capital of Chaonia, one of the three largest states (*koina*) in the Federation of Epirus. It was built on a hill which controlled the valley between Butrint to its south and the mountains which run into the Ionian Sea, to its north. It is first mentioned, in Greek sources, in 330BC; the walls surrounding it were built at the end of the 4th century BC and the beginning of the 3rd, with the huge polygonal stones common to Epirote cities (there are stretches of similar walls at Butrint). The middle of the 3rd century BC was the high point of Phoinike's power. The city became the capital (or one of the capitals) of Epirus in 232BC and minted its own coins. In 205BC, it was here that the peace treaty was signed which ended the First Macedonian War: the Peace of Phoinike.

The buildings on the acropolis are rather difficult to make sense of, because there are many layers built one above another, in periods ranging from the 4th century BC to the 4th century AD. The buildings around the edge of the acropolis were shops; in times of war, these were used to shelter citizens who lived outside the protective walls. Easier to understand is the theatre, built into the slope of the hill in a magnificent setting. It is much later than the main buildings on the acropolis, from the 2nd and 3rd centuries AD; it has not been fully excavated but is thought to have had a capacity of 12,000 spectators. The views from the acropolis and the theatre are superb; the Butrint Lagoon can be seen quite clearly, as can the southernmost villages of the Albanian Riviera.

The modern village of Finiqi is on a minor road which links the Saranda–Delvina road and the main Saranda–Gjirokastra road. From the village, an asphalted road leads up to the entrance of the site; it is steep, but a 4x4 is certainly not required. There is also a footpath up from the village, which is a 30–45-minute walk. Getting to Phoinike by public transport is difficult; all but the most budget-conscious will hire a taxi in Saranda for the round trip. There is one bus a day to Finiqi, but it leaves Saranda at lunchtime and does not return until the following morning. The village is a couple of kilometres from the main Saranda–Gjirokastra road.

There is little interpretation at the site, but the Regional Directorate for National Culture in Saranda produces a helpful leaflet; the tourist information office may have copies. Research at Phoinike has been led, since 2000, by archaeologists from the University of Bologna; those who read Italian might like to consult the archaeological mission's website (*www.phoinike.com*).

ISLAMIC HISTORICAL BUILDINGS, DELVINA Two very significant Islamic sites can be visited either with one's own transport or by taxi from Delvina, a small town about 20km from Saranda, high in the hills above the Bistrica Valley. The **Rusan Mosque** was mentioned by the 17th-century Turkish traveller Evliya Çelebi; its architecture is especially interesting, with several different levels of roof. Slim, agile visitors can climb the tightly winding stairs to the top of the minaret (the building is maintained by the Ministry of Culture and it is not a working mosque) where these can be seen more clearly. The hexagonal buildings nearby, whose tiled roofs look so attractive from above, are of later date, from when the site was used as a Bektashi *teqe* (see pages 22–3); one of them contains the graves of several Bektashi *babas*. The mosque's beautiful ceiling, inscribed with verses from the Koran, can be admired more closely from the gallery.

On the other side of Delvina is the recently restored **Xhermëhalla Islamic Complex**. The buildings within it include a mosque, a ruined *madrasa*, or Islamic school, a bathhouse and several Bektashi *tyrbes*, as at Rusan. During restoration work, a hitherto unknown fountain was revealed, below the entrance to the mosque and *madrasa*; this was where the faithful washed before entering the mosque to pray. There are good views from Xhermëhalla of the ruins of the Byzantine **Delvina Castle**, perched imposingly on a crag. It is possible to hike up to the castle, but there is not much to see once you get there apart, of course, from the views.

Both the Rusan Mosque and the Xhermëhalla Islamic Complex are very close to Delvina: only five or ten minutes' drive. Simple accommodation is available in Delvina at the Shameti Hotel (℡ *0815 22380;* $), centrally located with good views from the terraces on the upper floors.

THE BLUE EYE (*100 lek/car, 50 lek/person*) The Blue Eye (Syri i Kaltër) is an unusual underwater spring, set in shady woods 2km off the main road between Gjirokastra and Saranda. The water bubbles up through a deep pool, making a curious circular shape, deep blue at its centre and almost electric blue around the edges, like the pupil and iris of an eye. The rocks from which the spring rises are more than 45m below the surface and the pool has never been fully explored.

The Blue Eye is a pretty spot, with oak trees fringing the pool and flowers growing on the banks. It is surrounded by woodland and by streams and pools which flow from the spring. In the old days the area was reserved for the party élite to hunt and fish in, and ordinary Albanians were banned, which is usually a good indicator of how nice a place is.

The turn-off for Syri i Kaltër is indicated by a large brown 'tourist attraction' sign, after the Bistrica hydro-electric plant and just before the road begins to climb up to the Muzina Pass (as you come from Saranda). The road is asphalted; a path leads through the trees from the car park to the Blue Eye. There are several cafés around the park, with reasonable toilets.

GJIROKASTRA   *Telephone code: 084*

The austere and beautiful town of Gjirokastra began to spread downhill from its castle in the 13th century. The castle still broods on its hill, overlooking the whole city and the river valley below. From that vantage point, the grey stone of the houses below and the grey slates of their roofs blend into the hillside, distinguished from it only by their whitewashed walls. Gjirokastra's architecture and haunting atmosphere are described by one of the city's most famous sons:

This was a surprising city, which seemed to have come out of the valley unexpectedly, one winter's night, like a prehistoric being, and clambered up with difficulty, stitching itself on to the side of the mountain. Everything in this city was old and made of stone, from the streets and fountains right up to the roofs of its big houses, a century old, which were covered with stone tiles the colour of ash, like so many huge carapaces. It was difficult to believe that under these hard shells the soft flesh of life thrived and was renewed.

Ismail Kadare, *Kronikë në gur* (*Chronicle in Stone*), Onufri, 2000

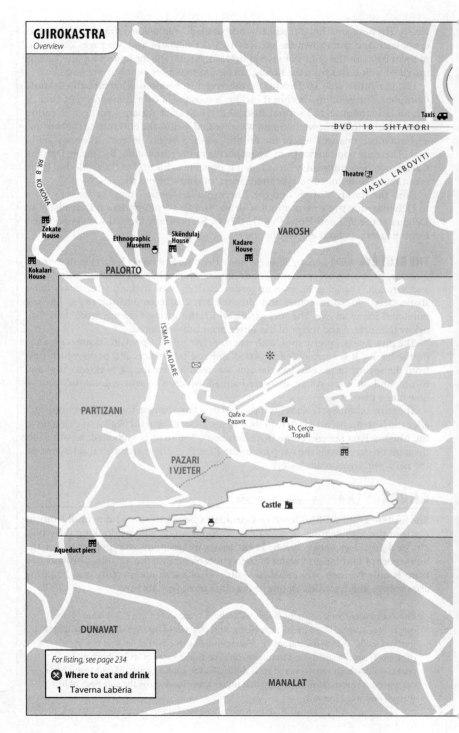

GJIROKASTRA
Overview

Taxis

BVD 18 SHTATORI

Theatre

VASIL LABOVITI

RR B KO KONA

Zekate
House

Ethnographic
Museum

Skëndulaj
House

Kadare
House

VAROSH

Kokalari
House

PALORTO

ISMAIL KADARE

PARTIZANI

Qafa e
Pazarit

Sh. Çerçiz
Topulli

PAZARI
I VJETER

Castle

Aqueduct piers

DUNAVAT

For listing, see page 234

⊗ **Where to eat and drink**

1   Taverna Labëria

MANALAT

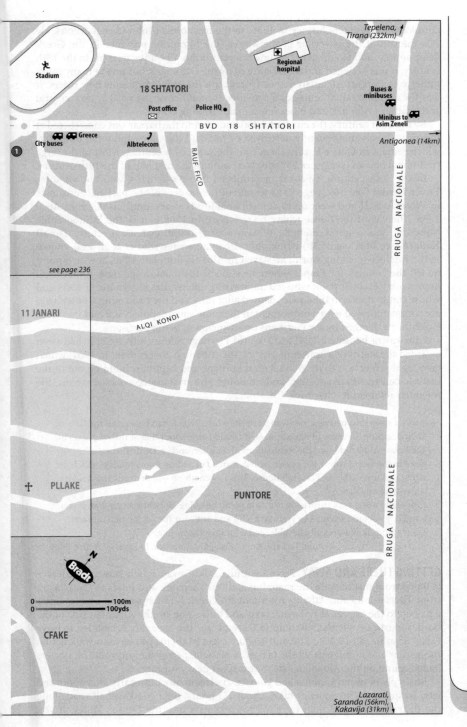

Tepelena,
Tirana (232km)

Regional
hospital

18 SHTATORI

Stadium

Buses &
minibuses

Post office   Police HQ

Minibus to
Asim Zeneli

City buses   Greece   BVD 18   SHTATORI

Albtelecom   Antigonea (14km)

RAUF FICO

RRUGA NACIONALE

see page 236

11 JANARI

ALQI KONDI

PLLAKE

PUNTORE

RRUGA NACIONALE

N

Bradt

0   100m
0   100yds

CFAKE

Lazarati,
Saranda (56km),
Kakavija (31km)

Gjirokastra first enters history in 1336, in the memoirs of John Cantacuzenus. He was the son of the governor of the Morea, the Byzantine province in the Greek Peloponnese, and would later become Emperor John VI Cantacuzenus. In the 15th century, it was besieged and then captured by the Ottomans, but unlike many other hitherto important Albanian towns, Gjirokastra flourished under its new rulers. It was the administrative centre of a province (*sanjak*) covering what is now central and southern Albania, and it became a major trading centre.

By the 17th century, the city had 2,000 houses, and the bazaar was constructed at this time. It was subsequently destroyed by fire, and the shops and other buildings which remain in Qafa e Pazarit date from the early 20th century. Most of the large traditional houses (see pages 237–40) were built in the first half of the 19th century.

In the 20th century, Gjirokastra produced two particularly well-known sons. **Enver Hoxha** (see box, page 83) was one of the leaders of the partisan resistance in World War II and went on to run Albania for 41 years, until his death in April 1985. The site of the house where he was born in 1908 is now the Ethnographic Museum, and a good example of Gjirokastra traditional architecture. **Ismail Kadare** (see box, page 238) is the only Albanian writer who is at all well known in the English-speaking world; he stayed in Albania until late 1990, at which point he left the country for France where he still spends most of his time. Other local heroes are Çerçiz Topulli, who led an uprising against the Ottomans in 1908 and whose statue stands in the square named after him, and the two young women who are commemorated with a monument in the same square, Bule Naipi and Persefoni Kokëdhima, hanged by the Germans on suspicion of being partisans.

Gjirokastra became a UNESCO World Heritage Site in July 2005. It had been awarded the status of a 'museum-city' by the Albanian government in 1961, which gave legal protection to its architectural heritage and kept new building out of the historic centre. Thanks to this, and no doubt also to its steep cobbled streets, the town has retained its charming atmosphere.

It was a steep city, perhaps the steepest in the world, which had broken all the laws of town planning. Because of its steepness, it would come about that at the roof-level of one house you would find the foundations of another; and certainly this was the only place in the world where if a passer-by fell, instead of sliding into a roadside ditch, he might end up on the roof of a tall house. This is something which drunkards knew better than anyone.

It really was a very surprising city. You could be going along the street and, if you wanted, you could stretch out your arm a bit and put your hat on top of a minaret. Many things here were unbelievable, and a lot was dream-like.

Ismail Kadare, *Kronikë në gur* (*Chronicle in Stone*), Onufri, 2000

GETTING THERE AND AWAY From Ioannina, 90km away, a daily **bus** service leaves at 06.00 from just outside the main bus station. There are also buses to Gjirokastra from Thessaloniki and Athens. Alternatively, Greek KTEL buses run several times a day up to the border at Kakavija; taxis and buses wait on the Albanian side of the border to run people the 30km up to Gjirokastra. The buses are scheduled to leave Kakavija at 07.30, 10.30, 14.00 and 16.30. To get to them, you have to walk across the border and uphill past all the taxi drivers to the petrol station; youthful porters hang around on the Albanian side to transport heavy luggage.

Buses ply between Saranda and Gjirokastra frequently until early afternoon, and later in summer. The journey takes about 1½ hours, on a good asphalt road along the Bistrica River and then over the Muzina Pass into the Drinos Valley. If you have your own transport, the alternative route through the town of Delvina offers good views across the Bistrica Valley, although east of Delvina the road is in poor condition. Mountain bikers might consider the track across the Mali i Gjerë range from Delvina to the village of Lazarati, a few kilometres south of Gjirokastra.

There are many buses from Tirana; they leave from a bus depot off Rruga e Kavajës (see the Tirana map on pages 62–3), until early afternoon. There are buses in the mornings between Gjirokastra and Përmeti; later in the day, you will need to change in Këlcyra. A bus runs every day except Sundays between Gjirokastra and Korça; it leaves Gjirokastra at 07.00. *Chapter 5*, page 131, has more information about this long (six-hour) but beautiful journey through the magnificent scenery of the Gramoz Mountains.

Gjirokastra's main bus terminus is beside the main highway, on the northern outskirts of town. The buses to Greece leave from a stop on Boulevard 18 Shtatori, opposite the stadium. Bus departure times and other useful information are displayed in the front window of the Sopoti Hotel, just off Sheshi Çerçiz Topulli.

GETTING AROUND Buses cannot drive up into the old town, but there are always taxis waiting to ferry people up from the bus terminus. Any bus coming from Saranda or Kakavija will drop passengers off at the foot of the hill going up to the old town. It is a very long, steep climb on foot. There are usually informal taxis hanging around at this junction. Alternatively, city buses ply between Boulevard 18 Shtatori and Sheshi Çerçiz Topulli, via the highway, with a flat fare of 30 lek. In the old town, there is a taxi rank in Sheshi Çerçiz Topulli.

People in Gjirokastra, like everywhere else in Albania, navigate by neighbourhoods (*lagja*) or landmarks. Those who are driving themselves should note that, in the old town, most streets are very narrow and steep; indeed, some are flights of steps. For pedestrians, these are useful short cuts between the old and new towns; driving a vehicle requires deep local knowledge and impeccable hill starts.

TOURIST INFORMATION A map of the old town is posted at the western end of Sheshi Çerçiz Topulli, next to the statue of Bule and Persefoni. Gjirokastra's tourist information centre has closed, but a couple of the shops on Qafa e Pazarit (eg: AlbTour) have taken over its role, selling guidebooks (including this one) and maps, and providing tour-guiding services in English and other languages. The website of the Gjirokastra Conservation and Development Organisation (GCDO), www. gjirokastra.org, has a wealth of information about the city, in English and Albanian. GCDO supports the **artisans** whose workshops are around Qafa e Pazarit and on Rruga e Kalasë ('Castle Street'). They include lacemakers, a woodcarver and a stonemason, who make exquisite pieces of art as well as small souvenirs.

Caravan Travel organises excursions on horseback, with English-speaking guides, to places of interest in the Gjirokastra area. For experienced riders, the highlight is a week-long tour along the old trading routes in the Zagoria and Pogoni mountains, with visits to Labova e Kryqit (see pages 243–4) and other beautiful churches, and finishing at Antigonea (see pages 240–1). Bespoke tours can also be arranged. See *Chapter 2*, page 31 for contact details.

 **WHERE TO STAY** *Map, page 236.*

Çajupi (34 rooms) Sh Çerçiz Topulli; ☏ 269 010; **m** 067 26 43 431, 067 26 44 397; **e** info@ cajupi.com; www.cajupi.com. English spoken at reception. Restaurant on top floor with good menu & views; bar with traditional décor; lift to all floors; Wi-Fi throughout. All rooms with nice en-suite bathroom with shower screens (some also bathtub), with AC, flat-screen TV; some have small balcony & city view, others overlook forest on castle hill. **$$$**

⌂ **Hashorva** (3 rooms) Lagja Varosh; 📞262 314; m 069 35 62 098; e hotelhashorva@yahoo.com. A traditional Gjirokastra house, partially modernised; bedrooms have carved wooden doors & other traditional architectural features; pleasant garden. 2 twin rooms share a large, simple bathroom, 1 dbl room has en-suite facilities. No TV, Wi-Fi or AC. **$$**

⌂ **Kalemi 1** (15 rooms) Lagja Palorto; 📞263 724, 267 260; m 068 22 34 373, 068 40 11 413; e draguak@yahoo.com; www.hotelkalemi.tripod. com. A traditional Gjirokastra house, lovingly restored by the owner; 1 dbl room has a beautiful carved ceiling. Magnificent views of the city & the castle from the balconies on the upper floors. Reliable electricity & constant hot water (solar). Restaurant/bar; Wi-Fi; parking; good English spoken. All rooms en suite (some have bathtub as well as shower), with TV, CH; some also AC. Lavish b/fast with fresh bread inc. **$$**

⌂ **Kalemi 2** (14 rooms, 2 suites) Qafa e Pazarit; m 068 22 34 373, 068 40 11 413; e draguak@ yahoo.com; www.hotelkalemi.tripod.com. Sympathetic restoration of a beautiful Category 2 house (see pages 238–9); re-roofed in slate; each room has a hand-carved wooden ceiling in a

different design. B/fast room, laundry service, good English spoken; Wi-Fi; magnificent views of castle from upper floors. Dbl & trpl rooms, all en suite with TV, AC; suites have bathtub as well as shower. **$$**

⌂ **Kotoni** (5 rooms) Lagja Palorto; 📞263 526; m 069 23 66 846; e info@kotonihouse.com; www.kotonihouse.com. Another traditional house, near Qafa e Pazarit; views of castle & old town; traditional décor in rooms. Friendly, welcoming management, English spoken; library of brochures & guidebooks for guests' reference; laundry service; restaurant & bar with traditional wooden ceiling & furnishings. All rooms en suite with TV, AC, Wi-Fi. Substantial b/fast inc. **$$**

⌂ **Babameto Hostel** (6 rooms) Lagja Pazari i Vjetër 📞262 090; m 069 36 55 915, 069 23 73 093; e info@gjirokastra.org; www. hostelbabameto.beep.com. A historic 19th-century Gjirokastra house, fully restored in 2013. Kitchen, bar, free Wi-Fi, lockers, ironing board; towels & sheets provided. Conference room, traditionally furnished sitting room, courtyard. 3-bed rooms & 6-bed dorms, sharing showers & toilets. **$**

⌂ **Sopoti** (17 rooms) Just off Sh Çerçiz Topulli; reservations through www.hostelworld.com. Laundry service; no Wi-Fi. Good-sized sgl, dbl & trpl rooms, sharing basic washing & toilet facilities. **$**

✗ **WHERE TO EAT AND DRINK** *Map, page 236, unless otherwise indicated.*

✗ **Fantazia** In a great location above Qafa e Pazarit, with wonderful views of the new town & of the castle. Serves pizzas, pasta, salads & the usual grilled meat dishes. **$$$**

✗ **Kodra** On the platform which, until 1991, supported a huge statue of Enver Hoxha, overlooking the Drinos Valley & mountains beyond. The owner (m *069 40 62 661*) hopes also to open a 13-room hotel built into the base of the platform, subject to negotiations with UNESCO. **$$$**

✗ **Kujtimi** Qafa e Pazarit. Good salads, traditional Gjirokastra dishes such as *qifqi*, plus whatever is available & fresh – fish, mussels, frogs' legs. Most tables outside on the lovely vine-shaded terrace. **$$$**

✗ **Gjoça** Qafa e Pazarit. Small restaurant with extensive menu – traditional Gjirokastra dishes, plus pasta, grilled lamb, fish. Friendly, helpful owners. **$$**

✗ **Sofra** Sh Çerçiz Topulli. Good range of traditional Gjirokastra dishes; small private dining room, hand-carved ceiling, traditionally furnished

with low seats & *sofra* (low wooden tables), annexe to larger, modern bar/restaurant. Family-run, good value. **$$**

✗ **Taverna Labëria** [map, page 231] In the new town, opposite the stadium. Specialises in chargrilled meat & chicken, innards, etc. **$$**

Out of town

✗ **Mulliri i Babait** Mashkullora; m 069 24 10 416. Nice rural setting, a few kilometres north of Gjirokastra. Serves spit-roasted lamb & other traditional meat dishes. **$$$**

✗ **Viroi** [map, page 217] On the lakeside just outside the city; 📞262 072. This popular restaurant & pizzeria, 5mins' drive from town, also has a few well-appointed hotel rooms with views of the lake. **$$$**

✗ **Terihates** Terihat; 📞0884 231 390; m 069 20 79 874/5. In a Greek-minority village to the south of Gjirokastra. Excellent traditional dishes such as *kukurec* (the Albanian equivalent of haggis) made from lamb or kid; also pasta, pizza, etc. **$$**

WHAT TO SEE AND DO

The castle (🕑 *May–Sep 09.00–19.00 daily, Oct–Apr closes earlier; 200 lek*)
Gjirokastra's castle perches above the city, controlling the Drinos Valley below and the passes through the Lunxhëria Mountains opposite. It is no longer inhabited, unlike the citadels of Kruja and Berati, but it was used as a garrison and a prison until very recently. Excavations indicate that the citadel may have been inhabited as early as the Iron Age, in the 8th–7th centuries BC; it was probably fortified in the 5th century BC and extended during the Despotate of Epirus (see page 9). Further enlargements and improvements were made in the early Ottoman period and in 1811 Ali Pasha Tepelena (see box, pages 246–7) undertook extensive building work. Much of what can be seen today is the work of Ali Pasha's architects and engineers.

The entrance to the castle can be reached via the steep, cobbled road which winds up the hillside from the top of Rruga e Kalasë ('Castle Street'), where the artisans' shops are. For those on foot, it is faster to use the steps which start almost exactly opposite the end of this street. The ticket office is just inside the castle entrance.

Turning right after the ticket office leads you into dark vaults built by Ali Pasha. The high tunnel to the left at the start of the vaults was originally the castle's main southern gate. A little further on, a Bektashi *tyrbe* (see pages 22–3) stands in a little garden, up some steps on the left. The rest of the vaults are fun to explore, but they are unlit and rather treacherous underfoot.

A left turn after the ticket office brings you into a dimly lit gallery lined with World War II artillery pieces. Right at the end of the gallery is a rare example of a Fiat L6/40 tank, used by the Italian army from 1941 to 1943. A collection of older weapons forms part of the exhibition in the **Museum of Armaments**, housed in the former prison above this gallery. Tickets (*200 lek*) are sold separately from admission to the castle; the museum ticket office is at the exit of the vaulted gallery, just after the Italian tank.

The prison was built in 1929 to accommodate King Zog's enemies, and then used enthusiastically by the Wehrmacht during World War II; in the summer of 1944, the Germans were holding 500 prisoners in the 50 cells here. The prison remained in use until 1968, when the first National Folk Festival took place in Gjirokastra Castle and it was felt that political prisoners were not entirely compatible with this happy event. The museum opened in 1971; the display focuses mainly on World War II, including many pieces taken from Italian or German troops, and some British weapons which were supplied to the partisans by the Special Operations Executive (SOE; see boxes, pages 13–15). After touring the exhibition, the guide will take you to see some of the prison cells: a chilling experience. A gruesome display case at the end of this section contains the clothes worn by Bule and Persefoni, the young women hanged by the Germans in 1944.

It will be with some relief that you emerge from the gallery on to a small terrace. In the corner sits a two-seater jet which the communist regime claimed was an American spy plane, forced down in 1957. The US Air Force's version of events is that the pilot, Major Howard Curran, 'strayed' into Albanian airspace during a routine flight to Naples from a US base in southern France and was forced to land by Albanian MIGs. Major Curran was released after being held for a couple of weeks; his plane, however, stayed where it was, at Rinas airport, before the Albanian government decided that it should be displayed in Gjirokastra. Beyond the plane, a path leads into an open area, largely taken up with the staging for the folk music festival which takes place here at rather random intervals (the next is scheduled for 2015). Another Bektashi *tyrbe* nestles against the castle wall, behind the staging.

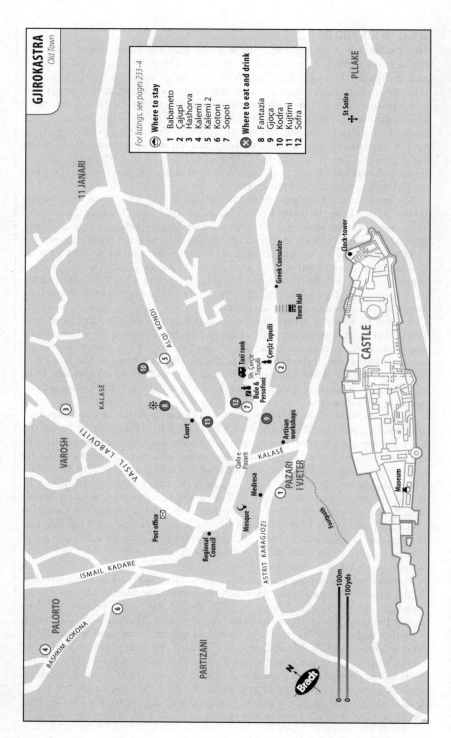

GJIROKASTRA
Old Town

For listings, see pages 233–4

Where to stay
1 Babameto
2 Çajupi
3 Hashorva
4 Kalemi
5 Kalemi 2
6 Kotoni
7 Sopoti

Where to eat and drink
8   Fantazia
9   Gjoca
10 Kodra
11 Kujtimi
12 Sofra

PLLAKE

St Sotira

CASTLE

Clock-tower

Museum

Greek Consulate

Town Hall

Çerçiz Topulli

Taxi rank

Sh. Çerçiz
Topulli

Bule &
Persofoni

Court

Artisan
workshops

KALASË

Qafa e
Pazarit

Medresa

Mosque

PAZARI
I VJETER

Foodbath

ASTRIT KARAGJOZI

Post office

Regional
Council

ISMAIL KADARE

ALQI KONDI

KALASË

VASIL LABOVITI

VAROSH

11 JANARI

PALORTO

BASHKIM KOKONA

PARTIZANI

100m
100yds

Bradt

Beyond the stage is the **clocktower**, another of Ali Pasha's improvements to the castle, although it was heavily restored in the 1980s. Below it, the structure of a very old church – possibly dating back to the Byzantine phase of fortification – has recently been identified. A viewpoint at the eastern extreme of the castle offers panoramic views of the Drinos Valley and the Lunxhëria Mountains beyond. A panel indicates the position of various points of interest, including Antigonea (see pages 240–1).

In addition to the vaults, the clocktower and other improvements, Ali Pasha also built an **aqueduct**, which brought water from springs on Mount Sopoti, 10km away, to huge cisterns under the central area of the castle. The aqueduct was demolished in 1932, unfortunately; the bases of three of its piers still stand at the southwestern tip of the castle, a few minutes' walk from the entrance towards the neighbourhood of Dunavat.

Gjirokastra dwelling houses The beautiful 19th-century houses of Gjirokastra are unique, and not just to Albania. Berati's houses are lovely too, but their architecture is different and the topography of the town makes them seem more uniform. In Gjirokastra, no traditional house is quite like another, although they have been classified according to certain design characteristics such as the number of wings which they have.

Many of the best examples of Gjirokastra domestic architecture were built in the first three decades of the 19th century. The Pazari i Vjetër (Old Bazaar) quarter, for example, dates mostly from around 1830. The houses are characterised by their defensively designed lower floors, with narrow entranceways and small windows set high in the wall. The entrance arches (*qemeret*) are made of dressed stone, often worked with great skill and refinement, and engraved with images of animals or birds; their wooden doors are also decorated with carvings. The ground floor of the house was traditionally used for storage and had a cistern (*stera*) into which rainwater was piped from the roof. The size of the cistern was an indicator of the status of the family that owned the house. The roofs themselves are of grey stone slates, supported on a wooden frame.

The living quarters, as is usual in Albanian vernacular architecture, are on the upper floors. In Gjirokastra there are usually two or three floors in total, with a few four-storey houses. Some of the houses are simple vertical structures; a widespread variant has a single wing added to this central structure, while the wealthiest families built houses with two wings. The Zekate house, right up at the top of the Palorto quarter and visible from many vantage points in the old town, is an outstanding example of the latter style.

Internally, each house is laid out in a way which reflects the family structure of the time. The main room was the 'winter room' (*dimërorja*), also called the 'fire room' (*dhoma e zjarrit*), with an ornate fireplace (*oxhaku*) which decorated the room as well as warming it. The number of chimneys and windows was another status symbol for Gjirokastra's wealthy families. One or more living rooms were used by family members for day-to-day activities. Guests were received in a separate room (*oda e miqve*), which was always the most beautifully decorated in the house. The walls were sometimes adorned with frescoes, and the ceiling was often of carved and sculpted wood. Reception rooms often had a wooden gallery – sometimes closed, sometimes open – where the women of the household could keep an eye on proceedings; this was especially useful when the men below were discussing the possible betrothal of their children. The rooms were linked by wide corridors and covered balconies (*nëndivani* and *divani i sipërm*), which were also used as living areas in hot weather. Three-storey houses with double wings also had open balconies set between the two wings.

On paper the traditional houses of Gjirokastra enjoy quite strict legal protection. Fifty-one of them have Category 1 listing, meaning that no external modifications are permitted; over 350 others are listed in Category 2, where some modification

ISMAIL KADARE

The Albanian writer who is best known outside the Albanian-speaking world is Ismail Kadare (the stress is on the last vowel of both his names), who was born in Gjirokastra in 1936. He studied literature at the University of Tirana and went on to study at the Gorky Institute in Moscow. He returned to Albania after the break with the Soviet Union in 1961 and worked as a journalist, as well as publishing a volume of poetry. His first novel, *The General of the Dead Army*, was written between 1962 and 1966, and brought him immediate renown. It was later made into a film, in which Marcello Mastroianni played the eponymous general, seeking the remains of Italian soldiers fallen during the Fascist occupation of Albania.

Following the success of his first novel, Kadare became the editor of the Albanian literary review *Les Lettres Albanaises*, and went on to write over a dozen novels, as well as short stories and essays. Many of his works are heavily allegorical and it is difficult for non-Albanians to grasp the layers of meaning in them; his novels *The Monster* (banned in Albania for 25 years) and *The Palace of Dreams*, and the work of literary criticism *Aeschylus*, are examples of these rather obscure, but ultimately rewarding, works. Some of his other novels, on the other hand, are much more accessible to the foreign reader and give very interesting insights into aspects of Albanian daily life in the latter half of the 20th century. *Chronicle in Stone*, about growing up in Gjirokastra, and *Broken April*, about the revenge culture of the northern highlands, are good to start with. *The Concert* sheds some light on Albania's break with China (see page 17) and how it affected Albanian professionals. *The Castle* is about Albania's resistance to the Ottoman invasion – the eponymous castle is Skanderbeg's seat at Kruja. The more recent (2003) works *Agamemnon's Daughter* and *The Successor* are fictionalised accounts of the fall from grace of Mehmet Shehu, Albania's prime minister from 1954 to 1981.

Ismail Kadare was allowed to travel widely by the communist government, and he could have defected from Albania on several occasions, but he chose not to. He was one of a group of writers and other influential people who lobbied for cultural liberalisation in the late 1980s. Towards the end of 1990, when communist regimes had collapsed all over central and eastern Europe, and it was obvious that even in Albania the end could not be far off, he left the country and obtained political asylum in France, where he still spends much of his time. Many young Albanians who took part in the struggle for democracy were hurt and baffled by what they saw as Kadare's abandonment of them. His 1991 book *Albanian Spring* (out of print in its English translation) outlined his reasons for leaving the country but, like much of Albania's recent history, it remains a very controversial matter.

Kadare is frequently mentioned as a contender for the Nobel Prize for Literature. In 2005, he was awarded the inaugural Man Booker International Prize.

is allowed as long as the façade is not altered. In practice, however, these beautiful buildings are at great risk from neglect, abandonment and fire. Some were wrecked in the civil unrest of 1997, the family house of the writer Ismail Kadare was destroyed in a fire in 1999, and every year more traditional houses are lost to collapse. Illegal building work also takes place within the supposedly protected Museum Zone of the town.

Traditional houses can be found throughout the old town, especially in the Partizani, Dunavat and Palorto neighbourhoods. Some have been converted into hotels – see the hotel listings on page 234 for details. Many others are unoccupied and can only be seen from the outside. Ismail Kadare has gifted the shell of his house to the Municipality of Gjirokastra, and its restoration is under way, albeit rather slowly; once it is completed, the house will then be opened to the public. Two original houses which have been restored and can be visited are described below; others may well open to the public in due course.

One way to see what a traditional house would have been like on the inside is to visit the **Ethnographic Museum** (⏲ *09.00–19.00 daily; 200 lek*), reconstructed on the site of the house where Enver Hoxha was born. The original building was destroyed by fire in the 1960s and it was rebuilt as a showcase for the classic features of a traditional Gjirokastra house. The museum contains many interesting items and has (old) maquettes of three types of traditional architecture, including the Zekate house.

The nearby **Skëndulaj house** (⏲ *09.00–19.00 daily; 200 lek*), built originally around 1700 and partly rebuilt in 1827, was formerly the Ethnographic Museum. It was confiscated in 1984 from the family who had lived in it for generations; they recovered it in 1992 and have restored it beautifully. The external architecture of this house has a couple of unusual features: lines of chestnut wood set into the wall every metre, to strengthen it, and a window and slit in the corner of the building through which the cistern could be cleaned and its water-level checked. The cistern has a capacity of 130,000 litres and is piped into the house through a tap. One wall of the cistern is also the wall of the pantry; an ingenious method of keeping food cool. Another interesting architectural feature is the underground shelter, a vaulted cellar; on the floors above it are kitchens whose ceilings are also vaulted, making the whole structure incredibly strong. Many of the household implements displayed in the kitchens – the coffee-roaster, for example – were used by the family until just a decade or so ago.

The Skëndulaj house has 64 windows, nine chimneys and six toilets (long-drop toilets, admittedly, but nonetheless quite impressive for the early 19th century). Some of the reception rooms also have an en-suite steam room (*hamam*), as well as galleries (*mafil*) and cupboards for storing bedding (*musandra*). The *divan*, or covered balcony, overlooks the city and connects with every room on that floor. It has a raised platform on which the mother of the household would sit in the mornings with her daughters-in-law to share out the day's tasks. The most elaborately decorated room, the *oda e miqve*, has no fewer than 15 windows, some with stained-glass lozenges. The frescoes on the fireplace, which are original, are full of symbolism: pomegranates and pomegranate flowers are believed to bring luck to your children, while candles symbolise the development of the family. The *mafil* was enclosed in glass in 1985, after the house had been requisitioned by the government; originally it had a wooden grille like the galleries in the other rooms. The *oda e miqve* was used for betrothal ceremonies, which would take place in the raised part of the room. The ceiling above this part of the room has two ceiling roses, rather than the usual single rose, to symbolise that two people will now live under the same roof.

The **Zekate house**, an imposing double-winged house at the top of Palorto, was built in 1810 by one of Ali Pasha Tepelena's administrators, Beqir Zeko. The tall arches of the entranceway support the weight of the upper rooms. On the ground floor, to the right of the entrance, is the large rainwater cistern; the family's status is further displayed by the stained-glass windows, elaborate fireplaces and carved wooden ceilings. The reception rooms have wooden galleries and *musandra*. The winter rooms have adjacent toilets and steam rooms (*hamam*). The top, third, floor is astonishing: the summer *divan* has spectacular views, particularly from the dais in the corner where the head of the household would sit with his most important guests. Finally, the remarkable reception room on this floor has beautiful frescoes on the walls and fireplace; an elaborate gallery and *musandra* over the entrance to the *oda* and its en-suite toilet; a magnificent carved and gilded ceiling; painted doors and coloured-glass windows. The Zekate house was restored in 2005. It does not have set opening hours, but the elderly couple who own it live next door and are usually somewhere around; admission is 200 lek.

The town hall air-raid shelter During the communist years, when town halls across Albania were known as 'Executive Committees', air-raid shelters were built under them so that the Committee Members and staff could continue to administer their town in the event of enemy bombardment. It is said that the shelters under the Executive Committee of Tirana, which nowadays houses the administration of the Albanian Parliament and other national institutions, were connected to Enver Hoxha's villa in 'The Block' (see page 82). Work has been going on intermittently to prepare the shelter under Gjirokastra's town hall so that it can be visited. At the time of writing, it is not yet in a condition which allows it to be open to the public – the dampness in the tunnels makes it impossible to run electric light into them, for example – but access can occasionally be arranged. (I am grateful to Mr Flamur Bime, the Mayor of Gjirokastra, for allowing me to visit it.)

The air-raid shelter is in fact a huge labyrinth of underground corridors with small offices opening off them. Many of the offices still have the signs on their doors indicating which department or functionary would have worked within; even the telephone switchboard operators would have relocated down to the bunker. The functionaries would have slept, as well as worked, in their little windowless offices. In the centre of the labyrinth is a large meeting hall, beyond which are the offices of the party officials who made up the Executive Committee itself. Private stairways (now blocked-up) led down to this VIPs' corridor from their offices above ground. The whole structure was designed to resist the impact of missiles of up to 6 tonnes; exploring the complex gives a unique and fascinating insight into the Hoxha regime's permanent state of alert for enemy attack.

Antigonea (🕓 *08.00–16.00 Mon–Fri, 09.00–15.00 Sat–Sun; 200 lek*) In 295BC, the king of the Molossians, one of the three main tribes of Epirus, founded a city and named it after his wife, a princess of both the Macedonian and Egyptian royal families. The Molossian king was Pyrrhus, whose later battles against expansionist Rome would come to be known as 'Pyrrhic victories'; his wife's name was Antigone and the new city was called Antigonea. For more than a hundred years, Antigonea was a major economic and cultural centre. Then, after Rome's victory in the Third Macedonian War (171–168BC), Epirus was unfortunate enough to be on the route of the victorious army's return home. Even though the Epirote state had not been involved in that phase of the war, 70 of its cities were sacked and 150,000 of its citizens were taken to Rome as slaves. Antigonea's neatly planned streets and luxurious houses were reduced to rubble and its walls reduced in height.

In a beautiful and highly strategic setting, on a mountainside overlooking the Drinos Valley opposite Gjirokastra, Antigonea is one of the few archaeological sites in Albania which has been extensively excavated and which has good interpretative materials for the non-specialist visitor. Well-designed information panels, placed at various significant points throughout the site, explain the history and function of the buildings.

The main things to see are the remaining sections of the city's fortifications and the remains of several impressive buildings. The best stretches of the city walls are those around the acropolis, near the site entrance, and right at the other, southern end, where you can see how the Romans destroyed the main gate to the city and pushed over the top of the wall. Near this gatehouse are the remains of a *stoa* (a covered walkway), which is a very clear example of the Epirote dry-stone building technique, using large polygonal stones. The path through the city takes the visitor past a group of houses. It was while excavating one of these houses, in 1968, that the site was identified as Antigonea, thanks to the discovery of 14 bronze *tesserae* imprinted with the name of the city; these are thought to have been voting tokens, used in the city's decision-making processes. The path continues down some steps to the so-called House of the Peristyle, with its colonnade which would have surrounded a garden or courtyard in the interior of the house. Note the large stone nearby with differently sized holes in it; this was for measuring out accurate quantities of various types of foodstuff such as oil, flour and so forth – the Molossians' Trading Standards Authority.

The city's main street ran north–south from the acropolis to the main gate; part of it can be seen below the House of the Peristyle, while excavations in 2013 revealed another section further to the south. In what was the centre of the city – the *agora* – another *stoa*, nearly 60m long and double-storeyed, was built up on an artificial terrace, above the line of the hill, so that it had spectacular views and could be seen from far around. Houses and workshops were built on a grid pattern around the *agora*, some of them with imposing columns which can still be seen. Almost at the end of the site is a palaeochristian basilica, triconch in shape and with mosaic floors (normally kept covered, unfortunately), from around AD500.

Maps of the site are posted outside the Archaeological Park's office in Asim Zeneli and near the turn-off in Gjirokastra; a useful leaflet, with the same map, site plans and information about the main buildings and fortifications, was produced some years ago and may be obtainable in Gjirokastra. The **website** (*www.antigonea. com*) gives brief information about the site, in English, and about other things to see in the area. It takes about half an hour to get to Antigonea by car from Gjirokastra; the road is signposted, for 'Parku Arkeologjik Antigone', from the main highway, near the bus terminus. The road is asphalted all the way to the site entrance. It is a lovely drive, through beautiful scenery and past several traditional villages with attractive Byzantine churches. A footpath starts at the park office and leads over the hills to the archaeological site; at the other end, the path begins behind the site office and the old fountain. It takes about 1½ hours to hike up to the park from Asim Zeneli.

Hadrianopolis Until a decade ago, it was an article of faith in Albanian archaeology that the country's ancient cities were never built in valleys, but always on the tops of hills. So when, in the 1970s, a landslide revealed the remains of a classical theatre in the Drinos Valley, south of Gjirokastra, academics were baffled as to what it was doing there. Ancient sources mentioned a city, built during the Emperor Hadrian's reign (AD117–38) and called Hadrianopolis after him, and located it somewhere between Apollonia and Butrint; but surely this theatre on a floodplain could not possibly have anything to do with a city? It was not until 2002, when the site of the theatre was drained and some of the area around it was excavated, that the first archaeologists began to realise that they really were looking at a city. They had, after all, discovered Hadrianopolis.

The lovely little theatre retains many of its original features – the entrances to the first and second rows of seating, the stage with its entrances for the actors and, below it, for the prompters, and the paved *orchestra*. Performances are occasionally staged in the theatre nowadays. Beyond the theatre, a beautiful stretch of wall, in a herringbone pattern, is part of the forum; there are hypocausts here, too, showing where the bathhouse was. Other buildings which have been excavated include part of the wall which surrounded the city, an ancient cemetery outside that wall and two temples. Hadrianopolis seems to have gone into some decline in the 3rd century, but the settlement survived into the 6th century. Its name lives on in the modern Albanian 'Dropulli', the collective name for the villages which flank the river between Gjirokastra and the Greek border.

The site, unattended, is about 15 minutes' drive up a rough track from the village of Sofratika, just off the highway to Greece. Minibuses serve Sofratika from Gjirokastra; it would be an easy walk to the site from the village, or from the junction on the highway.

LIBOHOVA   *Telephone code: 0881*

The small town of Libohova, in the Bureto Mountains on the other side of the Drinos Valley from Gjirokastra, would make an excellent base for a couple of days' hiking and sightseeing. It is easy to get to, has good accommodation, and there are several interesting things to do in and around the town. These include an early 19th-century fortress, a historic Bektashi *teqe* and an outstanding 6th-century church.

GETTING THERE AND AROUND There are buses to Libohova from Gjirokastra every morning. The journey by car takes about half an hour; the bus takes a bit longer. Getting *around* the area is another matter. To get to most of the places mentioned here, unless you have your own vehicle, you would need to negotiate a price with a Libohova taxi driver. Bikes would be ideal, as long as your thigh muscles are in good shape.

 WHERE TO STAY AND EAT The Hotel Libohova on the town square (*4 rooms;* m *068 26 50 658; all rooms en suite with TV & AC;* **$$**) is comfortable but rather small. If it is full, the 'Turizmi' (the communist-era hotel) on the other side of the square is more basic but much larger, and will almost certainly have rooms. Both have lovely views out over the Drinos Valley.

The owner of the Hotel Libohova also runs the terrace restaurant under the plane tree in the square. The salad ingredients are locally produced and delicious, as is the cheese which is processed at a factory at the foot of the hill.

WHAT TO SEE AND DO The main square in Libohova is dominated by the huge plane tree in its corner. This tree is said to be the largest of its kind (*Platanus orientalis*) in the Balkans, and to be 500 years old. It is 25–30m high and its branches extend for several metres in all directions. The terrace restaurant below it is made even cooler by the water which is channelled straight from the spring and past the tables. The views from the square across the Drinos Valley are spectacular on a clear day.

In the 19th century, Libohova was a much larger town than it is today, and the feudal landowners – the Libohova family – enhanced its importance through some clever diplomacy, marrying into the family of Ali Pasha Tepelena (see box, pages 246–7). This was a smart move which gave the town the protection of the most powerful man in southern Albania at the time and allowed it to prosper. Ali Pasha's sister, Shanishaja, is buried in the Libohova family's own graveyard, which is five minutes' walk from the town square, up past a Bektashi *tyrbe* and then down towards the stream. Unfortunately the graveyard has been neglected for many years and is very overgrown – you should ask someone to show you where it is, since if you try to follow directions you will probably walk right past it. It is no longer possible to tell which of the graves is Shanishaja's.

Ali Pasha's other legacy to Libohova was its fortress, the west wall of which can be seen from the road as you drive into the town. The entrance to the fortress is through someone's backyard (the owners seem to have no objection to tourists blundering through their property), downhill from the main square. There is nothing left of the interior of the fort itself, apart from some bricked-up archways, but the walls are very imposing – smooth blocks of grey stone about 2m thick in places.

St Mary's Church The original structure of the church in the tiny village of Labova e Kryqit (Labova of the Cross) dates from the middle of the 6th century, making it one of the oldest surviving churches in Albania. The parishioners of Labova say that its construction was ordered by the Emperor Justinian (AD527–65), who donated a fragment of the Holy Cross to the church and was married in it. It is built with red bricks laid in patterns, as is so characteristic of palaeochristian churches in Albania, and it is roofed with the grey slates which give Gjirokastra its beautiful austerity.

The church, dedicated to the Virgin Mary, is set in a walled garden, and both the garden gate and the church itself are kept locked. The key-holder's telephone number may be posted on the gate, or you can ask around the village for his house.

The front of the church has a simple exonarthex (portico) running the length of the front wall. Inside the church is a magnificent iconostasis of ornately carved and gilded wood, decorated with dragons and eagles and filled with ancient icons. On each side of the iconostasis, and behind it, are beautiful frescoes, and on the arch behind the throne are images which blend the pagan beliefs of the people with Christian symbolism. More frescoes decorate the walls of the nave. The works of art in the church have been conserved and restored, and when the restorers removed one of the icons for treatment, they found an astonishing icon hidden underneath it – a crowned figure representing, so the story goes, the Emperor Justinian himself (it is displayed next to the iconostasis, still slightly hidden in a corner). Another icon shows St Paraskevi, martyred in the 2nd century, with her head in a bowl (and a second head, still attached to her neck).

Subsidence over the centuries has made the cupola lean very noticeably, and the building has had to be reinforced on several occasions; an inscription indicates that such reinforcement was carried out in 1783, but it has continued into modern times. Some of the reinforcement work can be examined in the gallery of the church and the belltower. There is a padlocked box for donations just inside the church entrance, which is opened only when money is needed to pay for a repair.

This beautiful church can be reached by bus from Gjirokastra – there are two buses every morning – or by private car or taxi from there or from Libohova. Labova e Kryqit is about 40 minutes' drive from the main north–south highway. The road is not asphalted, and the last section is very steep and not always well maintained. It may be necessary to park on the roadside and walk up the last section, which takes about ten minutes. There is a public fountain and a café in the square.

The *teqe* at Melani As you come down the hill from Libohova towards the highway, a minor road off to your left leads to one of the holiest sites of Bektashism, the *teqe* at Melani. Built in the early 19th century, it occupies a splendid site, high on an isolated hill commanding glorious views of the Drinos Valley. Traces of fortification can be seen lower down around the hill, parts of which date back to the 4th century BC.

The teqe is a large building in which the faith's followers study, pray, meditate and listen to the teaching of the *baba* (father). The building is not always open, and the best time to visit is on one of the Bektashi holy days, when hundreds of believers make their way to Melani. These are social as well as religious occasions; people come with their family and friends, and bring picnics which they enjoy under the poplar trees which surround the teqe. There is a *tyrbe* (shrine) in front of the teqe, the burial place of one of the early *babas* there. You should remove your shoes before entering either the *tyrbe* or the teqe itself, and avoid stepping on the threshold.

The Melani teqe was damaged and looted during the atheism campaign of the late 1960s. When freedom of worship was restored, local believers collected money and materials and rebuilt the teqe with their own hands, sleeping in turns there every night to make sure their work was not vandalised. Many of those who helped with the restoration were from Lazarati, a Bektashi village a couple of miles south of Gjirokastra.

TEPELENA   *Telephone code: 0814*

Tepelena was the home town and secondary residence of Ali Pasha Tepelena, who was Governor of Ioannina from 1788 to 1822. Ioannina, now in northern Greece, was at the time the capital of the administrative district (*sanjak*) which covered much of southern Albania. Ali Pasha rebuilt the castle in Tepelena and then made it his secondary residence, after Ioannina itself. See the box on pages 246–7 for more information about Ali Pasha and his sticky end.

From the main square, where there is a large bronze statue of a reclining Ali Pasha, the castle is a few minutes' walk along Rruga Ali Pasha Tepelena. Its massive walls encircle an area of 4–5ha, dominating the valley of the Vjosa River below. The castle is still inhabited and there is no charge to visit it. A bar has been set up on the roof of one of the towers, from where there is a good view of the river valley and the bridge over the Vjosa, whose foundations are those built by Ali Pasha Tepelena. The flat roof of the Olindi Hotel is another good viewpoint.

GETTING THERE AND AWAY Tepelena is 30 minutes away from Gjirokastra and is linked with it by frequent buses and minibuses. It would also be an easy day trip from Përmeti (see pages 146–53). From the north, in addition to the buses and minibuses specifically for Tepelena, which go to the main square, it is also possible to alight from any vehicle heading for Gjirokastra or Përmeti. These stop on the main road below Tepelena; it is quite a stiff climb up from there to the town centre, but there are always taxis waiting where the buses stop.

 WHERE TO STAY AND EAT

Olindi (40 rooms) In the main square; \22368. The former 'Turizmi' hotel, now in private ownership. Restaurant & bar on ground floor. Friendly, professional management. Sgl & twin rooms, sharing showers & toilets. **$$**

THE RIVIERA

To the north of Saranda is a stretch of coast known as the Albanian Riviera, which is one of the most beautiful in the whole Ionian Sea. In any other country, it would have been completely swamped with high-rise hotels in the 1970s. There are not many good consequences of Albania's isolation and poverty under communism, but this unspoilt coastline is one. However, the country is making up for lost time by developing these lovely beaches as fast as it possibly can. Almost every little bay now has an access road and cafés and restaurants at the beach. There are hotels and rooms to let in every village along the coast road and temporary, summer-only campsites at many of the beaches. Prices increase dramatically in summer, when the demand for good hotel rooms far outstrips the supply, and it is advisable to reserve accommodation in advance. It is essential to carry sufficient cash. Almost none of the hotels on the Riviera accept credit cards and the only ATMs are in Himara.

The road out of Saranda begins inland and runs along the landward side of the mountains until the village of Shën Vasili (formerly called Përparimi). After Shën Vasili, the road begins to climb gradually above the deeply indented bays and the view from the road above is unforgettable. Rivulets run from the mountains and lose themselves in the fine sand of the beaches. The hillsides are full of orange trees and olive groves, planted on terraces which were cut by detachments of students from Tirana at around the same time as the villages of the Greek coasts were being covered in concrete.

GETTING THERE AND AWAY The journey from **Saranda** to Vlora takes about four hours by car; the road is well surfaced, but narrow and steep over the Llogoraja Pass. There are three coast-road buses every day; they usually display a sign on the dashboard reading *Bregdeti* ('coast'), to differentiate them from the buses which go via Tepelena and Gjirokastra. The first bus of the day leaves Saranda at 06.00 and continues to Tirana; then there are departures for Vlora at 11.30 and 14.30. In the other direction, from Vlora to Saranda, there are departures at 06.45 and 08.30; the bus from Tirana can be boarded on its way through Vlora, at around 10.00. Buses also run every day from Vlora to Himara (see pages 248–50) and Qeparoi.

Any bus will let you off in any of the small towns on its route, or at the road-ends for the beaches or the castles. Similarly, you can get *on* a bus anywhere along its route; ask locally for the time it is expected where you are. It is unwise to rely 100% on the last bus of the day, as it may unexpectedly be cancelled and perhaps leave you stranded without alternative transport.

The coast road is a lovely route for **cyclists**. There are some very steep stretches, but the magnificent scenery is a good excuse to stop for lots of rests. The Riviera buses will take bikes, if the gradients get too much; the appeal of this option is likely to grow as the Llogoraja Pass (see page 251) draws closer. Drivers are usually courteous to cyclists, but caution is required; cycling after dark is certainly not advisable. It is about 140km from Saranda to Vlora.

BORSHI Just before the village of Borshi, just over an hour from Saranda, a minor road up to the right leads up to **Borshi Castle**, sometimes also referred to as Sopoti Castle. The first written reference to it is in 1258 and the hill on which it stands was already fortified by the 4th century BC. However, what can be seen today dates from the 18th century. The mosque just within the entrance was built at that time; the painted ceiling and walls must have been beautiful when the fresco was in better condition. The whole castle is rather neglected and overgrown, but the views from it are spectacular, out across the Ionian to Corfu in one direction and, in the other, towards the mountains which run the length of the Riviera. There is a paved footpath up from the car park to just short of the castle entrance, with stone benches on which to rest and enjoy the views. If you are on foot, the best place to start is the Ujvara Restaurant; ask the waiters to show you the short cut up to the road. It takes about half an hour to walk up to the castle entrance from the restaurant. The Ujvara is a lovely place to stop for a meal (**$$$**) or a drink, with its tables arranged on terraces surrounded by waterfalls (the eponymous *ujvara*); the service is friendly and some English is spoken.

ALI PASHA TEPELENA

By the middle of the 17th century, the old system of provincial government in the Ottoman Empire had broken down. No longer did the governors of *vilayets* and *sanjak*s (provinces) work their way up through the ranks of the imperial administration. Instead, increasingly, they were appointed directly by the palace or by other great households; by 1630, only about a quarter of *sanjak* governors and governors-general had previous experience of provincial government. Rapid turnover in the administration also became common, with more than half of the governors-general in 1630 staying in their posts for less than a year.

In Albania, one outcome of these changes was the emergence of near-autonomous local rulers who were known as *pashas*. It was in the pasha's interest to expand the territory he controlled – his *pashalik* – whether by war or payment, because the larger it was, the greater his income and power. Towards the end of the 18th century, practically all of these small pashaliks had come under the control of two powerful pashas, one in southern Albania and the other in the north. See box, page 193 for information about the northern pashalik, whose capital was Shkodra.

The southern pashalik was centred on the city of Ioannina, which is now in northern Greece but at the time was in the same administrative region as much of southern Albania. In 1788, the sultan appointed as Governor of Ioannina a man from Tepelena called Ali. He had started his career as a brigand, and used his knowledge of other robber bands to curry favour with the sultan (ie: he shopped his friends), who rewarded him first with a small pashalik and then with Ioannina.

From there, Ali Pasha Tepelena used a combination of skilful diplomacy and ruthless violence to extend his authority throughout southern Albania and a large part of the Greek mainland. This was the period of Napoleon's expansions into Italy and Dalmatia, and Ali Pasha played the French and the British off against each other, consolidating his own power as he did so. In 1809, he captured Berati, and then Vlora and Gjirokastra. In that same year, Lord Byron visited Ali Pasha's court at Tepelena and described him in a letter to his mother:

> His highness is 60 years old, very fat, and not tall, but with a fine face, light blue eyes, and a white beard; his manner is very kind, and at the same time he possesses that dignity which I find universal amongst the Turks. He has the appearance of anything but his real character, for he is a remorseless tyrant, guilty of the most horrible cruelties, very brave, and so good a general that they call him the Mahometan Buonaparte.

Throughout the territory which Ali Pasha controlled, he built castles, aqueducts, bridges and mosques, many of which can still be seen. He was interested in

Where to stay

Golden Beach Hotel (12 rooms) Borshi; m 069 24 46 648; e goldenbeach-hotel@live.co.uk. In the village, not on the beach. The proprietor also has a small hotel at Borshi Beach (☺ *summer only*; $). Friendly, welcoming management; good English spoken; no restaurant. Rooms well finished & nicely furnished, all with good-sized en-suite bathroom (with shower curtain), 1 dbl & 1 sgl bed, bedside light switch, AC, TV, fridge, large balcony with drying rail & view of sea & mountains. **$$$**

BAY OF PALERMO After Borshi, the road drops down to the coast and rounds the Bay of Palermo, where Ali Pasha Tepelena (see box below) built one of his imposing

learning about new construction techniques, and hired European architects and builders to work for him. He converted to Bektashism (see pages 22–3) in about 1810, around the time when it was taking hold in Albania. His conversion allowed the Bektashi *babas* to preach more freely and to establish *teqes* throughout the territory under his rule.

By 1820, the huge area which he controlled was beginning to alarm the imperial authorities. He was dismissed as governor and ordered to hand his pashaliks back to the sultan's authorities. In a last audacious move, Ali Pasha then threw in his lot with a Greek revolutionary organisation. This was the last straw for the Ottomans. They besieged his castle at Ioannina and, after 17 months, in January 1822, he was killed and beheaded. His head was sent to Istanbul and his body was buried in Ioannina, next to that of his wife Emine.

AN ALI PASHA TOUR It would be relatively easy to self-assemble a short Ali Pasha tour, starting from either Ioannina or Corfu. Ioannina Castle houses Ali Pasha and Emine's tomb, next to the Fatih Mosque which he rebuilt in 1795. You can also look at the double-walled fortifications which his European engineers built. From Ioannina it is a short bus journey across the border to Gjirokastra, where Ali Pasha extended the fortifications and built a 10km-long aqueduct (demolished in 1932, sadly, although some traces are still visible).

Two impressive fortresses built by Ali Pasha, at his home town of Tepelena and at Libohova, are within easy reach of Gjirokastra and could be visited from there on day trips. See pages 242–4 for information about these towns and their castles.

At Butrint, on an island at the mouth of the Vivari Channel, which connects the Butrint Lagoon with the Corfu Channel, is a small fortress which Ali Pasha is said to have built in 1814, in response to Britain's capture of Corfu and the other Ionian islands. This castle can be visited by boat from Butrint; while you are there anyway, it would be perverse not to visit the main Butrint site, which is packed with wonderful things (see pages 222–7). Another Ali Pasha fortress stands at Porto Palermo, less than two hours north of Saranda up the beautiful coast road (see page 248).

Fairly frequent buses link Ioannina with Igoumenitsa, just across the strait from Corfu. Ferries and hydrofoils run every day from Corfu to Saranda (see page 215). There are direct buses from Ioannina to Gjirokastra (see page 232). If you have your own transport, you could return to Ioannina directly from Tepelena, via Përmeti and the Tre Urat border crossing (see page 146).

fortresses on what is practically an island: a promontory connected to the mainland by a narrow – and easily defensible – causeway. The promontory closes off part of the bay to create a sheltered harbour, still used today by local fishermen, and a pleasant pebbly beach. Cars can be parked either at the restaurant on the main road – a good place, with its shady terrace, for a drink or meal after your visit – or just beyond the causeway, beside a restored church (said to have been built by Ali Pasha for one of his wives, a Christian) and ruined 20th-century buildings, whose superb communist-era slogans are still visible under the more recent graffiti. It is a few minutes' walk up a rough track to the **castle** (*100 lek*).

The interior of the fortress consists of a huge vaulted chamber with archways leading off it into smaller rooms and dark tunnels (a torch will be useful), well worth exploring thoroughly. A stone staircase leads up to the battlements, from where part of the outer walls can be reached. The views are stunning. The islands which can be seen in the distance are Greek territory, lying off the northwest of Corfu. Not surprisingly, there are dense arrays of bunkers (see box, page 143) on the hillside overlooking the bay. The fortress itself was used as a military depot during the Italian occupation, and probably afterwards, too. From the castle (and at certain points along the road) you can see a huge tunnel blasted into the cliffs on the northern side of the bay. This was built as a shelter for the submarines which the Soviet Union based in the Adriatic from the late 1950s. When Albania broke off relations and sided with China (see page 16), the USSR reluctantly left most of the submarines behind.

HIMARA   *Telephone code: 0393*

Himara is the largest town between Saranda and Vlora, with a high school, district hospital, ATMs and so forth. Most of the inhabitants are ethnically Greek, and the whole area suffered large-scale emigration when Albania's borders opened in the early 1990s, as people rushed south to seek work in Greece. Greater stability in Albania and the economic opportunities provided by tourism are beginning to reverse this trend, and Himara, which only 15 years ago was a dusty ghost town, is now an attractive little resort with good hotels and restaurants. If you find Saranda overdeveloped, this is the place to come. The standard of service is better than at some other resorts on the Riviera, and the local people are friendly and helpful.

The swimming in Himara is excellent, with clear blue water which stays warm until late in the year. Non-swimmers, however, should note that the beach slopes very sharply into the sea, unlike the gentle Adriatic coast further north. The beach at the southern end of the town, Spile, is perfectly pleasant, with coarse sand and clear blue sea. Potami, about a kilometre out of town, is pebbled, but the hotels provide sun-loungers and the sea is crystalline. Both beaches can become rather dirty in the peak tourist season. Quieter beaches nearby include Livadhi to the north, 25 minutes' walk beyond the football pitch, and Llamani, a beautiful cove ten minutes' drive south.

Excavation in a cave near Spile (which means 'cave' in Greek, the mother tongue of most of the local people), revealed evidence of habitation in the 6th century BC. The castle above the town has revealed evidence of settlement in prehistoric times.

In Greek, *potami* means 'rivers', and the springs there are still the source of all of Himara's drinking water. The derelict pumping station behind the Likoka Hotel was built in the 1960s to irrigate the citrus trees and olives on the terraces above the town.

The Piazza Restaurant, on the boulevard in the town centre (see *Where to eat and drink*, page 250), sells maps and guidebooks (including this one).

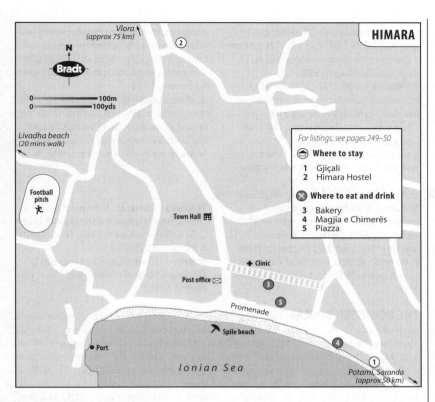

Vlora
(approx 75 km)

N

Bradt

0 ————— 100m
0 ————— 100yds

Livadha beach
(20 mins walk)

Football
pitch

Town Hall 🏛

For listings, see pages 249–50

🏠 **Where to stay**
1 Gjiçali
2 Himara Hostel

❌ **Where to eat and drink**
3 Bakery
4 Magjia e Chimerës
5 Piazza

✚ Clinic

Post office ✉

Promenade

Spile beach

Port

Ionian Sea

Potami, Saranda
(approx 50 km)

Getting there and away The road between Saranda and Vlora is asphalted and in good condition all the way. Himara is almost exactly halfway and the journey from either direction takes about two hours. See page 218 above for details of public transport on the coast road. There is also a daily departure from Tirana to Qeparoi, via Himara, at about midday and, in summer only, another at 17.00. Direct buses link Himara with Athens and other Greek cities.

🏠 **Where to stay** *Map, above.*

🏠 **Rapo's Resort Hotel** (48 rooms, 3 suites) Potami; ☎ 22857; m 069 20 62 842, 069 62 26 312, 069 89 73 986; e info@raposresorthotel. com; www.raposresorthotel.com. Lifts; restaurant with sea-view terrace; outdoor pizzeria in gardens; bar. English spoken; Wi-Fi; secure parking; credit cards accepted. Private beach, 2 swimming pools (1 big, 1 smaller). All rooms en suite, nicely furnished & well equipped with balcony, hairdryer, iron, minibar, safe, internet access, direct-dial phone, AC, cable TV. **$$$$$**

🏠 **Gjiçali** (12 rooms) Spile, just beyond the promenade as the road south starts to climb out of town; ☎ 22657; m 068 24 46 832, 069 29 59

318. Built out over the beach; the rooms on the lower floor are only a few metres from the sea. Steps down to the beach from the hotel's front door. English spoken; family-run. All rooms en suite, with TV, fridge & balcony with sea view & clothes-line for drying swimwear; most rooms have AC. **$$$**

🏠 **Likoka** (14 rooms) Potami, right on the beach at the far end; m 069 20 91 419, 079 22 11 484; e likokaanastas@gmail.com; www.hotel-likoka.com. The 1st hotel in Himara, still family-run; management very helpful; English spoken; Wi-Fi. Excellent restaurant with fresh locally caught fish; pasta, salads, meat also on menu; tables inside & out on raised veranda overlooking

The Southwest   THE RIVIERA

8

the sea. Rooms completely refurbished in 2014; some have 1 dbl & 1 sgl, other 1 dbl & 2 bunks; one 2-bedroom suite. All rooms en suite with AC, TV, fridge, furnished balcony. **$$$**

🏠 **Himara Hostel** (18 beds) m 069 51 71 901; e wehadsomuchfun@gmail.com; Facebook: Himara Hostel Albania. In the upper town, just off the main road to the left coming from Vlora. Lovely courtyard with fruit & citrus trees; spacious grounds with vegetable garden & chickens; water from well. Wi-Fi; computer with internet access;

equipped kitchen, washing machine; maps & local information available. Outdoor bar in evenings; bikes for hire; day trips organised. 2 dbls en suite; 1 dbl sharing with dorms; 3 dorms sharing 3 toilets & 2 showers, **$–$$**

⛺ **Himara Camping** Potami; m 068 52 98 940; www.himaracamping.com. Open only in summer. Kitchen, restaurant, washing machine, outdoor bar. Toilets & showers in outdoor booths, water heated by sun (low-tech, not solar panels!). **$**

✕ Where to eat and drink *Map, page 249.*

✕ **Piazza** In the town centre, on the promenade; tables outside on terrace with sea view; nicely decorated indoors. Wide range of seafood dishes, & pasta & pizza; huge portions; home-produced wine; fresh bread; good service, English spoken, Wi-Fi. Also has small bookstand. **$$$**

✕ **Magjia e Chimerës** At the end of the promenade, overlooking sea. Friendly staff, English spoken, Wi-Fi; fish & seafood, plus the usual pasta & grilled meat dishes. **$$$**

✕ **Baker** On pedestrianised street parallel to promenade. The usual range of bread & buns, plus excellent *byrek*. **$**

THE NORTHERN RIVIERA North of Himara, the marvellous scenery continues, with dramatic mountains rising up from the coast and the deep blue sea shimmering in the sunlight. The road goes through the pretty villages of Vunoi and Dhërmiu; below them, and below the road, are lovely beaches, with fine, clean sand, transparent blue sea, plenty of accommodation and lively nightlife in the summer. Jala Beach is 5km from the main road, just before the first houses in Vunoi; Dhërmiu Beach, sometimes known by its Greek name, Dhrimadhes, is 1.5km from the road. Both beaches are clearly signposted and both roads are well surfaced. There is no public transport to the beaches; those travelling by bus should ask to be let off at *Plazh* ('beach') and then walk, or try to hitchhike, down the hill.

A few kilometres beyond Dhërmiu, the road begins to climb towards the Llogoraja Pass. On the right, perched on the hillside, is the village of Palasa. To the left is Palasa Beach, where in 48BC Julius Caesar landed from Brundisium (now Brindisi), in pursuit of his rival Pompey in battle (see page 8). This is the northernmost beach on the Riviera, part sand, part pebble, and with wild flowers and oregano growing in the scrub behind the beach. Caesar led his legions from here over the Llogoraja Pass to Oricum; you can follow in their footsteps, more or less, although the paths are not at all clear. It would be easier in reverse, from Llogoraja; see opposite.

A short climb from the end of the beach leads to a series of huge tunnels blasted into the hillside facing the sea, their communist-era instructions still visible. At the time of writing, there are no permanent buildings at Palasa Beach, although in summer there is a small restaurant with a campsite at the end of the road. Wild camping is possible anywhere else along the beach. Asphalting of the road down to Palasa Beach was planned in 2014; it is about 3.5km from the highway to the restaurant.

🏠 **Where to stay and eat** There are many hotels and private rooms at both Jala and Dhërmiu beaches. In summer, finding somewhere to stay involves nothing more complicated than walking down the hill from the main road looking a bit foreign. People will call out to you from their gardens, pull up in their cars and send their English-speaking children to run after you in an effort to persuade you to stay in their house or their family's hotel. Temporary **campsites** open during the summer at these and most other beaches on the Riviera; some are quite luxurious and offer the option of renting a furnished tent, rather than pitching your own. Many hotels and guesthouses on these and other Riviera beaches can be reserved through the usual international booking websites or the Tirana-based Albania Holidays (*www.albania-hotel.com*; see page 31 for other contact details). Out of season, many guesthouses and hotels close; and from mid-July to mid-August it can be difficult to find accommodation anywhere on the Riviera without booking in advance.

🏠 **Shkolla Vuno** Vunoi; m 068 40 63 835; e shkollavuno@hotmail.com; www.tiranahostel. com; Facebook: Shkolla Vuno; ⏰ Jun–Sep. An initiative of the Outdoor Albania Association (see page 56), this backpackers' hostel is a repurposing of the old village school, which closed in 2011 due to the declining school-age population. Visitors can participate in activities to benefit the local community: clearing up litter, clearing paths, or repairing buildings. Hiking, kayaks available to rent, beaches (of course); English spoken; camping possible. **$**

LLOGORAJA The hairpin bends ahead of Palasa lead to the Llogoraja Pass, at more than 1,000m above sea level. To your right are the bare peaks of the Çika Mountains, with pines and firs shrouding the hillside below them; to your left the cliffs drop almost sheer into the Ionian Sea, as wine-dark as it was when Odysseus sailed it. The whole area around the top of the pass – over 1,000ha – is designated as a national park. It is rich in wildlife (roe deer, foxes, squirrels, wild boar and wolves are common) and would make an excellent base for a few days' hiking.

At the top of the pass, a path – steep in places, but no more than half an hour's walk – leads up to the phone masts on the clifftop to the west. On a clear day, the views from here are spectacular (unfortunately, because of the altitude and the proximity of the sea, it is very often misty here, when it is not actually raining). Hang-gliding from the clifftops out over the sea can sometimes be arranged (enquire at your hotel).

Possible hikes include the ascent of Mount Çika (Mali i Çikës, 2,045m) or Caesar's Pass (Qafa e Çezarit), where Julius Caesar is thought to have led his legions from their landing at Palasa to capture the city of Oricum (see page 262). A good circular hike goes up to Qafa e Thellë ('the Deep Pass'), along the ridge to the phone masts, then down to the top of the pass. The path starts from an obvious point between the Iliria restaurant and the Hotel Alpin; it has been paved and is generally in reasonable condition, although sensible footwear should obviously be worn. It is possible to hike over Qafa e Thellë to the start of the Karaburuni Peninsula and Caesar's landfall at Palasa, but the paths on the other side of the mountain are difficult and unclear; a local guide should be hired.

There is no public transport specifically to Llogoraja, but several buses and minibuses a day run between Vlora and Himara, Qeparoi or Saranda. See pages 218 and 253 for further details. If you do not plan to stay overnight, you should ascertain on arrival the expected time of the last bus on which you can return or continue onward.

🏠 **Where to stay and eat** There are several hotels within the national park, interspersed with restaurants all offering the same specialities of spit-roasted lamb and kid. Both hotels listed here have good restaurants.

🏠 **Llogora Tourist Village** (22 rooms, 3 suites, 16 chalets) 📞 033 225 790; 📱 069 33 44 400; 📧 info@llogora.com; www.llogora.com. Set in over 1ha of beautiful grounds on the edge of the forest, with a small herd of roe deer wandering freely. Restaurant with international menu as well as traditional dishes; bar, tennis court, indoor pool, gym, children's play area; babysitting service. Some English spoken; Wi-Fi in public areas. Guided treks, hang-gliding & jeep excursions can be arranged. Each chalet has 1 dbl & 1 twin bedroom, living room with satellite TV, CH, bathroom with shower, furnished veranda angled away from the chalet next door. Hotel rooms all en suite with TV, CH, good-sized balcony, bedside lights. **$$$**

🏠 **Hotel Alpin** (20 rooms) 📱 069 20 55 936, 069 23 90 561; 📧 info@hotelalpin-al.net; can be booked through www.albania-hotel.com. Helpful English-speaking management; hiking guides can be arranged; good restaurant, tables outside on large veranda in summer; no Wi-Fi. All rooms en suite with satellite TV, CH, fridge; some have balcony with views over national park. **$$**

VLORA   *Telephone code: 033*

The Bay of Vlora is where the Adriatic and Ionian seas divide, and the town has a real southern Mediterranean feel to it, with palm trees along the main road and the beach starting practically in the city centre. It has a long history, but its main claim to fame is as the place where Albanian independence was proclaimed in 1912. Vlora has three very different museums and is a good base for several interesting excursions. Its geographical position – roughly midway between Tirana and Saranda, and only 75km from Italy – and good transport links make it a convenient entry point into Albania.

Then known as Aulon, the town existed in antiquity – the Roman poet Martial, who wrote in the late 1st and early 2nd centuries AD, refers to it (in Epig. XIII. CXXV) as producing fine wool and wine; true to form, he says he'd rather have the wine. By the 4th century AD it is mentioned frequently as a landing port from the Italian ports of Otranto and Brindisi and, especially, as a stopping-off point on the road between Apollonia and Butrint (see pages 105–7 and 222–7). During the reign of the Emperor Justinian (AD527–65), it was one of the largest eight cities in the province of New Epirus and was the seat of a bishopric. It was taken by the Normans in 1081 and went on to suffer the same fate as Albania's other coastal cities, changing hands several times over the centuries. Vlora has always been a particularly attractive prize, because Sazani Island, in the Bay of Vlora, controls maritime access to the Adriatic.

It was the first Adriatic port to fall to the Ottomans, in 1417. Ali Pasha Tepelena (see box, pages 246–7) took it in 1810 and held it until he was captured and killed in 1822. On 28 November 1912, delegates from all over Albania met in Vlora and declared their country's independence from the Ottoman Empire. Unfortunately for the provisional government and its prime minister, Ismail Qemali, achieving independence was not quite as simple a matter as announcing it. Vlora and – of course – Sazani were occupied by Italy in 1914, and it was 1920 before they could be dislodged. Indeed, Albania's sovereignty over Sazani was not wholly secure until after World War II.

Vlora's recent past has been equally turbulent. In March 1991, while most of the world was concentrating on the Gulf War, 20,000 or so young Albanians commandeered ships in the harbours of Vlora and Durrësi and took them to Brindisi. In February 1997, riots in Vlora against failed pyramid-saving schemes developed into a civil uprising which engulfed the whole country and destabilised it for many months. At the same time, Vlora's proximity to southern Italy made it a natural base for Mafia-type operations, and it became the centre of an international network of clandestine emigration and the trafficking of women. For a few years, until a clampdown in 2002, it was effectively under the control of armed gangs. Vlora and the surrounding beaches are now safe and visitors need have no special concerns.

GETTING THERE AND AWAY

By sea Car ferries run daily between Brindisi and Vlora throughout the year, excluding Sundays in low season. They leave Brindisi at around 23.00 every night and dock in Vlora at about 07.00 the following morning. The return journey to Brindisi is faster; the ferries leave Vlora at around midday and arrive at about 17.30 (additional sailings in summer). A range of cabin accommodation is available. The one-way passenger fare in deck class ranges from €50 in low season to €70 in high season, plus embarkation taxes; return fares booked at the same time are reduced. Fares, schedules and online bookings are available on the Italian ferry websites www.traghetti.it and www.traghettiamo.it.

By land There are frequent **buses** to and from **Tirana**, from very early in the morning until mid-afternoon. In Tirana, they leave from the bus depot off Rruga e Kavajës; in Vlora, the terminus is near the railway station, quite a long way from the city centre. The journey takes about 2½ hours and the fare is 600 lek. There are also buses in the mornings to and from all other major towns in southern and central Albania. Buses and minibuses to Fieri and other nearby towns wait for passengers opposite the Muradia Mosque.

The journey from **Saranda** to Vlora takes about four hours by car; the road is well surfaced, but narrow and steep over the Llogoraja Pass. There are three buses every day, plus services to Vlora from Himara and other towns on the Riviera; for details, see the *Riviera* section (page 245). There are frequent minibuses up and down the coast as far as Rradhima and Orikumi until lunchtime (later in the summer).

GETTING AROUND
Vlora is a large city, and the distances between the sights in the centre, the port and the beaches are too great for all but the most enthusiastic walker. There are plenty of taxis, which can either be flagged down in the street or found at the many taxi ranks throughout the town. Urban buses are frequent, with a flat fare of 30 lek. The most useful route for the visitor is the 'Xhamia–Uji i Ftohtë', a half-hourly service which leaves from a bus stop behind the Muradia Mosque (*xhamia*) and runs out past Skela (the port) and Plazhi i Ri, as far as the Uji i Ftohtë post office. The hotels in Uji i Ftohtë are further on from here, but there are always taxis waiting where the bus terminates. The buses get very crowded and the only way to be sure of a seat is by boarding at the terminus at one or other end of the route.

TOUR OPERATORS
The tourist information office (⊕ *06.00–20.00*) behind the Independence Monument sells guidebooks and maps and can arrange car hire. The website of the Municipality of Vlora (*www.bashkiavlore.org*) has extensive information, in English, about things to do and places to visit in the area.

Travel agencies in Vlora can provide timetable information about, and tickets for, all ferry departures, from Saranda and Durrësi as well as from Vlora. They can also arrange tours of the area and excursions by boat to the Karaburuni Peninsula (see pages 259–61).

Colombo Travel Agency In the historic centre; ☎ 223 548; m 069 40 31 716

Dallandyshja Travel Skela, in the Riviera QTU shopping mall; ☎ 222 222; m 068 20 05 319

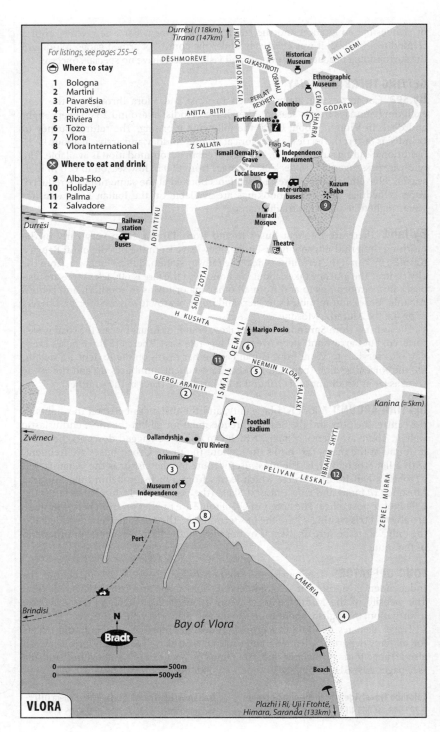

For listings, see pages 255–6

Where to stay
1 Bologna
2 Martini
3 Pavarësia
4 Primavera
5 Riviera
6 Tozo
7 Vlora
8 Vlora International

Where to eat and drink
9 Alba-Eko
10 Holiday
11 Palma
12 Salvadore

Durrësi (118km),
Tirana (147km)

DËSHMORËVE

Historical
Museum

ALI DEMI

Ethnographic
Museum

ANITA BITRI

PERLAT
REXHEPI

Colombo

GODARD

CENO SHARRA

Fortifications

Z SALLATA

Flag Sq

Ismail Qemali's
Grave

Independence
Monument

Local buses

Inter-urban
buses

Kuzum
Baba

Durrësi

Railway
station

Buses

ADRIATIKU

Muradi
Mosque

Theatre

SADIK ZOTAJ

H KUSHTA

Marigo Posio

ISMAIL QEMALI

NERMIN VLORA FALASKI

GJERGJ ARANITI

Kanina (≈5km)

Zvërneci

Football
stadium

Dallandyshja

QTU Riviera

BRAHIM SHYTI

Orikumi

PELIVAN LESKAJ

Museum of
Independence

ZENEL MURRA

Port

ÇAMERIA

Brindisi

N

Bay of Vlora

Bradt

0   500m
0   500yds

Beach

VLORA

Plazhi i Ri, Uji i Ftohtë,
Himara, Saranda (133km)

WHERE TO STAY *Map, opposite.*

Vlora's seafront hotels are strung out all along the coast, starting at the port (Skela), about 1.5km from the Muradia Mosque; running along the public beach of Plazhi i Ri, which is still within the city limits and is served by frequent urban buses; and in the nearby resort of Uji i Ftohtë, a short, inexpensive taxi ride from Vlora proper. There are also several comfortable hotels in the town centre. Choosing between them really comes down to what you want to do while you are in Vlora. The museums are in the centre and at the port, Plazhi i Ri is convenient for swimming and sunbathing and Uji i Ftohtë has good fish restaurants. Substantial reductions in room rates can often be negotiated outside the peak tourist season of July and August. For those hotels without their own websites, reservations can be made through the usual international booking sites or the Tirana-based www.albania-hotel.com.

Town centre

🏠 **Martini** (20 rooms) Rr Gjergj Arianiti; 📞224 017; m 069 20 83 049, 069 20 38 877; e hotel_martini@hotmail.com; Facebook: hotelmartinivlore. Signposted at the corner of the Boulevard with Rr Gj Arianiti. Restaurant serves traditional Vlora dishes as well as the usual fish & seafood. Roof terrace for guests' use; car park; friendly management. All rooms en suite with AC, TV, Wi-Fi; some have balcony. **$$**

🏠 **Riviera** (14 rooms) Rr Nermin Vlora, pranë Shkollës Industriale; 📞408 212; m 069 38 96 622, 069 62 25 202; e hotel.riviera@yahoo.com. Restaurant; some English spoken at reception. All rooms en suite with twin beds, AC, TV. **$$**

🏠 **Tozo** (15 rooms) Rr Vlorë-Skelë; 📞223 819; m 069 51 34 496. Set back from the main road behind the palm trees of the little Park of Hope. Restaurant with large terrace, room service also possible; parking; professional management. Good-sized rooms with large, well-equipped bathrooms, all with AC, TV, Wi-Fi, phone; some have balcony. **$$**

🏠 **Vlora** (15 rooms) Rr Justin Godard; m 069 33 43 947; www.hotelvlora.com. Restaurant, comfortable 1st-floor bar with large terrace overlooking Independence Monument; lift; some English spoken. Good-sized rooms, all en suite with LCD TV, AC, Wi-Fi, balcony, minibar. **$$**

Seaside

🏠 **New York** (85 rooms) 📞406 648/9; m 068 40 13 306; e info@hotelnewyork-al.net. A little beyond Plazhi i Ri, just before the Uji i Ftohtë Tunnel. Restaurant with picture windows, built out above the road on piers sunk into the sea; informal pizzeria; bars; conference room. Professional, helpful staff; good English spoken at reception.

Outdoor swimming pool, tiny private beach below restaurant, Wi-Fi, lift, laundry facilities, secure parking. Good-sized, comfortable rooms, all en suite with AC, safe, flat-screen TV, minibar, direct-dial phone, balcony; many have magnificent sea views. **$$$–$$$$**

🏠 **Bologna** (40 rooms) 📞409 600; m 068 20 34 103, 069 53 70 704; e hbvlora@gmail.com. Contemporary boutique hotel in fabulous setting right on the water's edge; large terrace bar & good restaurant overlooking sea; stylish reception area; parking; conference room; lift. Generously proportioned, beautifully designed rooms, all with nice en-suite bathroom, AC, Wi-Fi, flat-screen TV, minibar & balcony; most have great views across the Bay of Vlora, city-view rooms are cooler. **$$$**

🏠 **Pavarësia** (36 rooms, 2 suites) Rr Kosova, Lagja Pavarësia; 📞230 940; m 068 20 65 440/1; e info@hotelpavaresiavlore.com; http://hotelpavaresiavlore.com. Lift; restaurant & bar; English spoken; friendly, helpful staff; local honey & jam at b/fast. All rooms nicely laid out with good bathroom, balcony, AC, free Wi-Fi; TV. Suites (**$$$$**) have 1 dbl & 1 trpl room sharing 1 bathroom with jacuzzi. Credit cards accepted. Standard dbl **$$$**

🏠 **Primavera** (18 rooms) Rr e Ujit të Ftohtë; 📞229 664; m 069 20 65 610; e primavera.hotel@live.com; Facebook: Hotel "Primavera" Vlorë. Just off the promenade, on a side street opposite the Naval School. Friendly management; restaurant (**$$$**) & bar open to guests until late. All rooms en suite with AC, TV, phone, balcony with sea view. **$$$**

🏠 **Vlora International** (60 rooms, 6 suites, 6 apts) Rr Ismail Qemali, Lagja Pavarësia; 📞424 408; m 069 20 70 838; e hotel@vlora-international.com; www.vlora-international.com. 2 restaurants, bars, roof terrace; lift, large conference room, gym, business centre; indoor swimming pool, spa, sauna; English spoken. All rooms good sized with well-equipped bathrooms, AC, satellite TV, Wi-Fi, phone, minibar, balcony with sea view. Credit cards accepted. **$$$**

✕ WHERE TO EAT AND DRINK *Map, page 254.*

Almost all Vlora's restaurants have similar, Italian-influenced menus: pasta, risotto, veal escalopes, plus – as you would expect on the coast – grilled fish and seafood.

✕ **Holiday** Tables outside in lovely sheltered gardens; grilled meat, pizzas & generous salads. **$$$**

✕ **Palma** Rr Sadik Zotaj. Serves pizzas, pasta & other Italian-inspired dishes; tables outside in large garden. **$$$**

✕ **Tratori Salvadore** Rr Pelivan Leskaj. Large restaurant above fish wholesalers; signposted from corners of Rr Ismail Qemali & Rr Çamëria. Nicely decorated with 1st-class toilets; English spoken. Superb fresh fish & seafood, beautifully prepared & presented; outstanding value. **$$$**

WHAT TO SEE AND DO

Museum of Independence (*Lagja Pavarësia, Rr Ismail Qemali;* ⊕ *08.00–13.00 & 17.00–20.00 Tue–Sun; 100 lek*) When the First Balkan War started in October 1912 (see page 11), the Albanians realised that, if they did not obtain independence from the Ottoman Empire, their territory would be swallowed up by their Balkan neighbours. Ismail Qemali (1844–1919), one of 26 Albanians elected to the Ottoman Parliament after the Young Turk revolution of 1908, travelled to Vienna and Budapest to obtain diplomatic support for Albanian independence.

On his return to Durrësi, he found that Serbian troops were approaching the Adriatic, and he made his way across the treacherous marshes (now long since drained) of the Myzeqeja Plain to the relative safety of Vlora. It was thus that on 28 November 1912, Albanian independence was proclaimed in Vlora and Skanderbeg's ancient emblem, the double-headed black eagle, was raised at the spot which is now called Flag Square (Sheshi i Flamurit). Albania's first government, led by Ismail Qemali, set up its headquarters in the only building available, the former quarantine hospital in the port. This modestly sized villa is now the Museum of Independence.

The most interesting thing about the museum, for the majority of non-Albanians, is that several of the rooms have been kept as they were when they were used by those first ministers. Ismail Qemali's chair is still there behind his desk, and his bookcase still has books in it. On the long table in the Cabinet Room is the pen with which official documents were signed, and next to it, the government seal with its double-headed eagle symbol. Photographs of each of the first ministers hang on the wall; there are many other interesting pictures on display throughout the museum, including a famous one, taken by Albania's first photographer, Pjetër Marubi (see pages 193–4), of the independence ceremony in Shkodra. The Montenegrin army was not dislodged from there until May 1913, shortly before the First Balkan War ended.

In other rooms there are more photographs, maps of the territory which is now Albania at different stages in the process of winning independence, and reproductions of letters and government decrees.

A walk around the centre The building where the flag was first raised was badly damaged while the city was being bombarded by Greece in December 1912, and it was knocked down in 1932. The area cleared by this demolition has been kept as a large open space and is called **Flag Square**, or Independence Square. To the side of the square, near where the demolished house once stood, the Albanian flag flies from a small column, and beside it is the **Independence Monument**, an imposing bronze cast in the Socialist Realist style. Around its base stand various key figures in the independence movement, including Ismail Qemali and the Kosovar hero Isa Boletini (see page 12); above them, on a rock, a flag-bearer makes ready to hoist the double-headed eagle of Albania. Vlora's football team is called Flamurtari ('the Flag-bearer') in honour of the anonymous patriot who first raised the flag of independence.

Ismail Qemali himself is buried in the park behind the Independence Monument. On the other side of the park are a couple of short stretches of **medieval wall**, all that can now be seen of the octagonal turreted wall built to fortify Vlora in the 16th century. In the course of excavating sections of the wall, Roman tiles were found and so there may well have been an earlier fortification.

A little further down the main road is the **Muradia Mosque**, a beautifully proportioned little building with an elegant minaret of carved stone. It was built around the same time as the 16th-century fortifications and is thought to have been designed by the great architect Sinan (1489–1588). He built mosques, bathhouses, bridges and *han*s (inns) throughout the empire, and is considered to be one of the founders of Ottoman architecture. The minimalist decoration within consists of elegant plasterwork fluting and Koranic calligraphy on the ceiling dome.

If you continue down the main road, towards the port, you will pass the **theatre**. A hundred metres or so further, in a small park (the Park of Hope) on the same side of the street, is an attractive bust of a woman called **Marigo Posio**. She was born in 1878 and brought up in Korça, where she married and became involved in the nationalist movement. She and her husband attracted the attention of the Ottoman authorities, and moved to Vlora to shake them off. When the Labëria Patriotic Club was founded in 1908 (see below), Marigo Posio taught Albanian literacy at the night school there, under the outward guise of giving embroidery classes. Her real contribution to the art of embroidery was the double-headed eagle on the flag which was raised in Vlora on 28 November 1912 – a painting of her embroidering the Albanian flag hangs at the top of the stairs in the Museum of Independence. The original flag was handed down by Ismail Qemali to one of his many sons, and is now lost. Marigo Posio died in 1932 and was buried between two olive trees on the island of Zvërneci (see page 259).

Good views of the city can be enjoyed from two vantage points: Kuzum Baba and Kanina Castle. Like many places in Albania, Vlora has experienced a lot of new building in the past decade, and viewing the city from above is a good way to make sense of its geography. **Kuzum Baba** is the hill above the Muradia Mosque, so called for the Bektashi *tyrbe* on its summit (see pages 22–3 for more about Bektashism); a large restaurant, Alba-Eko (**$$$**), and a car park adjoin the *tyrbe*. Steps lead up to the restaurant from behind the minibus terminus. **Kanina Castle** is several kilometres from the city centre; the going rate in a taxi is 1,000 lek. Neatly paved steps lead up to the castle from the car park. Kanina was the seat of a bishopric in the 12th century and changed hands several times during the slow collapse of the Byzantine Empire (see pages 8–10), until it fell to the Ottomans in 1417. It was used as an Italian garrison during World War II and then, in the communist period, it was a surveillance centre for the Albanian air force. On a clear day, there are wonderful views over the city and out to Karaburuni and Sazani in the west; northwards to the Narta Lagoon and Zvërneci; and across the Vjosa River towards the mountains of Mallakastra in the east.

Ethnographic Museum (*Rr Ceno Sharra;* m *069 25 85 946;* ⊕ *08.00–15.00 Mon–Fri*) The Ethnographic Museum in Vlora is located in the house where, in 1908, the Labëria Patriotic Club was set up. Towards the end of the 19th century, after the crushing of the Prizren League, the Albanian nationalist movement switched its focus from political demands to cultural campaigning. 'Patriotic clubs' were set up in towns around Albania and in other Ottoman cities with a significant Albanian population, including Istanbul itself, where it was called the 'Albanian Committee'. The Labëria Patriotic Club was named after the region of which Vlora is the main town. It provided evening classes to people who wanted to learn how to read and write in Albanian, their mother tongue – no fewer than 50 Vloran women registered for these classes, and one of their teachers was Marigo Posio.

The signs to the museum around the city centre refer to it in English as 'House of Labëria Club'. However, the collection on display is mainly made up of ethnographic objects and traditional costumes.

The room on the left as you enter the house is devoted to agriculture; in addition to examples of milking stools, a tobacco-cutting machine and an olive press, it has a model of a farmstead, showing the layout used in this part of Albania, with separate buildings for the family, guests and livestock. The entrance hall contains various household items and, rather incongruously, some pieces of carved wooden iconostases, which the museum staff rescued from local churches during the atheism campaigns (see pages 16–17).

The room on the right acknowledges Vlora's role as a fishing town. The centrepiece is a boat carved about 30 years ago from a single tree trunk, an ancient technique which was still in use until very recently. Larger versions of the nets on display are still used – the circular net is cast from the boat over a shoal, and the fishermen move the mast up and down to lure the fish into the centre of the net, so that as many as possible are trapped before they pull it in. The long trap and the multipronged fork hung on the walls are used to catch eels in the lagoons of Narta and Pashaliman; the eel trap has two layers of mesh and, as the eel swims in, the pressure of its head tightens the inner layer so that it cannot escape. Of course these ingenious techniques are rather bad news for eels and fish, but they are a lot better than dynamite, which has replaced traditional fishing methods along much of the Albanian coast.

Upstairs, the 'men's room' of the house was where (male) guests were entertained, and some of the original furniture can be seen there, including a tray for serving raki and a *sofër* – a low, circular dining table – inscribed with the owner's name in the Greek alphabet and the date 1896. Guests sat in order of age on the cushioned seats around the walls; the host sat on the left of the fireplace and his most distant relative sat on its right.

The 'women's room', across the hallway, has some interesting examples of traditional Vloran costumes – as women grew older, they wore darker and darker shades of cloth – and dowry chests. The old tradition, still followed in more conservative Kosova, was that every bride had an Albanian flag and an embroidery of Skanderbeg (see box, pages 200–1) in her dowry chest, and some of these are exhibited, too. Finally, a display of textiles has as its centrepiece a genuine loom, used to make carpets and rugs as well as cloth.

Historical Museum

Historical Museum (*Rr Perlat Rexhepi;* ⏲ *08.00–15.00 Mon–Fri; 100 lek*) The Historical Museum is a good place to find out about the archaeological profile of the Vlora area, and also has some fascinating exhibits from recent history. During communism, it was called the 'War Museum' (Muzeu i Luftës), and many people in Vlora, including taxi drivers, still refer to it by this name. It was renovated in 2014 and the descriptions of the displays given below may have changed somewhat.

The first of the two rooms on the ground floor contains the museum's collection of Neolithic and Bronze Age artefacts. The most significant Bronze Age site in the

Vlora area is the Vajza tumulus, and some of the finds from that are on display here, although the best of them are in the national museums in Tirana. Vlora itself has seen little excavation, because it has been continuously inhabited throughout its history, but fragments of Roman artefacts are constantly unearthed whenever a building contractor or utility company digs more than 4–5m down. Some of these casual finds are displayed in a case near the door. Maps and photographs on the walls help to put the items displayed in context, although the maps and the labelling are in Albanian only. Across the hallway, the second room has several attractive Roman *stelae* (gravestones) and statues, and a selection of early Christian iconostases carved in stone.

The building in which the museum is housed was originally Vlora's town hall. The room on the first floor, which is now used for temporary art exhibitions, was once the mayor's office, and has been the scene of many historical events. The room beyond the mayor's office contains the museum's collection of 20th-century artefacts, including memorabilia from World War II. One of the most interesting objects is an example of the homemade mechanism which Vlorans used to get round the isolation which the communist regime imposed on them. In the 1980s, the Albanian authorities blocked the television signals from Italy, which otherwise can be easily picked up along much of the Albanian coast. The ingenious Vlorans improvised this little device to fit into their television sets and override the signal jam.

Another curious item on display is from the village of **Narta**, whose people believe they are descended from ancient Greeks and have several unique customs, as well as speaking a dialect of Greek which is quite different from the standard modern language spoken by other ethnic Greeks in Albania. One of Narta's traditions is a three-day carnival, at which masks like the one in the museum are worn. The museum also has a rare (for Albania) example of a Jewish gravestone inscribed in Hebrew, as well as stone inscriptions from mosques which were destroyed in 1967.

The museum carries a stock of different publications for sale, mainly in Albanian but some with English or French summaries, about local archaeological sites including Oricum.

Zvërneci The beach in Vlora starts pretty much as soon as you leave the port, but in the town it is dirty and covered in litter during the summer. The sea is a bit cleaner further south at Plazhi i Ri ('the New Beach'). However, if you want to spend time at the beach, it is better to head either down the coast road to Rradhima or Orikumi (see pages 261–2), or north towards the Narta Lagoon.

Leaving the port by Rruga e Sodës, you soon reach the long sandy beach at Soda. Behind the beach is a forest of pines and firs, covering the spit of land which forms one of the arms of the Narta Lagoon. At the end of this road is the island of Zvërneci, where there is a 14th-century monastery, St Mary's. The island is linked to the mainland by a new bridge and can be visited at any time. Zvërneci was once home to a group of Orthodox monks, but the last one left in 1966 and, during the atheism campaign the following year, the monastery library was burnt down. During the communist period, internal exiles were sometimes sent to Zvërneci. The monastery has now been restored and looks very attractive in its tranquil, wooded setting. Zvërneci is the traditional resting place of Vlora's most illustrious sons and daughters – Marigo Posio (see page 257) is one of those buried here.

KARABURUNI The northern tip of the Karaburuni Peninsula, Kepi i Gjuhëzës, is where the Adriatic and Ionian seas meet. The peninsula, which closes off the Bay of Vlora to the south, was a closed military zone during the whole of the communist

The Karaburuni Peninsula offers a fantastic opportunity to hike in one of the wildest parts of Albania. There are two ways to get to Karaburuni: by sea (see opposite for details) or on foot. Outside high summer, you will have to bring all your own food and – more importantly – drinking water with you. It might be possible to hire a donkey or mule in Orikumi, to carry your supplies. You could also try hiding some bottles of water in the bushes halfway along the peninsula, to collect on your way back.

A dirt track, which looks as if only the sturdiest of military vehicles would survive it, links the Pashaliman base with what remains of **Shëngjini**. Still to be found on some maps of Albania, Shëngjini was a military base during the communist period. All the buildings have been deliberately demolished, leaving only remnants of walls and a strikingly dense concentration of bunkers of various shapes and sizes. The 'bunker strategy' described in the box on page 143 can be seen clearly here, with large bunkers watching out over the shores dotted with smaller ones. Bunkers which contained heavier weaponry look out over the bay and Sazani. Their inner walls once carried instructions – now roughly painted over – on how to operate the weapons.

Before reaching Shëngjini, you walk through a smaller deserted military post. The pier leading from these barracks into the sea is now a popular picnic spot for Albanians. Around the military buildings are fig trees, perhaps planted by soldiers decades ago – a welcome treat, with their sweet fragrance, in this harsh environment. If you are planning to stay overnight, the ruins of Shëngjini would be a suitable spot to pitch your tent; just 100m beyond them, alternatively, is a rare field of something vaguely resembling grass – most of Karaburuni is covered with trees or thorn-bushes. There are many butterflies and other insects.

About 30km from Orikumi (it looks shorter on maps but the road keeps turning in discouraging bends) and 5–6km beyond Shëngjini, the Karaburuni Peninsula reaches its most remote point. The track passes high above Haxhi Aliu's Cave, at sea level; the steep cliffs mean the cave cannot be reached from above. At the cape, artificial caves overlook the narrow strait between Karaburuni and Sazani. Inside, posters explain how to set landmines, how to tell various chemical weapons apart and how to make a built-up area safe following a gas attack. Red-painted quotations by Enver Hoxha still grace the walls. Strange white flowers grow all around, 1.5m high, with huge red bulbs.

As you walk off the peninsula, a few kilometres before the Pashaliman base comes into view, you will come to some fishermen's huts. The fishermen will look perplexed to see somebody approaching from the west, but once they have restrained their dogs they will be glad to fill your empty bottles with water.

It is trickier than it seems to leave Karaburuni without walking into the naval base by mistake. After the fishermen's huts, you come to some military buildings. Beyond these, it looks at first as if you're walking straight into the base; however, this is the correct track for avoiding it. You descend nearly to sea level, past more buildings, and then turn right, slightly uphill, keeping the barbed wire to your left. A bend in the road will lead you slightly above the military base and around Pashaliman Lagoon. The detour around the lagoon adds at least 5km to the walk, but it is far quicker in the long run than being arrested and interrogated for trespassing on the base.

period. There is therefore no vehicular access; the only ways on to Karaburuni are from the sea or on foot. In recent years, it has become a popular destination for holidaymakers staying in Vlora and the resorts around the bay; between mid-June and mid-September, several companies run scheduled day trips to the beaches on the eastern shore. 'Pop-up' restaurants operate at these beaches in summer.

Most of these day-trips depart from the Orikum Yachting Club, between the resorts of Orikumi (see below) and Rradhima. Contact details for the Yachting Club can be found on page 33. The travel agencies in Vlora can book a day trip for you; see page 253 for contact details. One of the companies that operates these trips is **Plaku i Urtë** (m *069 51 04 101, 069 53 50 233;* e *plaku.urte@gmail.com*); its trips, for a minimum of ten people and a maximum of 25 and priced at 2,000 lek per person, depart from the Yachting Club at 09.30 and return from Karaburuni at 17.30.

Boats can also be hired to take you to one of the **sea caves** on the peninsula. The **Cave of Haxhi Aliu** was one of the hideouts of an 18th-century pirate from Ulqini (now in Montenegro). This is the largest sea cave in Albania, 30m long and with an entrance 10m wide. At Grama, on the western, seaward, shore of Karaburuni, thousands of inscriptions have been engraved on the rock face by passing sailors, soldiers and merchants – the earliest date from the 3rd century BC. During World War II, the British Special Operations Executive (SOE, see boxes on pages 13–15) used the cave at Grama as one of its bases. Code-named 'Sea Elephant', it was chosen not only for its extreme remoteness, but also because it was larger (and, one hopes, had fewer lice and scorpions) than the mission's previous base on the peninsula, code-named 'Seaview'.

It is possible to **kayak** from Orikumi or Rradhima to Karaburuni, but the currents are strong and the winds unpredictable. Only experienced sea-kayakers should contemplate this option. Outdoor Albania (see page 31) can give advice and arrange kayak hire if required.

For those wishing to **hike** in the wilderness of Karaburuni, accessing the peninsula from the sea is a much easier option than on foot: hiking in from Orikumi means a lengthy detour around the Pashaliman Lagoon to avoid the naval base (see *Hiking on Karaburuni* box, opposite). Alternative routes follow in the footsteps of the SOE agents over the mountains of Llogoraja (see pages 251–2), but the paths are difficult and unclear; they should not be attempted without an experienced local guide. Going in and out by boat would also solve the problem of carrying sufficient water – there are no springs on the peninsula itself – because you could bring some in on the boat and replenish your stocks as required at one of the beachside restaurants.

ORIKUMI *Telephone code: 0391* Beyond the Uji i Ftohtë Tunnel, the road continues along the Bay of Vlora, with the Karaburuni Peninsula and the island of Sazani, 9km offshore, closing the bay off to the west. During the communist period, the complex of villas at Uji i Ftohtë was reserved for senior party figures; several have now been converted into hotels.

A string of hotels lines the coast; almost every little cove has its own hotel. The village of Tragjasi, with its well-appointed **Grand Hotel** (*map, page 217; 21 rooms;* ✆ *0391 22039;* m *068 20 35 441; Facebook: Grand Hotel Tragjasi;* **$$$$**), is about 15 minutes' drive from the junction with the main road. This is Tragjasi i Ri ('New Tragjasi'), built to replace the old village which was burned to the ground by German troops in 1944, to punish the villagers for the presence of an SOE mission there (see boxes on pages 13–15). At the southern end of the bay, 18km from Vlora, is the small resort town of Orikumi and, at the far end of its beach, where the landward shore of Karaburuni begins to curl up to the north, is the archaeological site of **Oricum**.

The ancient city of Oricum was founded in the 6th century BC, by colonists from the Greek island of Euboea. It developed into an important trading post thanks to its geographical position and excellent harbour, protected by the peninsula which the Greeks called Acroceraunia, 'the thunder-riven heights', and the Ottomans named Karaburun, 'the black cape'. By the 3rd century BC, Oricum was minting its own coins and building a theatre for the entertainment of its citizens. Philip V of Macedon occupied it for a while during the First Macedonian War (214–205BC); later, during the Roman Civil War, it quickly surrendered to Julius Caesar after he landed with his troops at Palasa, on the other side of the Llogoraja Pass (see pages 251–2).

The original theatre was replaced in the 1st century AD, but its Hellenistic layout was retained and some of the stones were reused. This is the little theatre which can be seen today, whose capacity would have been around 400 spectators. Stone staircases led down to it from the acropolis, with shops and houses on either side of the steps. A beautiful flight of 27 steps, complete with a drainage channel carved into the rock on one side of the flight, has been excavated near the theatre; there are ten similar staircases around the city, running parallel to each other. Another can be seen near the entrance to the site, the so-called 'Western Staircase' (Shkalla Perendimore; signposted). Three deep wells have also been discovered, but there is no longer any water in them. The sea has advanced and retreated over the centuries and much of the ancient city is under the waters of the lagoon. This is what the Ottomans called Pashaliman, 'the Pasha's harbour', and the lagoon still bears this name, as does the nearby Albanian Navy base.

Although it is still in a military area, the archaeological site can be visited without prior arrangement (*200 lek*). However, visitors must travel in a vehicle, not on foot, and be accompanied; one of the guides is usually at (or near) the entrance gate to the base from about 09.00 until about lunchtime on weekdays. Not all the guides have their own cars; if they do not, they will arrange a taxi. If you are short of time and very keen to see Oricum, it would be advisable to call at the Archaeological Park's office in the modern town before you make your way to the base, to make sure that a guide is definitely available. Minibuses run frequently between Vlora and Orikumi until early afternoon – later in the summer. The journey takes about half an hour and the fare is 100 lek.

Appendix 1

LANGUAGE

THE ALPHABET Although the Albanian alphabet has a large number of letters (36), each consonant is always pronounced in exactly the same way, whatever its position within a word. A few of them do not have exact equivalents in English and, for these cases, approximations are given in the list below. Vowels can be long or short but, with one exception, they are very easy to pronounce.

The only vowel which might cause difficulty is ë, which represents the sound which philologists call '*schwa*'. It is the vowel sound a native English-speaker makes in the second syllable of the word 'understand'; a native French speaker makes the same sound in the first word of '*je comprends*'. For speakers of Slavic languages, it is like a vocalic 'r' without the 'r' sound (like the semivowel in the Serbo-Croat word '*trg*'). There are two problems with ë. One is that at the end of a word it is scarcely pronounced at all, but it can affect the length of the vowel in the previous syllable. The other is that, unlike most Indo-European languages, the *schwa* in Albanian can be stressed; this is hard for non-native-speakers to get right, because we are used to *schwas* snuggling in between consonants without anybody noticing they are there.

Fortunately, it is so unusual for any foreigner to be able to string together more than a few Albanian words that any slight mispronunciation of ë or anything else is invariably overlooked in the torrent of congratulations.

PRONUNCIATION

A as in c**u**t or c**a**rt
B as in **b**ig
C as the 'zz' in pi**zz**a
Ç as in **ch**urch
D as in **d**og
Dh the 'th' in **th**at
E as in g**e**t or as in s**ay**
Ë as in 'th**e**' in 'th**e** cat sat on th**e** mat'
G as in **g**old (always hard)
Gj – the 'du' in 'en**du**re' is an approximation
I as in h**i**t or m**ee**t
J the 'y' in **y**ear (not **j**am)
K as in **k**ite
L as in **l**og
Ll – a double 'l' sound, a bit like a Russian or Serbo-Croat 'dark' L
M as in **m**at
N as in **n**ot

Nj the 'ni' in 'u**ni**on'
O as in h**o**t or th**ou**ght
P as in **p**at
Q – the 'tu' in 'ma**tu**re' is an approximation
R as in **r**oad
Rr – a trilled double 'r'
S as in **s**un
Sh as in **sh**ine
T as in **t**in
Th as in **th**ick
U as in b**u**sh or m**oo**n
V as in **v**ote
X the 'ds' in ki**ds**
Xh as in **j**udge
Y – the French sound in '**tu**' or the German 'ü' as in 'd**ü**nn'
Z as in **z**oo
Zh – the 's' in 'plea**s**ure'

DEFINITE AND INDEFINITE ARTICLES In Albanian, the definite article ('the' in English) does not (normally) go before the word it defines but is suffixed to it. Thus, 'the Boulevard' is '*Bulevardi*', while any old 'boulevard' is '*bulevard*'. This feature is not unique to Albanian – it is found, for example, in Swedish and Romanian. Different prepositions, as well as taking different cases of the noun, also require either the definite or the indefinite form. This is not something which the visitor need worry about unduly, except to be aware that the rules apply to place names as well as to every other noun.

When they are speaking English or another foreign language, Albanians tend to use the definite form of place names – that is, they will refer to 'Gjirokastra' rather than 'Gjirokastër', and 'Kukësi' rather than 'Kukës'. When they speak Albanian, of course, they use whichever form of the word is grammatically appropriate, but most other languages do not have the grammatical framework which allows them to do that. This book therefore uses the definite form of all place names except for Butrint, which is so consistently called this in every English-language publication that it would be confusing to refer to it here as 'Butrinti'.

However, on road signs, bus signs, railway timetables and the like, the destination will always appear in the indefinite form. This is because it is invisibly governed by the preposition *në*, meaning 'to' or 'in', which must be followed by the indefinite. So, for example, the buses run *nga Tirana në Durrës* ('from Tirana to Durrësi') and then return *nga Durrësi në Tiranë* ('from Durrësi to Tirana'). All Albanian-produced maps, and most foreign-produced ones, too, consistently use the indefinite form. In many cases the difference is quite small and it is easy to tell which place is meant. Some which are not so obvious are listed at the end of this Appendix.

PHRASEBOOKS AND LANGUAGE COURSES The best phrasebook available commercially outside Albania is the *Albanian–English, English–Albanian Dictionary & Phrasebook*, by Ramazan Hysa, published in 2000 by Hippocrene Books.

Albanian grammar is difficult, and moving beyond simple phrases requires serious study. *Colloquial Albanian*, by Isa Zymberi, is the best book that is readily available in the UK and North America, although its idiom tends towards the Kosovar. It can be purchased with or without the accompanying CD (which is even more Kosovar). Other language course books can be purchased in Tirana.

WORDS AND PHRASES
Essentials

Good morning	*Mirëmengjesi* (until about 11.00)
Good afternoon	*Mirëdita* (until about 16.00 or 17.00)
Good evening	*Mirëmbrëma*
Good night	*Natën e mire* (when leaving people at the end of the evening)
Hello	*Përshëndetje*
Goodbye	*Mirupafshim*
What is your name?	*Si e keni emrin?*
My name is …	*Emri im është …*
Where are you from?	*Nga jeni?*
I am from …	*Jam nga …* [see town and country names in the next section, and use the definite form]
How are you?	*Si jeni?*
Pleased to meet you	*Gëzohem*
Thank you	*Faleminderit*
Please	*Ju lutem*
Don't mention it	*S'ka gjë*

Excuse me	Me falni
Cheers!	Gëzuar!
Yes	Po
No	Jo
I am looking for ...	Po kërkoj ...
I don't understand	S'kuptoj
Slowly, please!	Avash, ju lutem!
Do you understand me?	A me kuptoni?

Questions

how?	si?	when?	kur?
what [is ...]?	çfarë [është ...]?	why?	pse?
where?	ku?	who?	kush?
which?	i cili/e cila?	how much?	sa?

Numbers

1	një	11	njëmbëdhjetë
2	dy	12	dymbëdhjetë
3	tre	13	trembëdhjetë [etc]
4	katër	20	njëzet
5	pesë	21	njëzetenjë
6	gjashtë	30	tridhjetë
7	shtatë	40	dyzet
8	tetë	50	pesëdhjetë
9	nëntë	100	(një) qind
10	dhjetë	1,000	(një) mijë

Time

What time is it?	Sa është ora?
It's ...	Ora është...
am/pm	paraditës/mbasditës
today	sot
tomorrow	nesër
yesterday	dje
(the) morning	mëngjesi
(the) evening	darka

Days of the week

Monday	e hënë	Friday	e premtë
Tuesday	e martë	Saturday	e shtunë
Wednesday	e merkurë	Sunday	e dielë
Thursday	e enjtë		

Months of the year

January	Janar	July	Korrik
February	Shkurt	August	Gusht
March	Mars	September	Shtator
April	Prill	October	Tetor
May	Maj	November	Nëntor
June	Qershor	December	Dhjetor

Getting around
Public transport

Ticket (single/return)	biletë (vajtja/vajtja e ardhja)
I want to go to ...	Dua të shkoj në ... [and use indefinite form]
How much is the ticket?	Sa kushton bileta?
What time does it leave?	Në çfarë orë niset?
What time is it (now)?	Sa është ora?

from	nga	plane	avion
to	në	ferry	traget
bus station	agjencia (e udhëtarëve)	car	makinë
railway station	stacioni i trenit	taxi	taksi
airport	aeroporti	arrival	mbërritja
port	porti, skela	departure	nisja
bus	autobus	here	këtu
minibus	furgon or kombi	there	atje
train	tren	Bon voyage!	Rrugë të mbarë!

Self-drive

Is this the way to ... ?	Kjo është rruga për në ... [and then use indefinite form]?
Where is there a petrol station?	Ku ka pikë karburanti?
Please fill up the tank	Të lutem mbushe plot serbatorin
I'd like ... litres	Do desha ... litra
diesel	naftë
leaded petrol	benzinë me plumb
unleaded petrol	benzinë pa plumb
I have broken down	kam pësuar defekt

Road signs

Give way	Jep përparësinë	Exit	Dalje
Danger	Rrezik	Detour	Rrugë e tërthortë
Entry	Hyrje	One way	Rrugë një kalimshe
No entry	Nuk lejohet hyrja	Keep clear	Mos zij rrugën

Directions

Where is ... ?	Ku është ... ?	north/south	veri/jug
[then use definite form]?		east/west	lindje/perëndim
straight on	drejt	opposite	përballë
left	majtas	behind	prapa
right	djathtas	in front of	para
... at the traffic lights ... në semaforë		near	afër
... at the roundabout ... në rrumbullakë			

Signs

Entrance	Hyrja	Ladies (toilet)	Gra(të)
Exit	Dalja	Gents (toilet)	Burra(t)
Open	Hapur	Information	Informacion
Closed	Mbyllur		

Accommodation

Where is the XX hotel?	*Ku gjendet hoteli XX?*
Please show it to me on the map	*Ju lutem ma tregoni në hartë*
Do you have a ... room?	*A keni një ... dhomë?*
... single ...(room)	*... teke ...*
... twin ...	*... dyshe ...*
... triple ...	*... treshe ...*
... double ...	*... dopio/matrimonial ...*
with a bathroom	*me banjë*
How much per night/per person?	*Sa kushton nata?/veta?*
Where is the bathroom?	*Ku është banjo?*
Is there water?	*A ka uji?*
Is there electricity?	*A ka drita?*
Is there a generator?	*A ka gjenerator?*
Is breakfast included?	*E përfshihet mëngjesi?*
I'm leaving today	*Sot ikem*

Food

Do you have a table for X people?	*A keni tavolinë për X veta?*
I don't eat meat	*Nuk ha mish*
I don't eat fish	*Nuk ha peshk*
I don't eat dairy products	*Nuk ha bulmet*
[Please] bring me a ...	*me sillni një ...*
fork	*pirun*
knife	*thikë*
spoon	*lugë*
May I have the bill?	*Më bëni llogarinë?*

bread	*bukë*	meat	*mish*
butter	*gjalpë*	lamb	*... qengji*
cheese	*djathë*	veal	*... viçi*
olive oil	*vaj ulliri*	pork	*... derri*
pepper (ground)	*piper*	suckling pig	*... gici*
salt	*kripë*	kid	*... keci*
sugar	*sheqer*	chicken	*... pulë*
ice cream	*akullorë*		

Drinks

water	*uji*	tea	*çaj*
still mineral water	*uji mineral pa gaz*	coffee	*kafe*
sparkling water	*uji me gaz*	espresso	*kafe ekspres*
ice	*akull*	Turkish coffee	*kafe turke*
milk	*qumësht*	beer	*birrë*
fruit juice	*lëng frutash*	wine	*verë*

Shopping

I'd like to buy it	*Dua ta blejë*
How much is it?	*Sa kushton?*
I don't like it	*Nuk me pëlqen*
I'm only looking	*Po shikoj*
It's too/very expensive	*është shumë e shtrenjtë/*
	është shumë i shtrenjtë

It's cheap	është i lirë/është e lirë
I'll take it	Do ta merr
I'd like more	Dua më shumë
I'd like less	Dua më pak
I'd like a smaller one	Dua një më të vogël
I'd like a bigger one	Dua një më të madh

Where is ... ?
Ku është ... ?

... the bank	... banka
... the post office	... posta
... the church	... kisha
... the mosque	... xhamia
... the embassy	... ambasada
... the exchange office	... zyra këmbimi
... the telephone centre	... Telekomi
... the museum	... muzeu
... the archaeological museum	... muzeu arkeologjik
... the ethnographic museum	... muzeu etnografik
... the historical museum	... muzeu historik
... the art gallery	... galeria e arteve
... the castle/fortress	... kalaja

Emergencies

A&E clinic	Urgjenca
Please help me	Ju lutem më ndihmoni
Call a doctor	Thërrohuni mjekun
There's been an accident	Ka pasur një fatkeqësi
I'm lost	Jam e/i humbur
Go away!	Iku! (although the author's experience is that the annoying person is more likely to go away if s/he is addressed in a language which is not Albanian)
police	polici(a)
policeman	polic(i)
fire brigade	zjarrfikësit
ambulance	autoambulancë
thief	hajdut
hospital	spital
I am ill	Jam i sëmurë (if the speaker is male); Jam e sëmurë (if the speaker is female)

Health

diarrhoea	diarrea	suntan lotion	krem dielli
nausea	krupa	asthma	astmë
(a) doctor	mjek	epilepsy	sëmundja e tokës/ sëmundja e hënës
(a) prescription	recetë		
(a) pharmacy	farmaci	diabetes	sëmundja e sheqerit
painkiller	analgjesik	I'm allergic	Jam alergjik
antibiotic	antibiotik	... to penicillin	... penicilinës
antiseptic	antiseptik	... to peanuts	... kikirikesh
condom	prezervativ	... to bee-stings	... thumbëve bletësh
contraceptive	mjet kontraceptiv		

Other

I want to make a phone call	*Dua të bëj një telefonatë*
I do not understand	*Nuk kuptoj*
I do not speak Albanian	*Nuk flas shqip*
Do you speak English?	*A flisni anglisht?*
… French?	*… frengjisht?*
… Italian?	*… italisht?*
… Russian?	*… rusisht?*
OK	*Në rregull*
Of course	*Patjetër*

Adjectives (all in singular indefinite form)

beautiful	*i/e bukur*	hot	*i/e ngrohtë*
old	*i/e vjetër*	cold	*i/e ftohtë*
new	*e re/i ri*	difficult	*i/e vështirë*
good	*i/e mirë*	easy	*i/e lehtë*
bad	*i/e keq*	far	*larg*
early (in the day)	*herët*	near	*afër*
late (in the day)	*vonë*		

SOME PLACE NAMES IN ALBANIA

Definite	Indefinite	Italian	Greek (transliterated)
Shqipëria	Në Shqipëri	Albania	Alvania
Dibra	Dibër		
Durrësi	Durrës	Durazzo	Dhirrachion
Dhërmiu	Dhërmi		Dhrimadhes
Gjirokastra	Gjirokastër		Argirokastron
Himara	Himarë		Cheimarra
			or Chimara
Korça	Korçë		Koritsa
Ksamili	Ksamil		Eksamilion
Lezha	Lezhë	Alessio	
Llixhat	Llixhe		
Llogoraja	Llogara		
Saranda	Sarandë	Santi Quaranta	Agii Saranda
Shëngjini	Shëngjin	San Giovanni	
Shkodra	Shkodër	Scutari	
Tirana	Tiranë	Tirana	Tirana
Vlora	Vlorë	Valona	Avlona

SOME PLACE NAMES IN GREECE

Definite	Indefinite	English	Greek (transliterated)
Greqia	Në Greqi	Greece	Ellas
Athina	Athinë	Athens	Athina
Janina	Janinë	Ioannina	Ioannina
Korfuzi	Korfuz	Corfu	Kerkira
Kosturi	Kostur	Kastoria	Kastoria
Selaniku	Selanik	Thessalonica or Salonica	Thessaloniki

SOME OTHER USEFUL PLACE NAMES

English	Albanian
Europe	Evropa
England	Anglia
Great Britain	Britania e Madhe
Edinburgh	Edimburgu
Ireland	Irlanda
Northern Ireland	Irlanda e Veriut
London	Londra
United Kingdom	Mbretëria e Bashkuar
Republic of Ireland	Republika e Irlandës
Scotland	Skocia
Wales	Uellsi

The World	*Bota*
Australia	Australia
Canada	Kanadaja
New York	Njujorku
Istanbul	Stambolli
Skopje	Shkupi
USA	Shtetet e Bashkuara të Amerikës
New Zealand	Zelanda e Re

Appendix 2

FURTHER INFORMATION

BOOKS The London company I B Tauris is the most significant publisher of works about Albania in English. It is worth checking their website (*www.ibtauris.com*) from time to time to see if they have published anything new which interests you.

General history

Ceka, Neritan *The Illyrians to the Albanians* Migjeni, 2005. An authoritative and fascinating account of the ancient history of this ancient land.

Crampton, R J *The Balkans Since the Second World War* Longman, 2002. A readable introduction to a complicated area and a complicated history, covering Albania, Bulgaria, Romania and Yugoslavia, as well as Greece.

Durham, Edith *Burden of the Balkans*, 1905; available from various print-on-demand publishers. The history of the Balkans through Edith Durham's rather partisan eyes; at least you know which side she's on!

Durham, Edith *Twenty Years of Balkan Tangle* George Allen & Unwin, 1920; available from various print-on-demand publishers. Edith Durham's account of the historical developments in the Balkans during the disintegration of the Ottoman Empire, many of which she witnessed or even participated in.

Imber, Colin *The Ottoman Empire 1300–1650* Palgrave Macmillan, 2002. An excellent general history of the rise of the Ottoman Empire, with interesting chapters on its administration and military structure.

Malcolm, Noel *Kosovo: A Short History* Macmillan, 1998. Explains the later Ottoman period better than anyone else; also good on the political aspects of the Albanian nationalist movement.

Norwich, John Julius *Byzantium: The Decline & Fall* Penguin, 1996. The third and final instalment of Lord Norwich's accessible and reliable history of the Byzantine Empire, covering the confusing period when most of Albania changed hands several times. The family trees are invaluable; the bibliography is good, too.

Pettifer, James *The Kosova Liberation Army* Hurst & Co., 2012. A history of the KLA from 1958 to 2001, written by a defence specialist and Balkans expert. Mostly about Kosova, obviously, but also gives fascinating insights into Albanian military theory and the fevered atmosphere of Tirana in 1998–2000.

Vickers, Miranda *The Albanians: A Modern History* I B Tauris, reprinted 2001. Detailed, reliably researched and well written. An excellent guide to Albania's complicated history in the 20th century, and an indispensable companion for anyone trying to understand why Albania is the way it is now.

Vickers, Miranda and Pettifer, James *Albania: From Anarchy to a Modern Identity* Hurst & Co., 2nd edition 1999. Good account of the transitional period from the late 1980s to 1996.

A2

Vickers, Miranda and Pettifer, James *The Albanian Question: Reshaping the Balkans* I B Tauris, 2009. A carefully researched and riveting account of the last decade's events in the Albanian-speaking lands, including the pyramid-scheme riots in 1997 and the attempted coup in 1998, as well as the Kosova War and refugee crisis.

Winnifrith, T J *Badlands – Borderlands* Gerald Duckworth & Co., 2002 (out of print). Disentangles the confusing history and complicated heritage of southern Albania.

Winnifrith, T J *Tribes & Brigands in the Balkans*, I B Tauris, 2012. The first comprehensive history of northern Albania; unfortunately already out of print.

World War II

Bailey, Roderick *Smoke Without Fire? Albania, SOE & the Communist Conspiracy Theory* in S Schwandner-Sievers and B Fischer (eds), *Albanian Identities: Myth, Narrative and Politics* Hurst & Co. (New York), 2002

Bailey, Roderick *The Wildest Province: SOE in the Land of the Eagle* Jonathan Cape, 2008. The definitive account of what SOE did in Albania, based on recently declassified records and interviews with survivors.

Bethell, Nicholas *Betrayed* Random House, 1985. An account of the British and US attempts to infiltrate saboteurs into Albania between 1949 and 1953.

Foot, M R D *SOE: The Special Operations Executive 1940–46* Greenwood Press, 1984. Includes SOE's work in Albania.

Fischer, Bernd J *Albania at War 1939–1945* Hurst & Co., 1999. The only modern academic history of Albania from the Italian invasion of 1939 to the end of World War II.

Mangerich, Agnes Jensen, with Rosemary L Neidel and Evelyn M Monahan *Albanian Escape: The True Story of US Army Nurses Behind Enemy Lines* University Press of Kentucky, 2006. A stranded American nurse's account of occupied Albania.

Shehu, Mehmet *La Bataille pour la Libération de Tirana* Editions Naim Frashëri (Tirana). Detailed account of the Battle for the Liberation of Tirana in 1944, written by one of the participants. Hard to obtain, may be available in the UK through interlibrary loan.

Memoirs by SOE agents (see boxes on pages 13–15)

Amery, Julian *Approach March: A Venture in Autobiography* Hutchinson, 1973

Amery, Julian *Sons of the Eagle: A Study in Guerilla War* Macmillan, 1948

Davies, Edmund F *Illyrian Adventure: The Story of the British Military Mission in Enemy-Occupied Albania* Bodley Head, 1952

Glen, Alexander *Footholds Against a Whirlwind* Hutchinson, 1975

Hibbert, Reginald *Albania's National Liberation Struggle: The Bitter Victory* Pinter, 1991

Kemp, Peter *No Colours, No Crest* Cassell, 1958

Kemp, Peter *The Thorns of Memory* Sinclair-Stevenson, 1990

Oakley-Hill, D R *An Englishman in Albania* I B Tauris, 2004

Smiley, David *Albanian Assignment* Chatto & Windus, 1984

Historical background

Achtermeier, William O *The Turkish Connection: The Saga of the Peabody-Martini Rifle* in *Man At Arms Magazine* Vol 1, No 2, 1979.

Dumas, Alexandre (père) *Ali-Pacha* in *Causes Célèbres* Veuve Dondey-Dupré, 1840. Romanticised but fun version of Ali Pasha Tepelena's career. Available as an ebook in English translation for Kindle (*www.amazon.co.uk*). The French original has been digitised by Google.

Durham, Edith *Albania & the Albanians* I B Tauris, 2004. An edition, by Bejtullah Destani, of Edith Durham's articles and letters, most of them unavailable for over 60 years. A fascinating historical document.

Fleming, K E *The Muslim Bonaparte: Diplomacy & Orientalism in Ali Pasha's Greece* Princeton University Press, 1999. Critical biography of Ali Pasha Tepelena. Can be ordered through the publisher's website (*http://pup.princeton.edu*).

Lubonja, Fatos *Second Sentence: Inside the Albanian Gulag* I B Tauris, 2009. A memoir of life as a prisoner in the forced labour camp of Spaçi. Harrowing but essential reading.

Pettifer, James (editor) *Albania and the Balkans* Elbow Publishing, 2013. Essays in honour of Sir Reginald Hibbert, the SOE agent and (later) diplomat. Ambitious in scope, will have something to interest almost everyone.

Rees, Neil *A Royal Exile* Studge Publications, 2010. Published to mark the 70th anniversary of the exiled King Zog's arrival in England. Oral and archive history of the 'royal' family's six-year stay in the Thames Valley and Chilterns.

Tomes, Jason *King Zog* Sutton Publishing, 2003. Biography of Ahmet Zogu, who crowned himself King of the Albanians in 1928. Power struggles, intrigues, pistol fights and assassinations.

Cultural background

Allcock, John and Young, Antonia *Black Lambs & Grey Falcons* Berghahn Books, 2000. A collection of essays about women travellers in the Balkans, including Edith Durham, Margaret Hasluck and Rose Wilder Lane.

De Waal, Clarissa *Albania: Portrait of a Country in Transition* I B Tauris, 2013. A wealth of information and unique observation drawn from the author's anthropological fieldwork in rural Albania since the 1990s.

Kadare, Ismail. Almost anything by this great Albanian writer gives an insight into the culture and history of the country. *Broken April* and *Chronicle in Stone* are especially illuminating on the north and on Gjirokastra, respectively. His novel *The Successor* is a fictionalised account of the mysterious death of Mehmet Shehu, and is worth reading for that reason although it is not one of his best works. It and some of his other novels, translated into English from the French versions, are published by Canongate. Affordable paperbacks of the Albanian–French translations are published in the *Livre de Poche* series.

Kanun of Lekë Dukagjin. It is difficult to find good translations of the *Kanun*. The best is a parallel edition, with Albanian on one page and the English version opposite, published in the US by Gjonlekaj Publishing Co (1989). The International Bookshop in Tirana's Skanderbeg Square stocks it, but outside Albania it is hard to obtain.

Various authors *Albania: A Patrimony of European Values* Tirana, 2001. A useful overview of aspects of Albanian culture such as literature, fine art and music. On sale in Tirana bookshops.

Young, Antonia *Albania: World Bibliographical Series* ABC-Clio, 1997. A bibliographic guide to cultural and historical aspects of Albania. Out of print, but may be available in reference libraries.

Young, Antonia *Women who Become Men* Berghahn Books, 2000. Interviews with some of northern Albania's 'sworn virgins', a fascinating insight into this dying tradition.

Zymberi, Isa *Colloquial Albanian* Routledge, 1991. Language course which gives a thorough grounding in Albanian grammar.

Guidebooks

Ceka, Neritan *Apollonia: History & Monuments* Migjeni, 2001. Scholarly guide to the archaeology and history of Apollonia, an invaluable companion to the site. On sale in Tirana and in Albanian museum bookshops.

Ceka, Neritan *Buthrotum: History & Monuments* Migjeni, 2006. Scholarly guide to the archaeology of Butrint. On sale in Tirana and in Albanian museum bookshops.

Ceka, Neritan and Muçaj, Skënder *Byllis: History & Monuments* Migjeni, 2004. Scholarly guide to the history and buildings of Byllis; has photographs of the Byllis mosaics, usually kept covered. On sale in Tirana and in Albanian museum bookshops.

Gilkes, Oliver *Albania: An Archaeological Guide* I B Tauris, 2012. Detailed notes on archaeological sites, large and small, throughout Albania, especially strong on the southwest of the country. Includes many site plans and very useful advice on access.

Gilkes, Oliver *et al. Gjirokastra: the essential guide* Gjirokastra Conservation and Development Organization, 2009. A pocket guide to the city of Gjirokastra and the surrounding region. Small but full of information about the places to visit, some with site plans, and illustrated with modern and historic photographs.

Hansen, Inge Lyse (series editor) *Hellenistic Butrint, The Butrint Baptistery and its Mosaics, The Rise and Fall of Byzantine Butrint* and *Venetian Butrint* Butrint Foundation, 2007– 2009. An indispensable series of archaeological guides to the whole of the Butrint site, in English and Albanian. Scholarly and beautifully illustrated.

Zindel, Christian and Hausammann, Barbara *Hiking Guide Northern Albania: Thethi & Kelmendi* Huber-Verlag 2009. Detailed route descriptions of 17 hikes in the mountains of the far northwest of Albania, with good maps, GPS waypoints and difficulty grading. Also some general information about the geology, history and culture of the area. Companion hiking map also available from Huber-Verlag.

Travel writing

Carver, Robert *The Accursed Mountains* Flamingo, 1999. Sensationalist and negative account of travelling in Albania and meeting Albanians, none of whom the author appears to like. Albania was not like this in 1996, when he was there, and it is not like this now.

Cusack, Dymphna *Illyria Reborn* William Heinemann Ltd, 1966. An uncritical but fascinating glimpse of communist Albania before the atheism campaign – she hears church bells ringing and muezzins calling the faithful to prayer, and describes Tirana as being full of minarets. Her encounters with ordinary Albanians are described in a delightfully positive light.

Durham, Edith *High Albania* Edward Arnold, 1909; available from various print-on-demand publishers. Classic and enthralling account of travels in northern Albania in the early 20th century.

Hanbury-Tenison, Robin *Land of Eagles: Riding Through Europe's Forgotten Country* I B Tauris, 2014. An account of the journey on horseback by the author and his wife, from the far north to the far south of Albania, peppered with adventure and mishap, discovery and unexpected encounters.

Lane, Rose Wilder and Dore Boylston, Helen *Travels with Zenobia: Paris to Albania by Model T Ford* University of Missouri Press, 1983 (out of print). The authors – one the daughter of Laura Ingalls Wilder, the other the creator of the Sue Barton novels – drove across Europe to Albania in 1926.

Lear, Edward *Edward Lear in Albania – Journals of a Landscape Painter in the Balkans* I B Tauris, 2008. Lear, famous for his nonsense poetry, was a professional artist, who visited Albania in 1848 and 1857, and made a large number of drawings and watercolours of Butrint, Berati and elsewhere. This welcome reissue of his detailed and humorous journal of his 1848 trip is illustrated with some of his own sketches and paintings.

Ward, Philip *Albania* Oleander Press, 1983 (out of print). A rare record of a visit to communist Albania.

WEBSITES
Travel information

www.cemar.it/dest/ferries_albania.htm Italian maritime website, has links to the ferry schedules between Italy and Albania.

www.punetejashtme.gov.al The website of the Albanian Ministry of Foreign Affairs has information (in English) about entering Albania, the contact details for Albanian embassies throughout the world, and information about the Ministry's activities.

Tourist information

www.albania-holidays.com Offers tours throughout the country, city tours of Tirana and bespoke arrangements. Hotel reservations can be made through its sister website **www.albania-hotel.com**.

www.albaniantourism.com The Albanian Ministry of Tourism's website has information about archaeological and historical sites, cultural events and museums. Also contact information for selected hotels across the country, though these cannot be booked through the site.

www.hostelworld.com Reservation site for several Albanian hotels as well as hostels.

www.outdooralbania.com Outdoor Albania specialises in tours to the Albanian outdoors. Offers a range of hiking tours in the Albanian Alps and Tomorri Massif; kayaking and rafting trips; and one-day walks and hikes in Tirana and the surrounding mountains.

www.zbulo.org Hiking tours, mainly in northern Albania where Zbulo (Discover Albania) is based. Tailor-made and self-guided trips also offered. Can arrange Peaks of the Balkans cross-border permits.

General background

http://albania.usembassy.gov/index.html Information about the United States's activities in and policy towards Albania.

www.balkanspeacepark.org A network of academics, artists, environmental activists and local people living and working in the valleys and villages of Northern Albania, Montenegro and Kosova. See pages 56–7 for more about B3P.

www.bbc.co.uk Has general background information on Albania in its 'Europe' section and links to other sites. No longer broadcasts in Albanian, much to the dismay of its loyal listeners there.

http://bektashiorder.com Information in English about the Bektashi order, Albania's 'fourth religion'.

https://cia.gov/library/publications/the-world-factbook/geos/al.html The CIA factbook on Albania, with a reasonably up-to-date summary of recent history and the Agency's assessment of the current state of affairs.

www.frosina.org Designed for the Albanian diaspora in the US; has articles about Albania, folk tales and recipes.

www.gov.uk/government/world/albania News from the British embassy in Tirana.

www.instat.gov.al Albania's National Statistical Institute has a wealth of data on its website, much of it in English as well as Albanian.

www.iucn.org The International Union for Conservation of Nature & Natural Resources; gives information about endangered species all over the world, including Albania.

www.kishakatolikeshkoder.com The website of the Catholic Church in Shkodra. Mostly in Albanian; click on 'Zyra për Martirët' for information in English (and Italian) about Catholics who died for their faith during the communist years.

http://lcweb2.loc.gov/frd/cs/altoc.html US Library of Congress Country Study of Albania; from 1992, but useful historical background.

http://orthodoxalbania.org/old/ The Orthodox Autocephalous Church of Albania, information about the Church's activities and history, mostly in Albanian.

www.osce.org/albania Information about the mandate and the activities of the OSCE Presence in Albania.

http://reenic.utexas.edu/countries/albania.html The REENIC (Russia and East European Network Information Centre) site has links to a huge range of other websites.

www.tiranatimes.com and **www.albaniannews.com** The websites of Tirana's English-language newspapers. Most of the content is accessible only to subscribers, but they provide news summaries.

Index

277

INDEX OF ADVERTISERS